A
GENEVA
SERIES
COMMENTARY

DANIEL

A COMMENTARY ON
DANIEL

Edward J. Young

THE BANNER OF TRUTH TRUST

THE BANNER OF TRUTH TRUST
3 Murrayfield Road, Edinburgh EH12 6EL
PO Box 621, Carlisle, Pennsylvania 17013, USA

*

First published in U.S.A. 1949
First British edition published by the
Banner of Truth Trust 1972
Reprinted 1978
Reprinted 1988
ISBN 0 85151 154 6

*

Printed by offset lithography in Great Britain
at the University Printing House, Oxford

PREFACE

The present work is designed to serve the needs not only of the minister and trained Bible student, but also of the average educated reader of Holy Scripture. It aims above all to present a clear and positive exposition of the prophecy. In order to accomplish such an end it has been necessary to refute two common interpretations.

On the one hand the so-called "critical" position of the date and authorship of Daniel must be answered if the true view is to be established. On February 16, 1835 Dr. Caesar von Lengerke of Konigsberg could write in his commentary, " I have no further wish than that the work (i.e., his commentary) might contribute to the correct explanation of the difficult book and to the final establishment of the critical point of view." The "critical" view does indeed seem to hold the field today, but it is a position which is in basic error. One who claims that the book of Daniel is a product of the Maccabean age thereby denies that it is a work of true predictive prophecy as it purports to be. Furthermore, if the book of Daniel comes from the age of the Maccabees, I do not see how it is possible to escape the conclusion that the book is also a forgery, for it claims to be a revelation from God to the Daniel who lived in Babylon during the exile.

Another interpretation which is very widely held today, although maintaining the genuineness of the book, nevertheless interprets the prophecies in an extremely unwarranted manner by referring the fulfillment of many of them to an alleged period of seven years which is supposed to follow the second advent of the Lord. Those who espouse this position are sincere and zealous Christians, and it is only with hesitation that one writes against them. The present author hopes that advocates of this school of thought who study his commentary will understand the spirit in which he has discussed their views and will at least give serious consideration to the interpretation herein advanced.

The present work does not to any extent discuss philological questions. This has been admirably done by Montgomery, and the reader will discover that on almost every page the commentary is indebted to Montgomery's painstaking labors. It is a pleasure to make acknowledgement of such indebtedness. No student of Daniel can afford to ignore the writings of Montgomery and Rowley, and it is hoped that the frequent reference to these men in the following pages, even though it is so often by way of disagreement, will be regarded as a sign of the admiration and respect with which their labors are regarded by the author.

It is necessary also to acknowledge the great help which has been received from a study of Keil's commentary. This, I believe, is by far the best commentary on Daniel. Karl Friedrich Keil was born in Germany on February 26, 1807. In 1821 he went to St. Petersburg to become a carpenter, but was too small for the bench. Entering school, he distinguished himself in his studies and finally took up theology in Dorpat and Berlin, later becoming professor of theology in Dorpat. Throughout his long life (he died in 1888) Keil wrote commentaries in which he defended the authority and integrity of God's Holy Word.

The translation of Daniel herein given endeavors to bring out the exact meaning of the Hebrew and Aramaic. The reader who is unacquainted with these languages will find it profitable to compare this translation with the Authorized Version.

I would acknowledge indebtedness to Charles Scribner's Sons, to the Johns Hopkins Press, to the Yale University Press, to Mr. I. C. Herendeen and to Zondervan Publishing House for permission to quote respectively from the commentary of Montgomery on Daniel in the *International Critical Commentary Series, From the Stone Age to Christianity* by William F. Albright, *Nabonidus and Belshazzar* by R. A. Dougherty, *The Seventy Weeks and the Great Tribulation* by Philip Mauro, *The Great Parenthesis* by H. A. Ironside and *Daniel's Prophecy of the Seventy Weeks* by Alva J. McClain.

Lastly, it is indeed a pleasure to make acknowledgment to Miss Ruth Stahl for help given during the course of preparing this work.

EDWARD J. YOUNG

Feb. 1, 1949
Philadelphia, Penna.

TABLE OF CONTENTS

CHAPTER IV

CHAPTER V

CHAPTER VI

CHAPTER VII

CHAPTER VIII

CHAPTER IX

The Vision in the Third Year of Cyrus

CHAPTER X

The Revelation of the Future

CHAPTER XI

CHAPTER XII

APPENDICES

List of Abbreviations

(Common abbreviations together with those of the Biblical books have been omitted)

ABAT.: *Altorientalische Bilder zum Alten Testament,* Gressmann.
acc.: accusative case.
Add.: Additions.
Amm. Mar.: Ammianus Marcellinus, an historian of the 4th century A.D., born at Antioch. After an active life in the army he settled in Rome and wrote a Roman history of the years 96-378, thus forming a continuation of the history of Tacitus.
Ana.: Anabasis.
Ant.: Antiochus.
Antiq.: Antiquities.
AP: *The Apocrypha and Pseudepigrapha,* Charles.
Ass.: Assyrian.
AV.: Authorized Version.

BA: Beitraege zur Assyriologie.
Bab.: Babylonian.
Bab. u.. Ass.: *Babylonien und Assyrien,* Meissner
BDB: *Hebrew Lexicon,* Brown, Driver, Briggs.
BHT: *Babylonian Historical Texts,* Smith.

CA: Contra Apion.
CAH: Cambridge Ancient History.
CBA: *The Civilization of Babylonia and Assyria,* Jastrow.
com.: commentary.
Cy.: Cyropaedia.

DCS: *The Book of Daniel from the Christian Standpoint,* Kennedy.
DM: *Darius the Mede and the Four World Empires,* Rowley.
DP: *Daniel and His Prophecies,* Wright.
DS: Diodorus Siculus, a Greek historian and contemporary of Julius Caesar.

EJG: *Die Eschatologie der juedischen Gemeinde,* Volz.
Ep. of Jer.: The Epistle of Jeremiah.
ET: English Translation.

FSAC: *From the Stone Age to Christianity,* Albright.

GJV: *Geschichte des juedischen Volkes,* Schurer.

H: Ernst Wilhelm Hengstenberg, 1802-1869, a staunch defender of the Faith and author of many learned commentaries on the OT. In the words of B. B. Warfield, he was "—one of the most searching expounders of the Scripture that God has as yet given His church."
HBA: *History of Babylonia and Assyria,* Rogers.
Her.: Herodotus.

ICC: International Critical Commentary.
IOT: *Introduction to the Old Testament,* Pfeiffer.
ISBE: International Standard Bible Encyclopaedia.

JBL: The Journal of Biblical Literature.
JTS: The Journal of Theological Studies.

KAT: Keilinschriften und das Alte Testament.
KB: Keilinschriftliche Bibliothek.

LXX: The Septuagint, a pre-Christian translation of the OT into Greek. The portion on Dan. did not find favor in the Christian churches and was supplanted by the version of Theodotion. It is now extant in only one manuscript, the Codex Chisianus.

M: James Alan Montgomery, author of a com. on Dan., which, from the philological standpoint, is one of the finest.
Mas.: Masoretic.

NB: *Nabonidus and Belshazzar*, Dougherty.
nd: no date.
Neb.: Nebuchadnezzar.

PA: Pirke Aboth.
Pr.E.: Praeparatio Evangelica.
PG: *Patrologia Graeca*, Migne.
PL: *Patrologia Latina*, Migne.
PVA: A Persian Verse Account.
Poly.: Polybius.
Pr.G.: The Presbyterian Guardian.
prep.: preposition.
PTR: The Princeton Theological Review.

Q.Cur.: Quintus Curtius, a biographer of Alexander the Great, who lived during the 1st cent., A.D.

RA: *The Relevance of Apocalyptic*, Rowley.
Rs: *Die Religion des Judentums im spaethellenistischen Zeitalter, Bousset.*
RV: Revised Version.

SBD: *Studies in the Book of Daniel*, Wilson; I 1st Series, II 2nd Series.
SC: *Schoepfung und Chaos, Gunkel.*
SDJ: *The Self Disclosure of Jesus*, Vos.
SRB: The Scofield Reference Bible.
Sym.: Symmachus, an Ebionite who lived toward the close of the 2nd cent. A.D. He translated the OT into Greek.

Th.: Theodotion, a translator of the OT into Greek. Irenaeus speaks of him as an Ephesian, but practically nothing is known of him. In the 2nd cent. A.D. the version of Theodotion began to supplant the LXX of Dan. in the use of the churches.

TR: Theologische Rundschau.
tr.: translated.

Verr.: The Impeachment of Verres, an oration of Cicero.

WThJ.: The Westminster Theological Journal.

ZA: Zeitschrift fuer Assyriologie.

Introduction

INTRODUCTION

The book of Daniel comprises that portion of the Divine Revelation which relates certain historical events in the life of Daniel and certain dreams and visions concerning the future which were interpreted by him. In order properly to understand the life and activity of Daniel we must first consider the place of the Babylonian exile in the history of redemption. This period is regarded in the book of Daniel as a period of *Indignation* (Dan. 8:19), and this characterization receives support also from other passages of Scripture. Thus in Isaiah 10:5 we read, "O Assyrian, the rod of mine anger, and the staff in their hand is mine indignation." And again in the same chapter, verse 25, "For yet a very little while, and the indignation shall cease, and mine anger in their destruction." The exile, therefore, is to be regarded as a period in which the anger or wrath of God was manifested toward His chosen people.

This visitation of indignation, however, was not in any sense a manifestation of whim or caprice. When the nation Israel had been founded and established as the theocracy, Moses had clearly warned the people as to the consequences of sin and apostasy. "Then my anger shall be kindled against them in that day, and I will forsake them, and I will hide my face from them, and they shall be devoured, and many evils and troubles shall befall them; so that they will say in that day, Are not these evils come upon us, because our God is not among us?" (Deut. 31:17, Cf. also Deut. 32:9-44). This warning of the great human founder of the theocracy was repeated and enlarged over and over again by the prophets. These prophets were men who declared to the people the very word of the Lord. They spoke not in conflict with the foundational law of the nation, but rather based their messages upon this law. The words of the prophets may be rightly considered as expositions of this law. Like Moses, therefore, the prophets warned as to the consequences of sin and apostasy.

Despite these many warnings, the people fell constantly into rebellion against the LORD that had brought them forth out of the land of Egypt and out of the house of bondage. The book of Judges, for example, throws light upon the conditions of the people after their entrance into Canaan. It is a tragic picture. Despite the constant manifestations of the goodness of God in sending to them saviours, they forsook Him and His goodness and went after other gods. During this period jealousy begins to appear and finally breaks forth in the schism of the northern tribes. The wickedness of this act can hardly be overemphasized. "What portion have we in David? neither have we inheritance in the son of Jesse: to your tents, O Israel: see now to thine own house, David. So Israel departed unto their tents" (1 K. 12:16b). Thus ten tribes renounced the LORD and went their own way. The kingdom of Judah, although not officially departing from the theocratic position, nevertheless presents an admixture of good and evil. Finally, when the iniquity of the nation had run its course, the *Indignation* of the LORD fell upon it.

The apostasy of the people appears all the more heinous when one considers what Israel was destined to be. When man sinned against God, he not only forfeited all claim upon God's favor but also involved himself in an estate of sin and misery. Yet, from all eternity, God had elected some unto everlasting life, hence, He entered into a covenant of grace, whereby He might deliver man from his sin and misery and by means of a Redeemer bring him into an estate of salvation. Immediately after the fall, God revealed this gracious purpose. Since, however, the saving work was not right away to be accomplished, but only after mankind had been sufficiently prepared for the coming of the Redeemer, God chose a particular family from which the Saviour was to be born. The family grew until at Mt. Sinai the nation of God, the theocracy, was formally organized.

It must clearly be borne in mind that the revelation of the Law at Mt. Sinai is to be regarded as an administration of the covenant of grace. The moral law, which in the Ten Commandments is summarily comprehended, is the expression of truths which are eternal. Even the ceremonial law represents the expression of eternal truth. The covenant which God made with mankind was an everlasting one (see e.g., Gen. 17:18, 19) which was not to be changed or abrogated. The establishment of the theocracy, therefore, did not abrogate or nullify the covenant of grace (Gal. 3:17). Rather, in the theocratic arrangements, the eternal character of the covenant is expressly emphasized. Thus we may note the repetition of such phrases as "throughout your generations," "for ever," "statute of eternity," etc. These descriptions apply to the passover arrangements (Ex. 12:14,17,24); the day of atonement (Lev. 16:29,31,34); the other feasts (Lev. 23:14,21,31,41); the offering of sacrifice (Lev. 3:17; 10:15; Num. 15:15) and the rights and duties of the priests (Ex. 27:21; 28:43; 29:28; 30:21).

The exile brought to an end the independent existence of the nation as the theocracy. Its constitution *as a nation* which had been revealed at Sinai now disappeared, never again to be seen. Even when the people returned from Babylon and again erected the Temple, there was a difference. The soul of the theocracy was gone. The old Sinaitic constitution was never again really established.

Had the people remained true and loyal to the theocratic principles which the LORD had so graciously revealed at Sinai, the outward form of the nation might have longer continued. But their apostasy was so great that a change had to be introduced. No longer was the national Israel a light which should lighten the Gentiles and point them to Mount Zion, the dwelling place of the Holy God. Instead, she was a rebellious and stiffnecked people, ripe for judgment.

Although, therefore, the exile did bring to an end the outward organization of the people as it had been established at Sinai, it also introduced a new period. It introduced a period which may be regarded as transitional and preparatory, for the time of the *Indignation* led to the expectancy of the Messiah's coming. When the final days of this period were beginning to run their course, the LORD revealed to Daniel the time and definiteness of the Messiah's coming. Seventy periods of seven were determined in order to accomplish the Messianic work. In the end of the *Indignation* there would appear Antiochus Epiphanes with his fierce persecution. Then, the time of expectation and preparation would be completed. The axe would be laid unto the root of the trees. Christ would come and establish the kingdom that should stand forever. The exile therefore was the last great period of repentance before the coming of the Lord.

Not only would the abandonment of the outward theocratic form of the nation serve as a process to sift the chaff from the wheat among the people in order that a true remnant might return, but it would also serve as a benefit to the heathen nations of antiquity. These nations would now be faced more directly with the claims of the true God. Through the prophecies which Daniel uttered they would learn that no empire of human origin is eternal, for empire would succeed empire. They would learn also that no empire is of world wide dominion, for they would see rebellion after rebellion, nation rising against nation. And above all they would behold the vanity of the idols and the superiority of the God of Israel.

The exile constitutes the third great period of miracles in the history of redemption. There are four such periods: The time of the exodus; the age of Elijah and Elisha; the exile and the Apostolic age. It will be noted that two of these periods are times of establishment and foundation. Thus there is a correspondence between the exodus and the accompanying establishment of the nation as the people of God and the time of Christ and the Apostles when the early Church was established. Two of these are periods of conflict with heathen powers. During the days of Elijah and Elisha the religion of Israel came into serious conflict with the worship of the Tyrian Baal, introduced by Jezebel, and during the exile the religion of Israel was opposed by that of the Babylonians and the Persians. Furthermore there is a correspondence between the exodus and the exile. Both were times of great deliverance from heathen powers.

During the period of Egyptian oppression God wrought many mighty miracles for the purpose of breaking the pride of Pharaoh and showing forth His omnipotence. On the other hand revelation by dream was rare, and the emphasis upon God's omniscience was not so prominent (cf. Gen. 41). During the exile, however, the LORD sought to destroy the delusion of the nations that the God of Israel was just another god, a local, limited, tribal deity. It was necessary to show that the God of Israel was the true and living God, who possessed objective metaphysical existence, before Whom the gods of the heathen were vain, empty delusions, not having objective reality. Consequently, during the exile, more stress is placed upon revelations concerning the future than upon the performance of miracles as such. Three mighty miracles are recorded in the book of Daniel; the episode of the fiery furnace, the handwriting upon the wall and the deliverance from the den of lions. These are sufficient to establish the omnipotence of the LORD. But several revelations concerning the future are given in order that the nations might see that the God of Israel is the God in whose hand are held the sovereign dispositions of the affairs of men.

It was, therefore, at such a period that Daniel lived and labored. Of the man himself very little is known. He was of the royal seed (1:3), and was carried away, while yet a youth, during the third year of Jehoiakim. At the court in Babylon he received the name Belteshazzar, and was instructed in the wisdom and science of the Chaldeans. He remained steadfast in his devotion to God and distinguished himself by his ability and understanding. God gave to him particular gifts in the understanding of mysteries and the interpretation of dreams. These gifts he was enabled to employ in the interpretation of two remarkable dreams of the king Nebuchadnezzar (chs. 2 & 4). He was made ruler over the province of Babylon and chief of the governors over its wise men. During the last days of the empire, he interpreted a wonderful writing for Belshazzar, and was further honored. Under Darius the Mede he was one of the three presidents of the satraps. An attempt was made to do away with him, and he was cast into a den of lions from which he was miraculously delivered. He continued in high office until the first year of Cyrus, and apparently did not return to Palestine with his people but spent his last days in Babylon, with the assurance that he would continue in peace and await the resurrection at the end of the days.

Although the known facts of Daniel's life are so few, nevertheless he is revealed as a man of stalwart character and priceless convictions. He is willing at all times to stand up for what he believes, and is a true hero of the Faith. Coupled with this there is a gentle courtesy in his relations with others, and a simple and humble dependence upon the grace and power of the God Whom he worships.

Daniel was not placed in Babylon to do work among his own people. Rather, his whole training prepared him to be a statesman, and this he was. His personal integrity was so great that he could be heard and trusted even by those monarchs who did not believe in his God. In His sovereign providence God placed Daniel at the heathen court in order that he might declare to successive monarchs that the kingdoms of this world are temporal and fleeting but that the kingdom of God shall endure forever.

II

The book of Daniel was written by Daniel himself, as may be seen from the following considerations:

1. In the second portion of the book Daniel is named as the one who received the revelations and he also speaks in the first person (cf. 7:2,4, 6ff., 28; 8:1ff., 15ff.; 9:2ff., 10:2ff.; 12:5-8). Daniel is commanded to preserve the book in which the words are found (12:4).

2. The entire book is obviously the work of one writer, and if Daniel is named as the one who receives certain of the revelations, it follows that he must be the author of the entire book. That the book is a unit may be clearly seen:

a. The first part prepares for the second, and the second looks back to the first. Thus, ch. 7 develops more fully what is introduced in ch. 2 as also does ch. 8, yet neither 7 nor 8 is fully understandable without 2. Ch. 2 also prepares the way for the revelations in 9,10,11, and 12, and all of these chapters are based upon the earlier revelation in ch. 2. Cf. also 2:28 and 4:2,7,10 with 7:1,2,15.

b. The several sections of the same part also stand in mutual relationship. The reader should compare 3:12 with 2:49; the carrying away of the sacred vessels (1:1) prepares for the understanding of Belshazzar's feast in ch. 5; 9:21 should be compared with 8:15ff.; 10:12 with 9:23, etc. If the reader will read the book carefully, he will be deeply impressed with the remarkable manner in which the various parts interlock and depend upon one another.

c. The historical narratives uniformily have the purpose of revealing how the God of Israel is glorified over the heathen nations.

d. The character of Daniel is everywhere seen to be the same. It is one Daniel who appears throughout the entire book.

e. The literary unity of the book has been widely acknowledged by scholars of all schools of thought. It is naturally maintained by conservative scholars, but in recent times the following also have regarded Daniel as a unit; Driver, Charles, Rowley, Pfeiffer.

3. The Lord explicitly speaks of Daniel the prophet as having foretold the abomination of desolation (Matt. 24:15). In other passages also our Lord refers to the prophecies of Daniel and thus, at least indirectly, approves their genuineness. Cf. Matt. 10:23; 16:27ff.; 19:28; 24:30; 25:31; 26:64. On the use which the NT makes of Daniel see Wright, DP, pp. 97-100, and Kennedy DCS, pp. 5-28.

4. The Greek translation of the Pentateuch (3rd cent. B.C.) possibly shows the influence of Daniel. The book of Maccabees likewise makes reference to an episode in the life of Daniel himself and to the three youths in the fiery furnace. The book of Ecclesiasticus may possibly have known of Daniel, although it does not mention him by name. (For the development of this viewpoint see D. S. Margoliouth, *Lines of Defence of the Biblical Revelation*, New York, 1903, pp. 177-182).

5. The book reflects the background of the Babylonian and Persian empires. The historical objections which have been offered are not sufficient to overthrow this fact (see commentary and appendices for further discussion).

III

In our present Hebrew Bibles the book of Daniel is found, not among the Prophets but among the Writings. It is sometimes charged that the reason for this is that Daniel was composed after the canon of the Prophets had been completed. However, such is not the case. The reason why the book is not included among the Prophets is that Daniel did not occupy the office of a prophet, although he did possess the prophetic gift. He did not have the *munus propheticum* but did possess the *donum propheticum.*

A prophet must be an Israelite, raised up by the Lord in order to serve as a mediator between God and the people. Just as the priest would represent the people before God, so the prophet would represent God before the people. I "will put my words in his mouth; and he shall speak unto them all that I shall command him" (Deut. 18:18). In any correct definition of the prophet, therefore, this mediatorial character must be kept in mind.

The ministry of Daniel, as we have seen above, was not to the people of Israel, but to a heathen court. In this respect he stands in contrast with his contemporary, Ezekiel. Ezekiel was a man who occupied the prophetical office as well as a possessor of the gift of prophecy. But Daniel must be regarded primarily as a statesman. In referring to Daniel as a prophet, the NT uses the word in a broad sense, as it also does in the case of Balaam (2 Peter 2:16).

It is perfectly true that the book of Daniel may not always have been placed among the Writings. Indeed, there seems to be evidence that in some lists it was included among the Prophets. This fact, however, is not decisive. The character of the book and the station of its author show that it should properly be reckoned among the Writings. (The reader who is interested in pursuing this subject further should consult R. D. Wilson, "The Rule of Faith and Life," in PTR, Vol. xxvi. No. 3, July 1928; Solomon Zeitlin, *An Historical Study of the Canonization of the Hebrew Scriptures,* Philadelphia, 1933, and L. Wogue, *Histoire de la Bible et de l'Exégèse Biblique,* Paris, MDCCCLXXXI. The last named work discusses the question from the traditional Jewish point of view).

IV

The revelations concerning the future which are found in Daniel are given in dreams and vision in which symbolism plays an important part. There is a reason for this fact. These revelations were given at a time when the period of *Indignation* had begun. What was to be the future course of the people of God? Was God to cast them off utterly, to leave them dispersed among the nations? Or was He to fulfill His earlier promises in sending to the people a Redeemer? And, if He was to send the Redeemer, how would this be accomplished? In what relation would the people of God stand to the mighty heathen empires which were now appearing upon the scene? In answer to these questions, the book of Daniel reveals that God has not cast off His people. The nations will arise and become powerful, but they will nevertheless be subject to the all-controlling power of God. There will yet be much persecution for the people of the LORD, but when the appointed time has come, God will establish His own eternal kingdom.

Now, it is contrary to the nature and genius of prophecy to reveal the future as detailed history. In all prophecy there is an element of obscurity and perhaps even of ambiguity. The Lord had distinctly said that He would speak to the prophets in a manner less clear and direct than that in which He would speak to Moses His Servant (Num. 12:1-8). With the prophets He would speak in dreams and visions and — so it would seem — in dark and enigmatic sayings. In revelations which were given as visions, therefore, we should expect an abundance of imagery and symbolism. There are many instances of such revelation in the prophetical books (e. g., Isa. 24-27; Joel 3:9-17; Zech. 14; Ps. 2; Amos 7-9).

When one considers the standpoint of the writer of Daniel and the task which was his, it is to be expected that in his writing there should be an abundance of imagery and symbolism. The future of the people of God and its relation to the heathen nations was revealed to Daniel in a VISION. It is this fact which explains the abundance of symbolism in the revelations. The book of Daniel is often called an Apocalyptic writing. It is indeed such, but it must be sharply distinguished from the later Jewish Apocalyptic writings. There is only one other Apocalypse which may be compared with it, and that is the New Testament book of Revelation.

The book of Daniel towers far above these post-canonical apocalypses. In its use of imagery and symbolism it does not at all differ essentially from prophecy itself. Indeed, it should be regarded as presenting all the qualities of a true prophetical work. As we have already said, the form of Daniel is due to its subject matter. No other prophetical book of the OT speaks of the heathen nations and their relation to the people of God with the same fullness and definiteness as does Daniel. If, then, the book is to retain at all any semblance of mystery, it must make use of imagery. Its imagery, however, is employed for a didactic purpose, and sufficient explanation is given so that when the time of fulfillment comes, the reader may understand the meaning. The book, therefore, has an eminently practical purpose, and its basic, fundamental plan of the ages is clear to him who will read. (The reader who desires to pursue this subject further should consult SBD, II, pp. 101-116.)

V

The book of Daniel is written in two languages, Hebrew and Aramaic. 1:1-2:4a; 8:1-12:13 are written in Hebrew, and 2:4b-7:28 are written in Aramaic. It is difficult to determine exactly why two languages have been used, and many suggested solutions to the problem have been offered. All in all, the solution which seems to be most free from difficulty is that Aramaic, being the language of the world is used in those portions of the book which outline the future history of the worldly empires and their relation to the people of God, and Hebrew is used in those portions which interpret for the Hebrews the meaning of the visions of the world empires. The present writer is fully aware of the difficulties which are entailed in this position, and hence, has no desire to be dogmatic upon the point.

It is not the purpose of this commentary to discuss the textual and linguistic problems of the book. Nevertheless, it should be said that the Hebrew bears similarities to that employed by Ezekiel, the other great prophet of the exile. As far as the Aramaic is concerned, there is nothing which would preclude its having been written by Daniel at Babylon.

Concerning the languages of the book and their relation to the date of its authorship, Dr. Driver once wrote, "The verdict of the language of Daniel is thus clear. The *Persian* words presuppose a period after the Persian empire had been well established: the Greek words *demand,* the Hebrew *supports,* and the Aramaic *permits,* a date *after the conquest of Palestine by Alexander the Great* (B.C. 332)" *Literature of the Old Testament,* Edinburgh, 1909 p. 508. This statement would now have to be modified. There is nothing in the language of the book which would in itself preclude authorship in the 6th cent. B. C.

Even if it could be conclusively demonstrated that the Aramaic of our Bibles was from the 3rd cent. B. C., this would not preclude authorship by Daniel in the 6th. cent. For the present Aramaic may very well have been copied from the original, and later orthography introduced. However, it is not necessary to make such an assumption. Recent discoveries may require that many preconceived notions as to the characteristics of the Aramaic language will have to be modified.

One example will serve as an illustration of this statement. Certain words in the Aramaic portions of Daniel are spelled with d instead of z. For example, the relative pronoun (who, which, what) is spelled di, and not zi. This use of d in place of z has long been urged as an indication of lateness, for, so it was argued, the earlier documents employed z. In the light of the texts from Ras Shamra, however, this argument has lost its force. These texts (see App. IV) contain Aramaic elements and frequently employ d in place of z, just as Daniel does. The reader who is interested in this problem should consult:

H. H. Rowley, *The Aramaic of the Old Testament,* Oxford, 1929.

W. Baumgartner, "Das Aramaeische im Buche Daniel" in *Zeitschrift fuer die Alttestamentliche Wissenschaft,* 1927, pp. 81-133.

G. R. Driver, *The Aramaic of the Book of Daniel,* in JBL. 45 (1926), pp. 110-119; 323-325.

A defence of the early date of the Aramaic is given by R. D. Wilson, *"The Aramaic of Daniel"* in *Biblical and Theological Studies by the Members of the Faculty of Princeton Theological Seminary,* New York, MCMXII, pp. 261-305.

VI

That Daniel himself was the author of the book appears to have been the position both of the early Church and of the Synagogue. The first to cast doubt upon this view was the neo-Platonist Porphyry (See Appendix VIII). It was again criticized by Uriel Acosta (1590-1647), a Jewish rationalist, who considered the book to have been forged in order to favor the doctrine of the resurrection of the body. More serious, however, was the attack of the English deist, Anthony Collins, who in an appendix to his "Scheme of Literal Prophecy Considered" (1727), assailed the integrity of the prophecy. One of the first scientific presentations of the rationalistic viewpoint is to be found in the work of Leonhard Bertholdt (*Daniel, aus dem Hebraeisch-Aramaeischen neu uebersetzt und erklaert, mit einer vollstaendigen Einleitung and einigen histor. und exeget. Exkursen,* Erlangen, 1806-1808, 2 vols.). Bertholdt had studied at Erlangen and early showed an interest in the Oriental languages. This work brought him to the fore as a scholar. It is one of the first serious challenges to the traditional view of the authorship of Daniel. There were doughty champions of the Faith, however, who replied to Bertholdt's attack, most prominent of whom was Hengstenberg.

From this time on the battle was continued between two opposing schools of thought. One position, that which is represented in the present commentary, is that the book was written by Daniel himself in Babylon in the 6th cent. B. C., and that the contents of the book were given to Daniel by special, Divine revelation. The other view, influenced very largely by the accuracy of Daniel's description of the times of Antiochus, asserts that the book was composed by an unknown Jew at the time of Antiochus. Unfortunately, the controversy between the advocates of these two viewpoints has sometimes been carried on in too heated a manner, with the result that ridicule and abuse have at times been substituted for argument.

It is only just to assert that some of the scholars who have espoused the view to which this present book is opposed have been men of profound learning and scholarship. Some of them have also been men of true Christian faith. However much one may disagree with the positions which some have adopted, there is indeed reason to believe that the men themselves would have wished to disassociate themselves from the rationalism of a Collins or Porphyry.

Nevertheless, it is true that the negative view of the book of Daniel took its rise in a non-Christian atmosphere, and has been ably advocated by men who were opposed to the supernaturalism of Christianity.

There are, indeed, difficulties in the traditional view of the authorship of Daniel. Not to acknowledge this would be to close one's eyes to the facts. The present commentary does not profess to solve all the difficulties which are bound up in the traditional view. But there is, it would seem, a far greater difficulty in the negative position. If the book of Daniel is the product of the Maccabean age, then it is not a book of predictive prophecy, but a forgery. Whenever one makes such a statement, he is usually taken to task and told that he does not understand the nature of apocalyptic literature. Pusey, for example, has often been berated for his classic statement, "The book of Daniel is especially fitted to be a battle-ground between faith and unbelief. It admits of no half way measures. It is either Divine or an imposture" (p. 75). Pusey, however, was right, and his critics are wrong. The book of Daniel is not a romance, nor was it ever intended to be. It was received into the canon, and made part of the rule of faith and life. The later Jewish apocalypses were not thus treated, but the Jews did not doubt the canonicity of Daniel for an instant.

The book of Daniel purports to be serious history. It claims to be a revelation from the God of heaven which concerns the future welfare of men and nations. If this book were issued at the time of the Maccabees for the purpose of strengthening the faith of the people of *that* time, and the impression was thereby created that Daniel, a Jew of the 6th cent. were the author, then, whether we like it or no—the book is a fraud. There is no escaping this conclusion. It will not do to say that the Jews frequently engaged in such a practice. That does not lessen their guilt one whit. It is one thing to issue a harmless romance under a pseudonym; it is an entirely different thing to issue under a pseudonym a book claiming to be a revelation of God and having to do with the conduct of men and to regard such a book as canonical. The Jews of the inter-testamental period may have done the first; there is no evidence that they did the second.

Furthermore, and this is decisive, the usage of the NT shows that the NT writers did not look upon this book as a romance. It was none other than our LORD, the incarnate Son of God, Who spoke of Himself in terms taken from the book of Daniel. In the light of the decisive and authoritative usage of the NT, one is compelled to reject the idea that Daniel is a mere romance.

Despite this fact, however, the negative view is most prevalent in scholarly circles today. It is probably not an exaggeration to say that most scholars now believe that the book of Daniel, as we have it, comes from the days of the Maccabees.

Particular attention, however, should be directed to the theory of Gustav Hœlscher ("Die Entstehung des Buches Daniel" in *Theologische Studien und Kritiken* xcii, 1919, pp. 113-138). The composer of the book, thought Hœlscher, lived at the time of the Maccabees. He himself was the author of Daniel 8-12. He did not, however, compose 1, 2-6, or 7, since these chapters exhibit a background which is not that of the Maccabean age (The reader who does not read German will find an exposition of this general point of view in M). Nevertheless, this author took an old collection of five narratives, i. e., 2-6, provided these with an introduction (ch. 1), inserted ch. 7, and placed all of this material before his own work, thus producing the present book. Haller has adopted essentially this position, and since his comments are easily available, I have made reference in the commentary to his remarks upon the first eight chapters of Daniel.

This theory of Hœlscher's has found favor, it would seem, largely because it has been compelled to take cognizance of the fact that the background of chapters 2-6 is not that of the time of the Maccabees. This is great gain. But the theory breaks upon the assumption that chapters 2-5 contain narratives or legends which are not historical in character. In the comments upon the text I have sought to point out the weaknesses of this position as they appear in Haller's exposition.

VII

Analysis of the Book of Daniel

CHAPTER

I. a. vv. 1-2 The expedition of Nebuchadnezzar against Jerusalem.

b. vv. 3-7 The introduction of the four Jewish youths: Daniel and his three companions.

c. vv. 8-16 The first triumph of God's grace in Babylonia: Daniel and his companions abstain from the appointed food of the king.

d. vv. 17-21 The progress of the four youths in the Chaldean wisdom and their entrance into the king's service.

II. a. vv. 1-16 The dream of Nebuchadnezzar and the inability of the wise men to interpret it.

1) vv. 1- 6 Nebuchadnezzar the king dreams a dream by which he is greatly troubled and so summons the wise men of Babylon to tell him the dream and its interpretation.

2) vv. 7-12 The wise men ask the king to declare his dream. He refuses, and they confess their inability to tell the dream, protesting that he is asking the impossible. The king in anger orders the wise men to be put to death.

3) vv. 13-16 The decree to slay the wise men has gone forth, and in this decree Daniel and his three companions are included. Through Arioch's intervention Daniel obtains an audience with the king and promises to declare the dream and secures the deferring of the sentence of execution.

b. vv 17-23 Daniel prays to God for a revelation of the dream. His prayer is answered and He praises God.

1) vv. 17-19 Daniel enters his house to inform his companions of the state of affairs and to seek mercy from God. The secret is revealed to Daniel in a night vision.

2) vv 20-23 Daniel's prayer of thanksgiving for the mercy of God in revealing to him the secret.

c. vv. 24-45 Daniel is brought into the king's presence and declares his readiness to interpret the dream. He relates the dream and sets forth its interpretation.

1) vv. 24-30 Daniel is brought into the presence of Nebuchadnezzar and declares his readiness to interpret the dream.

2) vv. 31-35 Daniel relates the dream to Nebuchadnezzar.

3) vv. 36-45 Daniel's interpretation of the dream.

d. vv. 46-49 Nebuchadnezzar honors Daniel and his God and promotes Daniel.

III. a. vv. 1- 7 Nebuchadnezzar erects a golden image and requires that his subjects, upon penalty of death, shall worship it.

b. vv. 8-12 Certain Chaldeans inform the king that Shadrach, Meshach and Abed-Nego have not worshipped the golden image.

c. vv. 13-18 Nebuchadnezzar commands the accused men to be brought before him and asks them if the accusation is true. He repeats his edict, whereupon they reply that their confidence is in God.

d. vv. 19-30 Nebuchadnezzar, in rage, commands that the furnace be heated seven times hotter than customary, and that the three be cast into its midst. These commands are carried out. But in the furnace the king sees the men unharmed and accompanied by a Fourth. He thereupon commands them to come forth and blesses their God.

IV. a. vv. 1- 3 The proclamation of Nebuchadnezzar.
b. vv. 4- 9 Troubled by a dream, Nebuchadnezzar summons his wise men, who are unable to tell the dream. Lastly, Daniel is summoned.
c. vv. 10-18 The content of Nebuchadnezzar's dream.
d. vv. 19-27 Daniel interprets the dream.
e. vv. 28-33 The fulfilment of the dream.
f. vv. 34-37 The recovery of Nebuchadnezzar.

V. a. vv. 1- 4 The feast of Belshazzar.
b. vv. 5-12 The handwriting on the wall, the astonishment of Belshazaar thereat, and the inability of the wise men to interpret the writing.
c. vv. 13:28 Daniel is called before the king. He reads and interprets the writing.
d. vv. 29-30 The reward of Daniel and the death of Belshazzar.

VI. a. vv. 1- 9 Darius places Daniel in a position of authority. Aroused by jealousy, certain rivals devise a plot to destroy Daniel.
b. vv. 10-19 The accusation and condemnation of Daniel.
c. vv. 20-25 The deliverance of Daniel.
d. vv. 26-29 The decree of Darius.

VII. a. vv. 1-14 The vision of the four beasts.
b. vv. 15-28 The interpretation of the vision.

VIII. a. vv. 1-14 The vision of the ram and the he-goat.
1) vv. 1- 2 Introduction to the vision.
2) vv. 3- 8 The vision itself.
3) vv. 9-14 The interpretation of the vision.
b. vv. 15-27 The interpretation of the vision.
1) vv. 15-18 Gabriel is commanded to instruct Daniel as to the interpretation.
2) vv. 19-26 The angel's interpretation.
3) vs. 27 Daniel's sickness.

IX. a. vv. 1- 3 Introduction.
b. vv. 4-19 The prayer of Daniel.
c. vv. 20-23 The coming of the angel Gabriel to answer the prayer.
d. vv. 24-27 The revelation of the seventy sevens which Gabriel communicates to Daniel in answer to his prayer.
1) vs. 24 The announcement of the 70 sevens.
2) vv. 25-27 The three divisions of the 70 sevens.

X. a. vv. 1- 3 Introduction to the manifestation of God.
b. vv. 4- 8 The vision of God.
c. vv. 4-14 The introductory words of the heavenly Being.
d. vv. 15-11:1 Daniel is made capable of receiving the full revelation from the Messenger.

XI. 2-XII:3 The revelation of the future.
a. vv. 2 The kings of Persia.
b. vv. 3, 4 Alexander and the divisions of his kingdom.
c. vv. 5-20 The wars between the kings of the South and of the North for dominion over the Holy Land.
d. vs. 21-12:3 The revelation concerning Antiochus Epiphanes and the future.
1) vv. 21-24 The rise of Antiochus Epiphanes.
2) vv. 25-28 The first Egyptian campaign.
3) vs. 29 The next Egyptian campaign.
4) vv. 30-35 The persecution of the Theocracy by Antiochus.
5) vv. 36-39 The great arrogance of the enemy of God.
6) vv. 40-45 The final conflict .
7) 12: 1- 3 The final deliverance of Israel and the consummation.

XII. e. vs. 4 The final command to seal up the Book
f. vv. 5-13 The conclusion of the Prophecy.

"And in the days of these kings shall the God of heaven set up a kingdom, which shall never be destroyed: and the kingdom shall not be left to other people, but it shall break in pieces and overcome all these kingdoms, and it shall stand forever."

—Daniel 2:44

"Then the king made Daniel a great man, and gave him many great gifts, and made him ruler over the whole province of Babylon, and chief of the governors over all the wise men of Babylon."

—Daniel 2:48

"Now when Jesus was born in Bethlehem of Judea in the days of Herod the king, behold, there came wise men from the east to Jerusalem, Saying, Where is he that is born King of the Jews? for we have seen his star in the east, and are come to worship him."

—Matthew 2:1,2

THE PROPHECY OF DANIEL

A Commentary

CHAPTER ONE

a. vv. 1-2. The expedition of Nebuchadnezzar against Jerusalem

Vs. 1. *In the third year of the reign of Jehoiakim, king of Judah, came Nebuchadnezzar king of Babylon to Jerusalem and besieged it.* There are no satisfactory reasons for denying the historicity of these statements. Dan. apparently employs the Babylonian mode of reckoning the dates, and so says *third* instead of *fourth year.* See App. I for a discussion of the problem, and cf. 2 K. 24:1 and 2 Chr. 36:6. *Jehoiakim-* (Jehovah raises up) was the son of King Josiah and Zebudah, 2 K. 23: 34, 36. At the death of Josiah, the people anointed Jehoahaz, a younger brother of Jehoiakim as king. However, his reign lasted only three months, when he was deposed by the king of Egypt, who appointed Jehoiakim (whose original name was Eliakim) to be king and changed his name (2 K. 23:30-37; 2 Chr. 36:1-8). Jehoiakim was a wicked king, as is shown for example by his attitude toward Jeremiah's prophecy (Jer. 36). In his fourth year (2 K. 24:1; Jer. 46:1; Dan. 1:1, 2; cf. App. I) he became subject to Neb., and three years later revolted. After his revolt he and Jerusalem became the objects of predatory raids by roving bands, which were probably under Neb.'s direction (2 K. 24:2). Jehoiakim reigned eleven years, and was succeeded by his son, Jehoiachin (2 K. 23:36-24:9; Jer. 22:19; 36:30, *Antiq.* x:6,3). *Judah*]-a designation of the southern kingdom, comprising the tribe of Judah and most of Benjamin, which remained true to David's house at the time of Jeroboam's schism (Cf. 1 K. 12:16-19; 2 Chr. 10:16-19). *Came*] —not *set forth* as H, Keil, Zœckler. This translation is grammatically possible and not "opposed to Heb. usage" (Driver), but it is not necessary here (See App. I). *Nebuchadnezzar*]—(in Akkadian Nabu—kudurri—usur, Nebo, defend the boundary?). In Ezek. and Jer. spelled Nebuchadrezzar. Neb. was the son of Nabopolassar who in 625 B. C. founded the Neo-Babylonian Empire. In 605 B. C. Neb., after besieging Jerusalem as stated in this vs. ascended the throne of Babylon. *King*]—the statement is not inaccurate, but is used proleptically (Charles, Driver), as we say "In the childhood of President Washington." *Jerusalem*]—the capital city of the southern kingdom and dwelling place of Jehoiakim.

And besieged]—The duration of this siege is not mentioned, but Jerusalem was well protected, and difficult to capture (Cf. 2 K. 25:1-3). Ibn Ali suggests that Neb. either "stormed the city, as some think, or the people may have opened the gates. The latter is the more likely, as no battle is mentioned."

Vs. 2. *And the Lord gave into his hand Jehoiakim king of Judah and a part of the vessels of the house of God, and he brought them to the land of Shinar to the house of his god, and the vessels he brought to the treasure house of his god.*[1]

---

[1] Some commentators consider the text to be rough, and not accurately to represent the original. Various attempts have been made to restore what is supposed to be the original. Some, e.g., Driver, Charles, would delete with the LXX *to the house of his god.* But these words are found in Th. Their deletion does not remove any supposed difficulties, and so, we are not to regard them "as a gloss, intended originally to define the position of the 'treasure' house of clause *b,* which has found its way into the text in a wrong place" (Driver). Nor, does it help (with Behrmann) to delete 2b, *and the vessels,* etc. This procedure does not really have objective textual support. Furthermore, if the clause is not original, it is difficult to see why it was added, since it is the presence of this clause which constitutes the greatest difficulty in the vs. The objections which Charles raises against Behrmann's procedure, are largely subjective (See Charles, in loc.) The most drastic reconstruction of the text is that proposed by Charles, who asserts that the actual text presupposes in vs. 2 a definite mention of the transportation of captives to Babylon. Also, the text, according to Charles, is wrong in stating that God gave Jehoiakim and *only a part* of the vessels into the hand of Neb. What the original text meant, he thinks, was that *all* the vessels were given into Neb.'s hands, but that he transported to Babylon only a part of them and some of the most important classes of the Jewish population.

Since the phrase *the house of his god* presupposes that the suffix *them* refers only to the vessels, Charles would delete it, and presents the following reconstruction. "And the Lord gave J. King of Judah into his hand. And part of [the seed royal and of the nobles and part of] the vessels of the house of God he carried into the land of Shinar but the vessels he brought into the treasure house of his god." With respect to this reconstruction we would remark:

1. The presuppositions upon which it is based are purely gratuitous and subjective. There is no warrant for the assumption that vs. two must make some specific mention of the deportation of captives. When the text declares that God gave Jehoiakim into Neb.'s hand, this statement naturally implies the collapse of the Judean government. It certainly does not mean that only the king was taken and everyone else escaped. Consequently, the mere statement that Jehoiakim fell furnishes a sufficient preparation for the mention of captives in vs. 3.

2. How does Charles know that the writer meant to say that all the vessels were given into Neb.'s hands? All the ancient versions support the Heb. at this point. The Heb. word is used in a partitive sense (see below), and doubtless the point of the text is merely to describe what actually did occur. As a matter of historical fact, it should be noted that not all the vessels of the temple were carried away at this time. Some were taken later at the deportation of Jehoiachin (2 K. 24:13). and some were not removed until the destruction of the city at the time of Zedekiah (Jer. 27:19-22). Since upon hearing of the death of his father (See App. I) Neb. had to give up the siege and return to Babylon, it may very well be that the text is

The Lord]—not the covenant name, usually rendered in English, Jehovah, but Adonai, which means *lord, master.* Although Neb. was not conscious of the fact, he was nevertheless an instrument of the Divine will. God permitted this action, because ultimately it was for the good of His people. *Gave*]—It is not explicitly stated that the entire city was taken, but merely that the king and a part of the vessels were given into the hand of Neb. For the expression *to give into one's hand* cf. Ju. 3:10; Jer. 20:4, etc. *and a part etc.*]—Keil, Kranichfeld, Zœckler take this word as an abbreviation for the phrase *from end to end* (cf. Jer. 25:33; Gen. 47:21), and interpret the passage as meaning that from end to end the store of treasure contributed its share. But it seems best to take it (as does Maurer, who gives the best philological discussion) in a partitive sense as meaning *a part of the whole,* i. e., *some.* The strict interpretation of the words would seem to constitute strong evidence that at this time the entire city did not fall into Neb.'s hands. *Vessels of the house of God*]—i.e., the sacred vessels of the temple. Under Cyrus (Ezra 1:7) a portion of the treasures were returned, and again under Darius (Ezra 6:5). See App. II. The designation *house of God* is generally used by post-exilic writers (e. g., 52 times in Chr.), whereas exilic and pre-exilic writers employed

---

perfectly accurate in stating that the Lord gave only a part of the vessels into his hand. There are no objective grounds for Charles' assumption that the writer's purpose was to state that the Lord gave *all* the vessels into the king's hand.

3. Charles assumes that the words which he brackets in his reconstruction were omitted by a scribe through homoioteleuton. But there is no objective evidence for this assumption. These words, despite Charles, are not indispensable for this vs. Ewald had previously suggested the insertion of the words *with the noblest of the land* after the word *Judah* and with the remark *inserted by conjecture.* His suggestion, however, has not been widely received, since, like the addition of Charles, it appears to be based upon the unfounded assumption that vs. 2 must make some mention of the captives. See Ewald's note (Eng. Ed., vol. V, p. 310). The reason why this insertion has not met with widespread favor is that it does not actually remove the difficulties of vs. 2 (Cf. Driver).

4. By his reconstruction Charles has not really removed the principal difficulty of vs. 2, which is to be found in the disjunction between *a part of the vessels* and *the vessels.* If anything, Charles, by his removal of the suffix *them* and his substitution of *and part of the vessels* as the object of *he carried,* heightens this disjunction. The words of 2b, *but the vessels,* are not to be taken as explicative (Keil), but as adversative, as Charles rightly does. Because of their position, they are emphatic (Driver) and would at first sight seem to presuppose a previous reference to something else, as. e.g., *the captives* he took to Babylon, *but the vessels* to the treasure house. Now, it is precisely this *heightened disjunction* between the *vessels* on the one hand and the suffix *them* in *and he brought them* on the other, that constitutes the difficulty. And it is this difficulty which Charles, rather than having lessened, has actually increased, for now we must understand the text as declaring that on the one hand the king carried a part of the vessels to Babylon, but on the other he brought the vessels to the treasure house. To say the least this does not help. We therefore reject Charles' proposals and shall seek to interpret the text as it stands.

house of the Lord. Cf. however, Ju. 18:31. Dan. deliberately uses the word because of theological reasons. He wishes, it would seem, to emphasize the fact that this is the temple of the *true God,* in opposition to the false deities of the Babylonian court. Hence, he always prefixes the definite article, *the God,* an incidental evidence of the unity of the book. Since the phrase had already thus been employed in Ju. 18:31, appeal cannot be made to it here as supporting a late post-exilic date for the authorship of Dan.

And he brought them]—The most natural interpretation is to refer the suffix *them* to both Jehoiakim and the vessels. Against this it is argued that the phrase *to the house of his god* would be spoken only of the vessels. Why should Jehoiakim and the captives be brought to the temple? Some have suggested that the captives were exhibited as spoils of war, but this is mere conjecture. Hitzig seeks to solve the difficulty by taking the word *house* in the sense *land,* as in Hos. 9:15. But, as Keil indicates, this interpretation is not permissible here. If, then, the suffix does have reference to Jehoiakim, we must admit the difficulty caused by the presence of the word *house,* etc., and acknowledge that we are not able, at least for the present, to solve the difficulty, or else we must limit the reference of the suffix to include only the vessels, as do most of the commentators, e. g., Calvin, Maurer, Stuart, Rosenmueller, Keil, Hævernick, Driver. However, the adversative force of the phrase *and the vessels* tells against this. The language is difficult—but not corrupt—and, despite the difficulties involved, it perhaps is best to refer the suffix to both the king and the vessels. *The land of Shinar*]—i. e., Babylonia. The explanation of the name is uncertain. Prince and others regard it as a variation of *Shumer.* Other exilic writers speak of "the land of Babylon" (Jer. 51:29) or "the land of the Chaldeans" Ezek. 12:13, but this designation, which occurs also in Gen. 10:10; 11:2; 14:1, 9; Jos. 7:21; Isa. 11:11; Zech. 5:11, is well chosen as a designation of the land of Nimrod and the Tower of Babel "which is the antithesis of the theme of Dan." (M).

To the house of his god]—If any particular god is to be singled out, it is probably Marduk. *And the vessels*]—These, as booty, were placed in the treasure house of the god, probably as a *thank offering.* Cf. also Ezra 1:7; 5:14. According to Haller, the purpose of the introductory vv. is to give an historical background to the "collection of legends" in chs. 1-6. The narrator is supposed to use consciously the style of historical writing that is found in the book of Kings. In order to make the narrative appear as a piece of actual history, he placed the events in a period of antiquity and chose the exile as suitable for this purpose. The only evidence which Haller adduces to support this view is his assertion that the historical introduction is only "halb richtig" (But cf. App. I.).

b. vv. 3-7 The introduction of the four Jewish youths, Dan. and his three companions

Vs. 3. *And the king commanded Ashpenaz, the chief of his eunuchs to bring from the children of Israel and from the seed of the kingdom and from the nobles. Commanded*]—*lit.*, said to. The idiom is used principally in the exilic and post-exilic writings, and the verb has this sense in Arabic, Ethiopic and Aramaic, cf. Dan. 2:12, 46; 3:13, 19, 20; 4:23; 6:24. *Ashpenaz*]—Various etymologies have been proposed, *the man whose face is sad,* i.e., *harsh* (Saadia); *quick help* Simon (as given by Rosenmueller); LXX, *Abiezdri,* probably because of identification of this officer with the Melzar, v. 11 (see on v. 11); Syriac reads *Ashpaz; the goddess has formed the seed* (Lenormant); identified with Ashkenaz Gen. 10:3 (Hitzig, cf. Cheyne); *horse-nose, aspa—nasa* (Old Persian) so, (Zœckler). These identifications must be rejected. The word has also been found in non- Biblical texts, and its etymology is uncertain. It may possibly be a shortened form, like Asnapper (Ezra 4:10). Charles' statement "The word is corrupt, . . ." is too dogmatic. This officer was chief-marshal or majordomo of the court. *Chief* is the translation of *Rab,* which is used in the titles of Assyrian and Babylonian officials in 2 K. and Jer. Cf. Jer. 39:3. The word translated *eunuch* may be used in a broader sense, as of Potiphar, who was married, (Gen. 37:36). Etymologically, the word may represent the Babylonian sha reshi (of the heads) i.e., *leading men.* I am inclined to think that the word is broader in meaning here than *eunuch,* although in ancient times eunuchs did hold positions of great authority. At any rate, it is not necessary to assume with Josephus that the Jewish youths were made eunuchs. Theodoret suggests that this passage presents a fulfilment of Isa. 39:7, and this, I believe, is correct. The Targum on Isaiah renders the word as *nobles.* On the Isaiah passage Alexander remarks, "The fulfilment of this prophecy is recorded in 2 Kings 24:12-16 and Dan. 1:1-7, and that so clearly that the neologists are driven to their usual supposition of an interpolation, or of such an alteration as to make the tenors of the prediction more determinate."[2] *To bring*]—Rosenmueller, Stuart, Keil, and others would take this to mean that the Israelites were to be brought from Palestine to Babylon. But it is better, with Maurer, Driver, etc., to consider the command as referring to those who are already at Babylon.. Probably they are to be brought into the king's palace (as in 1:18). *Children of Israel*]—The name is not to be restricted to the southern kingdom, nor is it here used as a mere designation of the ten tribes. Rather, as Keil correctly indicates, it is here employed as the

---

[2] J. A. Alexander: *The Earlier Prophecies of Isaiah,* New York, 1846, p. 650.

theocratic name of the chosen people. The word *from* is used in a partitive sense. A number of commentators take the expressions of the vs. as correlative, thus finding three classes. If this be done, the three classes may be divided, one consisting of Israelites, and the others probably of Babylonians. This would seem to be the meaning of the LXX and Th. Or, the three classes may be referred to different groups of Israelites, and various modifications of this idea appear in different commentaries (Cf. Ibn Ali, Rosenmueller, Keil, Zœckler, etc.). Others, as Bertholdt, take the two *ands* in the sense of *either . . . or*, i. e., *Israelites, either . . . or*. But Hævernick seems to have indicated the correct view, and in this he is essentially followed by many. The designation *Israelites* is general, and the two subsequent phrases are explicative. Thus, we might paraphrase, "from the Israelites, both of the royal seed and nobles." Charles thinks that the Heb. is defective, and that the words *the exiles* should be added to the designation, *sons of the exiles of Israel.* Th. inserts *the captivity* and LXX *the chief men.* Charles is correct in saying that these glosses are needless, however, is it not likely that the Greek versions inserted the phrase because of its appearance in other Biblical passages, e. g., Dan. 2:25; Ezra 4:1; 6:19, 20, Jer. 24:5; 28:4; 29:22; 40:1, etc.? It should be noted that nowhere in the Bible is the theocratic phrase *children of Israel* broken by the insertion of words such as *exile* or *exiles.* We conclude that at this point the Greek versions are defective and the Heb. correct.

The seed of the Kingdom]—i.e., royal seed. Rosenmueller refers it to the seed of David's royal family. *Nobles*]—These were Israelitish, not Babylonian nobles, and the word, as M indicates, "may represent actual courtly use," in speaking of the Israelitish captives. That vs. 6 implies the presence of other than Israelitish captives does not militate against the interpretation here adopted.

Vs. 4. *Youths in whom there was no blemish, and good of appearance and intelligent in all wisdom and knowers of knowledge and understanding science and who had power within them to stand in the palace of the king and whom they might teach the literature and language of the Chaldeans. Youths*]—not *children,* as A. V., but *young men.* The term does not admit of a definite conclusion respecting the age. Possibly these were youths of 14 (Maurer) or 15 (Rosenmueller). The word is the direct object of *to bring* (vs. 3). "What is said in vs. 5 concerning a period of three years during which Daniel was in training, corresponds remarkably with these statements" (Zœckler). *Blemish*]—Physical imperfection, cf. Lev. 21:17, 18. Charles is probably correct in saying that such perfection could not be asserted of eunuchs. Youths of perfect physical form were chosen not only to grace the court but also because it was probably thought that they would have the best intellect. Cf. 2 S. 14:25; Song of Solomon 4:7. *Good of appearance*]—Good looking, cf. Gen. 24:16; 26:7. "Corporeal soundness and a handsome form were considered indispensable among the ancient Orientals for those who were destined for court service" (Zœckler). Apparently this has been the case in Turkey and Persia, even during the nineteenth century. *Intelligent*]—the ability to apply themselves to the Chaldean, not Jewish, subjects of wisdom. Hence, *discerning, understanding,* rather than *experienced* or *well versed.* The descriptive phrases do not designate three distinct mental functions, but are rather accummulative in force. Furthermore, they are not to be taken in a future sense, as though these were aptitudes which the youths were in the future to acquire, but they refer to aptitudes which have already been acquired. The intellectual and physical qualifications go hand in hand. The king desired those who possessed a *mentem sanam in corpore sano. Knowers of knowledge*]—a cognate acc. An emphasis and amplification of the preceding. *Understanding science*]—Perception or discernment in knowledge. All these phrases simply serve to emphasize the fact that the youths were skilled in all kinds of knowledge. *Power to stand*]—The ability or capacity, i. e., the requisite bodily and mental fitness and endowments "appropriately to stand in the place of the king, and as servants to attend to his commands" (Keil). For the meaning of *to stand* cf. Gen. 18:8; 41:46; Deut. 1:38. *To teach them*]—after *commanded* vs. 3. Lit., *He commanded . . . also to teach them,* better than to make the infinitive depend upon *ability,* i. e., *ability to teach them, for being taught. The literature*]—lit., *the book,* i. e., literary knowledge, letters. The word is not to be construed with *Chaldeans. Language*]—The cuneiform languages of Babylonia. This interpretation was first hinted at by Keil (1869). Probably the word is used in a broad sense to include not merely the original language of the Chaldeans, but also the cuneiform scripts generally. At any rate, the reference to Aramaic, held by many expositors must be rejected. (e. g., Jerome *chaldaicus sermo.* Until the rise of Assyriology this view prevailed). *Chaldeans*]—The writer believes that the term in this vs. is used in a broad ethnic sense, *the Chaldean people* or nation, rather than in its restricted sense, as, e. g., in 2:2.

M points out that "The royal court of letters played its part in ancient antiquity as well as in later civilizations; the Epistle of Aristeas represents the Jewish tradition of Ptolemy II's intellectual coterie of scholars; the Story of Ahikar proved how valuable the trained thinker was to the king in his political emergencies" (p. 121). Throughout their history, as M rightly indicates, the Jews (cf. the story of Joseph) were ready to accept secular education without doing despite to their religious beliefs. Certainly the Scriptures place no premium upon ignorance, and Dan. and his companions were but taking advantage of every opportunity in order the better to prepare themselves for the service of God.

Vs. 5. *And the king appointed to them a daily portion from the assignment of the king and from the wine which he drank; and to bring them up three years so that at their expiration they might stand before the king.* Charles, and probably Baumgartner, would transpose the latter half of this vs, to place it before the first half. The infinitive "to bring them up" would thus more regularly follow the infinitives of vv. 3, 4, each of which depends upon "commanded" in vs. 3, thus, "And the king commanded... to bring (vs. 3) ... and to teach (vs. 4) ... and to bring up (vs. 5)." It must be confessed that this would regularize the construction, but there is no objective evidence whatsoever to support it.

Appointed]—In the sense of numerical distribution (M).

A daily portion]—Lit., the thing of a day in its day. Cf. also Jer. 52:34; I Chr. 16:37. *From the assignment*]—The word is Old Persian, *patibaga,* which means *assignment.* (See M for the best philological discussion). Driver's rendering *delicacies* is thus not strictly accurate; although the *assignment* would doubtless include food of the best quality.

Wine which he drank]—lit., *of his drinking.* It was Oriental custom to feed officers of the court from the king's table, and this custom prevailed even in Israel. While it is true that some Greek writers speak of the ages at which the special training of Persian boys commenced and ended (see *infra* under *three years*), nevertheless our knowledge of the educational systems of ancient Persia and Babylon is scanty. Hence, there is no warrant for the suggestion that we are here presented with a picture of Persian rather than Babylonian life.

To be brought up]—The youths were to be brought up, lit., *made great.* The infinitive *to bring them up* depends not upon *he commanded* (vs. 3), but upon *he appointed* (vs. 5). Zœckler suggests that the primary reference may be to physical culture, but this does not necessarily follow. Both physical and intellectual education are included, cf. e. g., Isa. 1:2; 2 K. 10:6. *Three years*]—Plato, *Alcibiades* 1:121, states that the education of Persian youths began in their 14th year, and Xenophon, Cy., 1, 2 mentions the 16th or 17th years as the close. The Avesta says that a student for holy training should go to a master for three years. *To stand*]—i. e., to serve the king. The verb expresses the purpose of the training. It must be noted that this training was not specifically religious, but was to prepare the youths for serving the king in his court. Cf. Deut. 1:38; 1 K. 10:8; 12:8.

Vs. 6. *And there were among them (some) from the children of Judah, Daniel, Hananiah, Mishael and Azariah.* These four youths of Judah are named specifically since they are the subjects of the following narrative.

The mention of these four does not necessarily exclude the presence of other youths from Judah. *Daniel*]—probably means *God has judged,* although it is wise not to be dogmatic in asserting the meaning of proper names. The name occurs elsewhere, Ezek. 14:14, 20; 28:3; 1 Chr. 3:1, a son of David, and Ezra 8:2; Neh. 10:6, a priest. M gives some extra-Biblical occurrences of the name, to which may now be added its appearance upon the Ras Shamra texts (See App. IV).

Hananiah]—probably *Jehovah has been gracious.* The name appears elsewhere in the Bible, Jer. 36:12; 2 Chr. 26:11; 1 Chr. 25:23, etc., and also in extra-Biblical material (see M). *Mishael*]—not *who is God?* (Hommel); more generally it is taken to mean *who is what God is?* (e. g., Charles). M suggests that the first part of the name means *salvation.* This name also occurs elsewhere in the Bible, Ex. 6:22; Neb. 8:4. *Azariah*]—*Jehovah has helped?* occurs frequently in the O. T. M suggests that the absence of patronymics here indicates "a failure in historic verisimilitude." This is subjective, since each of these names occurs without patronymics in other passages, the historicity of which there is no sufficient reason to doubt.

Vs. 7. *And the prince of the eunuchs gave to them names, and he gave to Daniel Belteshazzar and to Hananiah Shadrach and to Mishael Meshach and to Azariah Abed-nego.* The term *prince* here is synonymous with chief (vs. 3). The custom of changing a person's name when he entered upon new conditions or positions in life, is, as Stuart pointed out, extensively developed in the O. T., e. g., Gen. 17:5; 41:45; 2 S. 12:24, 25; 2 K. 23:34; 24:17; Esther 2:7. "These names thus imposed anew, generally designate something which is intended to honor the persons who receive them, or to honor the god that is worshipped by him who imposes them, or to commemorate some event that is interesting, etc." (Stuart). Driver points out that this change of name, when a person enters public service in a foreign country, is well attested in the case of Egypt (Gen. 41:45). *Belteshazzar*]—possibly intended to represent the Babylonian Balatusu-usur *Protect his life! Shadrach*]—possibly an intentional perversion of Marduk. *Meshach*]—the word has not yet been satisfactorily interpreted. *Abed-nego*]—Servant of Nebo? Thus, the two names which bore the theophoric element—yah, are probably changed to contain the theophoric elements Marduk and Nebo. At any rate, in each case the change has the effect of obliterating the name of the true God. Calvin is doubtless correct in saying that "the design of the king was to lead these youths to adopt the customs of the Chaldeans, that they might have nothing in common with the chosen people."

Haller remarks that in the light of Dan. 2:1, with its mention of the 2nd year of Neb., there is no room for the three year period of training

(Daniels dreijaehrige Pagenzeit) of 1:3, 5, 18. The mention of a date is supposed to give the impression of true history, but in reality it indicates that we are not dealing with true history. So sehr der Verfasser auch bestrebt ist, den Eindruck zu erwecken, als schreibe er wirkliche Geschichte (z. B. durch die genaue Datierung der Ereignisse), so wenig hat doch seine Erzaehlung mit wirklicher Geshichtsschreibung gemein, wie sie in der Koenigzeit gepflegt wurde und auch sofort wieder erwachte, als das Judentum selbst Geschichte erlebte (I. Makk.). Seine Aufgaben sind wertvoll fuer eine Charakteristik des Judentums in der Diaspora, keinenfalls aber fuer die Kenntniss der Geschichte der Reiche, unter deren Herrschern er sein Helden auftreten laesst." These utterly incorrect remarks will be answered in connection with the discussion of 2:1.

c. vv. 8-16. The first triumph of God's grace in Babylonia: Daniel and his companions abstain from the appointed food of the king.

Vs. 8. *And Daniel laid upon his heart that he should not defile himself with the assignment of the king, and with the wine which he drank, and he sought from the chief of the eunuchs that he might not defile himself.*

Laid]—gave heed, cf. Isa. 42:25; 47:7; 57:1, 11; Mal. 2:2. Dan. here exhibits both his steadfast devotion to principle and his courteous common sense. To have partaken of the king's food and wine would, in Dan's. opinion, have involved self-defilement. The reason for this has been admirably expressed by Keil: "The partaking of the food brought to them from the king's table was to them contaminating, because forbidden by law; not so much because the food was not prepared according to the Levitical ordinance, or perhaps consisted of the flesh of animals which to the Israelites were unclean, for in this case the youths were not under the necessity of refraining from the wine, but the reason of their rejection of it was, that the heathen at their feasts offered up in sacrifice to their gods a part of the food and the drink, and thus consecrated their meals by a religious rite; whereby he who participated in such a meal participated in the worship of idols, but the meat and the wine as a whole were the meat and the wine of an idol sacrifice, partaking of which, according to the saying of the apostle (I Cor. 10:20f.), is the same as sacrificing to devils." To accomplish this end, Dan. displays no fanaticism or rudeness, but candidly states his purpose to the chief chamberlain and asks his help. At this point as throughout his life, Dan. exhibits himself as a true gentleman. He never yields in devotion to principle, but he does not permit devotion to principle to serve as a cloak for rudeness or fanaticism. He was a true hero of the Faith.

The view of von Lengerke, that this episode reveals a Maccabean background, has been adopted by others, e.g., Bevan, Charles. However, the aversion to defilement was certainly earlier, cf. Amos 7:17; Hosea 9:3f. It is perfectly true that loyal Jews did seek to resist the edicts of Antiochus which would compel them to eat unclean food (1 *Macc.* 1:47, 48, 62, 63. See also 2 *Macc.* 5:27.) Nevertheless, the account in Dan. is characterized by every absence of fanaticism (cf. also *Add. to Esther* 14:17; *Judith* 12:1, 2; *Tobit* 1:10, 11; Josephus, *Life* 3 for other illustrations). *To defile himself*]—Cf. Zeph. 3:1; Isa. 59:3; Mal. 1:7, 12.

Vs. 9. *And God made Daniel to find kindness and compassion before the chief eunuch.* The sequence of ideas is historical. Upon the request of Dan., God inspired the officer with favor toward him. *kindness*]—lit., *God gave Daniel to kindness, etc.* The chief eunuch recognized that Dan.'s request was made upon the basis of principle and he respected the request. This recognition was the result of divine grace. The word *God* has the definite article prefixed in order to show that this was the work of the true God. Cf. Gen. 39:21. God always honors the true witness of His faithful servants.

Vs. 10 *And the chief eunuch said to Daniel, I fear my lord the king who has appointed your food and your drink lest he should see your faces more gloomy than the youths who are of your age, and ye should make my head guilty to the king. Gloomy*]—in consequence of eating inferior food. Cf. Gen. 40:6 where the word is used of the butler and baker of Pharaoh, who were mentally disturbed. *Than*]—i.e., *than the faces of the youths.* The word *faces* is to be supplied. *Guilty*]—According to M the phrase means to "put (the responsibility) on my head," and does not necessarily imply capital punishment. Generally, however, the commentators suggest that capital punishment is involved. To my mind the evidence is not sufficient to enable one to speak dogmatically upon the question.

Vs. 11. *And Daniel said unto the Melzar whom the chief eunuch had appointed over Daniel, Hananiah, Mishael and Azariah. The Melzar*]—the word occurs only in this ch. According to some of the older versions it was regarded as a proper name. However, Saadia considered it as an appellative, and this view has generally held sway among Jewish and Protestant commentators (cf. e.g., Calvin's excellent discussion of the vs.) The etymological derivation of the word is difficult to determine. Attempts have been made to derive it from the old Persian and Arabic, and also to find its origin in the Assyrian massaru (nsr) *guardian.* M makes out a very convincing case to the effect that the word is an old Akkadian or Aramaic term for *guard.* At any rate, it should be regarded as the title of an official who was under the chief eunuch. He was probably a *steward* (Calvin) or *warden* (M); certainly not a *president of alumni* (Hitzig). Charles questions the genuineness of the Heb. text of this vs. on the grounds that Dan. has already been committed to the care of the chief eunuch and not to some third person called the Melzar. This position is essentially supported by the LXX, which reads: *And Daniel spake unto Abiezdri who had been appointed chief eunuch over Daniel,* etc. In answer to this position it may be remarked that although the chief eunuch had been set over Dan., is it not conceiveable that he could have appointed to a subordinate the specific responsibility for Dan.'s training? Apparently, that is what did occur. Since Dan.'s attempt to secure his wish from the chief eunuch had failed, he refuses to desist, but appeals to a subordinate, who doubtless knew of the chief eunuch's action and who, being a subordinate, would not run the same risk. "It is a clear and serious proof of our faith, when we are not fatigued when anything adverse occurs, and never consider the way closed against us" (Calvin).

Vs. 12. *Try, I pray thee, thy servants ten days, and let there be given us pulse to eat and water to drink. Try*]—This command is not a wager of faith (M), nor is Keil correct that it is merely an example of "the confidence of living faith which hopes in the presence and help of God." Rather, if Dan. had made this offer merely upon his own initiative, he would have been guilty of presumption. It seems to me that Calvin is correct in asserting that Dan. had received a special revelation from the Spirit of God and that, in speaking, he was acting in accord with that revelation. What warrant could faith have that at the expiration of a short period of time such a change would be apparent in the physical appearance of the youths as is suggested here? *Ten*]—a round number, as e.g., 1:20; 7:7; Amos 5:3; Zech. 8:23. *Let there be given*]—lit., *and let them* (i.e., those appointed for the purpose) *give. Pulse to eat*]—lit., *from the pulse that we may eat.* Driver is correct in referring this to vegetable food in general and in not restricting it to legumes, such as peas and beans. Although the word occurs only here, a somewhat similar word appears in Isa. 61:11 which means "the things that are sown." Here also the word means "the sown things". *Water to drink*]—lit., *water that we may drink.* From this vs. it appears not only that Dan. desired to abstain from food which in any sense might be regarded as dedicated to idols, but also that he wished for himself simple, frugal fare, and in this choice possibly evinced the desire that he might be free from the luxuries of the king's court.

Vs. 13. *And let our countenance be seen before thee and the countenance of the youths who eat the appointed food of the king, and even as thou dost see, do with thy servants! Countenance*]—lit., *that which is seen, appearance*. The verb *be seen* is pl., because of the two subjects. *dost see*]—i.e., as thou dost see fit, not, as thou dost see us. If, after the specified time, the appearance of Dan. and his companions is not better than that of the others, let the Melzar handle the situation as he sees fit.

Vs. 14. *And he hearkened to them in this matter and he tried them ten days. Hearkened*]—i.e., granted this request, cf. Gen. 19:21; 1 Sam. 30:24. *Matter*]—lit., *in regard to this matter*. The definite article is prefixed to the word matter, which lends intensity to the concept—*this very matter*.

Vs. 15. *And at the end of ten days their appearance was seen to be better and fatter of flesh than all the youths who ate the appointed food of the king. Fatter*]—pl. in the Heb. Rosenmueller regards this as dependent upon *was seen* (lit., showed *itself, appeared*) understood; thus, and it was seen that they were fatter etc. Hævernick (followed by Bevan, Charles and M) adopt essentially this position when they call this a *constructio ad sensum*, referring to the pl. suffix in *THEIR appearance*. The meaning of the vs. can best be brought out by means of paraphrase. "When the period of ten days had expired their appearance was seen to be better and they were fuller in flesh than all the youths who had been eating the food which the king had appointed." The participle, *eating*, denotes continuous action. As Deane very rightly remarks, "Thus was God beginning to assert His power among the Babylonians. This change in the appearance of Daniel was the effect of His free grace, not of the meat that came from the king's palace."

Vs. 16. *Thus the Melzar continued taking away their appointed food and the wine that they should drink and giving to them pulse. Taking . . . giving*]—The participles when construed with the finite verb express duration. Lit., *and it came to pass that he was taking away*, etc. The treatment proved to be so successful that it was continued, and this fact is remarked in order to emphasize more effectively the improvement in the youths' condition.

According to Haller, we are dealing in this section with legends which probably arose in the third century B.C. These legends were written to serve as an introduction to the entire collection, and reflect a time when Jew and heathen could have lived peacefully together under the protection of a universal empire. The lines of distinction between Judaism and heathenism are not so sharply drawn here as would have been the case in the Maccabean age. The four youths are represented as examples of Jews who are true to the Law, and the story is a song in praise of a Judaism that abides by the Law (Die Geschichte ist also ein *Loblied auf das gesetzestreue Judentum*). Particularly is it the purpose of the legend to show that the Jewish dietary laws are healthful.

It is gratifying to note the fact that Haller acknowledges that these vv. do not present a Maccabean background. However, if the period is that in which Jew and heathen may have lived together in peace, why may not this have been the case at Babylon in the sixth century B.C.? All the available evidence points to the fact that the description given in Dan. well accords with what is known of the status of the Jews in Babylonia. Cf. Ezek. 3:24; 8:1; 14:1; 20:1; Jer. 29:5. "The inscriptions found in the business house at Nippur contain also a goodly number of Jewish names, which shows how the Jews are becoming settled and taking part in the business life of the country" (Mœller, art. "Ezekiel" in *ISBE*).

Furthermore, the narrative does not possess the characteristics of legend, but presents itself as straightforward history. Dan. abstains from that which in any sense might be regarded as idolatrous and he also recognizes the value of simple fare. However, he does not break off all contact with the heathen court, but is willing to learn what it can teach him. He acts as any true believer in God would have acted under similar circumstances. Haller has not adduced one particle of objective evidence to support his contention that the narrative presents an unhistorical legend rather than true history.

d. vv. 17-21. The progress of the four youths in the Chaldean wisdom and their entrance into the king's service.

Vs. 17. *And as for these four youths God gave to them knowledge and intelligence in all literature and wisdom; and Daniel had understanding in every kind of vision and dream.* The emphasis in this vs. lies in the contrast between the words "four youths" and "Daniel". All four made progress in literature and wisdom, but Dan, in addition was favored with the understanding of visions and dreams. These attainments were not necessarily because of superior ability, but were gifts of God. As in vs. 9, *God* has the prefixed article to indicate that the Author of these gifts was the true God. The entire course of life of these youths was in the hands of God. *Knowledge*]—cf. vs. 4. Calvin suggests that the reference is merely to the liberal arts and not to the magical practices of Chaldea, since God would not approve of these latter. However, it is more likely that the *literature and wisdom* in which the youths were instructed did include superstitious practices. The knowledge and intelligence which God gave to them, therefore, was of a discerning kind, that they might know and possess the ability to accept what was true and to reject what was false in their instruction. That these youths might the more effectively serve the Lord at a heathen court, it was necessary that they should be deeply versed in all the Babylonian "wisdom" just as it had been necessary for Moses to be versed in the wisdom of Egypt (Acts 7:22) "so as to be able to put to shame the wisdom of this world by the hidden wisdom of God" (Keil). *Wisdom*]—i.e., "an intelligently arranged body of principles, or, as we should now say, *science*" (Driver). That the youths did not accept the superstitious and false elements in this *wisdom* is shown by the later examples of their steadfast faith in God (e.g., Dan. 3:6.), *Daniel*]—The statement concerning Dan. is somewhat in the nature of an introductory remark, to prepare the reader for his interpretation of Neb.'s dream in ch. 2. As Zœckler rightly points out, this ability is plainly a miraculous gift which should not be confused with the *donum propheticum* (See Introduction: III.). It is certainly true that Dan. himself possessed the ability to see visions and dreams (e.g., ch. 7), but the present vs. has reference to the ability of interpreting the dreams and visions of *others*, and thus it serves as a preparation for the events recorded in ch. 2. *Had understanding*]—attained readiness or facility in interpreting. "...Daniel was able to *discern* or *distinguish* the import of every kind of vision and of dreams" (Stuart). *Vision and dreams*]—By means of vision and dream God made known His will to true prophets (Num. 12:1-8). The term vision was also used as a synonym for revelation (cf. Isa. 1:1). However, the true method of revelation was imitated by false prophets and diviners (cf. e.g., Jer. 23:25ff.). Here the terms are broad and include both true and false visions and dreams. Thus, Dan. received the ability to tell whether a vision was from God and thus true, or whether it was a mere invention of the mind of man. In addition he was able to declare the true interpretation of the vision or dream. However, the words *had understanding* need not necessarily imply that Dan. was always able to interpret. The interpretation of Neb.'s dream was given to Dan. by means of a special revelation (cf. 2:19).

M's comments at this point are not strictly accurate and are likely to lead to confusion. He suggests that "Dan.'s specialty in visions and dreams does not belong to the highest category of revelation, that of prophecy; the Prophets had long since passed away, 1 Mac. 4:46 . . . " and "Dreams and visions belonged to a lower and often deceptive form of revelation, cf. Jer. 23, a fact recognized in Ecclus. 34:1ff." But M fails to distinguish between true revelation and pretended revelation. Those who were raised up of the LORD received their communications from Him by means of visions and dreams, and in this form of true revelation there was nothing deceptive. Those who pretended to have received dreams and revelations, as, e.g., the prophets described in Jer. 23, would naturally deceive. Furthermore, the reason why it was given Dan. to *have understanding* in visions and dreams was not that prophecy had long since passed away. Rather, it was the fact that Dan. had to live in an atmosphere where stress was laid upon dreams. In addition Dan. also possessed the *donum propheticum,* so that he was rightly called a prophet in the N.T. (Matt. 24:15). The emphasis upon dreams and visions is an accurate reflection of the Babylonian background of the narrative. Joseph had been placed in circumstances somewhat similar to those of Dan., and to him also had been given the power to *have understanding* in dreams.

Vs. 18. *And at the end of the days that the king had appointed for bringing them in, then the chief eunuch brought them in before Nebuchadnezzar. At the end*]—not "and toward the end of the time" (Von Lengerke) but as in vs. 5 (Bevan). *Appointed*]—lit., *said,*—i.e., *commanded,* to bring them in that they might begin their service in the court. *Them*]—the reference, as shown by vs. 19, is not merely to the four Hebrew youths but to all mentioned in vv. 3, 4.

Vs. 19. *And the king spoke with them and there was not found among all of them (any) like Daniel, Hananiah, Mishael and Azariah, and (so) they stood before the king. Spoke*]—i.e., by means of ordinary conversation the king sought to discover the abilities and progress of the youths. Ad explorandos eorum profectus (Rosenmueller). *Among*]—i.e., out of all of them. *Like*]—both in physical appearance and mental capacities. *They stood*]—As Hitzig pointed out, the force of the verb is inceptive, *they began to stand,* i.e., they entered into the personal service of the king (cf. vs. 5). "The king, by his own personal examination, fixed upon the very individuals as his personal waiters, whom Providence had distinguished by peculiar gifts which rendered them superior to the other children" (Stuart).

Vs. 20. *And in every matter of wisdom of understanding which the king sought from them, he found them ten times better than all the magicians (and) the astrologers who were in all his kingdom.* Lit., *And in everything which was a matter etc. Wisdom*]—Some versions would read *wisdom and understanding,* but the more unusual reading is probably to be preferred, and thus the intensity of the description is preserved, for "—the writer means to characterize the highest degree of acute discernment in matters abstruse and difficult" (Stuart). Wisdom, as here employed, refers to objective knowledge or science, and *understanding* to those powers of perception and insight which enable the mind to make proper distinctions and so to arrive at accuracy of knowledge. The force of the combined words is well given by Driver "wisdom determined or regulated by understanding." *Sought*]—i.e., inquired. *Ten times*]—lit., hands. *Better than*]—lit., above, i.e., superior to. *Magicians*]—The etymology of this word is obscure. It occurs also in 2:2, 10, 27; 4:7, 9; 5:7 and outside of Dan. (where it refers to the magicians of Egypt) in Gen. 41:8, 24; Ex. 7:11, 22; 8:7, 18, 19; 9:11. Perhaps the word as here employed does in some sense represent Egyptian magic, but Driver may be correct in asserting that it has reference to "men acquainted with occult arts in general." *Astrologers*]—the conjunction is omitted as in 5:15. A Babylonian term is used, which represents Babylonian magic. The two words are not here employed in a strictly technical sense.

Vs. 21. *And Daniel continued unto the first year of Cyrus the king.* This vs. has given rise to difficulty because of the statement in 10:1 that a revelation was made to Dan. in the *third* year of Cyrus. Various solutions of the difficulty have been offered. Ewald thought that some words had fallen out and that the text should read *So Daniel was at the king's court until the first year of King Cyrus.* Some would translate *he remained alive,* but this constitutes a flat contradiction of 10:1, since it implies that Daniel died in the first year of Cyrus. Some would actually emend the text to read *he lived* (so Hitzig). Ibn Ezra suggested "he remained in honor." But the true meaning of the text was set forth by Haevernick, namely, that Dan. continued until the first year of Cyrus. This use of the verb (lit., *was*) occurs also in Jer. 1:3, and Ruth 1:2, and the preposition *unto* does not exclude the remote future, cf. Ps. 110:1; 112:8. The thought is that Dan. continued until the time of Cyrus and beyond. Why, then, is the *first* year of Cyrus mentioned? The answer is that this was a period of particular importance. It was, for the Jews, the beginning of a new era (cf. Isa. 44:28; 45:1), the year of their deliverance. This great event was witnessed by Dan., about seventy years after his own captivity (cf. also 2 Chr. 36:22; Ezra 1:1; 6:3). The effect of the statement is that Dan. lived through the whole period of the Exile, per totum exsilii tempus (Maurer). Keil compares Jer. 1:2, 3 with its reference to the eleventh year of Zedekiah, although the book contains prophecies which date from after the taking of Jerusalem. "We are led to think of Daniel during this period holding high positions in the courts of Nebuchadnezzar, Belshazzar, and Darius, yet so using the things of this world that at the close of his life (Chap. 10:11) he became the man greatly beloved by God" (Deane).

Haller asserts that 1:21 contradicts 10:1 and concludes therefrom that the composer of ch. 1 was not acquainted with the second half of the book. However, as the above exegesis shows, there is no contradiction, and consequently, this conclusion does not follow. Ch. 1 is not to be regarded as an introduction merely to chs. 2-6 (Haller), but rather to the entire book.

According to Charles, 1:20 should properly occur after 2:49a for it "is at variance with all that precedes it in chapter 1, and with all that follows it in chapter 2 down to 2:49a." If the youths were *ten times* superior to the others, suggests Charles, why did not the king consult them? When placed after 2:49a, 1:20 would have reference not to Dan. but to his three companions who had been appointed officials and whom the king consulted, finding them ten times better than all the magicians and enchanters in his land.

In reply, however, it should be noted that 1:20 makes a distinct addition to the preceding. 1:17-19 relates the excellence of the youths in literature and wisdom and Dan.'s superiority in vision and dreams. 1:20 gives the additional information that this superior ability extended even to technical matters of science. It is, therefore, no mere recapitulation of the preceding. Furthermore, although upon this one occasion Dan. and his companions may have remarkably distinguished themselves, the king probably examined them but for a short time and might quite easily have forgotten them. That, in ch. 2, he should first call upon his own wise men is natural, since Dan. and his friends were still mere servants (Their promotion occurs in 2:48,49—I do not think we are to regard them, upon the basis of 1:19 as upon a level in rank with the wise men of Babylon).

Furthermore, whatever difficulty there may be is not resolved by transposing 1:20 in the manner that Charles desires. According to 2:48 Dan., because he has rightly interpreted the king's dream, has been elevated in position as ruler over the whole province of Babylon and also over the wise men. Dan. (2:49a) then requests that his three friends be given promotion, and the king set them over the affairs of the province of Babylon. Their promotion, apparently, was of a purely political nature. Now, if 1:20 be inserted at this point, it asserts that the king found these three (the suffix, according to Charles, would refer only to the three) in matters of wisdom and understanding ten times better than the magicians and astrologers. But what would be the point of such a comparison? Dan. was placed over the wise men, but the three were given purely administrative, governmental offices? What point is there in asserting that in matters of *technical science* (cf. the exegesis) these three, just appointed to political tasks, were superior to astrologers and magicians? We should expect rather a statement to the effect that these three showed themselves more capable in administering governmental affairs than any of the other governors. But, no, if this vs. be inserted after 2:49a, we are told that it was in matters of technical science that they distinguished themselves.

The comparison is pointless. It is clear that 1:20 does not belong after 2:49a but is in its proper place after 1:19, where, as the exegesis shows, it yields a good and satisfactory sense .

Nor does 1:21 belong after 2:49. As we have shown in the commentary, this vs. sets forth the fact that Dan. continued until the great event which occurred during the first year of Cyrus. Bevan's objection that this event is not alluded to elsewhere (save indirectly in 9:25) is beside the point. Why should there be allusion to it? 1:21 merely serves to give the reader a general idea as to the length of Dan.'s service. That Dan. himself (9:25) did not know when Jerusalem would be restored is no argument against the present position of this vs. If Dan. revised his whole book near the close of his life, why may not he *under Divine inspiration* have written this vs.? Or why may not this vs. have been inserted *under Divine inspiration* by the final editor of the book, if he were other than Dan.? At any rate, the presence of 1:21 is in no sense incongruous with the content of any of the subsequent portion of Dan.

CHAPTER TWO

a. Vv. 1-16. The dream of Nebuchadnezzar and the inability of the wise men to interpret it.

1. vv. 1-6. *Nebuchadnezzar the king dreams a dream by which he is greatly troubled and so summons the wise men of Babylon to tell him the dream and its interpretation.*

Vs. 1 *And in the second year of the reign of Nebuchadnezzar, Nebuchadnezzar dreamed dreams, so that his spirit was disturbed and his sleep left him.* The introductory *and* connects this ch. with 1:21. *The second year*]—This date is thought by some (e. g., Haller) to constitute a contradiction with what is said in ch. 1 about a three year period of training. If, so the argument runs, Dan. was brought to Babylon in the *first* year of Neb., and then entered upon a period of training which lasted *three* years, how could the events described in ch. 2 possibly have occurred during the *second* year of Neb.'s reign? Such is the argument, and varied indeed are the expedients which have been devised to answer it. Josephus (*Antiq.*, X: 10:3) speaks of this as the second year after the sack of Egypt. But the text clearly mentions the second year of the kingdom of Neb. Jehphet Ibn Ali says it is the second year after Neb. had become king of all the world (the 32nd year of his reign).

Some of the Jewish commentators believe that the reference is to the second year after the conquest of Jerusalem (Rashi, Ibn Ezra). Ewald, upon the basis of mere conjecture, offers the reading *twelfth* instead of *second.* Rosenmueller favors the view of Saadia that several dreams occurred during the second year and continued into the third (usque ad exactum annum tertium, quo demum tempore adolescentes Hebraei ad ministerium regium adducendi fuerant). Zœckler follows to the effect that Jer. 25:1 refers to the *first* year of Neb.'s co-reign, and the date in Dan. 2:1 to his second year as *sole* king. Thus, on this supposition, the date is about four years later than that in 1:1. M would read *six* for *two*, a reading which has much to commend it. The correct solution has probably been indicated by Driver, namely, the three years of training need not have been three full years but merely fractions of years, "By Heb. usage fractions of time were reckoned as full units: thus Samaria, which was besieged from the fourth to the sixth year of Hezekiah, is said to have been taken 'at the end' of three years (2 K. 18:9, 10); and in Jer. 34:14 'at the end of seven years' means evidently when the seventh year has arrived (see also Mark 8:31 etc.)" Thus, it is perfectly possible that the third year of training might fall in the second year of the kingship of Neb. A table will make this clear.

Years of Training		*Nebuchadnezzar*
First Year	=	Year of Accession.
Second Year	=	First Year.
Third Year	=	Second Year (in which dream occurred).

Upon this interpretation the first and third years are not to be regarded as full years. In the light of the above survey, the remarks of Prince are surely to be rejected, "All attempts on the part of the defenders of the authenticity of the Book to reconcile this assertion with C.1 are highly unsatisfactory." *Dreamed dreams*]—The s. occurs in vv. 3, 4, 5, and the use of the pl. has given rise to considerable discussion (Cf. also 4:2; 7:1). Butler thinks that the pl. indicates one dream containing "a succession of various events" and somewhat similarly Deane, one dream "in several parts". Keil calls it the pl. of intensive fullness "implying that the dream in its parts contained a plurality of subjects." Some of the rabbis referred the pl. to the dream and its interpretation. Stuart holds that the pl. indicates the dream was often repeated, and that this circumstance gave rise to the anxiety of the king. Barnes says that it is a mere popular use of words. M thinks that the pl. is indefinite, of a dream-state or dream experience. Probably we should paraphrase, "Nebuchadnezzar was in a state in which a dream came to him." This seems to be the force of the pl. rather than that it refers to several dreams, as Ewald translates, "had dreams." *Was disturbed*]—agitated, as in Gen. 41:8; Ps. 77:4. The verb, as M points out, indicates repeated strokes. Dreams were regarded in the ancient world as having significance and as portents of events yet to come. Cf. *CBA*, p. 266ff. See also Driver and M for a discussion of the importance of dreams in the ancient world. This dream, because of its content and vividness, greatly upset the spirit of the king. Perhaps, because it was no ordinary dream, but one which the Spirit of God caused the king to see, its vividness was particularly intense, so that the king's spirit was constantly smitten with terror. *His sleep*]—lit., *and his sleep was upon him*, as in 6:19. Aquila, Calvin and others have taken this to mean that the king's sleep returned to him, i.e., that he fell asleep again. But, in view of the agitation of Neb.'s spirit, this seems hardly likely. The words mean that the king, being disturbed by the dream, was unable to sleep, *his sleep brake from him*.

Vs. 2. *Then the king commanded to call the magicians and the astrologers and the sorcerers and the Chaldeans to make known to the king his dreams; so they came and they stood before the king.* Because of the agitation of his spirit, Neb. awoke from sleep. Perhaps the troubled spirit remained with him in the waking state, so he immediately summoned those whom he believed could tell the dream and its interpretation. *Magicians and astrologers*]—as in 1:20. *Sorcerers*]—throughout the OT this profession is condemned, cf., Deut. 18:10. It has been suggested that the word refers to those who prepare magical herbs. This is questionable, however, and it may merely designate the tone of voice in reciting an incantation. Prince translates, upon the basis of a comparison with the Babylonian, "reciters of incantations." M says "No scruple is felt at relating Dan. with this as well as with the other less obnoxious classes (although the sorcerers do not again appear); cf. 2:48, 4:9, 5:11, in which passages he appears as dean of the whole fraternity." This is to read into the text what is not to be found there. Cf. the exegesis of the passages referred to, and App. III.

The Chaldeans]—see App. III. The term is here used in a restricted, and not in an ethnic sense. The listing of the classes of wise men in Dan. is not intended to be given in a technical or exact sense, since the lists vary in order of statement. The fourfold mention here is evidently designed to include all the classes. Driver gives the following listings which occur.

- i.20 the magicians and the enchanters.
- ii.2 the magicians, the enchanters, the sorcerers, and the Chaldeans.
- ii.10b any magician, enchanter or Chaldean.
- ii.27 wise men, enchanters, magicians, (or) determiners (of fates).
- iv.7 the magicians, the enchanters, the Chaldeans, and the determiners (of fates).
- v.7 the enchanters, the Chaldeans, and the determiners (of fates).
- v.11 (of Dan.) 'master of magicians, enchanters, Chaldeans, (and) determiners (of fates).'
- v.15 the wise men, (even) the enchanters.

The term *wise men* occurs alone in 2:12, 13, 14, 18, 24, 48; 4:6, 18; 5:7, 8; *Chaldeans* occurs in 1:4; 2:4; 5:10a; 3:8.

To make known]—All four classes were intended to work together, supplementing one another, in order to state to the king what his dream had been and what was its meaning. Neb., in his ignorance, sought to do what was impossible. He sought for the explanation of a supernatural revelation by means of an appeal to those who had no real knowledge of the supernatural. Those who, like the magicians of Babylon, have no room in their thinking for the one true God, can never rightly interpret any revelation which He has given. *Stood*]—i.e., they stood before the king to serve him by interpreting the dream.

Vs. 3. *And the king said to them, A dream have I dreamed, and my spirit was troubled to know the dream.* Cf. Gen. 41. The king had not forgotten his dream (Calvin, von Lengerke, Gaebelein and Ironside hold that the dream was forgotten, apparently basing this assumption upon the translation of v. 5 in the A.V. "the thing is gone from me," nor did he have but a shadowy remembrance (Jerome). He remembered the dream, at least in its essentials. This seems to be established by his desire to test the wise men (vs. 9) to see whether their words were true. How could the king know whether the statement of the dream was true unless he remembered the dream? Charles calls attention to a similar occasion, related by Ibn Hisham (ed. Wuestenfeld, p. 9ff.) "And he (i.e., Rabia, the king of Yemen) saw a vision, and was terrified by it. So he assembled all the priests, and magicians, and augurers and star-gazers of the people of his kingdom, and said to them, 'Verily I have seen a vision, and was frightened by it. Tell it to me and its interpretation.' They said. 'Relate it to us, and we shall inform thee of its interpretation.' So he said, 'If I tell you it, I shall have no certainty as to what you tell me of its interpretation. Verily, no one knows the interpretation unless he knows it before I tell him (the dream)'." In this account, Rabia is obviously testing his wise men. So, it would appear, is Neb. It is not surprising that the king should not give complete trust to his servants. In his heart of hearts he must have known, as must the magicians themselves, that the religion of Babylonia was mere superstition and not the truth.

Vs. 4. *And the Chaldeans spake to the king,* [*in Aramaic*], *O king live forever, Declare the dream to thy servants and the interpretation we shall show. The Chaldeans*]—This term sums up the various classes of wise men. *In Aramaic*]—This word has occasioned considerable difficulty. The ancient versions construe the words *in Aramaic* with the verb *spake* to designate the language in which the Chaldeans addressed the king. This raises a question. If the Chaldeans spoke Aramaic at this point, why does the Aramaic continue throughout ch. 7 which describes the vision of Daniel? The statement that the Chaldeans addressed the king in Aramaic would not give a satisfactory explanation of the introduction of the Aramaic language at this point and its continued use to the end of ch. 7. It should also be noted that the king had addressed the Chaldeans in Hebrew (vs. 3), although in vs. 27 he spoke to Dan. in Aramaic.

Through a combination of this interpretation with 1:4 a gloss in the Greek text of 2:26 introduced the word "Chaldaic." This was followed by Jerome in his Preface. "Ab hoc loco usque ad visionem anni tertii regis Balthasar, quam Daniel vidit in Susis, Hebraicis quidem literis, sed lingua scribuntur Chaldaic, a quam vocat his *Syriacam.*" (i.e., From this place [2:46] on to the vision of the third year of Belshazzar which Dan. saw in Susa, they are written indeed in Hebrew letters but in the Chaldean language, which is called here *Syriac*). Aramaic was called Chaldean until the latter half of the nineteenth century.

It seems best, therefore, not to construe *in Aramaic* as modifying the verb. Driver adds the following reason, "it is besides quite certain that Aramaic, such as that of the Book of Daniel, was *not* spoken in Babylon." This statement of Driver's cannot be proven. Although we agree that 2:4 does not represent Aramaic as the court language of Babylon, nevertheless, it is quite possible that Aramaic was spoken in Babylon. Prince points out that both Assyria and Babylon had their own Semitic language, and that this would have been used. However, Xenophon (*Cy.* VII, 5, 31) asserts that the Babylonians spoke Syriac, by which he means a form of Aramaic. It is not necessary to discredit his testimony.[1] Aramaic may very well have been the language of common intercourse. As to the Aramaic in which Dan. is written, this was intended for Jewish readers, and there is no reason why it may not have been written by Dan. in Babylon during the sixth century B.C. This does not, however, necessarily mean that it was the common Aramaic of Babylon of the time, as Driver's statement seems to imply.

Hævernick construed *in Aramaic* with the verb and asserted that the Chaldeans deliberately spoke in Aramaic so as to hide their confusion from the presence of those in the court. This is not likely.

Some would substitute for *in Aramaic* the phrase *and they said* (e.g., Charles). But this is arbitrary, and without objective textual support.

It seems best to regard *in Aramaic* as a note, intended to warn the reader of the sudden change of language (see translation). Cf. Ezra 4:7 for a similar occurrence (so Driver, Wright).

O king]—used constantly in Dan. (3:9; 5:10; 6:6, 21). This greeting was common in Babylonian times. Prince refers to BA 1., p. 239, "May Nebo and Merodach give long days and everlasting years unto the king of the lands, my lord." Cf. also I K. 1:31; Neh. 2:3; I Sam. 10:24; also

---

[1] Cyrus, after having taken Babylon, ordered "those who understood Syrian to give notice to those in the houses to remain within." Cf. also Strabo 50:2 and 16.

(as suggested by Zœckler) Aelian, 1:31, Q. Cur. VI:5, Judith 12:14. "When the Chaldeans thus boldly promise to become good interpreters of the dream, they not only betray their rashness, but become mere impostors, who pretend to be proficients in a science of which they know nothing, as if they could predict by their conjectures the meaning of the king's dream" (Calvin).

Vs. 5. *The king answered and said to the Chaldeans, The thing is certain with me, if ye do not make me to know the dream and its interpretation, ye shall be dismembered, and your houses shall be made ruins. Certain*]—This difficult word, which occurs only here and in vs. 8 has given rise to various interpretations. The Greek evidently considered it as a verb and rendered *has gone from me.* Hence, the translation of the A.V. "the thing has gone from me," i.e., I have forgotten the thing (the dream). Maurer takes the word to mean, the thing has *gone forth* from me, i.e., *I have decreed* (cf. Isa. 45:23). For philological reasons, all these interpretations must be rejected. Keil would explain it as meaning "let the word from me be known," i.e., "be it known unto you." In recent times it has generally been assumed that the word which we have translated *certain* is of Persian origin and means *sure* or *certain.* This meaning was first expressed, I believe, by the Syriac. Thus, the king asserts his determination to punish the Chaldeans, if they do not interpret the dream. Keil's objection that since the royal commands were unchangeable, a declaration of the certainty of the king's word would be superfluous, would in ordinary cases be valid. However, it must be remembered that the heart of the king was gripped with terror, and for that reason he announced the certainty of his intention. *Dismembered*]—lit., made into limbs, i.e., ye shall be cut limb from limb. So the Peshitta, *limb, limb, ye shall be cut.* Cf. 3:29; 2 Macc. 1:16; *Ant.*, XV:8:4. *Be made ruins*]—Some would translate *a dunghill.* If this latter is correct, it need not be urged in its literal sense (Stuart), although such might have been the case (cf. 2 K. 10:27 and Hævernick). M, upon the basis of strong philological argument, suggests that the proper rendering should be *ruins,* and in this he is probably correct. "The bodies of the refractory wise men were to be dismembered, their houses pulled down" (M) The cruelty herein depicted was widespread in the ancient world, e.g., Her. III:79. "The violence and peremptoriness of the threatened punishment is in accordance with what might be expected at the hands of an Eastern despot; the Assyrians and Persians, especially, were notorious for the barbarity of their punishments" (Driver).

Vs. 6. *But if the dream and its interpretation ye do declare, gifts and a present and great honor ye shall receive from me: therefore declare (unto) me the dream and its interpretation. A present*]—The word is generally thought to come from the Persian and is recognized as a technical name for gifts. *Declare*]—as in 2:7, 9, 10, 11, 16, 24, 27; 4:2; 5:7, 12, 15. Dan. and his companions were not present. Threats and promises such as these would have meant little to them. "It is plain that God is shaping this matter to test the intrinsic futility of their (i.e. the Chaldeans') pretensions to superhuman knowledge, and to bring out in the most public manner his own infinite superiority over them all" (Butler).

2. vv. 7-12. ***The wise men ask the king to declare his dream. He refuses, and they confess their inability to tell the dream, protesting that he is asking the impossible. The king in anger, orders the wise men to be put to death.***

Vs. 7. *They answered a second time and said, Let the king tell the dream to his servants, and the interpretation we shall declare.* The request is repeated more respectfully, and seems to be reasonable, expecting a favorable reply.

Vs. 8. *The king answered and said, Of a certainty do I know that ye are buying the time, because ye see that the thing on my part is sure. Buying the time*]—not "to use the favorable time" (Hævernick), nor to become master of the situation at the present moment, but rather "to temporize and defer the fatal moment" (Charles) when their ignorance and inability would be brought to light. Cf. the Latin idiom *tempus emere,* as in *Verr.* 1:3. By their repeated request, they have convinced the king of their inability to declare either the dream or its interpretation.

Vs. 9. *That if ye do not make me to know the dream, there is (but) one law for you, and lying and corrupt words ye have agreed to speak before me, till the time be changed; therefore declare to me the dream, and I shall know that ye can declare to me its interpretation.* Vv. 8b and 9 should be connected; *ye see that the thing on my part is sure, that if,* etc., i.e., they see that the king is determined to punish them if they do not carry out his request. *One law*]—i.e., you can expect nothing else but the punishment which I have decreed. Not, as Hitzig, "one thing forms your object", or "one thing is your purpose" (Stuart). The word is Persian, lit., *your law is one,* i.e., the law against you is *one,* unchangeable, as Esther 4:11. *Lying*]—i.e., your claim to be able to interpret the dream if it is told you is false. The two words *lying and corrupt* strengthen the idea, *wicked lies* (Hitzig). *Ye have agreed to speak*]—ye have concerted (Charles). *The time*]—i.e., until "the king either drop the matter, or till they learn something more particular about the dream through some circumstances that may arise" (Keil). *Therefore*]—i.e., if you can relate the dream, I shall know that you can also properly interpret it.

Vs. 10. *The Chaldeans answered before the king and said, There is not a man upon the earth that is able to declare the matter of the king, forasmuch as no great and powerful king has asked a matter like this of any magician or astrologer or Chaldean. Great and powerful king*]—better than to find three classes, as the LXX, AV, Rose; *king, lord nor ruler.* The title *great king,* (cf. 2 K. 18:28) is, as Prince points out, reminiscent of "the old Assyro-Babylonian title so common in the inscriptions 'Great King, mighty King, King of Assyria,' (or of Babylon)." Perhaps the force is; no king, be he ever so great or powerful. The king's insistence compels the Chaldeans to acknowledge their inability, which, they say, is because the king is asking something beyond human power. Since no king has ever made such a request, they seem to conclude that the request is one which it is impossible to grant.

Vs. 11. *And the thing which the king asks is difficult, and there is not another that can declare it before the king except the gods whose dwelling is not with flesh. Difficult*]—lit., *heavy, weighty,* rather than *rare,* as Calvin and the AV. Since the matter was weighty, it was difficult to interpret. "Grave dicitus quod est difficile, quia quae gravia sunt difficulter portantur et sustinentur" (Rosenmueller). *Another*]—i.e., not another human. *Gods*]—Hævernick suggested that the thought is that the gods only act among men in certain events. Some commentators distinguish two classes of gods, those who dwell with flesh and those who do not (so e.g., Rose, Deane). But the Chaldeans are probably merely intending to assert that what the king asks is too difficult for men and can be answered only by the gods. It is "simply a confession of impotence on the part of the Chaldeans — no mortal man, only beings of a higher sphere, can perform the king's request" (Bevan). Thus the Chaldeans confessed the limitations of their art. It is possible that the pl. *gods* should be rendered *god,* and that the Chaldeans were using the term in a very vague sense, "We cannot do this; God alone can do it." "—for among all nations a persuasion has existed concerning a supreme God who reigns alone" (Calvin). It shows, moreover, that they had a distinct conception of a higher intelligence, some great mind or minds possessed of knowledge and forecast far beyond that of men" (Butler). For the philological evidence, see M. On the other hand, however, the words may contain nothing more than a general reference to polytheism. *Flesh*]—indicates weak and infirm human nature (Keil), cf. Isa. 31:3; Ps. 56:4; Jer. 17:5. The speakers include themselves in the designation *flesh,* in order to excuse themselves (Zœckler).

Vs. 12. *For this cause the king was wroth and very furious and commanded to destroy all the wise men of Babylon.* Since, in Gen. 40:2; 41:10, the same verbal root is used to indicate the anger of Pharaoh, it by no means follows, as Prince suggests, that this is an imitation of the story of Joseph. Apparently *Babylon* here refers only to the city and not to the province or the whole realm, cf. 2:49; 3:1. The excuse of the Chaldeans (vs. 11) does not influence the king favorably, for he sees in it a confession of impotence and orders the destruction of those who had made it.

3. vv. 13-16. *The decree to slay the wise men has gone forth, and in this decree Daniel and his three companions are included. Through Arioch's intervention Daniel obtains an audience with the king and promises to declare the dream and secures the deferring of the sentence of execution.*

Vs. 13. *And the decree went forth, and the wise men were to be slain, and they sought Daniel and his companions to slay them.* Cf. Luke 2:1. *To be slain*]—Probably the actual act had not yet occurred. Prince remarks "Such a sentence, implying the destruction of *all* the wise men, indicates that the author regarded them as a special class or order, of which he goes on to state that Daniel and his friends were members." But this sentence is inexact. There is not a word in the book of Dan. to indicate that the author regarded Dan. as a member of any order. Some scholars are too eager to make it out that Dan. was a heathen priest. Dan. had been trained under the Chaldeans but there is nothing in the text to indicate that he had yet been appointed or ordained as a wise man, except in the broadest sense. He was trained to stand before the king (cf. 1:5), not to be a priest or to perform religious duties. It is inconceivable, in the light of what is related in ch. one, that Dan. should have so compromised as merely to become a heathen priest. The command includes Dan., therefore, because he had been trained under the wise men, and, in a broad sense, could be designated as a wise man. The loose usage of the terms in Dan. should make commentators cautious in speaking about Dan's *membership* in any guild or order or class.

Vs. 14. *Then Daniel answered with counsel and discretion to Arioch the captain of the king's guard who had gone forth to slay the wise men of Babylon.* "Through Daniel's judicious interview with Arioch, the further execution of the royal edict was interrupted" (Keil). *Discretion*]—lit., *taste*, a figurative use of the faculty of discrimination. M, considering this to be a mere legend, asserts that good sense and prudence are "a characteristic of the Biblical saints." This remark is needless and not entirely correct. Cf. Abraham before Pharaoh, David and Bathsheba, etc. *Arioch*]—also in Gen. 14:1. An ancient name, not used elsewhere in this period. *Captain*]—Cf. 2 K. 25:8ff; Jer. 39:9; 52:12ff. lit., *captain* (chief) of the slaughterers (i.e., of animals). How the term came to be applied to the king's guard is not clear.

Vs. 15. *He answered and said to Arioch the captain of the king, Why is the decree so harsh from the king? Then Arioch made the matter known to Daniel. Answered*]—really a response to the circumstances rather than to any specific words. M suggests the use of the English "answer" in the sense of "correspond", to inanimate things. *Harsh*]—The translation *hasty* of AV, Hævernick, etc. is not correct. Nor is *urgent* (Stuart, RV) strong enough. The LXX more correctly rendered *bitterly;* the Aramaic word means *harsh, severe, cruel.* Stuart suggests that since Dan. wished to obtain Arioch's favor, he would hardly have used so strong a term. In answer to this, however, it may be said that we do not know all that Dan. said to Arioch.

Vs. 16. *Then Daniel went in and sought from the king that he would give him time, and the interpretation he would declare to the king.* The last clause *and the interpretation etc.* is to be regarded not as a final clause, *that he might declare* but as correlative with *went in,* etc. (See Charles for philological discussion). This last clause, therefore, represents a promise, not a request, upon Dan.'s part. M asks how Dan. entered the court without official intervention. The answer is (as Hævernick and others have indicated) that there probably was official intervention. If Arioch had learned that there was a possibility of Dan.'s interpreting the dream, he certainly would have arranged for Dan. to see the king. Furthermore, the fact that Dan. had previously made such a favorable impression upon the king doubtless eased matters. M points out that subsequently Dan. needs the aid of Arioch to present him to the king and "—now rather than later the terms of the etiquette are desiderated, while these terms in v. 25 are much belated." But it should be noted that in vs. 25 Dan. is not said to require the aid of Arioch. In vs. 25 Arioch is the principal character and *acts upon his own* in order that needless bloodshed may be avoided. Here, in vs. 16 Dan. upon his own initiative desires access to the king. Who is to say that he did not have proper official intervention? Furthermore, these "difficulties" which M thinks he finds are but evidences of the genuineness of the narrative. If a later writer were fabricating a romance or fiction, would he not have sought to smooth out these alleged difficulties?

This vs. exhibits the courage of Dan. Under ordinary conditions he might have been filled with terror, but he is convinced that the Spirit of God is with him. Men of deep faith are bold. Furthermore, as Deane points out, this vs. exhibits the humility of Dan. He makes no extravagant promise, but merely states that if the king will grant him time, he will declare the interpretation. Ewald suggests that he asked for a day, but this is mere conjecture. He merely asked for a specified time, in the conviction that the sovereign God, who previously had been with him in a special way, would not desert him now. The wise men had not even asked for an extension of time in which to consider the matter. *Interpretation*]—For the sake of brevity only the interpretation is mentioned although doubtless Dan. made it clear that he would also declare the dream itself.

b. Vv. 17-23. Daniel prays to God for a revelation of the dream. His prayer is answered, and he praises God.

1. vv. 17-19. *Daniel enters his house to inform his companions of the state of affairs and to seek mercy from God. The secret is revealed to Daniel in a night vision.*

Vs. 17. *Then Daniel went to his house, and to Hananiah, Mishael and Azariah his companions he made known the matter.* This vs. shows that the request was granted. *House*]—Whether this was an official or servant's dwelling, or a private residence, we do not know. At any rate, the four youths appear to have lived together.

Vs. 18. *And they would seek mercies from the God of heaven concerning this secret, that Daniel and his companions might not perish with the rest of the wise men of Babylon. And they would, etc.*]—This I take, as in vs. 16, not to be a final clause after *made known* (vs. 17) but a correlative clause. The force is best brought out by a paraphrase. "Dan. made known the matter, and so they undertook to seek mercies, etc." It is difficult to bring out the exact force of the Aramaic in English. (Cf. Charles, p. xcvi, although I do not agree with all of his conclusion. His description of the force of the idiom, however, appeals to me as being correct). Since the granting of the request would, of course, be an act of undeserved grace, it is described as mercy. "Whenever we fly to God to bring assistance to our necessities, our eyes and all our senses ought always to be turned towards his mercy, for his mere good-will reconciles him to us" (Calvin). *God of heaven*]—Cf. Gen. 24:7. This designation of the true God came into prominence at the time of the exile. (Cf. Ezra 1:2; 6:10; 7:12, 21; Neh. 1:5; 2:4; Ps. 136:26.) He is the God who is over the heavens, i.e., over the sun moon and stars which the Babylonians worshipped. The title is not a reminiscence of the Babylonian designation "the great gods of the heavens and the earth" (suggested by Prince), nor did it arise because of "the growing transcendence of Jewish thought regarding God" (Charles), nor did it appear because of the influence of Persian religion. *Companions*]—Dan. summons his companions to prayer that all might be delivered.

Vs. 19. *Then the secret was revealed to Daniel in a vision of the night; then Daniel blessed the God of heaven.* Dan. had prayed in faith, and an answer is given. The revelation was not made in a dream, but in a vision of the night. Such a vision was one which might come to a person in a waking condition. Cf. Job 4:13; 7 14 20 8; 33:15; etc. M characterizes the "dream" as "the lower means of communication to the pagan." But probably no such fine distinct on is to be drawn. Revelations were also granted to true prophets by means of dreams (cf. Num. 12:1-8).

2. vv. 20-23. *Daniel's prayer of thanksgiving for the mercy of God in revealing to him the secret.*

Vs. 20. *Daniel answered and said, May the name of God be blessed forever and forever, for wisdom and power are hi* Since God has so graciously answered his prayer, Dan. breaks out into grateful praise. *Answered*]—While this word is generally sed in the sense of commencing to speak (Driver) as in 3:9, 14 and Matt. 11 25 etc it would seem that in this case Dan. is actually answering by his prayer the revelation which God has given. "The revelation is of the character of an address from God, which Daniel answers with praise and thanks to God" (Keil). *Blessed*]—The language is that of Ps. 41:13, and was employed later by the Levites (Neh. 9:5). This leading thought of the prayer is first uttered (Hitzig), and thus emphasized. Throughout, the attitude of Dan. is *soli Deo gloria. The Name*]—i.e., the essence of God, which in itself is incomprehensible to men (cf. Ju. 13:17, 18). But in so far as God has revealed Himself, He may be known by man. When, therefore, Dan. here speaks of the Name of God, he probably refers both to the incomprehensible essence of God and also to all that may be known of God through His self-revelation. The meaning need not be restricted to the latter (as Charles). *For ever*]—i.e., eternally. *Wisdom*]—Dan. now proceeds to give the reasons why the Name of God should be eternally blessed. Cf. Job 12:13. The theme of this prayer is the wisdom and power of God. Vv. 21 c, d and 22 give examples of His wisdom, and 21 a, b exhibit His power (Charles).

By the mention of these attributes, the true God is distinguished from the idols of Babylon. God has wisdom — nothing is hid from Him — and He has power, for He governs all things. Calvin rightly says, "We must remember how God is defrauded of his just praise, when we do not connect these two attributes together — his universal foresight and his government of the world allowing nothing to happen without his permission."

Vs. 21. *And he (it is who) changes times and seasons; he removes kings and sets up kings, he gives wisdom to the wise, and knowledge to those who know understanding. He*]—emphatic, in order to stress the fact that it is God who controls history and not nature itself or the idols *Changes*]—the first exhibition of God's might. *Times*]—it is question able, whether a definite distinction between the words times and seasons can be made. The phrase is not an exhortation on the part of the autho to the effect that people should find comfort in the fact that better times will come, that Antiochus will not always be upon the throne (Hitzig) It means rather that the course of history lies in the hands of God. These critical periods which occur in the realm of time as such, are determined by God (Charles). It is not in heaven alone that we are to seek for evidences of God's power, but also on earth where this power is daily manifested in God's control over all things. *Removeth*]—i.e., God has sovereign determination of all political changes (M). "In this expression," says M, "lies a challenge to the fatalism of the Bab. astral religion a feature which in its influence long survived in the Graeco-Roman world.' In Babylon this astral religion was a real source of danger to the people of God. But is there any evidence that it was such years later in Palestine? If the author wrote in Palestine long years after the exile, what is the point of his making this specific endeavor to refute the Babylonian astral religion? That was not the great danger which faced the post-exilic Jewish community. This statement is suggested by the content of the dream of the king. Human history is in God's hands. In the prayer, Dan. gratefully acknowledges this fact. *Wisdom*]— Men have no wisdom but that which springs from God (Calvin). The word refers to the revelation of the deep and secret things of God. It is He who reveals to men His hidden counsels. Therefore, if a man appear as wise, he has received that wisdom from God. The *wise* here are not a caste, but wise men generally. "et animae quae fervet amare sapientiae, libenter spiritus Dei infunditur. In perversem autem animam non introibit sapientia (Sap. III)" (Jerome). *Knowledge*]— i. e., those who possess understanding of any matter receive this knowledge as a gift of God. All is of His grace. Cf. Prov. 4:1. There can be no objection to Dan.'s classifying himself as *wise* or as *one who knows* understanding, for Dan. freely acknowledges that what he has, he has received from God.

Vs. 22. *He reveals the deep and hidden things, he k ows wh t is in the darkness, and light dwells with him.* Cf. Job 12:22 *De p*]— God reveals Himself in the created universe and in the constitution of man. But, because of man's sinful rebellion, God has given a special revelation which has culminated in His Son. Calvin, therefor , is right when he refers this passage to the gift of Prophecy. It is more th n the re elation given in nature; it is the revelation of the plan of salvation, vouchsafed under the old covenant at sundry times and in divers manners to the fathers by the prophets, and now unto us by His Son The great truths which God has thus communicated to man are *deep*, a word which signifies their vastness and profundity, and the *hidden* things are specifically those which are to occur in the future and which are predicted by the prophets. The statement is thus a characterization of the plan of history and salvation revealed to Neb. The purposes of God were *deep*, and as yet *hidden* from men, so it was that the prophet should declare to the king these hidden purposes of God. *Darkness*]— i e, those things which are yet dark to man and unknown, are fully known to God. *Light*]— dwells with God as though it were a person, cf. Prov 8:30 As M points out, there is a certain crescendo here — *deep, hidden, dark*, so these mysteries must be regarded by man. For God, however, all is light since He alone is the author of wisdom, the omniscient One. Cf I John 1:7. Perhaps this description is intentionally employed to refute the notion prevalent among the Babylonians that their deities were givers of light. Among the later Jews this *light* was interpreted in a Messianic sense. Volz (*EJG*², pp. 364-367) gives a survey of the Jewish conceptions of light.

Vs. 23. *Thee, O God of my fathers, do I thank and praise, for wisdom and power Thou hast given to me, and now Thou hast caused me to know what we sought from Thee, for the matter of the king Thou hast caused us to know.* The Aramaic is empha ic THEE — *praising am I.* God is thus placed first. He is deserving of thanksgiving and praise, for He has answered the prayer. *Fathers*]— i. e, the God of Dan.'s ancestors, the Israelites. As in times past He has proven faithful, so also now. ***Wisdom***]— here refers specifically to the understanding of the dream, and *power* to Dan.'s ability to interpret it and to abide steadfast in the true religion. Dan , however, does not take credit for the answer to prayer. God has answered, not merely Dan.'s prayer, but also the prayers of his companions. "To his associates as well as himself he ascribes the successful supplications that had been made and when he becomes the honored instrument of disclosure, he takes no special credit to himself for this, but considers it as equally pertaining to them" (Stuart).

c. vv. 24-45 Daniel is brought into the king's presence and declares his readiness to interpret the dream. He relates the dream and sets forth its interpretation.

1. vv 24-30. *Daniel is brought into the presence of Nebuchadnezzar and declares his readiness to interpret the dream.*

V. 24. *Therefore, Daniel w nt in unto Arioch whom the king had appointed to destroy the wise men of Babylon; he went and thus he said o him, do not destroy the wise men of Babylon: bring me in before the king and the interpretation to the king I shall show. Therefore*]— i. e, because God had revealed the matter to him. After having thanked God for the answered prayer, Dan. is ready to approach the king The conf dence that he is to execute the will of God gives to him a holy boldness. This present statement is not proof that Dan had had no earlier au ence with the king (see comments at vs 16). For illustrations of Or ental etiquette, see *Bab. u. Ass.* I, 70.

Vs. 25 *Then Arioch in haste brought in Daniel before the king, and hus he said to him, I have found a man of the sons of the captivity of Judah who will make known the interpretation to the king.* We may reconst uct events somewhat as follows: In vs. 16 Dan., in the properly formal ay required by court etiquette, seeks audience with the king and reque ts time in order that he may ask mercy from God (vs. 16) In this vs. there is no particular need of mentioning the indiv dual steps in execution of the proper etiquette. Dan then prays and receives an answer to his prayer. He now again seeks access to the k'ng. But in the carrying out of proper court procedure the second time (vs. 25) Dan. finds that Arioch takes matters into his own hand and hastily b ings Dan. in befo e the king. Apparently Arioch desires credit f r himself. I have found,' he says, as though it were through his own effort that Dan. had been found It should also be noted that Arioch f cuses the king's attention upon the *man* Dan. rather than upon God D n. speedily deflects attention from himself, and points the eyes of the king to God.
Vs 26. *The king answered and said to Daniel whose name was Belteshazzar, Art thou able to make me to know the dream that I have seen. and its interpretation? Belteshazzar*]— This was the name which the king had imposed upon Dan. and that by which he knew him. *Seen*]— a fitting characterization of the dream, since the great image was the principal object presented to the king's vision.

Vs. 27. *Daniel answered before the king and said, The secret that the king asks cannot the wise men, astrologers, magicians, soothsayers show to the king.* Perhaps in these words Dan. is indicating the unreasonableness of the king's request and also showing sympathy for the Chaldeans, since the king has asked of them what they could not do. Man cannot perform that which is the prerogative of God alone. As Stuart observes, an excellent opportunity is presented "to vindicate the superior claims of the God of Israel; which he (i. e., Dan.) manfully and nobly uses to the best advantage."

Vs. 28. *But there is a God in heaven who reveals secrets and has made known to king Nebuchadnezzar what shall be in the latter days. Thy dream and the visions of thy head upon thy bed are these.* Although man cannot reveal such secrets, God can do so. He dwells in heaven, in opposition to the visible idols of Babylon, who cannot reveal secrets. God does reveal secrets and has revealed the explanation of this particular dream of Neb. which had to do with what should take place *in the end of the days.* In itself, this phrase denotes the uttermost part or segment of the days (i. e., of history) "the farthermost part of the days" (Vos). The word is also employed in a spatial sense (Ps. 139:9) "the uttermost parts of the sea." "It is a phrase that belongs to the field of eschatology and contains the note of epochal finality" (Vos). It thus has primary reference to that period which would begin to run its course with the appearance of God upon earth, i. e., the days of the Messiah. While it is true that the entire contents of the dream do not fall within the Messianic age, nevertheless, the principal point, the establishment of the Messiah's Kingdom, does fall therein

The age which was ushered in by the appearance of Christ upon earth is denominated in the New Testament "the last days," cf. Heb. 1:1; Acts 2:16, 17; I Tim. 4:1; 2 Tim. 3:1; I John 2:18. The reference here, then, is not merely to the future generally (Hævernick, de Wette), nor is the phrase to be equated with "the time of the end" of the latter portion of Dan., as is done by Gaebelein. This would be to place upon the phrase a meaning which it nowhere else bears. The content of the dream is *that which shall occur in the Messianic age. Visions*]—as in 4:5, 10, 13; 7: 1, 15. Perhaps the pl. is used because the *one* dream consists of a *series* of visions. *Of thy head*]—i. e., "as were entirely in accord with a thoughtfulness of the head actively engaged" (Kranichfeld).

Vs. 29. *Thou, O king,—thy thoughts upon thy bed came up, what should be after this; and the Revealer of secrets hath made thee to know what will be.* The thoughts here mentioned are to be distinguished from those mentioned in the next vs. They are not the dream itself (Hitzig). More likely the words refer to the king's thoughts before sleep came upon him. Probably as the king lay upon his bed, he was moved by thoughts concerning the future of his kingdom. It is not, therefore, correct to say that the dream was "the form into which, under Providence, his thoughts gradually shaped themselves" (Driver). Rather, it was the Divinely appointed answer to these thoughts. *After this*]—not a synonym for *in the last days,* but roughly equivalent to *in the future.*

Vs. 30. *And I—not through wisdom which is in me above all living is this secret revealed to me, but that the interpretation may be made known to the king and that thou mayest know the thoughts of thy heart.* The *Thou* and *I* of vv. 29 and 30 contrast the two principal characters. Dan. gives the entire glory to God, to whom it rightly belongs. The secret is not revealed to Dan. because of any wisdom that he possesses beyond others, but solely that the interpretation may be made known. In other words, unless there is specific supernatural revelation, the interpretation cannot be made known. *Made known*]—lit., *that they may make known.* Ibn Ezra suggested that *angels* were the revealers. However, this is a common impersonal construction in Aramaic, which should be rendered in English by the passive. The AV. translates incorrectly at this point.

2. vv. 31-35. *Daniel relates the dream to Nebuchadnezzar.*

Vs. 31. *Thou, O king, wast seeing, and behold! a great image; this image was mighty and its brightness was surpassing; (it) was standing before thee, and its appearance was terrible.* Charles argues that 28c "thy dream and the visions of thy head are these" is out of place and belongs here at the introduction to this vs. Logically, such a change might seem to be warranted, but it must be remembered that Hebrew writers did not always follow the order which to the Occidental seems to be that of strict logical sequence. There is no objective evidence to support Charles' proposal. The image seen is not an idol (Hitzig), but a statue in human form. Essentially, world powers are one, since they are human in nature; hence, the world powers are united in the *one* statue. *Brightness*]—because the statue was composed of metal. The appearance of the image was such as, because of its size and brightness, would inspire terror.

Vs. 32. *It—the image—its head was of good gold; its breast and its arms of silver; its belly and its thighs of brass. It*]—i. e., as for the image. *Good*]—i. e., pure gold. *Brass—*] i. e., bronze or copper.

Vs. 33. *Its legs were of iron; its feet, part of them were of iron and part of clay.* From the head of gold to the feet of clay there is steady deterioration. Fine gold, silver, bronze (M refers to Her.'s description of the lavish use of bronze in Babylonia, Her., 1,181 and Meissner, *op cit.*, I, 265ff.) iron, clay. Note further that only the head constitutes a unified whole. The origin of this symbolism must be found in Divine revelation.

As far as is known, there were no precursors from which the symbolism could have been borrowed.

Vs. 34. *Thou didst continue seeing until a stone was cut out without hands, and it smote the image upon its feet of iron and clay and crushed them.* This vs. does not state from *what* the stone was cut; the words *of a mountain* should not be inserted here (Charles). Evidently, as Stuart suggests, the image in all its parts was completely formed before the stone was cut. *Without hands*]— i. e., without human power or assistance. "The blow of the stone, although it directly fell upon the feet of iron or clay, was so vehement, that the *whole* image, by violent concussion and consequent fall, was reduced to powder" (Stuart).

Vs. 35. *Then there were crushed together the iron, the clay, the bronze, the silver and the gold and they became like chaff from the summer threshing floors, and the wind took them away, and no place was found for them; and the stone which smote the image became a great mountain and filled all the earth.* Charles would change the order of the first two expressions to read, *the clay, the iron.* Such a change is without warrant. The present order shows its genuineness. *Threshing floors*]—As Driver remarks, these "were generally on exposed or elevated spots, where the chaff might readily be cleared away by the wind." Cf. Hos. 13:3; Isa. 41:16.

4. vv. 36-45. *Daniel's interpretation of the dream.*

Vs. 36. *This is the dream, and its interpretation we shall declare before the king.* The pl. *we* has called forth various interpretations, "I and His wisdom" (Rashi), a pl. of majesty or authority, Dan. here includes his companions (Keil, Charles). It seems to me that M is correct in comparing Paul's use of "we," in 1 Cor. 2:6, as employed with a certain humility, for the message was not Dan.'s own. Also, there is no evidence that Dan.'s companions were present before the king, hence, it does not seem correct to include them in this reference.

Vs. 37. *Thou O king, king of kings, to whom the God of heaven hath given a kingdom, strength, and power and honor.* The phrase *king of kings* stands in apposition to *O king.* The remainder of the vs. and all of vs. 38a constitute a parenthesis. Thus, the force of the passage is *Thou O king, king of kings, thou art the head of gold.* M states that this form of address was Persian and appears upon the Assyrian inscriptions, but quotes Prince to the effect that it was "not the customary Bab. form of address." Prince quotes the East India House Inscription, "Nebuchadnezzar, King of Babylon, the exalted prince, the beloved of Marduk." In the first place, however, it should be noted that this inscription presents merely the king's designation of himself. He is not here being addressed by others. Secondly, various documents from the neo-Babylonian empire describe the king merely as "King of Babylon" (See *KB*, pp. 176-259). From this it would appear that there is not extant sufficient evidence to indicate how a subject would address the king when speaking to him. Thirdly, the inscription of the Persian king Ariyaramna (610-580 B. C.) describes the king as "king of kings." If this was a specific Persian form of address, it is quite possible that it might also have been employed at Babylon by Dan. There is not extant sufficient evidence to warrant the conclusion that Dan., living at the time of Neb., would not have addressed the king as "king of kings." This same designation is employed of Neb. in Ezek. 26:7. *Kingdom*]—these things had been given to the king by God.

Vs. 38. *And wherever dwell the sons of men, the beast of the field and the birds of the heavens, he hath given (them) into thy hand, and caused thee to rule over all of them; thou art it—the head of gold.* "Neb. as the type and crown of Man has been invested by God with man's charter of dominion over all living creatures, Gen. 1:28, Ps. 8:17." (M) This is a fitting designation for the first great representative of world power. The claim of universal dominion had been made by the Assyrian kings, cf. "king of the four quarters," which designation Sennacherib employs of himself. The wild animals are mentioned, as Driver rightly points out "in order to represent Nebuchadnezzar's rule as being as absolute as possible." Cf. Jer. 27:6; 28:14.

It is perfectly true that Neb.'s kingdom did not hold sway over the entire earth, but in the sense that it did include much of civilized Asia, and laid pretension to universality, it might properly be designated as Dan. has done. The *SRB* is incorrect in interpreting this vs. to mean merely that the empires are able to possess the inhabited earth. The universal character of these kingdoms (in so far as they contained within them the true elements of universality) is stressed in order to bring out the contrast between these kingdoms and *The Kingdom,* which alone is truly universal. *Thou art*]—The reference is not to the king as an individual, since it is immediately stated that another kingdom (not king) will stand in Neb.'s place, but to the empire itself. In what sense, then, is this reference to be taken? Hitzig is one of the principal advocates of the view that the reference is merely to the king himself, since this view, he thinks, alone does justice to the words of the text. Also, he maintains, the "after thee" of vs. 39 cannot very well be addressed to a kingdom, hence he concludes, the king himself is intended. As an exegetical curiosity the view of Ewald may be stated. Ewald held that a writer living at the time of Alexander the Great wrote a prophecy which he attributed to Dan. who lived, says Ewald, in Nineveh during the Assyrian period. The four empires of this prophecy were the Assyrian, Chaldean, Medo-Persian and Greek. During the time of the Maccabees, the prophecy was re-edited, and Dan. was thought to have lived at the time of Neb., hence, the four empires became, Neb., Media, Persia, Greece. Lacunza held that included in the head of gold were the Chaldean and Medo-Persian kingdoms. However, there has been more or less agreement that the reference is to the Neo-Babylonian Empire, so: Ephraim of Syria, and the early fathers, Irenaeus, Hippolytus, Origen, Eusebius, Jerome, Chrysostom, Augustine, also, Ibn Ali, Ibn Ezra, Luther, Calvin, Eichhorn, de Wette, Maurer, Rosenmueller, Delitzsch, H. Keil, Hævernick, Stuart, Zœckler, Wright, Boutflower, Bevan, Kuenen, Driver, M, Charles, Rowley, Haller, SRB, and the dispensationalist school. It must be noted, however, that a personal form of address is employed. The empire in the person of its ruler, stood before Dan. and would therefore be addressed as *thou.* Also, in a certain sense, the king was the empire, for he had built it up. It is, therefore, the neo-Babylonian empire, represented in the person of its monarch, to whom Dan. makes his address. *Gold*]—refers to the dignity of the kingdom, the first of the great world empires, a dignity which, as vs. 37 shows, was bestowed by God.

Vs. 39. *And in thy place shall stand another kingdom lower than thou; and another, a third, kingdom of brass which shall rule over all the earth.* These kingdoms are merely mentioned here, the fuller designation being reserved till chs. 7, 8 and 10. *Shall stand*]— a more accurate translation than *shall arise,* for as M indicates, "there is nothing mobile in the scene." *Lower*]—i.e., possesses a lower degree of dignity. But how was such inferiority manifested? Calvin sought to discover this in the moral sphere; Kliefoth in the fact that the second kingdom was smaller than the Babylonian, Keil in a lack of inner unity. I am inclined to think that Keil is correct. The symbolism itself appears to suggest this. Thus, Babylon is represented by one head; the 2nd kingdom by breast and arms, the 3rd by belly and thighs and the 4th by legs and feet. In this sense, it seems to me (and this is also borne out by the symbolism of chs. 7 and 8) there is progressive inferiority.

Various identifications for the second kingdom have been proposed. The Romanist scholar Goettsberger finds the reference in Belshazzar; Lacunza applies it in this ch. to the Grecian empire; it is referred to the Median empire alone by Ephraim of Syria, Maurer, Delitzsch, Bevan, Prince, Hitzig, Driver, Haller, M, Charles, Rowley. It has, however, generally been referred to the Medo-Persian empire; so the church fathers,

Jerome and Porphyry, Luther, Calvin, Stuart, Rosenmueller, H, Pusey, Keil, Hævernick, d'Envieu.

The third kingdom is referred to Neriglissar by Eerdmans, Medo-Persia by Goettsberger, Persia by Ephraim of Syria, von Lengerke, Maurer, Bevan, Hitzig, Prince, Driver, Haller, M, Charles, Rowley. Lacunza found the reference to the Roman empire. The following interpret of Alexander; Porphyry, Stuart, Rosenmueller, Zœckler. It is referred to the Grecian empire by the church fathers, Ibn Ali, Luther, Calvin, H, Hævernick, Keil, Auberlen, Pusey, Kliefoth, d'Envieu, Wright, SRB and the dispensationalist school. This position is adopted in the present commentary.

Vs. 40. *And a fourth kingdom there shall be, strong like iron, inasmuch as iron breaks and smashes wholly; and like iron which breaks, all these will it crush and break.* Eerdmans referred the fourth kingdom to Nabonidus and Belshazzar; Ibn Ezra to the Mohammedan rule; Lacunza to the powers of Europe. By the following it is applied to the empire of Greece, Ephraim of Syria, von Lengerke, Maurer, Hitzig, Delitzsch, Bevan, Prince, Driver, Haller, M, Charles, Goettsberger. On the other hand Porphyry, Rosenmueller, Stuart, Zœckler, apply it to the successors of Alexander. The traditional interpretation, which is also adopted in this commentary, is to refer the fourth kingdom to the Roman empire. This view has been held by Josephus, the church fathers, Chrysostom, Jerome, Augustine; Ibn Ali, Luther, Calvin, Bellarmine, H, Hævernick, Caspari, Keil, Pusey, Auberlen, Kliefoth, Fuller, Wright, Boutflower, d'Envieu.

In recent times another interpretation has been making its appearance. This interpretation is known generally as dispensationalism. It is to the effect that the fourth monarchy represents not only the historical Roman empire, but a *revived* Roman empire, which will come to an end by a sudden catastrophic judgment, after which the kingdom of God (i.e., the millennium of Rev. 20:1-6) will be set up.[1] The destruction of the Gentile world power, according to this view, occurs not at the first coming of Christ, but at His second advent.

Thus "He (i.e., Christ at His first advent) did not smite the image; the image, so to speak, smote Him."

"The stone strikes the image, when the ten toes, the final ten kingdom division of the Roman Empire, are in existence."

---

[1] A strange and exegetically untenable interpretation of the colossus has been set forth by G H. Lang, *The Histories and Prophecies of Daniel*, London, 1941. Lang rejects the idea of a revived Roman empire but substitutes what might be called a revived Babylonian kingdom, with Babylon as the capital of Antichrist.

"The stone which falls from above is the Second Coming of our Lord Jesus Christ, His coming in great power and Glory" (Gaebelein).

I have quoted thus extensively from Gaebelein, and shall continue to do so, as, in my opinion, he is one of the ablest representatives of this school. The following table presents the interpretation which is adopted in this book. (Cf. App V. for a defense of the position that the fourth kingdom is Rome and not Greece).

The head of gold	—	The neo-Babylonian Empire
The breast and arms	—	The Medo-Persian Empire
The belly and thighs	—	The Grecian Empire
The legs and feet	—	The Roman Empire

THE STONE

Darby is correct when he says, "We may first observe that the Gentile kingdoms are seen as a whole. It is neither historical succession nor moral features with respect to God and man, but the kingdoms all together forming, as it were, a personage before God, the man of the earth in the eye of God—glorious and terrible in his public splendour in the eyes of men." *Strong*]—The power of this empire to crush is compared with iron, and the account of this kingdom is more definite than that of the others, in order to bring out the contrast. This kingdom—strong as iron—is crushed by something far stronger than iron—the power of the sovereign God. *Breaks in pieces*]—The word in Syriac means *to break with the hammer, to forge. All these*]—object of *will it crush and break*, thus, *it will crush and break all these* metals which represent the previous kingdoms. With iron strength it will crush them, not at one blow, for they do not exist together at the time of appearance of the fourth kingdom, but in the sense suggested by Kliefoth, "The elements from which the Babylonian world-kingdom was made up, the countries, peoples, and civilization which were comprehended in it, as its external form, would be destroyed by the Medo-Persian kingdom, and carried forward with it, so as to be established in a new external form. Such, too, was the relation between the Medo-Persian and the Macedonian world kingdom, that the latter assumed the elements and constituent parts not only of the Medo-Persian, but also therewith at the same time of the Babylonian kingdom."

Vs. 41. *And as thou sawest the feet and the toes, part of them of potter's clay, and part of them iron, the kingdom will be composite, and there shall be some of the firmness of iron in it, inasmuch as thou didst see iron mixed with miry clay.* One part was of clay, the other of iron. *Composite*]

—This word is generally translated *divided,* as though the kingdom were divided in two. On the basis of this many scholars, e.g., Driver, refer to the successors of Alexander, the Ptolemies and the Seleucids, whereas others find the reference in some division of the Roman Empire, such as East and West. Ibn Ali thinks the division is between Romans and Arabs. Buxtor however, rightly translates, *regnum diversum erit,* i.e., the kingdom will be composite or diverse. The firmness of iron does not characterize the entire kingdom. Only *some* of the firmness of iron will be in it since the iron was mixed with miry clay. *Clay*]—The vs. comes to its climax in the words *miry clay,* rendered by M, *the tile work of clay.*

Vs. 42. *And as the toes of the feet were part of iron and part of clay, so part of the kingdom will be strong and part of it will be broken.* Some commentators find difficulty over the repetitions of these vv. This vs. particularly is placed under suspicion, because it is regarded as a doublet of vs. 41. But objective grounds for suspecting it are not present, and when Baumgartner suggests "v prb add" as a footnote to this vs., he is engaging in mere conjecture. This vs. merely indicates how thoroughly composite is the nature of the kingdom, a diversity extending even to its toes. This composite nature of the toes is a further evidence of the composite nature of the entire kingdom.

Vs. 43. *As thou sawest iron mingled with miry clay, they shall mix with the seed of men, but they shall not cleave together, this with that, see! even as iron does not mix with clay.* This vs. is generally taken to refer to intermarriage. Many commentators find the allusion to the marriages contracted between the Ptolemies and Seleucids (11:6, 17). However, the expression need not be limited to marriages. "The figure of mixing by seed is derived from the sowing of the field with mingled seed, and denotes all the means employed by the rulers to combine the different nationalities, among which the *connubium* is only spoken of as the most important and successful means" (Keil). However, this mixing together will fail.

Vs. 44. *And in the days of those kings the God of heaven will set up a kingdom that shall never be destroyed, and the kingdom shall not be left to other people: it will crush and bring to an end all these kingdoms, but it shall stand forever.* Driver refers the phrase *in the days of these kings* to the Seleucids and Ptolemies. Others find the reference to kings of the Roman Empire. Keil specifically applies this to the kings of the world kingdoms last described. The view adopted by SRB is that *these kings* refers to the ten kings of Dan. 7:24-27. Thus, it is argued, the time of the prophecy is fixed as being, not the first but the second Advent of Christ. According to this position, there must first be a revived Roman Empire, the signs of which, it is alleged, are already to be discerned. "In that day the iron of imperial power will be mixed with the brittle pottery of socialism and democracy; but they will not cleave together" (Ironside). Christ will then come *for* His saints; the Church will be caught up to heaven, and the Stone will fall. This view must be rejected as being exegetically untenable. It makes too much of the symbolism. We are not expressly told that there are ten toes. The *ten* kings can be derived only from the ten horns of Dan. 7:24-27. That there are ten toes is merely inferred from the fact that the colossus appears in the form of a man. Furthermore, the image was not smitten upon the toes but upon the feet (2:34). Now the feet and legs are to be taken together (2:33), and since the image is smitten upon the feet, the blow should fall, if the dispensationalists were consistent, at the time when the kingdom was divided into the Eastern and Western Empires. (See *SRB*, p. 901, note 1, where the two legs are interpreted as the Eastern and Western empires.) Lastly, the phrase *in the days of these kings* cannot refer to the ten toes (Gaebelein), for the toes are nowhere identified as kings. Nor does it refer to the kings of the fourth monarchy, for no such kings are mentioned; the only kings or kingdoms mentioned are the four empires. The correct interpretation has been set forth by Allis, " . . . the words 'in the days of those kings' would refer most naturally to the four kingdoms or kings represented by the image. This interpretation is clearly involved in the symbolism of the image (vs. 45) and is permissible because, while distinct, these four kingdoms were also in a sense one. Medo-Persia conquered and incorporated Babylon. Greece did the same to Medo-Persia. And while Rome never conquered all of Alexander's empire, she did conquer much of it and the extent of the Roman Empire was far greater and more world-wide than any of the others. It was while the image was still standing that the blow was struck. So we may say that it was in the period of those four empires as together representing Gentile world dominion but in the days of the last of the four that the kingdom of Messiah was set up." It is while the colossus is standing that God will set up His kingdom. The striking of the feet is symbolical, and does not necessarily have any particular reference to the fourth kingdom. The image is struck on the feet, because such a blow will cause it to totter and fall. Where else would one strike a blow that would cause the entire image to fall?

The kingdom of God is of Divine *origin* and eternal *duration.* For this reason, it cannot be the millennium, which is but 1000 years in length. Since the kingdom is divine, it is therefore eternal. It will furthermore not be conquered by others, but will ever be in the hands of the same people, the true Israel of God, the Church. On the other hand it will break in pieces and destroy other kingdoms. The contrast may be represented as follows:

THE KINGDOMS OF THE COLOSSUS	as to	THE KINGDOM OF GOD
Human	ORIGIN	Divine
Temporary	DURATION	Eternal
Overcome by each succeeding kingdom	POWER	Unconquerable

This kingdom which God establishes is the sphere of His reign or sovereignty among men.

Vs. 45. *Inasmuch as thou sawest that from the mountain a stone was cut out without hands and crushed the iron, bronze, clay, silver and gold, the great God hath made known to the king what will be after this; and sure is the dream and faithful its interpretation.* According to Jerome, Porphyry and the Jews refer the stone to the people who will become a great nation. Jerome himself sees the fulfillment in the Virgin Birth, "absque coitu et humane semine, de utero virginali." Essentially this view is held by Justin Martyr, Tertullian, Irenæus and Ephraim of Syria. Most Christian expositors find the reference in Christ and the progress of His kingdom, and this seems to me to be correct. The stone is represented as not being cut out of the mountain by hands in order to show that it is prepared, not by men, but by God. The blow which it delivers strikes the metals in the reverse order from which they had first been described, "as if its effects would not only reach onward, but backward on the remnants of former earthly greatness" (Rose). The kingdom of God will completely triumph, and the kingdom of men (as represented by the image) will be completely destroyed. *The God of heaven*]—in this instance, the words may be indefinite, *a God*, but, since Dan. has already identified this God, the definite article in English is to be preferred (see discussion in Keil). *After this*]—i.e., after this present time during which the dream had occurred. This revelation is a remarkable instance of God's goodness to a heathen monarch. *Sure is the dream*]—This is not spoken because the king has forgotten the dream, but rather to impress him that the matter is true, should be taken to heart and glory given to its Author. Cf. 8:26; 10:21. Keil further points out that this remark also " . . . assures the readers of the book of the certainty of the fulfillment."

According to Haller, the purpose of this ch. is to show how Dan. had the opportunity of employing his wisdom in interpreting dreams (Traumdeutekunst). The connection with ch. one, however, is said to be loose since there is a conflict over dates (1:18 with 2:1—but cf. the discussion *supra* of 2:1).

The account, thinks Haller, consists of a framework, 2:1-30 and 46-49, and a kernel. According to the narrator in the framework, dreams were supposed to be divine revelations, the interpretation of which was a secret art. The framework also serves the purpose of justifying faith in Yahweh as over against the heathen culture and science, a thought which is well expressed in Dan.'s prayer (2:20 ff.). The wisdom which the Jewish God bestows is far superior to all heathen art and knowledge, and Neb.'s judgment upon the magicians is a fine stroke (besondere Feinheit) of the writer. Second Isaiah likewise despised the black art of the wise men of Babylon (Isa. 47:12 ff.).

As to the account of the dream itself, it is, thinks Haller, but a variation of the favorite oriental legend-motif of a dreaming king and a wise dream interpreter, which motif had already appeared in the Old Testament in the story of Joseph (Gen. 40 ff.). The demand of the king for the content of the dream is an oriental touch (Das ist orientalisch gedacht.) and, to prove this statement, Haller refers to the Yemenite king, discussed above (under 2:3). The form which Neb. saw was a kind of colossal statue, of which the ancient Orient knew many, such as the colossus of Rhodes or the image in the temple of Bel at Babylon (Her. I:183). However, Haller is in error here; neither of these can really be compared with the colossus of the dream. This latter was unique, and, so far as the present writer knows, there was nothing in the ancient world with which it could be compared.

The writer held Babylon in a favorite light and so represented it in the symbolism by the most valuable metal. The middle kingdoms, the Median and the Persian, and the Macedonian are indicated, but stress is placed upon the fifth, the diadochoi, which was mixed with the iron firmness of the Macedonians and the vacillation of the Asiatic hordes. To this dream additions were made which come from the time of the Maccabees. Haller sets his position forth in dogmatic fashion. It is up to him to prove that we are here in the realm of Oriental legend, and this he has not done.

d. Vv. 46-49. *Nebuchadnezzar honors Daniel and his God and promotes Daniel.*

Vs. 46. *Then the king Nebuchadnezzar fell upon his face and bowed down to Daniel, and tribute and sweet odors he commanded to pour out unto him.* Porphyry criticized this vs. as not being true to life, in that it represents a most haughty king adoring a mere captive. Jerome replied to this by citing the attempt of the Lycaonians to worship Paul and Barnabas. Porphyry further criticized Dan. for receiving these rewards, and Jerome replied by commenting upon the magnitude of the task which Dan., as a boy, had accomplished, and sought to exonerate

Dan. from all blame. *Fell upon*]—in itself a mark of respect. Bevan, I think, is correct in saying that "Nebuchadnezzar at the feet of Daniel represents the Gentile power humbled before Israel (cf. Ps. xlix: 23; lx. 14)." *Bowed down to*]—This word is used of worship and adoration to a god (cf. 3:5, 6, 7 etc.) although it need not always have this connotation. As Stuart says, the word " . . . is not decisive of religious worship." It must be remembered that the king was in an aroused state of mind, and probably his desire was to honor Dan. as the accredited representative of the true God who had revealed to His servant the dream. Thus, as Jerome first indicated, through Dan. the king would adore the God of Dan (*Non tam Danielem quam in Daniele adorat Deum, qui mysteria revelavit*). In the *Antiq.* (11:8:5) Josephus records that Alexander the Great bowed before the high priest of the Jews, and when asked by his general, Parmenio, as to the meaning of his action, replied, "I do not worship the high-priest, but the God with whose high-priesthood he has been honored."

At any rate, whatever may have been the precise purpose of the king, we may be sure that a man of the stalwart character of Dan., whose sole desire was for the glory of his God, would not have taken to himself honor which belonged to God alone. *Tribute*]—a present, offered as a mark of respect, and also, generally, an oblation. *Sweet odors*]—lit., a savour of rest or contentment. The homage due to a god is bestowed upon Dan., who, probably as the representative and in the Name of his God, accepts it.

Vs. 47. *The king answered Daniel and said, Of a truth your god is God of gods and Lord of kings and a revealer of secrets, inasmuch as thou hast been able to reveal this secret. Of a truth*]—i.e., I know of a truth. *Your*]—the pl. probably because the king is addressing Dan. and his companions. *God of gods*]—more accurate than *a god of gods.* The expression indicates the superlative. Among all the gods your god is *God.* The supremacy of Dan.'s God over other gods is thus expressed. The title, lord of the gods (bel ilani) was applied, also by Neb. to Marduk The profession of the king, however, was nothing more than the profession of a polytheist. He had not yet come to see that Dan.'s God is the only God. However, the superiority of Dan.'s God is recognized when the king calls Him a *revealer of secrets,* and the reason why he bestows this epithet is that Dan. (and here the s. is used) was able to reveal this secret.

Vs. 48. *Then the king made Daniel great, and large and numerous presents (he) gave to him, and made him ruler over all the province of Babylon and chief overseer over all the wise men of Babylon.* Dan. is promoted by way of reward. Provinces such as Babel etc., were ruled by an official known as shakkanaku (Meissner I, 121). Dan. is called a *rab signin,* i.e., chief overseer. Those who deny the historicity of the account find this vs.

to bristle with difficulties (see M). But the words of Stuart are still to the point, "What the particular duties of this office were, we do not know. That Daniel so managed them as to keep clear of divination by sorcery or astrology, and of the performance of heathen rites, would seem to be implied by the account of his demeanor which is given in the book of Daniel."

There is no particular reason why Dan. should refuse the rewards of the king. But, if these words were written at the time of the Maccabees or at any other period of *strict* Judaism, it is difficult to understand why the author, supposedly a strict Jew with an abhorence of everything pagan, would represent his Jewish hero as receiving such honors from a pagan king.

Vs. 49. *And Daniel requested from the king and he appointed over the business of the province of Babylon Shadrach, Meshach, and Abed-Nego, and Daniel was in the gate of the king.* The three companions had assisted Dan. in prayer, and he requests their promotion to be under-officers to himself that he might serve in the court of the king. *Gate*]—Oriental terminology for royal offices, cf. Turkish "Sublime Porte." The mention of the three companions also prepares the way for the narrative related in ch. three.

CHAPTER THREE

a. vv. 1-7. Nebuchadnezzar erects a golden image and requires that his subjects, upon penalty of death, shall worship it.

Vs. 1. *Nebuchadnezzar the king made an image of gold, whose height was sixty cubits (and) its breadth six cubits; he erected it in the plain of Dura, in the province of Babylon.* The LXX and the translation of Th. date this event in the 18th year of the king's reign, apparently intending to place it in the year of Jerusalem's downfall. However, this is probably suggested by Jer. 52:29 and is not original. We do not know in what year of his reign the king erected the image. *Nebuchadnezzar*]—In Dan. the proper name generally precedes the title, but cf. 2:28, 46; 3:16; 4:28, 5:9, 11; 6:9. Charles appeals to this variety of usage as evidence of the lateness of language. But if a later writer were endeavoring to make his composition appear archaic, a product of the 6th century B.C., why would he not use the invariable order *Nebuchadnezzar the King?* Being an educated man, he would have had before him the documents of ancient Hebrew and Aramaic. It is questionable whether the papyri to which Charles makes appeal for evidence of earlier usage are really determinative. The phrases *X the King* in these papyri appear in headings, and are more or less stereotyped. But in a long document, a work of literature, such as the book of Dan., variation would naturally be introduced to avoid monotony. Hence, it does not seem that this variation in itself is any indication of the date of the book.

The LXX adds the words, "when he had brought under his rule cities and provinces and all that dwell upon the earth from India to Ethiopia." This addition is accepted by Charles, but is obviously intended to furnish a reason for the erection of the image. *Made*]—"It was a common practice of the Assyrian kings to erect images of themselves with laudatory inscriptions in conquered cities, or provinces, as symbols of their dominion, the usual expression in such cases being *sa-lam sharru-ti-a* (*shur-ba-a*) *ipu-ush.* 'A (great) image of royalty I made'; see KB, i.69, l.98f.; 73, 1, 5; 99, l.25, 133, l.31; 135, l.71; 141, l.93; 143, l.124; 147, l.156; 155, l.26, &c (all from the reigns of Asshur-nasir-abal, B. C. 885-860, and Shalmaneser II, B.C. 860-825)" (Driver). The text does not state that this was an image of the king himself. Hippolytus (2.15) suggests that the idea of the imag was induced by the vision of ch. 2. When Dan. called the king the "head of gold," the king became puffed up with pride and decided to erect a golden image. Thus, the image represented the deified Neb. (So also Jerome *ut ipse adoretur in statua*). It is quite possible that, overcome with pride because of his conquests (and the downfall of Jerusalem may now have been included in these) and also, influenced by Dan's identification of himself as the head of gold, the king erected this image which may possibly have been of himself. It was, however, erected to do honor to his god as well as to himself. *Of gold*]—probably because in the dream the king had been identified as the head of gold. Many have been the objections which have been urged against this description. Such an image would be too expensive, it has been alleged. However, it need not be maintained that the image was of solid gold. "The gold consisted in overlaid plates" (M). Cf. Ex. 38:30; 39:3ff of the golden altar, and Isa. 40:19ff; 41:7; Jer. 10:3ff. Her. (1:183) "... there is a second temple, in which is a sitting figure of Jupiter, all of gold. Before the figure stands a large golden table, and the throne whereon it sits, and the base on which the throne is placed, are likewise of gold. The Chaldeans told me that all the gold together was eight hundred talents' weight. Outside the temple are two altars, one of solid gold, on which it is only lawful to offer sucklings; the other a common altar, but of great size, on which the full-grown animals are sacrificed.—In the time of Cyrus there was likewise in this temple the figure of a man, twelve cubits high, entirely of solid gold" (Her. I: 183, Rawlinson's translation). Cf. also Pliny, 33:24, 34:9ff., and the Epistle of Jeremiah 7, 54, 56; Bel and the Dragon, 7. Such references afford sufficient background, and the consideration that the statue need not have been of solid gold amply refutes the objection "But the amazing, the incalculable, the unbelievable expense of such an image of *gold!* It surpasses all faith, except an *a priori* one, like that of Hengstenberg" (von Lengerke). *Its height*]—Many objections have been raised against the proportions of the statue, which are said to be grotesque, 90′ in height x 9′ in breadth. Driver says that this disproportion has not been satisfactorily explained. But M is correct when he says, "At all events, it is not necessary to charge the narrator with an obvious absurdity." It is conceivable that the statue may have been in the form of an obelisk, nine feet in breadth at the base. The form would then be grotesque, it is true, but grotesqueness seems to have characterized a considerable portion of Babylonian sculpture. In DS II:9 Ctesias mentions a statue of the god which was forty feet in height and weighed 1000 Babylonian talents. The Colossus of Rhodes was 70 feet in height. However, it is quite possible that included in these dimensions was a base or pedestal, which would greatly detract from the grotesqueness of the proportions. At any rate, the dimensions given certainly present no objection to the historicity of the account. "In truth, if the account before us is so monstrously incredible as some critics of a recent class assert; if the incongruities are so staring, and in such high relief, then what kind of a witling was he, who wrote the book of Daniel at so late a period?" (Stuart). An evidence of genuineness is seen in the expression of the dimensions in terms of the Babylonian sexagesimal system. (cf. Meissner, II, p. 385ff and Ezek. 40:5 *six cubits*). *He erected it*]—This same phrase is used in the inscriptions of Palmyra and the Hauran, e.g., "This statue is that—which there erected to him, etc." (De Vogue, no. 4 as given in Cooke, p. 270). However, the usage is not consistent in these inscriptions, the word 'avad being used almost interchangeably with 'akim. This word is employed in Hebrew of the establishment of institutions, cf. Amos 9:11. *In the plain*]—i.e., a broad plain between mountains. The exact location has not been determined. The word duru means an *enclosing wall,* and is of common occurrence. It has been pointed out that the tablets mention three localities which bear the name Duru, and that several Babylonian cities have names compounded with Dur. The archaeologist Oppert (*Expedition Scientifique en Mesopotamie,* 1:238ff) declared that S. S. E. of Hillah, at a distance of about 12 miles, there were some mounds called Tolul Dura (the mounds of Dura). One of these, known as el-Mokhattat, consisted of a rectangular brick structure 45′ square and 20′ in height, which according to Oppert, may have formed the pedestal of a colossal image. If this ch. is a mere legend, composed in the second century B. C. as a "polemic against the heathen worship and in particular against idolatry" (Bevan), how account for the presence of this word *Dura?* The appearance of the word is in reality an evidence of genuineness in that it seems to presuppose some knowledge of the Babylonian geography. *In the province*]—These words help to identify the location of the plain of Dura. The name Dura has occurred in classical sources; Polybius 5:48, Amm. Mar. 23:5, 8; 24:1, 5 mention a Dura at the mouth of the Chaboras where it empties into the Euphrates, but this can hardly be reckoned as being in the province of Babylon, and another Dura is mentioned as being beyond the Tigris not far from Appollonia, Polybius 5:52 and Amm. Mar. 25:6, 9. This also would be too distant. Oppert has probably suggested the approximate location. He says, "On seeing this mound, one is immediately struck with the resemblance which it presents to the pedestal of a colossal statue, as, for example, that of Bavaria near Munich, and everything leads to the belief that the statue mentioned in the book of Daniel (ch. III:1) was set up in this place."

Vs. 2. *And Nebuchadnezzar the king sent to gather the satraps, prefects, governors, judges, treasurers, counsellors, sheriffs, and all the rulers of the provinces to come to the dedication of the image which Nebuchadnezzar the king had erected.* It was, apparently, a universal custom of antiquity to observe dedication rites. Of particular interest is it to note that this account is in keeping with what is known of the ancient Babylonian rites, "In the matter of local color this dedication ceremony is correct" (M). To this ceremony the officials of the kingdom are invited. Meissner I:71 tells of Sargon's action after the completion of his palace at Dur Sharrukin. "Sargon made himself secure in his palace with the princes of all lands, the rulers of his land, the governors, presidents, magnates, honorables and senators of Assyria, and instituted a feast" (Sargon's Prism, 178f.). *Sent*]—By messengers employed to give publicity to the summons. *Satraps*]—The word is from old Persian 'kingdom-guardian.' The use of these Persian words here is not necessarily an anachronism (Charles). For one thing, such Persian terms may have been employed in the neo-Babylonian empire due to Persian influence. The earliest extant old-Persian inscription is c. 610—580 B. C. If Dan. had written his book after the taking of Babylon, it is quite conceivable that he might have employed Persian terms. Certainly, the use of these words is not necessarily evidence for a later date. The two words *governors* and *prefects* are Semitic. *Sheriffs*]—probably "a minor judicial title" (M). Apparently these titles reveal a certain gradation in rank. Why was Dan. not present in this group? Various answers are given to this question. Hippolytus supposed that Dan. might have been present, but was not particularly watched. Calvin suggests that the accusers could more easily attack the others since Dan. stood in peculiar favor with the king. Others say that the source of this story was independent of the Dan. sagas, but was incorporated into these latter by their compiler who exhibited little concern as to the whereabouts of Dan. during the episode. This view of course, does not regard the book as historical and is therefore to be rejected. As a matter of fact, we do not know why there is no mention of Dan. in this ch., and it is useless to speculate on the matter.

Vs. 3. *Then were gathered together the satraps, prefects and governors, the judges, treasurers, counsellors, sheriffs and all the rulers of the provinces to the dedication of the image which Nebuchadnezzar the king had erected, and were standing before the image which Nebuchadnezzar had erected.* Such repetition is characteristic of Semitic style. Hitzig has objected that if the officials of the province were thus gathered, it would put a stop to the government of the country. But surely soldiers would have remained at their posts throughout the province to quell any uprisings. Cf. Esther 1:3ff. This *dedication* doubtless possessed religious significance, by which the image was consecrated as a symbol of the world-power "and (in the heathen sense) of its divine glory" (Keil).

Vs. 4. *And a herald proclaimed with strength; to you it is commanded oh! peoples, nations, and tongues.* The three words placed together denote all nations, no one in the whole kingdom was to be exempt from obeying the command. The expression recurs in 3:7, 29; 4:1; 5:19; 6:25; 7:14 and cf. Rev. 5:9; 7:9; 10:11; 11:9; 13:7; 14:6; 17:15. All these nations are represented by officials.

Vs. 5. *At the time that ye hear the sound of the horn, flute, harp, trigon, psaltery, bagpipe and all kinds of music, ye fall down and worship the image of gold that Nebuchadnezzar the king has erected.* Philologically, this is an extremely interesting vs. The word *kind* is of Persian origin. Two of the names of the musical instruments are Semitic (*horn* and *flute*); three are probably Greek, and one (*bagpipe*) is of uncertain origin. *Horn*]—The curved ram's horn, as in Jos. 6:16. *Flute*]—From a root meaning to *hiss or whistle*. *Harp*]—or lyre, *Trigon*]—the Greek instrument was of triangular shape with four strings. Greek writers say that this instrument was of Syrian origin (Athenaeus 4:175 d, e). *Psaltery*]—said to be a stringed instrument of triangular shape. *Bagpipe*]—a word of uncertain meaning. Here it evidently refers to a musical instrument, but Polybius employs it to describe the music which Antiochus Epiphanes used on festive occasions (Polybius 26, 31, "going to feasts with horn and *symphony*").

The presence of Greek words—if such they are— is no argument against the early date for the authorship of the book of Dan. "The idea that Greece and Hellenic culture were little known in Western Asia before Alexander the Great is difficult to eradicate. Actually, as we know from recent archaeological discoveries, there was not a century of the Iron Age during which objects of Greek origin, mostly ceramic in character, were not being brought into Syria and Palestine. Greek traders and mercenaries were familiar in Egypt and throughout Western Asia from the early seventh century on, if not earlier. As early as the sixth century B. C. the coasts of Syria and Palestine were dotted with Greek ports and trading emporia, several of which have been discovered during the past five years. None of these could begin to approach the prosperity of the great Hellenic harbors of Naucratis and Daphne in Egypt. There were Greek mercenaries in the armies of Egypt and Babylonia, of Psammetichus II and Nebuchadnezzar" (FSAC p. 259). *Fall down*]—Prostration "is both a preparatory act for worship, and one which accompanies worship itself" (Stuart). These words make clear the religious character of the act.

Vs. 6. *And whoever does not fall down and worship, at that moment he will be cast into the midst of a furnace of burning fire.* This command evidently pre-supposes that there will be instances of refusal. Among the Assyrians and Babylonians, cruel punishments were practised. Cf. Jer. 29:22. Refusal to do homage to the image, since it was erected by the king and for his glory, would be regarded as equivalent to treason to the state. In so far as the image may have represented the gods of the king, it would not go against the scruples of heathen captives to bow down to it, since this would simply involve the acknowledgment that the gods of Babylon were more powerful than their own gods, and this the heathen of antiquity could easily grant. But for devout Jews to worship this statue would have been to deny their cherished conviction that there is One alone to whom worship is due. The edict of the king, therefore, was certain to work hardship upon the faithful Jews. There is, however, in this edict, nothing which could be compared with the religious persecution practised by Antiochus Epiphanes. *Furnace*]—Hævernick calls attention to the description of the traveller Chardin (*Voyage en Perse*, VI), who was in Persia 1671-77, and who notes that two furnaces of fire were kept burning for a month for consuming those who overcharged for food. M suggests that this furnace " . . . must have been similar to our common lime-kiln, with a perpendicular shaft from the top and an opening at the bottom for extracting the fused lime."

Vs. 7. *Because of this at the time when all the people were hearing the sound of the horn, flute, harp trigon, psaltery and all kinds of music, all people, nations, and tongues were falling down, worshipping the image of gold which Nebuchadnezzar the king had erected.* In this repetition the bagpipe is omitted. The love of the Babylonians for music is attested by Isa. 14:11, Ps. 137:3, Her. 1:191, Q. Cur., 5:3.

b. vv. 8-12. Certain Chaldeans inform the king that Shadrach, Meshach and Abed-Nego have not worshipped the golden image.

Vs. 8. *On account of this at that time there drew near certain Chaldeans, and accused the Jews.* The three companions had not fallen down before the image, so *on account of this* fact, the accusation was brought. *Drew near*]—to the king. *Chaldeans*]—Here the term is employed in an ethnic sense; Chaldeans in contrast to Jews. *Accused*]—lit., *they ate their pieces,* a common Semitic idiom for *calumniate, slander.* Probably this accusation was motivated by jealousy due to the high position of the three.

Vs. 9. *They answered and said to Nebuchadnezzar the king, oh! king, live forever.* Cf. 2:4, for the form of address.

Vs. 10. *Thou, oh! king, hast made a decree that every man who hears the sound of the horn, flute, harp, trigon, psaltery and bagpipe and all kinds of music shall fall down and worship the image of gold.*

Vs. 11. *And whoever does not fall down and worship shall be thrown into the midst of a furnace of burning fire.*

Vs. 12. *There are certain Jews whom thou hast appointed over the service of the province of Babylon, Shadrach, Meshach and Abed-Nego, these men have paid no heed to thee, oh! king; thy god they do not serve, and the image of gold which thou hast erected they do not worship.* Hitzig rightly remarks: "These Chaldeans knew the three Jews, who were so placed as to be well known, and at the same time envied, before this (von frueher her). They had long known that they did not worship idols; but on this occasion, when their religion made it necessary for the Jews to disobey the king's command, they make use of their knowledge" (translated by M. G. Easton). Implied in this accusation is the charge of ingratitude. The king, it is argued, has honored these men but they have paid no heed to him as may be seen by the fact that they do not honor the king's god, nor worship his image.

c. vv. 13-18. Nebuchadnezzar commands the accused men to be brought before him and asks them if the accusation is true. He repeats his edict, whereupon they reply that their confidence is in God.

Vs. 13. *Then Nebuchadnezzar in rage and fury commanded to bring Shadrach, Meshach and Abed-Nego; then these men were brought before the king.* The furious rage of the king shows that the Chaldeans have succeeded in their object.

Vs. 14. *Nebuchadnezzar answered and said to them, Is it true, Shadrach, Meshach and Abed-Nego, that my gods ye do not serve and the image of gold which I have erected ye do not worship?* The question *is it true* has often been translated, *is it of purpose* or *of design.* This is because the precise meaning and etymology of the words have been unknown. However, this word has now been found on an Aramaic ostrakon where the context clearly shows the meaning. The king thus is willing to give the accused an opportunity to deny the charge, since possibly he suspected the motives of the accusers.

Vs. 15. *Now, if ye are ready that, at the time when ye shall hear the sound of the horn, flute, harp, trigon, psaltery and bag-pipe, and all kinds of music, ye will fall down and worship the image that I have made—and if ye do not worship, in that instant ye shall be cast into the midst of a furnace of burning fire, and what kind of a god can deliver you out of my hand?* The apodosis of the first sentence is omitted; we should expect some word such as *well.* The aposiopesis of the apodosis, however, lends force to the statement. Cf. similar examples, Ex. 32:32; Luke 13:9; 19:42; 2 Thess. 2:3ff. Cf. also the *Iliad* I:135ff. Haevernick tries to avoid the aposiopesis by translating, "if ye will hear ... then ye will fall down." But this is not grammatically correct, nor does it yield a good sense; it further destroys the disjunction between *ye will . . . worship* and *ye will not worship.* "This narrative clearly assures us, how kings consult only their own grandeur by a show of piety, when they claim the place of their deities" (Calvin). Probably the king discerned the look of refusal upon the faces of the accused. In his rage, he suggests that no god can deliver from this punishment. Had he paused to reflect, he would have realized that the God of the Jews was unlike his own deities, but rage does not reflect; instead, it threatens.

Vs. 16. *Shadrach, Meshach and Abed-Nego answered and said to the king Nebuchadnezzar, we have no need with respect to this matter to make defence before thee.* There are difficulties in this vs., partly occasioned by the Massoretic pointing. If the word *Nebuchadnezzar* be taken as a vocative, as the Massoretes pointed it, then the three accused ones are made to be guilty of disrespect. It is inconceivable that men of the character of these should at such a time engage in such familiarity. The difficulty is easily resolved by translating as above. Jerome had noted the omission of the word king (In Hebraeo non habet regem, sicut in LXX). *We have no need*]—This response has also occasioned difficulty. Von Lengerke believed that it was an evidence of the Maccabean date of the book, when the Jews thought it a glory to suffer martyrdom rather than to obey Antiochus. But this is to miss the meaning of the response. Arrogance is entirely lacking in this reply and so is that fanaticism which characterized the martyrs of the Maccabean age. The three are simply acknowledging the correctness of the indictment laid against them and declaring that there is no defence or apology that need be made. They cast themselves utterly upon God. It is a case where they are compelled to serve God rather than man, and for their noble faith, they are evidently honored by the writer of the epistle to the Hebrews as those who by faith "quenched the violence of fire" (Heb. 11:34).

Vs. 17. *If our God whom we serve is able to deliver us from the furnace of burning fire and from thy hand, oh! king, he will deliver.*

Vs. 18. *But if not, be it known to thee, oh! king, that thy god we are not serving and to the image of gold which thou hast set up we will not bow down.* The translation given here is difficult, because it seems to imply a doubt as to the ability of God to deliver from the furnace. Various attempts have been made to circumvent this difficulty. Jerome translated, "For behold our God," and Maurer remarks that all the interpreters except von Lengerke adopt this translation. The other ancient versions begin the translation with for. Some commentators render, as the AV, "If it be so, our God . . ." Charles regards the Massoretic text as corrupt. He thinks that the original (as reconstructed upon the basis of the versions) was, "For there is a God, whom we serve, who is able to deliver us," and this, he thinks, provides a satisfactory answer to the question of the king (in vs. 15). However, the versions are apparently paraphrases or expansions of the text made for the sake of clearing away the difficulty. Hence, the Aramaic text, it would seem, is to be preferred, and I have translated as above, because that translation alone seems faithfully to represent the Aramaic original.

If, however, this translation be adopted, we must inquire as to its meaning. M believes that the language does betray a lack of absolute confidence in the Divine omnipotence. If this assumption is correct, it certainly presents a picture far removed from the fanaticism of the Maccabean age. However, I do not think that any doubt as to God's omnipotence is intended. Keil has stated the true interpretation when he says that the reference is to "... *ethical ability,* i.e., the ability limited by the divine holiness and righteousness, not the omnipotence of God as such." Thus, the thought is, "If, in His *sovereign good* pleasure, our God can deliver us, He will do so." "The three simply see that their standpoint can never be clearly understood by Nebuchadnezzar, and therefore they give up any attempt to justify themselves. But that which was demanded of them they could not do, because it would have been altogether contrary to their faith and their conscience. And then without fanaticism they calmly decline to answer, and only say, 'Let him do according to his own will'; thus without superstitiousness committing their deliverance to God" (Kliefoth, as given in Keil.) Cf. also Isa. 43:1, 2. The noble comment of Barnes on this passage is worthy of quotation in full, "This is the *religion of principle;* and when we consider the circumstances of those who made this reply; when we remember their comparative youth, and the few opportunities which they had for instruction in the nature of religion, and that they were captives in a distant land, and that they stood before the most absolute monarch of the earth, with no powerful friends to support them, and with the most horrid kind of death threatening them, we may well admire the grace of that God who could so amply furnish them for such a trial, and love that religion which enabled them to tak a stand so noble and so bold." The remark in the SRB that these three youths are typical of the Jewish remnant, faithful in the last days in the furnace of the great tribulation is wholly gratuitous and devoid of any Scriptural support whatsoever.

d. vv. 19-30. Nebuchadnezzar in rage commands that the furnace be heated seven times hotter than customary, and that the three be cast into its midst. These commands are carried out. But in the furnace the king sees the men unharmed and accompanied by a Fourth. He thereupon commands them to come forth and blesses their God.

Vs. 19. *Then Nebuchadnezzar was filled with anger, and the fashion of his face was changed with respect to Shadrach, Meshach and Abed-Nego; he answered and commanded that the furnace be heated seven times beyond what was wont.* The king's command is absurd, the result of his anger. In his pride, he can brook no opposition. *Fashion*]—The word literally means *image,* and is the same that is employed to designate the image of gold. Here, it must mean the *form,* or *appearance* of his countenance. *Seven times*]—lit., *one-seven,* i. e., 1 x 7; the phrase employed may be reminiscent of expressions used in the Babylonian multiplication tables. This type of expression also occurs in the Syriac translation of Dan. 11:8, 13. The number *seven* is taken by some to be the indefinite expression of a round number (Hævernick); by others to indicate intensity (Kranichfeld), but probably, as Zœckler points out, it has a *judicial* bearing as indicating fulness of satisfaction or atonement See Lev. 26:18-24; Prov. 6:31; Matt. 18:21ff. *Wont*]—i. e., beyond the point to which it was customarily heated. Zœckler suggests that a better meaning is, *more than appropriate or necessary.* Probably the word *wont* best expresses the meaning The furnace is to be raised to an *extremely intense* heat.

Vs. 20. *And certain strong men that were in his army he commanded to bind Shadrach, Meshach and Abed-Nego and to cast (them) into the furnace of burning fire.* Since the task was not without certain danger, the king ordered the strongest men of the army to carry it out. Probably the choice of *men of strength* was also intended to forestall any intervention either of human or of Divine power.

Vs. 21. *Then these men were bound in their mantles, their trousers and their hats and their garments and they were cast into the midst of the furnace of burning fire.* The three had been present in court dress, and, bound in their clothes, were cast into the furnace. Of the words for clothing here employed, only that for hats seems to be of certain meaning. See M for full philological discussion.

Vs. 22 *On this account because the command of the king was peremptory and the furnace exceeding hot, those men who had brought up Shadrach, Meshach and Abed-Nego,—them did the flame of fire kill.* The executioners had taken the three men up to the top of the furnace to cast them in, and were themselves killed by a flame of the fire. The point is not that the three were carried, but that they were *taken up* to the opening at the top of the furnace to be cast in there. Through an opening at the bottom the furnace could be heated, and the men within could be seen, but the men were cast into the furnace from the opening at the top.

Vs. 23. *And these three men Shadrach, Meshach and Abed-Nego were fallen down into the midst of the furnace of burning fire bound.* The verb sets forth the circumstances existing at the time of the action of the main verbs in vs. 24. The thought may be paraphrased as follows: "These three men were fallen down bound, when the king wondered and rose up in haste." The vs. serves to emphasize the difficulty of deliverance. *In a fiery furnace—bound!*—This was the state of things from which only the power of God could deliver. The vs. serves to set forth the mighty contrast between the desperate plight of the men and the miraculous deliverance which produced the king's astonishment. Nevertheless, Charles considers the vs. to be an interpolation, but confesses that he cannot account for its insertion in the text. His principal grounds for its rejection are that it does not appear in the LXX, it contributes no fresh fact to the narrative, and it does not serve as an introduction to vs. 24. However, we have already pointed out the purpose which the vs. serves, and we would call attention to the fact that it does occur in Th. The LXX does contain a vs. 23 which is largely made up of phrases from the Mass. vs. 22. Furthermore, the versions at this point appear to be very corrupt. Hence, the preponderance of weight of evidence is in favor of retaining this vs.

At this point the Greek translations insert the "Prayer of Azariah" and the "Song of the Three Youths" with some introductory vv. This prayer begins with the theme of praise to God, and acknowledgment of His justice in the judgment which has befallen Israel and then continues with a request for deliverance, and for the punishment of the enemies of Israel. After this prayer the interpolation continues with a narrative of the further heating of the furnace and the descent of the Angel of the Lord. This narrative is followed by the "Song," which is an ascription of praise to

God, most of the vv. ending with the refrain "Sing His praise and highly exalt Him forever."

For further information on these interpolated vv. see AP; Driver, pp. xviiiff., xcviiiff.; Bevan, pp. 43 ff.

Vs. 24. *Then Nebuchadnezzar the king wondered and rose in a hurry; he answered and spake to his counsellors, Did we not cast three men into the midst of the fire bound? They answered and said to the king, True, oh! king.* Through the opening at the bottom of the furnace by means of which it was heated, the king could see within. What he saw put him in astonishment, causing him to rise up in a hurry to ask of his counsellors whether three men had been cast into the fire. *Counsellors*]—ministers. The word is probably of Persian origin, and its precise signification is unknown. The question of the king is elicited by the fact that he now beholds four men in the furnace.

Vs. 25. *He answered and said, Lo! I see four men loose, walking in the midst of the fire and there is no harm upon them, and the appearance of the fourth is like that of a son of the gods.* Apparently the king alone saw the fourth Being, which accounts for his behaviour. *Loose*]—i. e., the fire had devoured the bonds, but left the men themselves untouched. Their freedom is emphasized by the statement that they are *walking*. *Son of the gods*]—The translation of the AV, the *Son of God* is not grammatically defensible. The meaning is, *son of deity*, i. e., a Divine Person, one of the race of the gods, a supernatural being. The fact that this Being is called an angel in vs. 28, does not detract from this interpretation, since in Aramaic the word angel may stand as a designation of deity, somewhat in the sense of the Angel of the Lord in Gen. It must be remembered that we do not have before us the exact words of Neb., but only an Aramaic translation of the same. No doubt the king spoke "in the spirit and meaning of the Babylonian doctrine of the gods" (Keil). He recognized in the presence of the fourth Person one who was a superhuman being, in the sense that he was Divine. The Aramaic endeavors to reproduce these thoughts, and does so by means of the language of paganism (See M for philological discussion and literature). The theological question remains, What was the identity of the fourth Person? Since the language of the text would have us understand that a supernatural Person was present, we must ask whether this supernatural Person was merely an angel (Jewish expositors) or whether we are face to face with a pre-incarnate appearance of the second Person of the Trinity. The early Christian expositors adopted this latter view. Perhaps, upon the basis of the available evidence, the question cannot definitely be settled, although I incline toward the latter view. Jerome suggests that the wicked king did not deserve to see the Son of God (*nescio quomodo rex impius Dei Filium videre mereatur*), but the appearance was primarily for the benefit of the three. When God's people are called upon to pass through the waters of affliction, it is He Himself who has promised to be present with them (cf. Isa. 43:1-3).

Vs. 26. *Then Nebuchadnezzar drew near to the door of the furnace of burning fire; he answered and said, Shadrach, Meshach and Abed-Nego, servants of God most High, come forth and come out. Then Shadrach, Meshach and Abed-Nego came out from the midst of the fire.* The king approached the aperture through which the furnace was heated and commanded the men to come forth. *Most High*]—The king does not rise above the level of paganism. So, the Greeks called Zeus the Most High. Neb. does not acknowledge that the Lord alone is God, but merely that the God of the Confessors is the highest of Gods. Even the performance of this mighty miracle does not convert him.

Vs. 27. *And there were gathered together the satraps, prefects, governors and counsellors of the king; and they saw those men upon whose bodies the fire had no power, and the hair of whose heads it had not injured, and whose garments had not changed and upon whom the smell of fire had not come.* There is a gradation noticeable in this description; the *hair* is not singed, the *garments* were whole, and *themselves* were free from the smell of fire

Vs. 28. *Nebuchadnezzar answered and said, Blessed be the god of Shadrach, Meshach and Abed-Nego who has sent his angel and delivered his servants who trusted in him, and the word of the king they have set at naught and have given their bodies that they should not serve nor worship any god except their god.* This statement constitutes at least an acknowledgment of the fact that there is a god who can deliver from the king's hand (cf. vs. 15). It is an expression of awe called forth by the miracle, but it is not the utterance of a truly converted heart. "Convictions wrought by the display of miraculous power, seem better adapted to arrest the attention and check the daring course of the transgressor, than to work a permanent change in his mind" (Stuart). *Set at naught*]—lit., *changed.*

Vs. 29. *And by me is a decree established that every people, nation and tongue that speaks anything amiss against the god of Shadrach, Meshach and Abed-Nego shall be cut in pieces and his house shall be made a dunghill; because there is no other god that can deliver like this.* Cf. 2 K. 10:27. "The idea is that the utmost possible dishonour and contempt should be placed on their houses by devoting them to the most vile and offensive uses" (Barnes). Possibly however, the punishment may merely refer to the destruction of the houses. Cf. 2:5.

Vs. 30. *Then the king caused Shadrach, Meshach and Abed-Nego to prosper in the province of Babylon.* Probably he caused them to prosper in the offices which they already held.

Haller considers the third ch. of Dan. to contain a popular history of martyrs. It is purely legend, and is divided into five scenes. Possibly chs. two and three present two variations of one and the same legend. Probably the writer, in describing the great statue, had in mind the statue which Antiochus Epiphanes IV had erected in Daphne. During the diaspora, thinks Haller, there were probably many stories of faithfulness to the Law in times of persecution going about from mouth to mouth. The narrator could employ such stories, which were sometimes based on Bible passages such as Jer. 29:22, and could easily adapt them to his purposes.

A didactic purpose is visible, thinks Haller. The Jew must not only abstain from heathen practices, but must positively oppose them. Thus, he will be saved by God in a miraculous fashion.

However, sober exegesis reveals that the book of Dan. is not composed of legends. Haller has not one whit of objective evidence with which to support his ideas. The best refutation of such vagaries is to be found in careful exegesis of the book.

CHAPTER FOUR

a. vv. 1-3. The proclamation of Nebuchadnezzar.

Vs. 1. *Nebuchadnezzar the king to all peoples, nations and tongues that dwell in all the earth, May your peace be multiplied.* In the Aramaic text 4:1-3 is numbered as 3:31-33. This same order is also followed in the Greek and Latin versions. However, these vv. properly belong with ch. 4 and are so treated here. *All the earth*]—i. e., the known, inhabited world, from Elam and Media in the east to Egypt and the Mediterranean sea-coasts in the west. Cf. Jer. 25:26; 27:5-6. The Assyrian and Babylonian kings regarded themselves as kings of all the earth, and in their inscriptions were accustomed thus to speak of themselves. This practice was also in vogue among the Persian rulers. *Your peace*]—as in 6:25.

Vs. 2. *The signs and wonders that God Most High has wrought for me, it seemed good to me to show.* These signs were events of an extraordinary or miraculous nature, and the word *wonders* serves to designate the effect which they produced. Stuart paraphrases "miraculous events which call forth wonder."

Vs. 3. *How great are his signs, and his wonders how strong! His kingdom is an everlasting kingdom, and his rule for ever and ever.* "In ascribing an *eternal kingdom* to God, Nebuchadnezzar evidently means to contrast it with the mutable and perishing nature of a dominion like his own" (Stuart). M states that "As an edict the document is historically absurd; it has no similar in the history of royal conversions nor in ancient imperial edicts." Driver says that the phraseology of the decree betrays its Jewish author.

It must be confessed that there are difficulties in the study of this edict. It is perfectly true that a considerable familiarity with Biblical thought is expressed. The doxology (4:3) agrees almost word for word with Ps. 145:13. Zœckler, therefore, believed that the edict was composed, not by Neb., but by Dan. himself. To support this position, he further argued that the remainder of ch. 4 was written in a style similar to that of the other narrative portions of the book, and that 4:25-30 spoke of the king in the third person, rather than in the first, as elsewhere, and that the designation of the palace as being "at Babylon," indicates at least that the writer was writing for other than Babylonians. On the other hand, H,

Keil and others believe that the theocratic language of the edict is due to the instruction and influence of Dan. I am inclined to agree with Keil. The edict is genuine, but it was probably prepared under the influence of Dan. This would account for the theocratic coloring which is considerable. Cf. 4:3,34 with Ps. 72:5; 145:13; Dan. 7:14, 27 and 4:34ff., with Isa 24:21; 40:17; 41:12, 24, 29; 43:14; 45:9; Job 9:12; 21:22. On the other hand, if the decree was merely the work of a Jewish author, it is difficult to understand, particularly if this author lived at the time of the Maccabees, that pagan elements of thought would be permitted to appear. Cf. expressions in 4:5, 6, 10, 14, 15, 20.

Nor can it be maintained, when the purpose of the king is considered, that the publication of such a decree was an absurdity. The concern of the king was to testify, not to his madness, but to the grace of God which is able to abase those that walk in pride. The publication of this edict sheds interesting light upon the open, magnanimous character of the great king. He upon whom the efficacious grace of God has come cannot but declare His praise and wonders. How different this is from the mean, little character of Antiochus Epiphanes! "If the writer of the book of Daniel did indeed mean to hit off Epiphanes in the sketch that he has given us of Nebuchadnezzar, he was one of the most unskillful of all the *likeness-painters*, with whom it has been my lot to form an acquaintance" (Stuart). Jerome presents an interesting comment. The decree (epistula) of the king is inserted in the volume of the prophet, he says, in order that it may be believed to be from Daniel himself, and not from another, as the sycophant (Porphyry) maintains.

b. vv. 4-9. Troubled by a dream, Nebuchadnezzar summons his wise men, who are unable to tell the dream. Lastly, Daniel is summoned.

Vs. 4. *I Nebuchadnezzar was at rest in my house, and flourishing in m palace.* This statement of the king's condition is designed to set fort more vividly the contrast with the events to follow. *At rest*]—i. e., fre from care, at ease. Contentment and security are suggested by the word *Flourishing*]—*growing green*, used of the growth of a tree; hence *prosperous, flourishing.* "Here plainly the word is chosen with referenc to the tree which had been seen in the dream" (Keil). Cf. Ps. 92:12. Th LXX prefaces this vs. with the words, "In the 18th year of his reig Nebuchadnezzar said." However, these words are not given by Th. or b the other versions. They are probably not original. They might easil have been added by a copyist who desired to date each historical even

A similar dating is given in the Greek translations of 3:1. The shorter reading of the Mass. text is therefore to be preferred. (See Charles for the opposite opinion). *In my palace*]—i. e., he was secure upon his throne.

Vs. 5. *A dream I beheld and it terrified me, and the imaginations upon my bed and the visions of my head troubled me.* "The abrupt manner in which the matter is here introduced well illustrates the unexpected suddenness of the event itself" (Keil). *I beheld*]—i. e., the dream was presented to my mind. *Imaginations*]—images, fantasies of the dream. In later Aramaic the word is used to refer to evil imaginations. *Troubled*]—i. e., agitated the whole being of the king. The word is stronger than the word translated *terrified.* Cf. 2:28 for *visions of my head.*

Vs. 6. *And by me a decree was made to bring before me all the wise men of Babylon, that they might cause me to know the interpretation of the dream.* The king here apparently desires to know only the interpretation of the dream and does not demand of the wise men that they also tell the dream itself.

Vs. 7. *Then came in the magicians, the astrologers, the Chaldeans and the soothsayers, and the dream I related before them, and its interpretation they did not make known to me.*

Vs. 8. *Until at last there came before me Daniel whose name is Belteshazzar according to the name of my god and in whom is the spirit of holy deity, and I related the dream before him.* Behrmann translates *Und ausser anderen,* i. e., *and besides, in addition to others.* Bevan would translate, *and yet another entered.* Hitzig renders *bis als letzter,* i. e., *until as the last one.* M follows Hævernick, who first correctly explained the Aramaic word. Upon the basis of this explanation I have followed M and translated as above. However, I disagree most strongly with M when he sees in this entrance of Dan. the gaining of "a higher dramatic end," in that Dan. is triumphant and the colleagues nonplussed. The text is the record of sober history and not a romance or legend. *Belteshazzar*]—This is the name by which Dan. would be known to the king's subjects. *Spirit of holy deity*]—Behrmann translates *in welchem der Geist heiliger Goetter ist* (i.e., *in whom is the spirit of holy gods*) and considers the statement to be similar to that of Pharaoh in Gen. 41:38, and Driver remarks that the king expresses himself as a polytheist. So also AV, and Jerome who expressly opposes Th. ("holy gods and not holy god," says Jerome). But Th. first rightly interpreted the phrase as a s., rather than as a pl. M presents a wealth of philological evidence to support this position. The king recognized that the God of Dan. was different from his own gods. The thought is, "That which is truly God is to be found within Dan." The epithet *holy* does not here have reference to moral purity, but is, rather, roughly equivalent to our word "divine."

Several questions are called forth by this vs. Why did Dan. appear only after the wise men had failed to interpret the dream? Why, if Dan. was so well known for his ability to interpret dreams, and if he occupied a position of prominence over the wise men, was he not summoned first of all? It should be noted that this difficulty, if such it be, is a mark of genuineness. If the account had been a mere legend, intended to glorify the pious Jew, Dan., it would probably have had Dan. appear first of all. The LXX does precisely this. It omits vv. 6-10a. "The LXX, by thus omitting all mention of the wise men and representing the king as at once consulting Daniel in 4:15 (18) puts the action of the king in a reasonable light" (Charles). But this omission is perhaps due to a desire to avoid the alleged difficulty of the Mass. text and therefore the LXX, at this point, does not present a better text. Surely, if the author were a mere literary artist and nothing more, he would have striven to remove this alleged difficulty. The fact that it remains is, it would seem, evidence for the genuineness of the text.

Keil seeks to answer the difficulty by asserting that the king had forgotten his former dream and Dan.'s interpretation. Several years, he argues, had elapsed, and the disquietude caused by the present dream would cloud the memory, so that the king would not think of Dan. However, if the king had forgotten his previous experience, would not the present dream have served, rather, to call it to mind?

I think that Calvin has hinted at the true solution, which has been developed more fully by Kranichfeld. The king, on this interpretation, had not forgotten Dan. Rather, his dream apparently caused him to realize that he would suffer humiliation, and probably this humiliation would be at the hands of Dan.'s God. How could the king have forgotten the dream recorded in ch. 2 and the marvelous manner in which it had been interpreted? This would have impressed him with the greatness of Dan.'s God. Add to this the miraculous events described in ch. 3 and it is difficult to understand how the king could have failed to recognize that Dan.'s God was a God indeed. This is further borne out by the description which the monarch applies to Dan., "a man in whom is the spirit of Deity." With this God, Neb., as yet, wanted no dealings. If others can interpret the dream, he will go to them rather than to Dan. As Calvin says, it is "extreme necessity" which compels the ruler to turn to Dan. "And hence we gather that no one comes to the true God, unless impelled by necessity" (Calvin).

Vs. 9. *Oh! Belteshazzar, chief of the magicians, in whom I know is the spirit of holy Deity, and no secret is too difficult for thee, behold! my dream that I have seen and its interpretation declare.* The ordinary translation (e. g., AV.) *tell me the visions etc.*, seems to bring this vs.

into conflict with what follows, where the king himself relates the dream. The difficulty is removed if the word commonly translated *visions* is rendered *behold!* This change is philologically sound (see M for discussion). The manner in which Dan. is addressed seems to show that the king has not forgotten his ability to interpret dreams.

c. vv. 10-18. The content of Nebuchadnezzar's dream.

Vs. 10. *As for the visions of my head upon my bed, I was beholding, and lo! a tree in the midst of the earth and its height was great.* When the dream came upon the king, he was beholding, i. e., regarding attentively that which was being presented to him. The tree which he saw was *in the midst of the earth,* i. e., occupying a central position on the earth. Apparently, as Barnes suggests, it stood by itself, remote from any forest. Thus, its central position would attract attention. Possibly, Babylon was regarded as the center of the earth. This position of the tree would then indicate its importance for the entire earth. It is probable that by this figure of the tree the king recognized himself. Although dreams were common in the ancient Orient, and although the figure of a tree was used as a symbol of royalty, it must be insisted that this present dream was placed in the mind of the king *ab extra.* It was a divinely imposed dream, a revelation from God. Now, it is quite conceivable that in the giving of this dream, the Spirt of God permitted the mind of the king to reflect upon images and thoughts which had previously impressed him. Thus, the dream might appear to be merely the result of impressions which in waking hours had been made upon Neb.'s mind. But, if such impressions constituted to some extent the *materia* of the dream, it must be insisted that they were wrought into the form of *this* dream in a supernatural manner. The dream might appear to the king to be merely the result of natural causes, like other dreams. In point of fact, it was supernaturally imposed.

Ezek. 31:3ff. compares the Assyrian with a cedar of Lebanon. However, the tree of this dream seems to have been one of many in a forest. It is not a tree standing alone in the midst of the earth. Cf. also Ezek. 17:1ff., especially vv. 22-24, and Isa. 2:13; 10:18, 19; Jer. 22:7, 23. "Nothing is more obvious than the comparison of a hero with a lofty tree of the forest, and hence it was natural for Nebuchadnezzar to suppose that this vision had a reference to himself" (Barnes). Among the commentators Hævernick particularly has illustrated the fondness with which the Orientals depicted the rise and fall of human power by means of the symbol of a tree. Thus, Her. 7:19 relates a dream of Xerxes, who, ready to set out against Greece, beholds himself crowned with an olive shoot, the branches of which stretch out over all the earth, but afterward the crown disappears; in 6:37 Croesus says that he will destroy the men of Lampascus "like a fir" since this tree when cut down, sends forth no fresh shoots, but dies outright; in 1:108 Astyages the Mede dreamed of a vine which grew from the womb of Mandane, his daughter, and spread over the entirety of Asia, the vine being Cyrus. Hævernick makes allusion also to Arabic and Turkish sources. However, these accounts merely serve to show the significance of the tree among the Orientals. The utterly *unique* character of the present dream must be insisted upon.

Vs. 11. *The tree was growing and becoming strong, and its height was reaching to the heavens, and its appearance to the end of all the earth.* The verbs indicate not a fixed state (e. g., Driver, *was grown*) but rather a state of becoming. Before the eyes of the king the tree is growing, so that its visibility reached unto the ends of the earth. The language is hyperbolical, in keeping with the language of universality with which the Assyrian and Babylonian kings described their reigns. "In the more chastened style of the west, Nebuchadnezzar would have said, that the tree was very high, and could be seen at a great distance" (Stuart).

Vs. 12. *Its foliage was fair, and its fruit abundant, and food for all who were in it; under it the beasts of the field take shade, and in its branches are dwelling the birds of the heaven, and from it all flesh takes nourishment.* The meaning is not that the tree had food for all (e. g., Maurer, cibus in ea erat pro omnibus, non: cibus erat pro omnibus qui in ea erant [avibus]), but rather, *there was food for all who were in it.* The Massoretes have joined the words *for all* with *in it,* thus intending that the two should be taken together. The tenses of the verbs denote continuous or habitual action, "—and therefore might be observed as taking place continuously at the time of the dream" (Driver). *All flesh*]—An expression which comprehends all beasts and fowl, but is a symbolical reference to mankind, "—thus imaging all of the human race that were united under the sceptre of Nebuchadnezzar" (Zœckler).

Vs. 13. *I saw in the visions of my head upon my bed, and behold! a watcher, and a holy one from heaven was descending.* A new incident is indicated by the words *I saw.* The dream, which hitherto has transpired rather quietly, now takes a new and sudden turn. Stuart, however, thinks that the king had awakened from a first dream and now beholds a "second and continuous dream." But this is to ignore the force of *I saw;* cf. the use of this phrase in 7:7. Rosenmueller rightly explains *videbam autem porro. A watcher*]—who was *holy,* the word *holy* being epexegetical. The word translated *watcher* occurs in the OT only in this ch. Its fundamental significance is *a vigilant.* According to Bousset we are here deal ing with a narrative which is founded upon an old polytheistic saga, and, at this point the original polytheism breaks through. (*Hier schaut der urspruengliche Polytheismus der uebernommenen Erzaehlung noch deutlich hindurch*" RJ, p. 322). These watchers, thinks Bousset, are clearly considered as a college of astral deities ("...*so sind die Waechter deutlich als ein Kollegium von Goettern und zwar von Gestirngoettern gedacht*," p. 322). I cannot accept such a position. If the book of Dan. comes from the Maccabean age, as Bousset holds (p. 11), and the first part of the book contains legends which the composer has worked over for the purpose of strengthening the people's faith in difficult times (—*den Glaubensmut des Volkes in schweren Zeiten zu staerken*"), why was he not more careful to eradicate such "polytheistic" traits from his work? This ch. particularly, according to Bousset, betrays a non-Jewish background. But would not pious Jews have detected such a pagan background and consequently rejected the book? Instead of that, according to Bousset's theory, the book of Dan. became the foundation of the Apocalyptic style.

I do not understand such an explanation, since it seems to be psychologically improbable. If the "unknown" author were endeavoring to strengthen the faith of his people, would he not do all in his power to make his hero appear as a real person? He would have banished from his writing every trace of the fact that he was merely working over old legends, some of them of pagan origin. He was not writing to entertain, but to convince. And certainly there would be some among his readers who would detect the true nature of his writing. Apparently, however, such was not the case. The "legendary" Dan. had remarkable success among the Jews.

The paganism of this language, therefore, is not to be explained in the manner adopted by Bousset. The king speaks as a pagan, and the Aramaic word which Dan. employs is one consciously chosen to represent the thought of the king. This pagan thought is that which was common both to Babylon and Persia. Stuart quotes the Bun-Dehesh, to show the presence of angels called watchers in the religion of Zoroaster. The king is probably referring to the angels which were known to him through the Babylonian religion.

Some have attempted to find the identification in the *theoi boulaioi* of DS. 2:30, beings who keep watch over the universe. d'Envieu, the Roman Catholic expositor, would identify the *watcher* with the second Person of the Trinity. But this cannot be correct, for Dan., in interpreting the king's dream, says that the decree is from the Highest (vs. 24) and not from the watchers (vs. 17). This is an express repudiation of the king's pagan interpretation. For further study of the subject, see particularly Hævernick.

Vs. 14. *He cried with strength, cut down the tree and break off its branches; strip off its foliage and scatter its fruit; let the beasts wander away from under it, and the birds from its branches.* As a herald, the watcher cries with strength, i. e., aloud. To whom, however, is this proclamation addressed? Hitzig maintained that it was to subordinate angels. Stuart, to "the implied attendant retinue of the *watcher*," M thinks that the subjects of the pl. verbs are "the celestial executors of the decree," whereas Keil takes the verbs as impersonal. I am inclined to follow Keil. The force of the verbs would then be best expressed in English by the passive, e. g., *the tree shall be cut down, etc. Strip off*]—lit., *cause to fall off*, as of withering leaves. *Scatter*]—probably uttered contemptuously, as though the fruit were valueless and not worth the trouble of gathering. Since the tree is cut down, the beasts which had found shelter under it flee away, "... a lively image of subjects alarmed by the fall of their sovereign..." (Zœckler).

Vs. 15. *But leave the stump of its roots in the earth and with a band of iron and brass, in the grass of the field, and let him be wet with the dew of heaven, and with the beast let his portion be in the grass of the earth.* The tree is not to be completely destroyed. *Stump*]—the trunk that remains after the tree is felled, which is attached to the roots. The stump refers not to the royal dynasty (Hævernick) but to the king himself, "who as king shall be cut down. but shall as a man remain, and again shall grow into a king" (Keil). *Band*]—the reference is to something which Neb. would have to suffer during his madness. It is difficult to tell precisely what this is. Some of the principal interpretations may be noted: 1) "... a figure of speech for the stern and crushing sentence under which the king is to lie" (Bevan; so essentially M and Charles); 2) the band was to be placed around the tree in order to keep it from splitting (von Lengerke, Stuart); 3) the bond of darkness which would overshadow the king's spirit (Hitzig); 4) the chain with which madmen were wont to be bound (—*omnes furiosos, ne se praecipitent et alios ferro invadant, catenis ligari*, Jerome); 5) "... the withdrawal of free self-determination through the fetter of madness," cf. Ps. 107:10; Job 36:8 (Keil). I lean toward Keil's interpretation, although one cannot be dogmatic. *Let him be wet*]—With these words a departure from the symbolism is made, and the interpretation is begun.

Vs. 16. *Let his heart be changed from man's, and let the heart of a beast be given to him, and let seven times pass upon him.* This vs. sets forth the means by which the king is to be brought into the condition described in vs. 15. *From man's*]—Von Lengerke adopts the unusual interpretation that this means *away* from men; i.e., while the king is far away from men, his heart will be changed. But the word *from* is privative in force; his heart will be changed *away from* that which is human. The meaning is that the crowning glory of the king, his reason, will be taken from him, and he will become like an irrational creature, a lower animal. " . . . his intelligence is to be dehumanized," (M). The heart, in the OT, is the seat of reason, cf. Jer. 5:21; Hos. 7:11. *Seven times*]—expresses the duration of the king's insanity. How long a period is indicated by the word *time?* Hippolytus mentioned a view which identified a time with one of the four seasons, " . . . seven times of three months each which change. For the year has four seasons, winter, spring, summer, fall. Seven such times now passed over the king." Theodoret and others, following a Persian mode of reckoning, suggest six months, or two seasons. M thinks that the figure may have been conventional, as in Greek lore nine years was the term for the were-wolf. The most common interpretation is to identify the word with a year, thus seven years. This procedure is as early as the LXX, and is adopted by Jerome. Possibly there is truth in Hævernick's assertion that underlying these times there were astrological periods. Calvin thinks that the expression merely means "a long time." H and Keil take the word as indicating a definite period, the exact length of which cannot be determined. Keil argues (correctly) that from vs. 26 the length of the *times* cannot be determined, and he further maintains that in 7:25 and 12:7 the times are not years. M says "It is vain to expect to know what was meant." However, this is perhaps too strong. The Aramaic word means a fixed and definite period of time. But I do not see how it is possible to determine the length of such a period. All that is meant is that seven such periods must pass before the king's reason returns to him. Possibly *years* are intended but this is by no means certain. d'Envieu gives a full discussion of the interpretations. Gaebelein finds that this humiliation for seven "years" points to the end of the Gentile age, i. e., to the alleged period between Christ's coming *for* and His coming *with* His saints. This period is supposed to be for seven years, and is that which most dispensationalists identify as Dan.'s 70th week. (See com. in loc.). However, there is no Scriptural evidence to support the view that this madness of the king had any typical significance whatsoever (See Allis on Dan. 4).

The positive teaching of this vs. is simply that for a definite period of time, the exact length of which is not stated, Neb. will be deprived of his reason.

Vs. 17. *By the decree of the watchers is the command, and (by) the word of the holy ones is the decision, until that the living may know that the Most High is ruler in the kingdom of men, and to whom he wills he gives it, and the humblest of men he raises up over it.* It must be remembered that the king is here speaking as a pagan. *Most High*]—Gaebelein's suggestion that this is the millennial name of God has no foundation in fact.

Vs. 18. *This dream, I, king Nebuchadnezzar, have seen, and thou, oh! Belteshazzar, declare the interpretation, because none of the wise men of my kingdom are able to cause me to know the interpretation, and thou art able, for the spirit of holy deity is in thee.* After stating the content of the dream, the king, somewhat appealingly, commands Dan. to interpret it.

d. vv. 19-27. Daniel interprets the dream.

Vs. 19. *Then Daniel whose name was Belteshazzar was perplexed for a moment and his thoughts were troubling him. The king answered and said, oh! Belteshazzar, let not the dream and its interpretation trouble thee; Belteshazzar answered and said, my lord, may the dream be for thy enemies and its interpretation for thy adversaries.* "As Daniel at once understood the interpretation of the dream, he was for a moment so astonished that he could not speak for terror at the thoughts which moved his soul. This amazement seized him because he wished well to the king, and yet he must now announce to him a weighty judgment from God" (Keil). *Was perplexed*]—Dan. understood the dream, and evidently showed his astonishment plainly. The root idea of the verb seems to be "to be motionless." Jerome translates "was silent" (tacitus), but the verb (cf. 8:13) evidently intends to express the idea of embarrassment or perplexity. *For a moment*]—lit., one hour, and thus it is rendered in the AV. However, the words are merely an idiom. *Were troubling*]—Dan. realized that the dream was unfavorable to the king. Perhaps, because of his admiration for Neb., he hesitated to declare the interpretation. It is not likely that his agitation was due to fear of any possible consequences which might come upon himself (as Hitzig suggests). *The king*]—the courtesy and respect with which the king speaks seem to present ample evidence that he had not forgotten Dan. He courteously desires that whatever the interpretation may be, Dan. should relate it. By his previous courage and steadfast adherence to principle, Dan. has won the confidence and respect of the king. *Belteshazzar*]—Dan. here calls himself by the name which Neb. has given him. This is probably done in order to avoid confusion in the narrative. With equal grace and courtesy Dan. expresses his wish that the dream might be to the king's enemies. By this wish he makes it known that the dream is unfavorable to the king.

Vs. 20. *The tree which thou sawest that became great and strong, so that its height reached to heaven, and its appearance to all the earth.*

Vs. 21. *And its foliage was beautiful, and its fruit abundant and there was food for all who were in it; under it dwelt the beast of the field and in its branches lodged the birds of heaven.*

Vs. 22. *It is thou, oh! king, that hast grown great and become strong, and thy greatness has increased and extended to heaven and thy sovereignty to the end of the earth.* The tree symbolized the king himself, in the pride and extensiveness of his sovereignty.

Vs. 23. *And that the king saw a watcher and a holy one descending from heaven who commanded: Cut down the tree and destroy it, only the stump of its roots leave in the earth, and with a band of iron and brass in the grass of the field, and let him be wet with the dew of heaven, and with the beast of the field his portion, until seven times shall have passed over him.*

Vs. 24. *This is the interpretation, oh! king, and the decree of the Most High it is which has come upon my lord the king.* It should be noted that Dan. sets forth the true state of affairs. The decree is from God, not from the watchers. As Neb. spoke from the background of his paganism, so Dan. spoke as a believer in God Most High.

Vs. 25. *And thee will they drive from men, and with the beast of the field will be thy dwelling, and herbs, like oxen, will they feed thee, and from the dew of heaven will they drench thee, until seven times shall pass over thee, until thou shalt know that the Most High is ruler in the kingdom of men, and to whom he will he gives it.* Although I have translated these verbs as pl., in order to keep as close to the exact form of the Aramaic as possible, it should be noted that the pls. are impersonal. The verbs may then be rendered freely in English, *thou shalt be driven, thou shalt be fed, thou shalt be drenched.* The purpose of this experience, therefore, is to bring the king to the knowledge of the truth that God, as the Most High, is sovereign in His providential dealings with men.

Vs. 26. *And that they commanded to leave the stump of the roots of the tree, thy kingdom is abiding for thee, after that thou shalt come to know that heaven rules.* The fact that the stump was to be left shows that the king will not utterly be deprived of his kingdom, but that it would remain for him and again be his after the time when he has come to know that God and not himself is the real ruler. This description certainly does not apply to Antiochus Epiphanes who, as M points out, came to the recognition that man should not act as God (2 *Macc.* 9:11, 12) only upon his deathbed. *After that*]—These words express the certainty that the king will attain to this knowledge. *Heaven*]—The word is employed in this sense nowhere else in the OT. It is obviously used as a surrogate for God, perhaps to convince the king that the true Ruler is spiritual and above this earth, and that the true Power is heavenly and not earthly. In the NT the phrases "Kingdom of heaven" and ""Kingdom of God" are synonymous. The word in this sense came into popular usage in later pagan and Jewish literature (See Schuerer, II. 268 n. 47 and von Lengerke).

Vs. 27. *Wherefore oh! king, let my counsel be acceptable to thee, and break off thy sins by righteousness and thine iniquities by compassion to the afflicted, if there may be a lengthening to thy prosperity.* After interpreting the dream, Dan. urges the king to repent (i. e., to break off his sins by well-doing and mercy) in the hope that his period of tranquility may be lengthened. Commentators generally assume that Dan. is telling Neb. that if he gives up his evil doing, the threatened judgment may be averted. To support this position, appeal is made to the fact that certain predicted events such as the destruction of Nineveh and the death of Hezekiah had been averted by repentance and prayer (See Jonah 3:10; 2 K. 20:1-5; Jer. 18:7, 8).

It is indeed perfectly true that repentance may serve to avert a predicted judgment, but I am not entirely convinced that such was Dan.'s meaning in speaking to the king. Hence, with some hesitation I find myself unable to accept the common interpretation of the purpose of Dan. in speaking as he did. It should be noted that the predicted madness of the king is to come *for the express purpose* of bringing him to the knowledge of the Truth. The judgment is for the purpose of converting Neb. Dan. exhorts the king to repent so that the period in which he will reign prosperously may be lengthened. The predicted experience is to come (that the king may be brought to the knowledge of the Truth), but Neb., if he ceases to do evil and learns to do well, may enjoy a longer period of prosperity upon the throne. The text says nothing of an averting of the predicted judgment, but merely speaks of a lengthening of a period of tranquility. In these words, therefore, we see an expression of the truth that God's judgments are directed against men according to their conduct.

It is a gross perversion of the text to force it to teach salvation by th merit of good works. Jerome gave classic expression to this false view,— "et peccata tua eleemosynis redime, et iniquitates tuas misericordii pauperum, forsitan ignoscat Deus delictis tuis" (—and redeem thy sins b almsgiving, and thine iniquities by showing mercy to the poor, perhap God will ignore thy sins). This translation, however, is inaccurate. *Brea off*]—The verb does not mean *to redeem.* The translation *to redeem* oc curs in the LXX, and is adopted by many, e. g., Syriac, de Wette, Hitzi Zœckler, but the meaning *to redeem* is not original, but is one which cam later to be attached to the verb. The correct meaning is *to break off, ca away.* Bevan points out that the metaphor is taken from the breaking of yoke, Gen. 27:40. This usage occurs in the Mishnah, "whoever break off the yoke of the Law," P. A. 3:9. *Righteousness*]—"The chief virtue a ruler in contrast to the unrighteousness of the despots" (Keil). With th exercise of righteousness is coupled the practice of mercy to the poor. In the OT these two virtues are frequently associated, cf. Isa. 11:4; Ps. 72: 4; Isa. 41:2. If the king is to have a lengthening of prosperity, he must give up his injustice and cruelty to the poor and must practice righteousness and mercy. Some commentators would translate *well-doing* instead of *righteousness.* But in the OT the word never has this sense, which apparently developed later. In *Tobit* 12:9; 14:11 righteousness and almsgiving are almost equated, and in the Talmud the word has the meaning of *almsgiving.* In the Taima inscription, the word means "the due" (c. 5th cent. B. C.), and on the Keret text from Ras Shamra (I:12, 13) it occurs in the probable sense of "legitimate" or "lawful." But the meaning of the word must here be determined from the OT itself.

e. vv. 28-33. The fulfillment of the dream.

Vs. 28. *All this came upon Nebuchadnezzar the king.* A comprehensive statement of the fulfilment of the dream.

Vs. 29. *At the end of twelve months, he was walking upon the royal palace of Babylon.* After twelve months had expired the king was walking upon the flat roof (cf. 2 Sam. 11:2) of the palace of his kingdom which was in Babylon. The inclusion of the words *of Babylon* does not indicate that the book was written in Palestine, but probably does show that the narrative was intended primarily for those who were strangers in Babylon. The words are included with special reference to the statements which follow, and do not indicate that the king had been living at a distance from Babylon, or that the writer was not at Babylon (so Maurer,—scriptorem non fuisse Babylone).

Vs. 30. *The king answered and said, Is not this Babylon the great, which I have built for a royal residence, by the might of my power, and for the honor of my majesty?* The accuracy of this statement has been remarkably confirmed. For early historical references to the great buildings of Neb. in Babylon see the statements of Berosus as reported by Josephus (*Antiq.* 10:11: 1 and CA, 1:19 and of Abydenus as reported by Eusebius (*Pr. E.* 9:41, *Chronicon* 1). The discovery of the cuneiform inscriptions has remarkably confirmed the accuracy of this vs. From these we learn that Neb. was primarily, not a warrior, but a builder. In the famous East India House Inscription, for example, Neb. relates how he renovated the two temples of Marduk in Babylon, and of Nebo in Borsippa. He then declares how he restored fifteen other temples in Babylon and completed the two great walls of the city, adding a large rampart. Then he rebuilt the palace of Nabopolassar and in only fifteen days constructed a palace, with which was connected the famous hanging-gardens. He declares, "Then I built the palace, the seat of my royalty (cf. with the language in the present vs.), the bond of the race of men, the dwelling of joy and rejoicing" (KB iii, 2, p. 39) and, "In Babylon, my dear city, which I love, was the palace, the house of wonder of the people, the bond of the land, the brilliant place, the abode of the majesty in Babylon" (KB iii, 2, p. 25, cf. M). *Answered*]—This does not necessarily mean that the king had been meditating upon the dream. It is almost equivalent to "began to speak." *The great*]—This description is applied in Rev. 14:8; 18:2. *Built*] —i.e., built up or enlarged. Babylon was founded, as related in Gen. 11:5-9. *By the might*]—The pride of the king is exhibited by these words.

Vs. 31. *While the word was still in the mouth of the king, a voice fell from heaven; to thee it is declared, Oh! Nebuchadnezzar the king, the kingdom has passed from thee.* When pride fills the heart of the king and manifests itself in his utterance, the divine voice is heard within, and the prophecy begins its fulfilment. *A voice*]—i. e., a revelation from God. *Fell*]—as in Isa 9:8. *Passed*]—The perfect indicates that the matter is finished.

Vs. 32. *And from men they shall drive thee, and with the beast of the field will be thy dwelling, herbs as oxen they shall feed thee, and seven times shall pass over thee, until thou shalt know that the Most High is ruler in the kingdom of men, and to whom he wills he gives it.*

Vs. 33. *At that instant the matter was fulfilled upon Nebuchadnezzar, and he was driven from men, and herbs as the oxen he ate, and from the dew of heaven his body was bathed, until his hair grew as eagles' and his nails like those of birds.* The prophecy is fulfilled. *Was fulfilled*]—lit., *was ended*, i. e., it came to an end in that it was completed or fulfilled, *with respect to* Neb. The result of the madness is described in the bestial-like appearance of the king. His hair grew until it resembled the feathers of eagles and his nails became long and sharp like the claws of birds.

As might be expected, objections have been urged against the historicity of this account of the king's madness. It has been asserted that it is not historical because no other writer of antiquity has mentioned it. Such an objection, if true, would hardly be conclusive, since the records from the reign of Neb. are quite imperfect. Is it, however, strictly accurate to assert that there is no other mention of the king's madness coming from antiquity?

There is a passage in the *Pr. E.* (9:41) which is worthy of careful study. Eusebius presents a quotation from Abydenus, which reads as follows, "And afterwards, the Chaldeans say, he went up to his palace, and being possessed by some god or other uttered the following speech: 'O men of Babylon, I Nebuchadnezzar here foretell to you the coming calam ity, which neither Belus my ancestor, nor Queen Beltis are able to persuade the Fates to avert.

" 'There will come a Persian mule (i. e., Cyrus), aided by the alliance of your own deities, and will bring you into slavery. And the joint author of this will be a Mede, in whom the Assyrians glory. O would that before he gave up my citizens some Charybdis or sea might swallow him up utterly out of sight; or that, turning in other directions, he might be carried across the desert, where there are neither cities nor foot of man, but where wild beasts have pasture and birds their haunts, that he might wander alone among rocks and ravines; and that, before he took such thoughts into his mind, I myself had found a better end.'

"He after uttering this prediction had immediately disappeared" (Gifford's translation).

The last portion of this account seems to have reference to the king's madness and is covered up under the form of a prediction. The tradition underlying this prediction probably is derived from the *fact* of Neb.'s insanity. How did such a prediction concerning Cyrus come to be attributed to Neb? "The least that we can now make of all this is, that in Abydenus' time there was still, among the Chaldees, a tradition about something extraordinary and peculiar in the closing part of Nebuchadnezzar's life" (Stuart). Note the following similarities (based on Stuart):

1. The extraordinary event occurred after the king's conquests and shortly before his death.

2. In both Dan. and Abydenus, the king is on the top of his palace.

3. The king was seized by some divinity. (This is supported by the Armenian Version of the *Chronicon*).

Of interest also is the statement of Berosus, "After beginning the wall of which I have spoken, Nabuchodonosor fell sick and died, after a reign of forty-three years" (CA, 1:20, Thackeray's translation). The very mention of the sickness before death seems to imply that this sickness was of an unusual nature. Sickness before death is so common that there would be no point in mentioning it, were it not of an unusual kind. As Stuart points out, the Greek conveys the idea of being *suddenly invaded by sickness*. I have quoted these passages merely to show that they reflect, through garbled tradition, upon the tragedy which overcame the king. H gives a thorough discussion of them.

It has also been objected that if the king were sick for seven years, a revolution would probably have occurred, and the kingdom would have been lost. But as pointed out, the text does not necessarily say that the malady lasted for seven years. Furthermore, we may be sure that wise provision had been made for the administration of the kingdom while Neb. was ill. Quite possibly the Chaldeans had charge of affairs. Such was the case when the king was called home from his expedition in the west. Cf. *Antiq.* 10:11:1 "—the affairs which had been managed by the Chaldeans, and the royal authority which had been preserved for him by their chief."

The disease which came upon the king is known technically as Lycanthropy, in which the sufferer imagines himself to be changed into an animal and, to a certain extent, acts like that animal. Apparently Neb. had that form of the disease which would be called Boanthropy, i. e., he thought himself to be an ox, and so ate grass like an ox. Pusey in his extremely valuable work has collected considerable data on the subject. He asserts that one of the earliest witnesses to Lycanthropy is a Greek medical writer of the 4th century A. D. Other early writers also give examples of the disease in one form or another. This is a disease from which recovery is possible. Furthermore, as Pusey remarks, ". . . not even the extreme form of insanity interferes with the inner consciousness, or, consequently, with the power to pray." "The inner consciousness remains unchanged, while, up to a certain point, the sufferer thinks, speaks, acts, as if he were another." Pusey adduces the remarkable case of Père Surin, who believed himself to be possessed, yet maintained communion with God. It is true to fact, then, that Neb., although under the influence of this strange malady, could lift up his eyes unto heaven. Pusey well says, "There is scarcely any stronger internal evidence of truth, than circumstances, on the surface unlikely, which, on careful examination, appear to be in harmony with the rest of history. And this the more, when the scientific knowledge of that truth belongs to a later age."

f. vv. 34-37. The recovery of Nebuchadnezzar.

Vs. 34. *And at the end of the days I Nebuchadnezzar did lift mine eyes to heaven, and my understanding returned to me, and I praised the Most High, and I honored and glorified Him that liveth forever, for his dominion is an everlasting dominion, and his kingdom for ever and ever.* After the expiration of the predicted seven times, here called the end of the days, the king lifts his eyes to heaven, and his reason returns. This lifting of the eyes indicates the first return of human consciousness (see notes on previous vs.). This does not mean that he had gone about on all fours and was now standing on his feet (Hitzig), but merely that he now recognized that heaven was the source of his help and lifted his eyes thereunto. With the return of his reason, his first thought was to praise God as the eternal One, whose dominion is without end.

Bevan calls attention to a passage in the *Bacchae* of Euripides (1265ff.) where Agave on looking up to heaven in her madness has her reason restored. "The resemblance is the more remarkable because the Bacchants, like Nebuchadnezzar, are in some sort assimilated to animals—they not only wear the skins of beasts but also suckle young fawns and wolves (*Bacchae,* 669). Both in Daniel and in Euripides the looking heavenwards indicates a return to humanity" (Bevan). But whereas in Euripides the looking heavenward may merely be indicative of popular superstition, in Dan., the king lifts his eyes to heaven for he now knows that the eternal God alone is his help (cf. Ps. 123:1).

Vs. 35. *And all the inhabitants of earth are reputed as nothing, and according to his will he doeth in the army of heaven, and (among) the inhabitants of earth; and there is none that will stay his hand, or say to him, What doest thou?* The vs. presents the content of the king's praise and blessing. It is a remarkable declaration of the sovereign omnipotence of God. Cf. Isa 24:21. *Stay his hand*]—lit., *smite his hand,* "derived from the custom of striking children on the hand in chastisement" (Keil). What the origin of the phrase may be is not really known but in later language it comes to have the meaning *to reprove* or *to interfere with.* Here it means that none can oppose God's action.

Vs. 36. *At that moment my understanding returned to me, and for the honor of my kingdom, my glory and brightness returned unto me, and my counsellors and magnates sought me, and I was established upon my kingdom and excellent greatness was added to me.* The statement *my understanding returned* is repeated in order to show that the king regains his former temporal glory. In vs. 34 it indicated a spiritual conversion. *For the honor*]—i. e., my glory and brightness returned to me for the sake of, i. e., to promote the honor of my kingdom. *Sought*]—Some expositors have maintained that the king had been permitted to roam about at will, and that his counsellors, not knowing where he was, were seeking to find him. Upon the basis of such an interpretation, objections have even been adduced against the historicity of the narrative. Suffice it to say that such an interpretation is utterly unwarranted. All the vs. means is that, since the king's reason has returned, his counsellors once again seek him for advice and consultation. These counsellors are probably the ones who had carried on the government during the king's insanity.

Vs. 37. *Now I Nebuchadnezzar praise and extol and honor the king of heaven, all whose works are truth and his ways judgment, and those that walk in pride he is able to abase.* The climax of the edict is reached in this public confession. It has been debated among Christian interpreters whether Neb. was truly converted. Calvin denied the conversion, and in this he has been followed by H, Pusey and Keil. The matter is difficult to determine and perhaps cannot be determined. Nevertheless, there are certain considerations which would lead to the conclusion that the king did, after all, experience in his heart the regenerating grace of God.

(1) There is discernible a progress in his knowledge of God. Cf. 2:47 with 3:28 and finally with 4:34, 35.

(2) The king acknowledges the utter sovereignty of God with respect to his own experience (4:37b).

(3) The king utters true statements concerning the omnipotence of the true God (4:34, 35).

(4) The king would worship this God, whom he identifies as King of heaven (4:37a). These reasons lead me to believe that, although the faith of Neb. may indeed have been weak and his knowledge meagre, yet his faith was saving faith, and his knowledge true.

It is not certain whether any of the comments of Porphyry upon this ch. are preserved. However, in his discussion of vs. 7 Jerome mentions certain *contemptores historiae* (among whom Porphyry is probably to be reckoned) who believe that the description of the vastness of Neb.'s empire is greatly overdrawn.

CHAPTER FIVE

a. vv. 1-4. The feast of Belshazzar.

Vs. 1. *Belshazzar the king made a great feast for a thousand of his magnates, and before the thousand he drank wine.* "This chapter is notable for its historical inconsistencies" (Charles). Such a sweeping statement, however, will not stand the test of close investigation. We prefer to write "This chapter is notable for its remarkable accuracies." *Belshazzar*]—the Babylonian Bel-shar-usur, i.e., "Bel, protect the king." The versions confuse this name with Dan's. name, Belteshazzar. The spelling in the Aramaic text is not consistent. The identity of Belshazzar had long caused difficulty to the commentators. Some have denied his historicity. However, this was before the discovery of his name upon the cuneiform tablets. Others sought to identify him with Evil-Merodach, son of Neb. (Kranichfeld, Zœckler, Hævernick, Kliefoth, Keil), or with a grandson of Neb., or a brother of Evil-Merodach. Other identifications were also attempted. Keil presents a remarkably learned discussion of the problem. The king's name, however, has now appeared upon the cuneiform documents, so that there can be no question as to his historicity. This is the first point at which this ch. exhibits its remarkable accuracy. *The king*]—One of the latest objectors to the historicity of this designation is Rowley ("The Historicity of the Fifth Chapter of Daniel" in JTS, Vol. XXXII, pp. 12-31.) who says that the representation of Dan. that Belshazzar was "the monarch of that empire (i.e., the Neo-Babylonian)" "... must still be pronounced a grave historical error" (p.12). Rowley's extremely able and learned article is worthy of careful study. He insists, rightly, that on the cuneiform inscriptions, Belshazzar is never called "king" and he seeks to prove that Belshazzar "was not associated with his father on the imperial throne," nor was he "placed by his father on the subordinate throne of Babylon." The occasion of Rowley's article was the appearance of Dougherty's learned work, *Nabonidus and Belshazzar*, 1929, in which the cuneiform evidence was made available, and the essential historicity of the fifth ch. of Dan. was defended. The question to be answered then, is, Are we in a position positively to declare that the author of Dan. made an historical mistake in calling Belshazzar "king"? This, and this alone, is the question. The burden of proof rests upon those who declare that the author of Dan. did make such an error. The book must be assumed to be *innocent* until proven *guilty.* We must regard it as *true* until it is shown to be *false.* The presumption that Dan. is *guilty* until proven *innocent* must be rejected. Can Dan., therefore, be proved at this point to be in error? The facts, based upon the now available evidence, are as follows:

1. Dan. calls Belshazzar "king" (5:1; 8:1), "king of the Chaldeans" (5:30); "king of Babylon" (7:1).

2. Dan. speaks of the "kingdom" or "reign" of Belshazzar (8:1).

3. Dan. dates events in Belshazzar's reign: "in the first year" (7:1) and "in the third year" (8:1).

4. All the available cuneiform evidence (see Dougherty) speaks of Belshazzar as the "son of the king" (mar sharri).

5. In the cuneiform evidence, the designation sharru (king) is never applied to Belshazzar.

6. The available cuneiform evidence dates the documents according to the years of the reign of Nabonidus, father of Belshazzar, whom it calls "the king" (sharru) and "king of Babylon" (shar Babili*ki*), e. g., the twenty-sixth day, the fourteenth year of Nabonidus, the king of Babylon.

7. During the absence of Nabonidus on campaign, on the 7th, 9th, 10th, and 11th years of his reign, the New Year's Festival was not celebrated. In a document called *A Persian Verse Account of Nabonidus* (in BHT, 1924) Nabonidus declares his purpose of building the temple of Sin at Harran, and the New Year's feast is to cease until this project is completed.

8. The PVA. explicitly states that Nabonidus entrusted the kingship to his son Belshazzar. "He freed his hand; he entrusted the kingship (ip-ta-kid-su sharru-tam) to him. Then he himself undertook a distant campaign."

9. The PVA. seems to imply that Nabonidus established his residence at Tema. Note the following lines: "Then he himself established his dwelling (su-bat-su); the power of the land of Akkad . . . That city he made glorious;—they made it like the palace of Babylon."

10. Belshazzzar performed important functions (some of them regal) while Nabonidus was in Tema.

a. Business negotiations in the interest of Belshazzar were carried on by his servants in the city of Babylon. One text suggests that Belshazzar had income apart from his business interests. Apparently some of these interests were to be managed by Belshazzar's agents because he himself had higher interests to attend to (cf. NB., pp. 81-86).

b. Belshazzar appears to have exhibited concern for the upkeep of places of worship in Babylonia.

c. Nabonidus, in prayer for length of days, associates Belshazzar with himself in a unique manner.

d. Oaths are taken in the name of Nabonidus and Belshazzar. Note a phrase such as, "the decrees (a-di-e) of Nabonidus king of Babylon and Belshazzar, son of the king." This close association of the two names is, to my mind, sufficient evidence, that Belshazzar is to be regarded as occupying *regal* status. Is it conceivable that one of *lesser* status could be thus closely associated with Nabonidus?

e. An astrological report similarly connects the two names.

f. In the delivery of royal tribute the two names are closely associated.

g. In one text (NB., pp. 101-103) Belshazzar possesses subordinate officials equal to those of the king.

h. Belshazzar's *regal* power is further shown by his granting of leases, his issuing of commands, his performance of an administrative act concerning the temple at Erech.

Such, in very brief compass, is a summary of the most important data now available. The gratitude which is due to Dougherty for assembling the cuneiform material is truly great. How, then, is this material to be interpreted? It seems to me that we can best interpret this data by positing a co-regency in which Belshazzar occupied a subordinate position. Is this a contradiction in terms? No doubt, if the word "co-regency" be pressed, it can only refer to a joint-rule in which the two kings possessed equal authority. Such a co-regency might be theoretically possible, but human nature being what it is, it would not work out in practice. Hence, we shall use the term as referring to a joint-regime, in which Belshazzar, in theory, at least, occupied a subordinate position. Dougherty is perfectly correct when he writes, "One can conceive of a co-regency which would grant far from equal power to the person of lower rank raised to a position of partnership in governing the empire" (*NB.*, p. 104).

Technically, therefore, Belshazzar occupied a position somewhat subordinate to that of Nabonidus. This would account for the fact that in *official* documents, events were dated according to the reign of Nabonidus. This technical subordination would always be preserved in *official* documents. To change this would be to give cause for suspicion of treason, and there is no available evidence that Belshazzar desired any such thing. All the evidence seems to indicate that Belshazzar and Nabonidus were on the best of personal terms. Does not this explain the reason why Nabonidus *in official documents* is always called "king" and Belshazzar "son of the King"? Why should Belshazzar have desired a change? What would he have gained thereby?

Although, technically, Belshazzar occupied a position of authority subordinate to that of Nabonidus, actually, he seems to have had nearly all the prerogatives of monarch. As the extant evidence shows, his word was regarded with utmost deference. He actually was entrusted with the kingship, and he managed it like a king. It is quite possible that Nabonidus was content to have it so, as long as his superior status received technical recognition (i. e., through dating according to his reign, and through receiving the designation sharru.). Ultimately, of course, the final word would rest with Nabonidus, as is shown bv the fact that during his absence, the New Year's Festival, apparently at his request, was not observed. But, practically, Belshazzar was king, and he was so regarded by the people.

Now the book of Dan. is not an official document of the Neo-Babylonian Empire. It was written for the Jews, the people of God, who had to deal with the man who ruled in Babylon. This man was Belshazzar—not Nabonidus. The man whose royal word could affect the Jews was Belshazzar. The man in regal status who desecrated the vessels of the Lord's temple was Belshazzar. Very properly, therefore, he is called "king" and "king of Babylon." In the light of the available evidence, I do not see how anyone can call such a designation inaccurate. Dan. does not describe Belshazzar as monarch or sole king. He merely calls him king.

As to the fact that Dan. twice dates the reign of Belshazzar, it should again be remembered that the book of Dan. is not an official Babylonian document. Since Belshazzar was the king with whom Dan. had to do—and not Nabonidus—it is to be expected that Dan. would date his dreams according to the years of Belshazzar's reign. When Dan.'s purpose is taken into consideration, I do not see how there can be objection to his practice. What other word could Dan. have employed to denote a man whose status was *regal?* The term crown-prince, from the Jewish viewpoint, would not have been sufficient. In the designation of Belshazzar as *king*, therefore, we see the second example of remarkable accuracy which this ch. exhibits.[1] *Feast*]—lit., *bread*, probably an archaic use of the word. *Thousand*]—Royal feasts in antiquity were often huge. "The invitation to a thousand officers of state corresponds to the magnificence of Oriental kings" (Keil). Athenaeus, (4:10) relates that the Persian king daily fed 15,000 men from his table (cf. Esther 1:4, 5). M refers to a marriage festival of Alexander, at which 10,000 guests were present and to a similar feast for the last Ptolemy, and to the characterization of Q. Cur., 5:1, "Babylonii maxime in vinum et quae ebrietatem sequntur effusi sunt." The word *thousand* must be considered as a round number, to indicate the enormity of the feast. In thus describing the feast as so large, this ch. exhibits for the third time its remarkable accuracy. *Before the thousand*]—in accordance with Oriental custom, at which the king sat at a

[1] See *SBD* I, pp. 83-127 for a discussion of the senses in which the Aramaic word "king" might be employed. The word itself need not bear the connotation of absolute monarch.

separate table on an elevated place, so that the guests were before him. Cf. Athenæus 4:10. "The drinking of wine is particularly noticed as the immediate occasion of the wickedness which followed" (Keil). A fourth point of accuracy appears in this mention of the fact that the king drank before his guests. In such feasts the drinking of wine was the predominant element.

Vs. 2. *Belshazzar commanded, while tasting the wine, to bring the vessels of gold and silver that Nebuchadnezzar his father had brought out from the temple that is in Jerusalem that the king and his magnates, his wives and his concubines might drink from them.* The king "when he began to feel the influence of the wine" (Driver), apparently lost all sense of decency and sought to desecrate the temple vessels. Hævernick suggests that the vessels were brought in order to propitiate the God of the Jews, but this is contrary to the express statement of the text. *Concubines*]— This term in Aramaic refers to the inferior class of women in the harem. Stuart adduces considerable evidence from the classical writers to show the lasciviousness of such feasts. "What sort of a banquet Belshazzar was engaged in, seems to be sufficiently evident from such testimonies. Hence the aggravation of the insult to the God of heaven" (Stuart). It was the custom in Babylonia to admit women to the drinking feasts (cf. Q. Cur. 5:5; *Cy*. 5:2:28.)

Some have sought to discover an historical inaccuracy in the statement that Neb. was the father of Belshazzar. But the usage of this word was vague in Oriental languages. R. D. Wilson (SBD. I, pp. 117-122) shows that the word was capable of being employed in at least eight different ways, and M says, "There are indeed all sorts of possibilities and combinations." Is it not possible that Belshazzar may have been the adopted son of Nabonidus? It should be remembered that the author of Dan. was acquainted with Jeremiah (cf. Dan. 9:2). Now Jeremiah expressly mentions the fact that Evil-merodach was king of Babylon, and places his reign after that of Neb. (Jer. 52:28-31). Would not the author of Dan. have noted this fact? Yet he calls Neb. the father of Belshazzar. He must, therefore, use the word "father" in the sense of ancestor. There seems to be no suitable reason for disputing the accuracy of this designation. See SBD, I, for a thorough discussion of the question.

Vs. 3. *Then they brought the vessels of gold which had been brought from the temple of the house of God that is in Jerusalem, and out of them drank the king and his magnates, his wives and his concubines.* Only the vessels of gold are mentioned, although some of the versions include the words *of silver*. But the one term is sufficient as a designation of all. *Temple*]—

the temple proper as distinguished from the temple area, cf. I K. 6:3; Ezek. 41: 4.

Vs. 4. *They drank wine and they praised the gods of gold and silver, brass, iron, wood and stone.* Cf. Rev. 9:20. The drinking of wine is again mentioned in order to connect it with idolatry. "The wickedness lay in this, that they drank out of the holy vessels of the temple of the God of Israel to glorify their heathen gods in songs of praise" (Keil). Hævernick believes that this was a particular religious festival, but more likely it was merely a drinking bout at which songs in celebration of the idols were sung.

b. vv. 5-12. The handwriting on the wall, the astonishment of Belshazzar thereat, and the inability of the wise men to interpret the writing.

Vs. 5. *At that moment there came out the fingers of the hand of a man, and they were writing before the candelabrum upon the plaster of the palace wall of the king, and the king saw the extremity of the hand that wrote.* "The royal table was doubtless set on a dais and against a wall, and that quarter of the hall was lit with a great candelabrum, the light of which was reflected on the plastered wall behind the royal seat" (M). Prince says that in the ruins of the palace at Nimroud, "a thin coating of painted plaster was discovered by Layard, the colours of which when first found were still fresh and brilliant." There is now available the testimony of Koldewey who notes that the walls of the palace at Babylon were covered with white plaster (as given in M). This mention of *white* plaster is interesting, because the Aramaic word translated *plaster* literally means *chalk*. Any dark object moving across this *white* surface would stand out particularly. The description in this vs. is another example of the accuracy of the book of Dan. *Extremity*]—i.e., the hand from the wrist to the tips of the fingers.

Vs. 6. *Then the king's color changed, and his thoughts troubled him, and the joints of his loins were loosed, and his knees knocked one against another.* The sight alarmed the king out of his drunkenness, for he evidently believed that it was a sign of supernatural intervention. *Color*]—lit., *brightness* as in 3:19. The color faded from his face because of terror. *Thoughts*]—probably called forth by a guilty conscience. *Joints*]—cf. Isa. 21:3; Nah. 2:10; Ezek. 21:12; Ps. 69:23, the emotions of fear and suffering were ascribed to the loins. *Knees*]—cf. Nah. 2:10.

Vs. 7. *The king called aloud to bring in the magicians, the Chaldeans, and astrologers. The king answered and said to the wise men of Babylon, Any man that will read this writing and will make known its interpretation will be clothed with purple, and a necklace of gold will be upon his neck, and he shall rule as Triumvir in the kingdom.* Only three classes of wise men are here mentioned—an evidence of genuineness, for if this had been a fictitious work the author would consistently have used a standard category. It is difficult to say why only these three classes are here mentioned. It has been suggested that the purpose was to avoid summoning Dan., but this does not seem probable. *Purple*]—the color of royalty in ancient times, cf. Xen., *Ana.* 1:5, 8 with Esther 8:15, *Cy* 1:3, 2; 2:4, 6. *Necklace*]—an ornament worn by Persians of rank, *Ana.* 1:5, 8; 8:29, presented by one king to another; 1:1, 27. "—the decoration could be worn only when presented by the king" (M.). *Triumvir*]—Many have interpreted this word as the ordinal numeral, *third* (tertius), thus AV; the LXX renders, *the third part.* But it has been early recognized that the translation is difficult (e. g., Jerome, vel tertius post me, vel unus ex tribus principibus). M argues at length to show that "the term is a true reminiscence of old Bab. officialdom." The philological argument cannot be reproduced here, but the Aramaic term is the equivalent of the old Akkadian shalsu—a thirdling or triumvir, "one of three." The Triumvirate would then include, in order of authority, Nabonidus, Belshazzar, Dan. But probably it is wise not to be too dogmatic concerning the precise meaning of this word.

Bevan argues that a man who of his own authority can make anyone "third ruler in the kingdom," must be supreme in the state. This conclusion, however, does not necessarily follow. It is possible that a man with delegated authority could have made such an appointment, provided that delegated authority was very great, as, in the case of Belshazzar, it was. This could be so, even if Nabonidus had returned from Tema and was performing some of the functions of government. Whatever the precise relationship as to government between Nabonidus and Belshazzar, we may never know, but there is no evidence available to contradict this representation of Dan. Rowley considers it to have been "grim humour" for anyone to have received such an honor when the empire was ready to fall. For such an honor would have placed its recipient in grave danger (see *op. cit.*, p. 20). Such may very well have been the case, but it must be remembered that the king was in terror. He was desperate, and not acting as a result of calm reflection.

Vs. 8. *Then came in all the wise men of the king, and they were not able to read the writing and to make known the interpretation to the king.* It has been suggested that the handwriting consisted of characters similar to those of Phoenician. These would be unknown to the Babylonians, but Dan. would easily recognize them. However, this is to interpret the miracle on naturalistic principles. "The characters employed in the writing must have been altogether unusual so as not to be deciphered but by divine illumination" (H).

Vs. 9. *Then the king Belshazzar was greatly agitated, and his color was changed upon him, and his magnates were perplexed.* The failure of the wise men threw the whole company into confusion. The king was deeply disturbed, and the magnates were upset and tumultuous.

Vs. 10. *The queen—because of the affairs of the king and his nobles, had come in to the banquet hall; the queen answered and said, oh! king, live forever! let not thy thoughts trouble thee and let not thy color change.* Who is this new figure that is suddenly introduced? Porphyry maintained that she was the wife of the king (Jerome says, "*Evigilet ergo Porphyrius, qui eam Balthasaris somniatur uxorem, et illudit plus scire, quam maritum*"). But the text explicitly states that the wives of the king were already present. The stately manner in which she makes her appearance also seems to imply that she is not the king's wife. Josephus had suggested that she was the grandmother of the king, and Origen that she was the queen mother. This would account for the fact that she had known past events of which the king was ignorant. Probably she was the wife of Neb. The exalted position of the queen mother in the court is shown by Meissner (*op. cit.*, p. 74), who asserts that the queen-mother held the highest rank in the royal house, particularly if she understood how to play a role in politics. Meissner gives interesting examples to support this statement. Cf. also I K. 15:13; 2 K. 10:13; 24:12, 15; Jer. 13:18; 29:2. The high station of the queen is further shown by the fact that she entered the banquet hall (lit., *house of the feast*) of her own accord.

Vs. 11. *There is a man in thy kingdom in whom is the spirit of holy deity, and in the days of thy father—illumination and understanding and wisdom like the wisdom of God was found in him; and the king Nebuchadnezzar, thy father, appointed him as chief of the magicians, astrologers, Chaldeans, soothsayers; thy father, the king.*

The language of the queen mother is reminiscent of the language used by Nebuchadnezzar in addressing Dan., 4:5. *Illumination*]—an abstract noun which literally means *light.* Possibly the queen had reference to *insight. Like the wisdom*]—The queen meant that Dan.'s wisdom was superhuman, to be compared with the wisdom which God alone possesses. The last words *thy father the king* are probably to be omitted. They are difficult to construe as they stand, and are not supported by Th.

Vs. 12. *Since an excellent spirit and knowledge and understanding, the interpreting of dreams and resolving of dark sayings, and dissolving of knots was found in this same Daniel whom the king named Belteshazzar, now let Daniel be called and let him show the interpretation.* Since the abilities of Dan. are so great, call him in now, that he may interpret the writing. *Interpreting*]—The ability to interpret dreams had been already exhibited, ch. 2. *Resolving*]—The words refer to the ability to expound riddles or hard sentences. *Dissolving knots*]—i. e., knotty, difficult problems, such as that which now called for solution.

c. vv. 13-28. Daniel is called before the king. He reads and interprets the writing.

Vs. 13. *Then Daniel was brought in before the king; the king answered and said to Daniel, Thou art Daniel then, who art from the children of the captivity of Judah whom my father the king brought from Judah?* The queen's advice was immediately followed, and Dan. was brought before the king. The manner in which the king speaks shows that he was acquainted with Dan's. origin. It seems also to show that Dan. was no longer chief of the magicians. The king apparently in addressing Dan. seeks to avoid the name Belteshazzar, which was so similar to his own.

Vs. 14. *And I have heard concerning thee that the spirit of deity is in thee, and illumination and understanding and excellent wisdom has been found in thee.* Belshazzar omits the epithet "holy" from before deity."

Vs. 15. *And now there have been brought up before me the wise men, astrologers to read this writing and to make me to know its interpretation, and they were not able to show the interpretation of the matter.*

Vs. 16. *And I have heard concerning thee that thou art able to show interpretations, and to dissolve knots, now, if thou art able to read the writing and its interpretation to show me, with purple thou shalt be clothed, and a necklace of gold shall be upon thy neck, and as Triumvir in the kingdom thou shalt rule.* There is a tone of egoism and haughtiness in these words, as is shown by the emphatic, introductory *I.*

Vs. 17. *Then Daniel answered and spake before the king; let thy gifts be to thyself and thy favors give to another, nevertheless, the writing I shall read to the king and the interpretation I shall cause him to know.* The response of Dan. is not to be construed as pert or rude. Nor does he speak contemptuously. Nor does Dan. refuse the gifts because of any fear for his own safety, as Hitzig suggests. Rather, he rejects the gifts because he wishes to make it plain that he has no desire for earthly or personal gain or advantage. Furthermore, by his refusal, he makes it abundantly clear that, come what may, he is determined to declare the truth. How this must have impressed the king, who evidently expected Dan. to be a seeker after reward like the Chaldean wise men!

Vs. 18. *Thou, oh! king,—God most High gave to Nebuchadnezzar thy father, a kingdom, and greatness and honor and glory.* "The absolute position of the vocative" (Thou, oh! king) "at the beginning of the sentence, places the king rhetorically in a living relation with the facts reported in the following clause, with regard to his father Nebuchadnezzar" (Zœckler).

Vs. 19. *And because of the greatness which He gave to him, all nations, peoples, and tongues trembled and feared before him; whom he willed, he killed, and whom he willed, he kept alive, and whom he willed, he exalted, and whom he willed, he abased.* A remarkable and graphic description of the arbitrary and despotic power of an Oriental monarch. For the exercise of this power, however, as the next vs. shows, the king was responsible to God. Without doubt, this statement is intended to impress upon the mind of Belshazzar the fact that he was not the equal of Neb. in power. Yet, not being the equal, Belshazzar had become puffed up with pride in that he had not honored the one God who abases and exalts kings. I am inclined to think that this vs. actually constitutes an accurate allusion to the historical situation. Belshazzar, although he might be called king, was not an absolute monarch like Neb. (cf. I Sam. 2:6, 7).
Vs. 20. *And when his heart was lifted up, and his spirit became strong with pride, he was brought down from the throne of his kingdom, and honor was taken from him.* The words heart and spirit are employed here as synonyms. His spirit became unyielding. *With pride*]—lit., that he dealt proudly. The word is an infinitive, not a noun. *Was taken*]—lit., they took.

Vs. 21. *And from the sons of men he was driven, and his heart was made like the beasts, and with the wild asses was his dwelling; they fed him grass like oxen, and his body was wet with the dew from heaven, until he knew that God most High is ruler in the kingdom of men, and whomsoever he wills, he establishes over it. Sons of men*]—i.e., mankind. *Wild asses*] —cf. Gen. 16:12: Job 39:5-8, "An untameable animal, which roamed in the open plains" (Driver). This fact is not mentioned in 4:32, but is probably now added by Dan. in order to make a stronger impression upon the mind of Belshazzar. *Ruler*]—In the original the order is very emphatic, *until he knew that RULER is God, etc.*

Vs. 22. *And thou, his son, Belshazzar, hast not abased thy heart, although thou knowest all this.* Despite the fact that thou dost know these incidents in the life of thy father, thou hast sinned more deeply. No respite or pardon is offered to Belshazzar. "There is no finer example of the preacher's diction in the Bible than this stern and inexorable condemnation" (M). The fact that Belshazzar had such full knowledge of the life of Neb. supports the accuracy of the designation, *his son.*

Vs. 23. *But against the Lord of heaven thou hast lifted up thyself, and the vessels of his house have been brought before thee, and thou, and thy magnates, thy wives and thy concubines have drunk wine in them, and the gods of silver and gold, brass, iron, wood and stone, which see not, and hear not, and know not, thou hast praised, but the god in whose hand is thy breath, and to whom are all thy ways, thou hast not glorified.* The king's sin of pride is now more clearly set forth. Not only has he not humbled his heart, but he has actually vaunted himself against God by defiling the vessels of His temple. His act has been one of folly for he has praised gods which are inanimate, but has not glorified the true God who has given him life. The description of the idols is based upon Deut. 4:28; also cf. Ps. 115:5ff.; 135:15ff.; Isa. 44:9; Rev. 9:20. *In whose hand*]—i.e., in whose power or disposal is thy life. *Ways*]—i.e., destinies. Note the force of this vs. as seen in the contrast between *the gods* and *the god* at the beginning of each clause and *thou hast praised* and *thou has not glorified* at the conclusion of each clause. These words well illustrate the folly of any way of life which is not founded upon true theism, for all idols, whether they be of wood or stone, the creation of men's hands, or finely-spun philosophies, the creation of men's minds, cannot see nor hear nor know. Unbelief is folly.

Vs. 24. *Then from him was sent the extremity of a hand, and this inscription was written.* From God (lit., *from before him*) was sent the hand. *Then*]—temporal, not causal. When thou didst exalt thyself, then God sent forth.

Vs. 25. *And this is the writing which was written, MENE, MENE, TEKEL, UPHARSIN.* The writing had apparently remained upon the wall. *Written*]—i. e., inscribed.

Vs. 26. *This is the interpretation of the matter, MENE, God has numbered thy kingdom and brought it to an end.* There is question as to the precise form of the inscription. The LXX is confused, and Th. simply renders, MENE, TEKEL, PHARES. This is followed by the Vulgate (Mane, Thecel, Phares), and also by Josephus (*Antiq.* X:II:3). However, the repeated MENE is probably for the sake of emphasis. As to the word UPHARSIN, the U is the common Aramaic conjunction "and," and PHARSIN is a pl. form, which is perhaps secondary and may be accounted for as the work of a scribe who perhaps had in mind the word *Persians* (vs. 28). The original probably read, MENE, MENE, TEKEL UPERES.

Why were Belshazzar and the Chaldeans unable to read this writing? Some of the rabbis have suggested that the characters were written vertically instead of horizontally, thus:

P	T	M	M
R	K	N	N
S	L	'	'

(The writing would have consisted only of consonants). It has also been suggested that some unfamiliar form of Aramaic character was used. However, as Charles remarks, "The writing may have consisted of ideograms; for according to the text even expert Babylonian scholars could not decipher it." Whatever was the case, it was necessary that the text be both read and interpreted.

In 1886 M. Clermont-Ganneau pointed out (see *Journal Asiatique*, Juillet-Aout, 1886, p. 36ff., and Noeldeke *ZA*, Vol. I, pp. 414-418) that the inscription consisted in reality of names of weights, thus: MENE was the maneh of Ezek. 45:12 and Ezra 2:69; TEKEL was the Hebrew shekel; PERES was thought to represent the PERAS or half-maneh. The inscription is then supposed to read, a maneh, a maneh, a shekel and a half-maneh. The interpretation given in vv. 26-28 amounts to a play upon words, and in vs. 28 the play is a double one. Bevan, who adopts this view of Clermont-Ganneau's remarks, "Why these words are here introduced, whether they have any special reference to the situation of Belshazzar or to the times of the author of Daniel, remains altogether obscure." One is also inclined to ask why the illogical order, mina, shekel, half-mina is given.

Prince suggests that the mina alludes to Neb., whereas the shekel which was of far less value, referred to Belshazzar, and the half-minas to the Medes and Persians. He would then interpret, "There have been fixed by fate the reigns of the great king Nebuchadnezzar, the Mina; of the insignificant Belshazzar his wicked successor, the shekel; and the dominion of the Medes and Persians, the half minas, whose combined power is to equal that of Nebuchadnezzar." Prince thinks that the meaning of the proverb, which was originally Babylonian, was probably understood by the author, but that he was merely interested in presenting an explanation rather than a translation.

However, if there is in these words an allusion such as Prince suggests, there is no evidence of that fact in the text. Nor does the appropriateness of such a cryptic reference seem pertinent in a message directed primarily to Belshazzar. At any rate, the text treats these words merely as passive participles, and in each of them it finds a double sense. MENE *numbered,*

God has numbered (MENA) the days (i. e., the length or duration) of the kingdom and finished it, i. e., "its duration is so counted out that it is full, that it now comes to an end" (Keil).

Vs. 27. *TEKEL, thou art weighed in the balances and art found wanting.* Cf. for the figure of the balances, Job 31:6. Ps. 62:9; Prov. 16:2 etc. *Wanting*]—lacking, deficient in moral worth. "As if he had said, Thou thinkest thy dignity must be spared, since all men revere thee; thou thinkest thyself worthy of honour; thou art deceived, says he, for God judges otherwise; God does not use a common scale, but holds his own, *and there thou art found deficient;* that is, thou art found a man of no consequence, in any way" (Calvin).

Vs. 28. *PERES, thy kingdom is divided and given to the Medes and the Persians.* Some have wrongly held the meaning to be that the kingdom should be equally divided, one part being given to the Medes and the other to the Persians. But the thought is that the kingdom shall be dissolved or destroyed, which calamity was to be brought about by the united power of the Medes and Persians under Cyrus. In the naming of the Medes before the Persians there is to be seen an evidence of historical accuracy (cf. also 6:8, 12) for from the time of Cyrus on the Persians were named before the Medes (cf. Esther 1:3, 14, 18, 19). In the word PERES (*divided*) there is an allusion to PARAS (the word which is translated *Persians*), which would seem to indicate that the Persians were the dominant power in the *dividing* or *dissolving* of Babylon.

d. vv. 29-30. The reward of Daniel and the death of Belshazzar.

Vs. 29. *Then Belshazzar commanded, and they clothed Daniel with purple, and the necklace of gold was upon his neck, and they cried concerning him that he should be the third ruler in the kingdom.* Driver speaks of the unconcern of Belshazzar as being "scarcely consistent with historical probability." But how does Driver know that Belshazzar was unconcerned? The text merely relates that he fulfilled his promise concerning Dan. The proclamation need not have been made publicly upon the streets of the city. Quite possibly it was announced only to the assembled multitude. The action of Belshazzar shows that, although he was apparently not a regenerate man, he did nevertheless believe the truth of what Dan. had said. This explains why he honored Dan. instead of putting him to death. Nor can there be any ground for attacking the narrative upon the basis of the fact that Dan. now receives the gifts which formerly he had rejected. In vs. 17 Dan. rejects the gifts since he is not interested in personal advancement. His personal disinterestedness has now been made abundantly evident and there is no reason why the gifts should at this time be refused.

Vs. 30. *In that night was Belshazzar king of the Chaldeans slain.* Haller maintains that the powerful catastrophe, mentioned in this vs., is unhistorical (Von einer gewaltsamen Katastrophe, wie sie hier v. 30 berichtet wird, kann keine Rede sein). But this vs. does not speak of a powerful catastrophe, unless the murder of the king, in itself, be regarded as such. According to Her. (I:190:191) Cyrus was a long time in preparing for the siege of Babylon, and the Babylonians advanced to meet him. Being worsted, they retreated and shut themselves up in their city. Finally, Cyrus diverted the waters of the Euphrates so that his troups could cross the shallow water. The city fell when a festival was being celebrated.

Xenophon (*Cy.*, VII: 5:1-36), mentions the deflecting of a stream which flowed through Babylon. Finally, when the Babylonians were observing a night festival with drinking and revelry, Cyrus turned aside the course of the river and entered the city. The entrance was made by Gobryas, who entered the palace and slew the wicked king. Xenophon represents the Babylonians as being extremely hostile to Cyrus.

Berossus (*CA*, I:20) relates that Nabonidus met the approaching Cyrus and being defeated, fled to Borsippa. Cyrus then captured Babylon and razed its walls. Nabonidus surrendered and was sent to Carmania where he died in exile.

The Nabonidus Chronicle (see *NB*, pp. 168-175) mentions that in the month Tishri (i.e., October) Cyrus fought and destroyed the people of Akkad at Ophis on the Tigris river; on the 14th day he captured Sippar without fighting. Nabonidus fled; on the 16th day Gobryas (Ugbaru), the governor of Gutium, and the troops of Cyrus without fighting (ba-la sal-tum) entered Babylon.

Cyrus also (in the Cyrus Cylinder) states that he entered Babylon without encounter or battle.

It is not our purpose here to try to harmonize these various accounts, but it may be remarked that the divergence between the Greek and the cuneiform sources is not as great as at first sight might seem to be the case. It is interesting to note the tradition of a festival preserved in Xenophon. It is also interesting to note that Dan. does not speak of a battle in connection with the downfall of Babylon. The mere statement of the murder of Belshazzar is in perfect keeping with all that is known from other sources.

According to Haller, we are dealing in the fifth chapter of Dan. with a legend, in which the narrator employs a popular tradition (eine volkstuemliche Ueberlieferung) of the end of Babylonian rule as a historical background for his stories about Dan. The whole episode is an advance (Steigerung) over what has preceded, and so the interpreter of the mysterious writing appears greater than the interpreter of dreams. The legend bears the characteristic traits of similar types of legends. Thus, the thought of the revenge of the gods against those who mock them is common to mythology (ein gut mythologischer). But the spirit, which bound the various elements of this legend together, is Jewish.

The earliest part of the Belshazzar story is said to be the inscription, which must be separated from its interpretation, which was added later. The inscription (Haller follows essentially Prince's view) was a proverb (Volkswitz) in which was comprised the history of the period after Neb. Haller, of course, elaborates his theory, but presents no objective evidence to support it. The remarkable accuracy of the fifth of Dan. is a strong obstacle in the path of those who regard the ch. merely as legend.

CHAPTER SIX

a. vv. 1-9. Darius places Daniel in a position of authority. Aroused by jealousy, certain rivals devise a plot to destroy Daniel.

Vs. 1. *And Darius the Mede received the kingdom, being about sixty-two years old.* This vs. belongs to ch. 6 rather than to ch. 5 (as in AV, Bevan, Stuart—Jerome treats 5:30 and 6:1 as one vs.), as it both forms a connecting link between the events narrated in ch. 5 and those in ch. 6 and provides the historical basis for the events of ch. 6. *Darius*]—the identification of this king is as yet unknown, since secular historical sources are silent concerning him. The fact that hitherto it has been impossible to identify him does not prove that he never lived or that the figure in any sense represents a conflation of confused traditions. It should be remembered that men once spoke in terms of doubt concerning Belshazzar as some now speak of Darius. (See App. VI). *The Mede*]—The word stands in contrast to the expression, "king of the Chaldeans" (5:30) and in anticipation of "the Persian" (vs. 29). It cannot be used to support the view that the author of Dan. believed in the existence of a separate Median kingdom, since it is not said that the kingdom was Median, but merely that Darius was a Mede. Vs. 29 seems to show that both Darius and Cyrus were kings over the same kingdom. (See App. V). *Received*] —Charles, Haller and others take this to mean that Darius received the kingdom from God; Keil, Boutflower, Wilson, that he received it from Cyrus. But the phrase in itself merely means that he succeeded upon the throne.

If subsequent discovery should make it plain that Darius was as a matter of fact entrusted with the kingship by Cyrus, there is nothing in this statement which would run counter to that fact. (See SBD, I, pp. 128-144 and DM, pp. 51-53). About *sixty-two*]—The statement concerning Darius' age seems to have been added to show that Darius' reign was not of long duration, but soon gave way to that of Cyrus the Persian. Keil suggests that the word *about* "intimates that the statement of the age rests only on a probable estimate."

Vs. 2. *It seemed good before Darius that he should establish over the kingdom an hundred satraps, which should be throughout the kingdom.*

This statement has caused difficulty, and its accuracy has been denied many. On the Annalistic Tablet of Cyrus, it is said that Gubaru appoin governors in Babylon. Her. (III:89ff.) speaks of the division of empire into 20 satrapies under Darius Hystaspis. Esther 1:1 mentions 1 provinces (cf. also 8:9), but the province should be distinguished from satrapy, and hence, these figures are not necessarily out of harmony w those which indicate that the empire of Darius was divided successiv into 21, 23 and 29 satrapies (so the inscriptions of Darius). The Gre writers (see Keil, in loc.) do not attribute the origin of the division ir satrapies to Darius Hystaspis, as has sometimes been assumed, hen they are not in conflict with the statements of this passage. It is not sa that Darius the Mede divided the kingdom into 120 satrapies, but o that he appointed 120 satraps (kingdom-protectors) who should be d tributed throughout the kingdom. It is quite possible that these satra were given the special mission of caring for the newly conquered count because of fear of the hostility of the land to the conquerors. In ot words, this may have been a temporary arrangement, and not at al description of a formal organization of the country into 120 satrapi These governors may very well have had responsibility for and jurisd tion over districts which were smaller than those commonly designat as satrapies. It is not inconceivable that satraps may thus have be appointed to special missions. Thus, Darius speaks, "There was a m Dadrsis by name, a Persian, my subject, satrap in Bactria, him did I se etc." Even, however, if the text does intend to represent an organizati of the countries into 120 satrapies, it cannot be shown to be at fault.

Vs. 3. *And over them three presidents of whom Daniel was one, in or that those satraps might render an account to them, that the king mi suffer no loss.* There is no known parallel to this arrangement of the th presidents. Probably it was an expedient adopted to meet the needs the existing situation, after the pattern of that which had been used the days of Belshazzar (5:7). *Loss*]—particularly with respect to reven

Vs. 4. *Then this Daniel was distinguishing himself over the preside and satraps, because an excellent spirit was in him, and the king minded to set him over all the kingdom.* Dan. distinguished himself (*was preferred*) in his duties because of the spirit that was in him (5:12). This spirit is described as *excellent or surpassing.* It refers r merely to Dan.'s own determination faithfully to perform his tasks, f as Calvin correctly remarks, "It does not always happen that those w are remarkable for prudence or other endowments obtain greater author and rank," but it refers also to the fact that God had bestowed upon D a greater portion of His Spirit. This resulted in Dan.'s excellence bei noted by the king, who *planned* (the Aramaic word I regard as a pass participle which may have an active meaning) to advance Dan. to a position superior to the presidents and satraps.

Vs. 5. *Then the presidents and the satraps were seeking to find a pretence against Daniel, in regard to the kingdom, but they were not able to find any pretence or fault, because he was faithful, and no error or fault was found against him.* In the discharge of his governmental duties Dan. was found dilatory in no respect.

Vs. 6. *Then those men said, We shall not find any occasion against this Daniel, unless we find it against him in the law of his god.* A typical trick of the corrupt politician. "This is high testimony in favor of Daniel's integrity and piety. It would seem, that even his rivals apprehended that he would remain firm and unwavering in his religious duties" (Stuart). An honest man of conviction in the midst of government or ecclesiastical politicians stands out like a fair flower in a barren wilderness. *Law*]—i. e., religion.

Vs. 7. *Then those princes and satraps came in concert to the king, and thus they said to him, oh! Darius, the king, live forever!* The AV. renders *assembled together*, the RV. *came tumultuously*. This last however would not be appropriate for the description of an appearance before the king. In a long philological note, M shows that the meaning is "they acted in concert, harmony."

Vs. 8. *All the presidents of the kingdom, the governors, the satraps, the counsellors, and the prefects have taken counsel together that the king should establish a decree and should confirm an interdict that anyone who makes a request of any god or man for thirty days except from thee, oh! king, shall be cast into the den of lions.* All the presidents of the kingdom, of whom there were four classes (not merely the three presidents of vs. 2) consult together and conclude that the king should make a decree (not *to establish a royal statute*, AV.) to the effect that anyone who makes religious request of any but the king will be cast into the den of lions. *Make a request*]—not any kind of request, but a religious request. The thought is that the king was to be regarded as the sole representative of deity. This account is regarded as unhistorical by many expositors: "Nothing can be more unfortunate than the attempts of apologists to make these things appear probable" (Bevan). Under the Hellenistic kings, it is said, such a condition might have been possible, but not under the Persian kings. Of course there is difficulty in the account, but who is to say that an oriental despot, yielding to the subtle flattery of such a proposal, might not, in a weak moment, have agreed to it? This is not the first time in history that men have acted foolishly and entered upon an ill-considered plan of action, only to regret it later.

Vs. 9. *Now, oh! king, do thou establish the interdict and inscribe the writing which cannot be changed, according to the law of the Medes and Persians, which altereth not.* In order that the securing of their end may be made sure, the instigators request the king to put the decree in writing. *Cannot be changed*]—i. e., it was irrevocable, cf. Esther 1:19; 8:8. "Bochart, *Hierozoicon,* I, 748, cites a passage from Diodorus Sic., xvii, 30, ed. Didot, concerning Darius III's attitude toward his sentence of death upon Charidemos: 'immediately he repented and blamed himself, as having greatly erred; but it was not possible to undo what was done by royal authority' " (M).

b. vv. 10-19. The accusation and condemnation of Daniel.

Vs. 10. *Therefore, the king Darius inscribed the writing, even the interdict.* The king thus carried out the proposal. "—the object of the law was only to bring about the general recognition of the principle that the king was the living manifestation of all the gods, not only of the Median and Persian, but also of the Babylonian and Lydian, and all the gods of the conquered nations. — All the nations subjected to the Medo-Persian kingdom were required not to abandon their own special worship rendered to their gods, but in fact to acknowledge that the Medo-Persian world-ruler Darius was also the son and representative of their national gods. For this purpose they must for the space of thirty days present their petitions to their national gods only in him as their manifestation" (Kliefoth, as given by Keil). It will thus be seen that such an interdict would work grave hardship upon a pious Jew such as Dan. in that, if he obeyed it, he would not be able to pray directly to God, and if he disobeyed it, he would appear to be disloyal to the king whom he faithfully and devotedly served. The conspirators had done their work well.

The action of Darius was both foolish and wicked. What led him to yield to the request of the ministers can only be conjectured, but probably he was greatly influenced by the claim of deity which many of the Persian kings made. Q. Cur. (VIII:5) says, "The Persians worshipped their kings among the gods"; Arrian VI:29; Plutarch, Themistocles, 27; Her. 1:99 and *Cy.* I, 3, 18; Aeschylus, *Persians,* 157, 855 (see further references in H's *Authentie,* p. 127 ff). The statement of Stuart appears to be justified, "*Parsism* did not indeed require men to regard the king as a god in his own proper nature, but to pay him supreme homage as the *representative* of Ormusd. Such being the state of the case, it is easy to see that the account of Darius' behaviour, when he was importuned by his courtiers and nobles, wears no special marks of improbability."

Vs. 11. *And when Daniel knew that the writing was inscribed, he went up to his house, and he had windows opening in his roof-chamber toward Jerusalem, and three times a day he was kneeling upon his knees, and praying and making confession before his God, even as he had been accustomed to do before this.* Even after he had learned that the king had signed the decree, Dan. continued his custom of prayer. In so doing he was not tempting God nor guilty of hypocrisy or ostentation. His manner of prayer was the result of his deep piety, and could be discovered only by spies who were on the lookout for such things. Dan. went to the roof-chamber of his house (cf. 2 Sam. 18:33, I K. 17:19) which had *open* windows (i.e., probably cut in the wall and not closed with lattice work, cf. Ezek. 40:16) fronting Jerusalem. The custom of facing Jerusalem in prayer began after the dedication of the temple by Solomon, cf. I K. 8:33, 35. Spies could thus discover that Dan. prayed by an open window which faced Jerusalem. In prayer Dan. kneeled, as a sign of humility and abasement before God and prayed three times, cf. Ps. 55:17. The custom of praying three times daily went over into the Church, *Didache* 8. *Before his God*]—These words fitly characterize the entire course of Dan.'s life. In his prayer there was nothing forced or mechanical, but he uttered his petitions as in the very presence of God. The higher the task to which God calls a man, the more does he feel the need of prayer. It was Dan.'s custom to offer his prayer with thanksgiving, cf. Phil. 4:6.

Vs. 12. *Then those men came together and found Daniel praying and seeking grace before his God.* Many commentators retain the idea that the spies acted tumultuously. Thus Driver, "flocking tumultuously about Daniel's house." But, as in vs. 7, the verb means merely that the men acted in concert or conspiracy. It was their determined purpose to have Dan. put to death, and part of their conspiracy was to "discover" Dan. at prayer.

Vs. 13. *Then they drew near and spake before the king concerning the interdict of the king, Didst thou not sign an interdict that any man who asks from any god or man for thirty days except from thee, oh! king, shall be cast into the den of lions? The king answered and said, The matter is fixed, according to the law of the Medes and Persians, which changeth not.* Perhaps the first *king* should be vocative, *oh! king, didst thou not etc.*

Vs. 14. *Then they answered and spake before the king that Daniel who is from the children of the captivity of Judah, hath not regarded thee, oh! king, nor the interdict which thou hast signed, and three times a day he maketh his petition.* The despicable character of the accusers is brought to light by the manner in which they make their accusation. They describe

Dan. as an exile, rather than as the appointed head over the presidents and satraps, in order that, by calling to mind the fact that he is a foreigner, they may insinuate that he is politically unfaithful to Darius. Furthermore, they first state that Dan. has been unfaithful to the king and then that he has broken the interdict. The matter is thus presented in as bad a light as possible, a common trick of corrupt politicians.

Vs. 15 *Then the king, when he heard this matter, was greatly vexed, and with regard to Daniel, he set his mind to deliver him, and unto the sunset he was striving to rescue him.* The AV., *was displeased with himself* is incorrect. The vb. is impersonal, lit. *there was vexation upon him.* The folly of his action was now manifest, and Darius, like a trapped wild animal, striving to free itself, was struggling to deliver Dan. M suggests that he consulted the lawyers and tried to browbeat the conspirators.

Vs 16 *Then those men came in concert upon the king, and said to the king Know, oh! king, that the Medes and Persians have a law that any interdict or decree that the king establishes does not change.* "This is a very discourteous reminder to the king that he is bound by his own law, which has the tradition of the past behind it" (Charles).

Vs. 17 *Then the king commanded and they brought Daniel and cast him into the den of lions; the king answered and said to Daniel, May thy God, whom thou dost worship continually, deliver thee.* The king is thus forced to carry out the decree which he had made. Perhaps he has heard of the wonders which God has already performed through Dan., and so utters the faint hope that God will deliver Dan. Calvin thinks that the king is interested in saving Dan. only because of the benefits which he received from him However, it is more likely that a deep personal attachment for Dan. had grown up on the part of the king "His law demands that Daniel be cast before the lions, his heart filled with love towards Daniel demands that he be saved" (Gaebelein). This is a dilemma which the king is unable to resolve. "Well may we think here of another Law and another Love" (Gaebelein).

Vs. 18. *And a stone was brought and placed upon the mouth of the den, and the king sealed it with his signet and with the signet of his magnates that the affair concerning Daniel might not be changed.* By closing the mouth of the pit with a stone and sealing it, the execution of the sentence was rendered sure. Some critics have raised objections to this passage. Hitzig, for example, thinks that the den was a mere cistern, with one opening in the top, patterned after that into which Joseph was thrown. It should be remarked, however, that we know nothing about the constructions of such lions' dens. This den may have been a subterranean cavern, with an opening in the top, and possibly also one at the side, through which the animals were admitted. It may well have been that the opening at the side was closed with a stone. This does not exclude the fact that there might have been a gate which served for ordinary purposes,—such as the entrance of the keepers to feed the lions, etc. But upon this occasion something stronger than an ordinary gate was necessary. In order that Dan. might not escape, the stone was set and sealed. The king stood above the pit to converse with Dan. and Dan. was lifted up (vs. 24) out of the den through the top opening probably because the king wanted to free him as soon as possible and did not wish to wait for the removal of the stone. Most of the objections to this account are based upon the assumption that the pit must have been constructed in a certain manner. These objections are not impressive. The act of sealing the stone certified the official character of the transaction. It was not necessarily performed in order to frustrate any designs that the king may have had for delivering Dan. The king seems to have exhausted his resources for setting Dan. free, and appears now as a thoroughly frustrated man. Furthermore, the accusers doubtless had their guards on hand to see that no one tried to gain access to Dan. The mouth of the den, being sealed up, would make impossible any escape on Dan.'s part. On the other hand, the opening in the top of the pit through which the king later conversed with Dan., was doubtless too high for any escape.

Vs. 19. *Then the king went to his palace, and spent the night fasting, and diversions were not brought before him, and his sleep fled from him.* What the usual diversions of the king were is not stated. Some, upon the basis of an Arabic derivation, and others, by emending the text, would read, *concubines.*

c. vv. 20-25. The deliverance of Daniel.

Vs. 20. *Then the king rose very early in the morning and went in haste to the den of lions.*

Vs. 21. *And as he drew near to the den, he called to Daniel with a pained voice; the king answered and said to Daniel, oh. Daniel, servant of the living God, is thy God, whom dost worship continually, able to save thee from the lions?* Probably the king calls from the top of the den, since he could not be heard if he had called through an entranc on a lower level which had been stopped up with a sealed stone. His voic is full of anxiety and concern as he desires to know whether the living God (the God who preserves life) has been able to deliver Dan.

Vs. 22. *Then Daniel spoke with the king, oh! king, live forever.*

Vs. 23. *My God hath sent his angel, and shut the mouth of the lions, and they have not harmed me, forasmuch as before him innocency was found in me, and also before thee, oh! king, have I done no injury.* God has recognized Dan.'s innocence and hence has sent His angel to stop the mouths of the lions, Ps. 34:7; 91:11ff. *Innocency*]—not that Dan. was sinless, but he was innocent of the charge of which he had been accused, namely, disloyalty to the king.

Vs. 24. *Then the king was very glad, and he commanded to bring up Daniel from the den, and Daniel was brought up from the den, and no injury was found in him, for he had trusted in his God.* Probably because the king does not wish to wait to have the stone removed, he has Dan. lifted up through the entrance in the roof of the den. The words need not necessarily mean *to bring up* and may merely indicate that Dan. was brought forth from the den. Dan.'s innocency is stressed by the statement that no injury was found in him.

Vs. 25. *And the king commanded, and they brought those men that had slandered Daniel, and into the den of lions they cast them, their children and their wives, and they had not come to the bottom of the pit before the lions had power over them and broke all their bones.* The accusers were thrown into the den, evidently from the opening in its roof, and before they reached the ground, the lions had seized them. That the entire body of 120 satraps was cast into the den is a purely gratuitous assumption. The accusers were only a small group of special enemies of Dan. Vv. 5 and 6 refer to the accusers merely as *presidents, satraps, those men.* It is possible that all the presidents had agreed to the establishment of the decree, although the statement in vs. 7 may have been a falsehood uttered by the chief accusers. The plot was the work of a few men. *Slandered*]—lit., *had eaten the pieces;* the accusation was false, and therefore amounted to slander or calumny. The punishment of the wives and children was in accordance with Persian custom, cf. Her. III:119; Amm. Mar. xxiii; 6, 81, ("some laws are abominable, through which, because of the crime of one person, all his relatives are put to death").

d. vv. 26-29. The decree of Darius.

Vs. 26. *Then Darius the king wrote to all people, nations and tongues that dwell in all the earth; May your peace be multiplied!* Darius, like Neb., regarded his empire as universal.

Vs. 27. *I make a decree that in all the dominion of my realm men tremble and fear before the God of Daniel, for he is the living God and abides for-*

ever, and his kingdom (is one) which shall not be destroyed, and his dominion shall be unto the end. Darius does not rise above his polytheistic background. He does not confess Dan.'s God to be the only true God, but merely raises Him above other gods. Thus, he does not condemn the worship of these other gods. In demanding that men fear and tremble before Dan.'s God, Darius requires no more than Neb. had apparently demanded for himself (cf.5:19 where the same words are used). How tragic it is that in the presence of his mighty miracles, men do not acknowledge God to be the only true God! In the statements made concerning God and His kingdom, Darius is probably influenced by the events of the immediate past and by the instruction which he had received from Dan. His words, while true enough in themselves, could only have had a hollow meaning for himself.

Vs. 28. *He rescues and delivers and doeth signs and wonders in the heaven and on the earth, who has delivered Daniel from the hand of the lions.* Vs. 29. *And this Daniel was prosperous in the reign of Darius and in the reign of Cyrus the Persian.* The same Dan., whom the accusers would destroy, was not destroyed but prospered, not only during the reign of Darius the Mede, but also during the reign of Cyrus the Persian. The two rulers of the kingdom were of different races, one a Mede and one a Persian. The kingdom, however, was the same. The designation *the Persian* is in accordance with the usage of the Persian kings. Thus, Ariyaramna (c. 610-580 B.C.) speaks of himself as "Ariyaramna, the great king, the king of kings, the Persian king."

Thus concludes the historical portion of the book. The author's purpose has been to exhibit the wonder-working power of the sovereign God among those who held the people of God in bondage and thus to prepare the way for the deliverance of the latter. But a further lesson is also enjoined, and I cannot do better than to state it in the words of Thomas Myers, the editor of Calvin's superb commentary. "Throughout these LECTURES (i.e., on Dan. 1-6) we are ever taught that we can see God only by being pure in heart. The preparation for spiritual insight into holy mysteries is purity of conscience and singleness of eye. But even these able comments do not clear up everything. Our lot on earth must be to walk more by faith than by sight. This is the chief exercise of the soul, which is essential to its vitality and growth. We must have at times our mountains of vision as well as our valleys of the shadow of death. Never let us doubt the essential permanence of justice, and righteousness and truthfulness. By this we shall be borne up through regions of cloud into realms of light. Thus will our spirituality be strengthened and refined:

thus we shall be permitted to obtain larger perceptions of God's character and maturer judgments of his purposes."

Haller regards this ch. as a geniune martyr-legend, which is built (as ch. 3) on the theme of a miraculous deliverance of the Jews who are true to their profession of faith. However, here it is the hatred of the people rather than the anger of the king which places the Jews in danger. The essential theme is the same as in ch. 3, and Haller asserts that, just as the prophet-legends grew up about different men (e.g., he thinks that the same miracles are related in similar form concerning Elijah and Elisha), so the Jewish narrators liked to repeat such stories of deliverance over and over again. The same motif appears in the NT in connection with the deliverance of Peter and Paul from prison.

Haller acknowledges that the narrator possessed a certain knowledge of the late Persian period, but that he was in the dark about the beginning of that period. There is no need to reproduce the elaboration of Haller's theory in detail. For our part, we believe that a careful exegesis of the book will make it clear that we are dealing with a record which is history and not legend.

CHAPTER SEVEN

a. vv. 1-14. The vision of the four beasts.

Vs. 1. *In the first year of Belshazzar, king of Babylon, Daniel saw a dream and visions of his head upon his bed; then he wrote the dream, (and) the sum of the matters he related.* "Here Daniel begins to offer instruction peculiar to the Church" (Calvin). This vision was seen during the first year, not shortly before (Hitzig), of the reign of Belshazzar. It has the same subject as does that of ch. 2. In the 2nd year of his reign, at the height of power, Neb. had his dream, but this vision is given to Dan. in the first year of Belshazzar, when the glory and might of the kingdom had begun to wane. It should be noted that Dan. does not adhere to the chronological order hitherto employed, but reverts to a date anterior to that of ch. 5. The visions, therefore, (chs. 7-12) are not intended to be a continuation of the narratives (1-6). *King*]—It has already been shown that this usage of the word is not inaccurate (cf. comments on 5:1). Since Belshazzar is the king with whom Dan. and the people of God had to do, his name is here employed in dating. Let it be repeated; this is not an official Babylonian document, but a prophecy written for the Church of God. *Saw a dream*]—i.e., he had a mental perception of a dream. Cf. Isa. 2:1, "he saw a word." *Visions*]—(Cf. 2: 28; 4:2, 10—the similarity of the phraseology is an argument in favor of the unity of the book). This dream vision came to Dan. as he lay asleep upon his couch. The text does not mean that the visions of the dream had their origin in the brain (*head*) of Dan. Rather, this was a divinely imposed dream. *Wrote*]—Upon awakening, Dan., under the sovereign influence of the Spirit of God, wrote out accurately the contents of the dream which had come to him during his sleep. *Sum of the matters*]—This phrase is particularly difficult. Keil takes it to mean that "by means of writing down the vision he said, *i.e.* reported, the chief contents of the dream, omitting secondary things, e.g. the minute description of the beasts." This is perfectly possible, and may be correct. However, upon the basis of some of the early translations, and the usage of the word translated *sum* in Palmyrene Syriac, it is said to be possible to regard the phrase as indicating the beginning of what Dan. wrote. Thus, *Beginning of the composition.* But this is questionable, and I incline toward Keil's explanation.

Vs. 2. *Daniel answered and said, I was beholding with visions of the night, and lo! the four winds of heaven burst forth upon the great sea.* Dan. would again affirm that the message which he is about to deliver was given him of God, and was not merely the product of his own subconscious mind. *Of the night*]—i.e., visions which come with the night, as 3:33; Ps. 72:5 and the well known line of Ovid, "Cum sole et luna semper Aratus erit (*Ars Amatoria* I: 15, 16). *Lo!*]—cf. 2:31. *Four Winds*]—cf. 8:8; 11:4; Zech. 2:6; 6:5. These are the four cardinal winds. Cf. "The south-wind, the north-wind, the east wind, the west wind." These are called the four winds (irbit-tim sare) in the Bab. Creation Tablets, IV: 42, 43 (ed. Langdon, p. 133; Heidel, p. 28); ". . . it is the common phrase to speak of four winds blowing from the four quarters or regions of the globe" (Calvin). Do these winds have any particular symbolizing significance? Jerome regarded them as symbolizing angelic powers; Keil suggests that they represent the "heavenly powers and forces by which God sets the nations of the world in motion." Other commentators see no particular symbolical significance. However, it is rather generally assumed that the "great sea" does signify mankind. Hence, since it is the four winds which stir up humanity, it would seem that they must be regarded as winds specially controlled by God. By means of these winds God at this time stirs up the nations. To be rejected is the view of W. R. Smith (as mentioned by Bevan—I have not been able to check the reference) that the ideas of this vs. are "borrowed from the ideas of cosmogony then current in the ancient East," and of Gunkel *SC*, p. 328ff., that the ch. goes back to the Babylonian myth of Tiamat, and that the "wind" is an ancient motif (Hier ist also ein uralter Zug treu bewahrt). *Burst forth*]—i.e., were breaking forth, not *strove.* The root of the word refers to the bursting forth of water. Calvin rightly translated *commovebant.* Cf. the vivid description of a storm at sea by Vergil, *Aeneid* I:82ff.,

> ". . . ac venti, velut agmine facto,
> qua data porta, ruunt et terras turbine perflant.
> Incubere mari totumque a sedibus imis
> Una Eurusque Notusque ruunt creberque procellis
> Africus et vastos volvunt ad litora fluctus."

Great sea]—not the Mediterranean (Gaebelein, Lang, Hitzig, Bertholdt), although in Josh. 1:4 the term is used, for such a specific geographical reference is here out of place. Rather, it is the world-sea or great abyss, the boundless ocean, Isa. 51:10; Rev. 17:8. As Hippolytus first indicated, it symbolizes the world of nations in a tumultuous state, cf. Isa. 17:12ff.; Jer. 46:7ff.; Rev. 17:15; 21:1. This interpretation is specifically supported by vs. 17 of the present ch. where it is said that the kings shall arise out of the earth. "The imagery is allied to the tropical use of *overflowing rivers* and *mighty waves,* for the designation of invading armies which overrun a country without control" (Stuart).

Dan., therefore, declares that in the vision which came to him by night he was beholding, and the four cardinal winds were breaking forth upon the vast ocean and stirring it up.

Vs. 3. *And four great beasts were ascending from the sea, diverse one from another.* "Oecumenical commotions give rise to oecumenical kingdoms" (Kliefoth in Keil). As a consequence of stirring up the sea, four beasts arise. But, as the subsequent context reveals, not simultaneously. These beasts, although differing one from another, have this in common, that each arises from the sea, i.e., represents a kingdom of human origin and nature. (Cf. Rev. 13:1 where the symbolism is based upon Dan.). These beasts are described as *great,* i.e., *monstrous* (Ewald), not *ravenous* (Kranichfeld). Their diversity is mentioned, in order to call attention to the importance of the symbolism by which each individual kingdom is represented. In the OT the gentile nations are frequently symbolized by beasts, cf. Ezek. 29:3ff.; Isa. 27:1; 51:9. In this picture of the beasts, belonging to the water, but ruling also on earth, Gunkel, as might be expected, thinks that he finds a mythologizing strain (ein uraltes Motiv). The diversity is one of worth, as Theodoret and M point out.

Vs. 4. *The first was like a lion and had eagle's wings. I was beholding until its wings were plucked off, and it was lifted up from the earth, and upon two feet like a man it was made to stand, and the heart of a man was given to it.* The first beast corresponds to the head of gold of ch. 2 and stands for Babylon, particularly as represented in the reign of Neb. The symbol of the winged lion is especially appropriate. Hitzig first called attention to the winged lion with a man's head which was excavated at Nimrud.

Neb. had been compared to a lion and eagle, cf. Jer. 4:7; 49:19; 50:17, 44; 49:22; Lam. 4:19; Hab. 1:8; Ezek. 17:3, 12. If the book of Dan. was composed by an unknown Palestinian author of Maccabean times, whence did he derive his knowledge of this symbol? It is certainly a remarkable thing, if on the basis of the above Scripture passages alone, the author constructed this symbol (Prince), and his symbol has turned out to be such an accurate representation of Babylon! No, the accuracy of this symbol is evidence that the book was written by someone who knew Babylon well. "These discoveries may be referred to as evidence that this book was composed in Babylon, and also as explaining the Babylonian colouring of the dream" (Keil). The lion as king of the beasts and the eagle as king of the birds, well corresponds with gold (ch. 2) the most precious of metals. Thus, Babylon is represented by the lordliest of creatures.

As Dan. beholds, a change comes over the beast. Its wings were plucked off, and thus it is deprived of its power of flight. No longer as a conqueror can it fly over the earth, nor as a ruler hover over it. *Lifted up*]—not removed from the earth (Calvin), nor destroyed (Jerome), but raised up from the ground to stand upon two feet. The Aramaic employs the dual, and this I have sought to preserve in the translation. *Heart of a man*]—i.e., its beast nature was changed to that of a man; it was humanized. Thus, both inwardly and outwardly, this humanizing process takes place.

The particular reference of this humanizing process is probably to Neb.'s humiliation. Charles, however, thinks that this is impossible because in 4:13, Neb. is not given the heart of a beast until after his conquests, whereas in 7:4 the beast is given the heart of a man during its period of conquest. But is this not to become over literal and pedantic? For it was precisely the giving to Neb. of the "beast's heart" (ch. 4) which humbled him. By Neb. receiving a "beast's heart", the Babylonian empire was given a human heart. "As in 2:38, Nebuchadnezzar and his Empire are treated as identical. The Babylonian Empire, on its first appearance, has a purely animal, i.e. heathen, character, but after a while the animal attributes disappear, the Empire is, as it were, humanized in the person of its representative" (Bevan).

Vs. 5. *And behold! another beast, a second, like to a bear, and it was raised up on one side, and three ribs were in its mouth between its teeth, and thus they said to it, Arise, devour much flesh.* This beast came into sight after the lion. It is said to be *another*, i.e., one which differed from the first, and a *second*, i.e., second in the order of appearance. Cf. Rev. 14:8, "another second angel." Next to the lion, the bear is selected for its strength and fierceness. In Scripture the two are often grouped together, e.g., Hos. 13:8; Amos 5:19; Prov. 28:15.

Yet, as Driver remarks, the bear "is inferior to the lion in strength and appearance, and is heavy and ungainly in its movements." *Was raised*]—not *it raised itself up. On one side*]—The language is difficult. It does not mean "it established a dominion" (Kranichfeld) nor that it stood on its hind feet (Hævernick), nor stood aloof from harming the Hebrews (Jerome) nor, stood by the side of the lion (Rosenmueller), but stood with the feet on one side raised for the purpose of going forward (Keil). "The animal then is pausing to devour a mouthful before springing again on its prey" (M). The device of an animal raised on one side is not distinctive of any one nation, but is here chosen, probably to indicate the double sided nature of a kingdom ready to march forward in conquest. In ch. 8 this double sided nature is represented by the two horns, one of which rises after the other and higher. The animal itself, the bear, represents the Medo-Persian empire, and the double sided nature of this empire is symbolized by the beast lifting itself up on one side.

According to many expositors, the kingdom represented by the bear is merely the Median. It is true that Dan. represents Belshazzar as succeeded[1] by a Median ruler, Darius, but as the proper exegesis of 6:29 shows, Darius the Median and Cyrus the Persian were both rulers in the same kingdom. See App. V. *Three ribs*]—not three tusks (Bertholdt) nor three classes of teeth (Hævernick). Jerome referred these to three kingdoms, Media, Persia, and Babylon, but since the bear itself represents the Medo-Persian empire, what it devours must be something else. Maurer found the illusion to the three chief satrapies of 6:3 (opinor, tres, in quas Darius Medus universum regnum distribuit provincias majores). But since Maurer regards this beast as Media, this is tantamount to saying that the beast is devouring itself, for the three chief provinces are those which a Median erected. For the same reason, we must reject the reference as to the "three Median kings" (Ewald). Likewise, Hitzig's interpretation is unlikely,—Nineveh, Larissa and a third city. Those who regard the second empire as Medo-Persian, have generally taken the ribs to be Babylon, Lydia and Egypt. This fits in well with the symbolism and may be correct. Hitzig says that those who cannot explain the number three, consider it to be a round number. I probably fall under this condemnation, for it seems to me, as Calvin long ago pointed out, the insatiable nature of the beast is indicated, since, not being content with one body, it devoured many. If however, a definite reference is intended, that to Babylon, Lydia and Egypt is satisfactory, whereas those who regard this empire as the Median, seem to have found no satisfactory identification of the three ribs. *Arise*—not a summons to go forth upon a career of further conquest, but to devour the flesh of the ribs which were already in the mouth. The beast must wholly consume what it has seized. *They said*]—may be rendered, it was said. The command is given by God, thus showing that Divine Providence overruled in the affairs of the mighty human kingdom.

Vs. 6. *After this I was beholding, and lo! another like a panther, and it had four wings of a bird upon its back, and the beast had four heads,*

---

[1] L. Waterman (*A Gloss on Darius the Mede* in *JBL*, Vol. LXV, March 1946, pp. 59-61) calls attention to the difficulty of the language of this phrase and suggests that the correct translation is *and it furnished a single ruler* (i.e., Darius the Mede). If this translation is correct, and I do not believe that it is, it would provide an interesting connecting link to show the unity of chs. 5, 6 and 7.

and dominion was given to it. The third empire, the Macedonian, is represented in the vision by a panther, an animal noted for its agility and intelligence, cf. Jer. 5:6, Hos. 13:7. *Upon its back*]—The word may also be rendered *sides.* Possibly, therefore, the animal is to be conceived as having wings upon its sides, as in the representations of the winged beasts from Babylon. Since there are only two pairs of wings, but four heads, we are probably to regard the heads as having a signification independent from that of the wings. The wings, as expositors generally recognize, denote swiftness. However, since these are merely the wings of an ordinary bird, and not those of an eagle, the swiftness in conquest of this empire is not as royal or noble in quality as was that of Neb. On the other hand, since the first beast had (presumably) but one pair of wings and this one has two, this empire is to be considered as possessing greater rapidity in its conquests. This is in accordance with the historical facts. "In this (i. e., rapidity of conquest) Nebuchadnezzar excelled much, but Alexander outstripped all other conquerors in the East or West" (Stuart). Those who would refer the 3rd beast to Persia may point to the rapidity of Cyrus' movements and appeal to Isa. 41:3. However, this is not to be compared with the panther-like swiftness and lightning-like rapidity of the rise and fall of the Macedonian empire of Alexander. As Kliefoth has well pointed out, the same gradation which was found in ch. 2 in the relation of the brass to gold and silver, here appears in the subordination of the panther to the lion and bear. *Four heads*]—Not the four Persian kings of ch. 11:2 (Charles, Bevan). Nor do the heads refer to the four successors of Alexander, Ptolemy, Seleucus, Philip, Antigonus (Jerome, Calvin), nor to the four principal divisions of Alexander's conquests, Greece, Western Asia, Egypt and Persia. It is true (8:5ff.) that Alexander's kingdom did thus become four-fold, but here the four heads, representing the four corners of the earth, symbolize the ecumenicity of the kingdom. In Dan., kings are generally symbolized by horns, rather than heads (but cf. 2:39). *Dominion*]—This agrees with 2:39 "it shall bear rule over all the earth." In its rapid conquest, however, the third kingdom is under the Providence of God. It can conquer only because God gives it the power so to do.

Vs. 7. *After this I was beholding in visions of the night, and lo! a fourth beast, fearful, and terrible and strong exceedingly, and it had great iron teeth; it was devouring and crushing, and trampling the residue with its feet, and it was diverse from all the beasts that were before it; and it had ten horns.* The vision of the fourth beast is introduced with special solemnity. There can be no question but that it is intended to be identical with the iron of the image of ch. 2. Here "the point of destructiveness is particularly pressed" (M). This beast is nondescript, because in the entire world of nature, no proper similitude could be found. The conquering ability is indicated by mention of its massive iron teeth. Thus, it used these teeth to devour and crush, and what could not be destroyed in this way was stamped upon with its feet. Its particular characteristic is its rage for destruction. Wherein the precise diversity of this beast from its three predecessors consists, is not indicated in the symbolism. Perhaps it is to be found in the intensity of its destructive power. A participle is used in the Aramaic, *was acting diversely*. Upon the basis of reasons given in App. V I think that the beast represents the Roman Empire. *Ten horns*]—These represent ten kings, vs. 24. Like the number *four* in vs. 6, the number *ten* here is to be taken in a symbolic sense as indicating "a multiplicity of rulers, or an indefinitely large number of kings" (Zœckler), "comprehensive and definite totality" (Keil). The horn is also the symbol of power (cf. Deut. 33:17; I Sam. 2:1, 10; Ps. 18:2), and so in the ten horns the power of the kingdom comes forth in full display. Since the number *ten* indicates completeness, we need not regard the horns as representing ten specific *contemporary* kings. It should be noted that whereas the number ten is explicitly mentioned here, it is only by inference that we can say the image of ch. 2 has ten toes.

Vs. 8. *I was contemplating the horns, and, behold! another horn, a little one, was coming up among them, and three of the first horns were uprooted before it, and behold! eyes like the eyes of a man in this horn, and a mouth speaking great things.* The horns attract the particular attention of the seer, and, as he regards them contemplatively, he beholds another horn, a little one, coming up among them. The special manner in which this little horn is introduced serves to bring to the fore its importance. The reader's attention is thus detracted from the beast to that which grows out of it, the little horn. *I was contemplating*]—The idea is that of continued contemplation, being lost, as it were, in observation. *A little horn*]—Unlike the little horn of ch. 8, this horn is not described as growing in stature. As a little horn, it makes war with the saints and prevails against them (vs. 21). Why, therefore, is it said to be little? This is not to indicate its small beginning (Driver), since it is not described as growing. Rather, the designation *little* serves all the more to focus attention upon the eyes and mouth, which are the principal features of this horn. This little horn, therefore, represents a small kingdom whose power is concentrated in its king, here represented by the eyes and mouth (The symbolism is interpreted later in vv. 21 ff.). *Were uprooted*]—i. e., were displaced. According to Porphyry, who regarded the fourth beast as a symbol of the successors of Alexander, the little horn is Antiochus Epiphanes, who overthrew the three horns, Ptolemy Philometor, Ptolemy Euergetes and Artarxia, king of Armenia. Jerome remarks that Porphyry attempts this identification in vain (frustra) since the first two of these rulers were dead before the birth of Antiochus, and even after a certain Antiochus had fought against Artarxia, he continued to reign. This interpretation of Porphyry may be mentioned as an historical curiosity. For other interpretations, see App. V. In general, it may be said that those who regard the fourth beast as symbolizing some aspect of the Grecian empire, consider the little horn to be identical with the little horn of ch. 8 and to symbolize Antiochus Epiphanes. *Eyes of a man*]—This description is not intended merely to indicate that the horn signified a man, but principally to guard against the little horn being considered as possessing more than human characteristics. The sagacity of the little horn is so great, and his rule and government so terrible that he might be mistaken for a supernatural being, whereas in fact he is but a man. So Jerome long ago expressed the true meaning, "that we may not, according to the notion of some, think it to be a devil, or a demon, but one of those men in whom the whole of Satan is to dwell bodily" (unum de hominibus, in quo totus Satanas habitaturus sit corporaliter). *Mouth*]—a proud, presumptuous mouth, which uttered words of "boasting, haughtiness, contumacy" (Stuart). These things were spoken against God and His people. Cf. Ps. 12:3; Obadiah 12; Rev. 13:5, where the beast with ten horns has "a mouth speaking great things and blasphemies." Pride and self-exaltation are the principal characteristics of the little horn.

It should be noted that with regard to the fourth beast, Dan. sees not only certain characteristics but also the unfolding of a history. In fact, within the history there appear to be three distinct phases or periods.

1. The beast itself is first presented to the vision. "For the living creature which represents this, there is no name. No one creature can express its terribleness, not even if the attributes of different creatures, (as in the symbol of the lion with eagle's wings) were combined to picture it" (Pusey). After attention is called to the stupendous strength and crushing power of the fourth beast, the statement is made that it had ten horns.

2. The period of the ten horns. Although, in order to indicate the essential unity of the fourth kingdom, the horns appear upon the head of the beast, it is obvious that these horns represent a later phase of the beast's existence. After the characterization given in vs. 23, with its emphasis upon the conquering power of the beast (as in vs. 7), it is stated (vs. 24) that ten horns shall come *out of* this kingdom. This accords with the mention of the horns in vs. 7 *after* the description of the crushing power of the beast. "*The kings* then or *kingdoms* which should *arise out of* this kingdom, must, from the force of the term as well as from the context, be *kings* or *kingdoms* which should arise at some later stage of

its existence, not those first kings without which it could not be a kingdom at all" (Pusey). Although these horns need not be exact contemporaries, one with another, nevertheless, they all belong within this second period of the beast's history.

3. The period of the little horn. All the ten horns "are prior in time to the little horn which is to arise out of them" (Pusey). While the period of the ten horns is in existence, there arises *among* these kingdoms another, which uproots three and then holds sway. Thus, the eleventh horn comes up among the others, yet is after them. There will be a period when the kingdom of the little horn, particularly in the person of its king, will hold dominion over all the earth.

To what does this symbolism refer? The beast itself stands for the Roman Empire as it appeared at the birth of Christ and in the years subsequent. This well agrees with the symbolism. Like no empire before her, Rome permanently subdued her conquered territory. Her conquests were universal in a sense that was true of no nation before her. See Pusey (p. 129).

Following the historical Roman Empire is the period represented by the ten horns. In this period the strength of the beast is expressed in full display. These kingdoms in one sense or another, arise historically from the ancient Roman Empire. This does not mean that each one of the empires must be able to trace its origin immediately to Rome. The kingdoms of modern Europe, for example, might be said to have come from the Roman Empire, but certainly not directly. Yet, they may trace their origin back to Rome, as Medo-Persia, for example, could not trace its origin back to Babylon, or Greece to Medo-Persia, or Rome to Greece. This is certainly not to deny that elements other than Roman have contributed to form the present European governments, but it cannot be doubted that modern Europe may in a very legitimate sense have arisen from Rome.

As I have previously tried to indicate, we are not to look for ten kingdoms which shall exist side by side when the little horn appears. If the number ten is to be pressed, all we need insist upon is that, from the time when the fourth empire lost its beast form (i. e., the destruction of the Roman Empire) to the appearance of the little horn, there have been ten kingdoms which truly partake of the character of the beast. If, however, the number ten be regarded merely as the symbol of completeness, as I am inclined to regard it, the vs. means that from the time of the destruction of the Roman Empire to the appearance of the little horn there will be a number of kingdoms, which may truly be said to originate from the ancient Roman Empire. To seek to identify these kingdoms, when Scripture furnishes no clue as to their identity, is very precarious and probably unwarranted.

Toward the close of the second period there appears another kingdom, symbolized by the little horn. This kingdom or government uproots some of the others (I am not sure that the number three is to be pressed). This kingdom fades into the background as far as significance is concerned, and all importance is given to its head, which arrogates unto itself prerogatives that belong to God alone. For the third period it shall hold sway. It is, I believe, that one of whom Paul spoke, "Let no man deceive you by any means: for that day shall not come, except there be a falling away first, and that man of sin be revealed, the son of perdition; who opposeth and exalteth himself above all that is called God, or that is worshipped; so that he as God sitteth in the temple of God, shewing himself that he is God" (2 Thes. 2:3, 4). This one is the Anti-Christ. Thus, in one remarkable picture, the entire course of history is given from the appearance of the historical Roman Empire until the end of human government.

Vs. 9. *I was beholding until thrones were placed, and the Ancient of days did sit; His raiment was like white snow, and the hair of His head like pure wool; His throne-flames of fire; its wheels-burning fire.* Vv. 9-14 constitute a unit and treat of the Divine judgment upon the Gentile nations. "In contrast with the chaos of Great Ocean, its hurricanes and portentuous monsters, appears the august vision of God come to judgment" (M). The scene of judgment is conceived majestically. Upon this passage is based the description in Rev. 4:2ff. Later apocalyptic has also used this scene as a model. The imagery of this magnificent scene is largely derived from the OT (I K. 22:19 ff.; Psa. 51; 82; Joel 3:15, 16) although the description itself is without prototype, for the source of this vision is to be found in immediate Divine revelation. *I was beholding*]—The action is continuous. As Dan. beheld, the mouth in the little horn continued speaking, but the scene shifted, and Dan.'s eyes were lifted to heaven. *Thrones*]—The word is pl., which would imply that the scene is that of a heavenly court or session. Who then, besides the Occupant of the fiery throne, constituted the court? Various suggestions have been offered. The Son of Man (*Enoch* 37-71); David (Akiba in *Sanhedrin* 38b); the elders of Israel (a Jewish interpretation); glorified men (H); angels who are to be distinguished from the multitude of vs. 10 (Keil, in appeal to Ps. 89:8); the Persons of the Trinity (d'Envieu). The Scriptures do mention attendants of the Lord as Judge, cf. Isa. 6:2; Rev. 1:4; 8:2 and 4:4. Christians also are said to judge, Luke 22:30; I Cor. 6:2; Rev. 3:21. If, therefore, the pl. is to be stressed, the thought is most likely that those who occupy the thrones are angels. M, following Maldonatus,[2] suggests that the pl. is not to be stressed ("for only One took his seat") and appeals to Ps. 122:5. On this interpretation the pl. is to be regarded as a pl. of majesty. I am inclined to think that the pl. should be stressed, and that the thrones were occupied by angels whose position naturally would be subordinate to that of Him who sat upon the throne. *Were placed*]—Calvin remarks that some have translated, "thrones were removed" and refer it to the four monarchies. But the verb does not mean to remove but to place. The AV "were cast down" is incorrect. *Ancient of days*]—lit., one advanced in days, i. e., advanced in years. Cf. Gen. 24:1 "had come into years," and Cicero, *de Senectute* 3:10, *aetate provectus*. It is therefore not to be regarded as a superlative, "He who is most ancient as to days," i. e., the Eternal (Stuart), nor as a designation to contrast Him with *younger* associates, or with the little horn or with recent gods of the heathen (Zœckler, appealing to Deut. 32:17; Jer. 23:23). The correct meaning has been set forth by Keil "—an old man, or a man of grey hairs, in whose majestic form God makes Himself visible (cf. Ezek. 1:26)." Since age inspires veneration and gives the impression of majesty, such a figure is used. He who sits upon the throne is a venerable Person. *Raiment*]—The white garment of a judge indicates both majestic dignity and purity (cf. Isa. 1:18; Ps. 51:7; Rev. 3:5; 4:4, 6; 19:8). *Hair*]—a further symbol of purity and majesty, although the white hair of an aged person would be natural, as Driver suggests, cf. Rev. 1:14. *Throne*]—Fire often accompanies the presence of God, cf. Ex. 19:18; 20:18; 3:2; Deut. 4:24; 9:3; 18:17; Ps. 18:8; 50:3; Ezek. 1:4, 13, 27; Heb. 12:29; Rev. 4:5. Here the fire represents the power to destroy and also splendor and majesty. It is the agent through which the beasts are to be destroyed. *Wheels*]—Apparently the throne appeared as a chariot as in Ezek. 1:15-28. Here, however, the throne and wheels are represented as being of fire. Although there are similarities with the vision of Ezek., the vision of the throne does not belong "to a common stock of tradition coming down from Eze." (M), but is the product of Divine revelation.

Vs. 10. *A river of fire was flowing, and coming forth from before Him; thousand thousands were serving Him, and myriad myriads were standing before Him; the court sat, and books were opened.* The fiery streams flowed forth from before the throne. In Rev. 4:5 the lightnings and thunderings and voices proceed from the throne itself. Cf. also *Enoch* 14:19.

---

[2] Juan Maldonado was born in 1533 in Spain and died at Rome in 1583. He first taught at Salamanca and later at Paris. He was an excellent theologian and a man of sound learning and wrote several Biblical commentaries. His work on Dan. (*Commentarii in Prophetas IV* i.e., Jeremiah, Baruch, Ezekiel, Daniel) was published in 1609 at Lyons.

Various interpretations of the symbolism have been offered. Jerome treats this phrase as belonging to vs. 9 and translates "a fiery and rapid stream was proceeding forth from His face," and concludes that the purpose of the stream was to carry sinners to hell (ut peccatores traheret in gehennam). Calvin suggests that the symbolism is intended to inspire the prophet with fear, in order to humble him so that he may the better comprehend God's majesty. Ewald considers the fiery stream to be a symbol of the command of God for judgment to begin. Hitzig conceives of the stream as constituting a floor for the judgment scene, otherwise the entire appearance would hang in the air without support. But Keil seems correct in indicating that the stream consumes all that is opposed to God and renders glorious His people and kingdom. Cf. also Ps. 50:3; 97:3. *Thousand thousands*]—The numbers are not to be taken as definite; they indicate rather that a vast multitude, an innumerable host, stood ready to serve the majestic Figure that was seated upon the throne. Cf. Deut. 33:2; Ps. 68:17. *The court sat*]—lit., the judgment sat. The abstract noun is used for the concrete. So, in Latin, *Verr.* 2:18. Gaebelein maintains that this is a judgment which preceded the final judgment by 1000 years. He identifies the Ancient of Days with Jesus Christ, but also identifies the Son of Man with Jesus Christ. This is an impossible interpretation, as the subsequent discussion will endeavor to point out. *Books*]—The actions of men are recorded in books (cf. Isa. 65:6; Jer. 17:1; Mal. 3:16; Luke 10:20 and Rev. 20:12), but here the reference is particularly to the deeds of the four beasts and the little horn. Gunkel believes that he discerns a mythologizing strain in this description of the throne, but presents no details. Again, let it be emphasized, the origin of this particular vision is to be found only in Divine revelation.

Vs. 11. *I was beholding then from (the time of) the voice of the mighty words that the horn was speaking; I was beholding until the beast was slain, and its body destroyed, and it was given to the burning of fire.* For the translation of this vs., I have followed M. The word *from* is often taken in the sense of *because,* as giving the reason why Dan. continued beholding. But this is difficult, and so it is more generally taken to give the reason for the judgment that follows. However, Kliefoth (in Keil) gives the correct interpretation "from the time of the words, or from the time when the voice of the great words made itself heard." From the time when the mouth in the little horn began to speak Dan. had been beholding. Evidently (since there is no warrant for regarding the judgment scene as a separate vision, as does Gaebelein, who heads this section "The Third Night Vision") all the while that Dan. beheld the vision of judgment, he heard the presumptuous words of the little horn. If this representation be correct, it surely adds to the drama of the entire scene. The second

I was beholding simply means that Dan. continued watching the scene until the judgment was executed. This judgment (in the vision) falls first upon the fourth beast. By mention of the *body* being destroyed, the *utter* destruction of the beast is intended. It will exercise no further power in any sense, since it is to be completely done away. This, it seems to me, is a serious objection to finding the primary reference of the little horn to Antiochus, for after Antiochus' time, there were other Syrian kings who afflicted the Jews. But with the destruction of the little horn, the power of the fourth beast disappears *entirely*. It will not do, with Stuart, to say, "The minutiae of subsequent history are out of his (i. e., Daniel's) circle of vision, and aside from his design." What warrant is there for such a statement? *Fire*]—a further symbol of utter and complete destruction. It is the fire of judgment from God which completely triumphs over the fourth beast (cf. Isa. 9:5; 66:24; Rev. 19:20; 20:10). Since it is the destruction of empires and not of individuals as such which is described, it is probable that the primary reference is not to the fire of hell. Rather, it is the majestic and full triumph of Divine judgment which is pictured. This involves, of course, eternal punishment for some members of the fourth empire, but such is not the principal thought in this symbolism.

Vs. 12. *And the rest of the beasts—their dominion was taken away, and extension in life was given to them for a time and a season.* Dan. speaks now of the first three beasts. Nothing had been said about their disappearance from the scene as each successive beast arose. Apparently, therefore, we are to regard them as having remained in the vision all the while. Some expositors refer these beasts to the seven horns which were not uprooted by the little horn. But this is impossible, for the complete destruction of the fourth beast has just been described. Rather, the reference is to the first three beasts which appeared in the vision, the lion, bear and leopard. Why then is the destruction of the fourth beast narrated first, whereas in actual fact the first three kingdoms perished before the fourth? The answer is that the destruction of the fourth beast—the power which, in the appearance of the little horn, so blatantly opposes God, is to be emphasized. It constitutes, in one sense, the heart of the vision. As far as flagrant and presumptuous opposition to God was concerned, the first three beasts were insignificant in comparison with the fourth. For the sake of emphasis, then, the utter destruction of the fourth beast is first mentioned. The fate of the first three beasts is not as terrible as is that of the fourth. They lose their power to rule, but they are permitted to continue alive until the time, determined in the counsel of God, should come. At the appointed time, therefore, the dominion of each of the beasts was taken away. So Keil. "the first three beasts also had their dominion taken away one after another, each at its appointed time; for to each God gave its duration of life, extending to the season and time appointed by Him." The words *for a time and season* (as in 2:21) simply express the idea of a predetermined time.

Vs. 13. *I was beholding in visions of the night, and lo! with the clouds of heaven One like a son of man was coming, and unto the Ancient of days He came, and before Him He was brought.* This remarkable vision is introduced by the phrase *I was beholding in visions of the night.* It is not to be regarded as a fourth vision (Gaebelein), but as the climax of the one vision. The judgment which Dan. beheld does not end in the destruction of the world-powers. It is continued in the foundation of the kingdom of God by the Son of Man. *With the clouds*]—i. e., in connection with the clouds, whether on or in them is not stated, but "surrounded by clouds" (Keil). Probably the LXX has rightly expressed the thought "upon the clouds," although this must be regarded merely as an interpretation. Th. reads "with." M suggests that "Position *upon* the clouds, which the writer avoids, would rather be the attribute of Deity, e. g., Is. 19:1, Ps. 104:3." But this is to press the symbolism too far. It is the coming in accompaniment with clouds (which certainly does not exclude position upon them) that is indicative of Deity. (Cf. Rev. 1:7 *With the clouds*]—This passage in the NT which obviously is based upon Dan. 7:13, clinches the matter. There can be no question, but that Deity is intended here); Mark 13:26; Matt. 24:30; 26:64; also Ps. 104:3; 18: 10-18; 97:2-4; Isa. 19:1; Nah. 1:3. Driver, therefore, is correct in interpreting "in superhuman majesty and state." Among the Jews the Messiah came to be known as 'anani "Cloudy One" or bar nivli "Son of a Cloud." *A son of man*]—The AV is incorrect. Lit., one like (or the likeness of) a son of man, i. e., one like a man, a figure in human form. The words "son of man" in Syriac or Aramaic simply mean "a man." It is not expressly stated that the heavenly Figure *was* a man but merely that He was *like* a man and not like the beasts. M thinks that the human being presents a contrast with both the Ancient and the beasts, thus, God, man, beast, as in Ps. 8. In Ezek. this designation is commonly applied to the prophet himself. But here, the language is employed to signify a new kingdom and one of an entirely different character from that represented by the beasts.

The prophet employs the word *like* in order to stress the distinction between the heavenly Figure and the beasts. The word also serves to describe the Person who comes on the clouds. He is a human-like Personage.

Some of the older commentators, e.g., Calvin take the word *like* as indicative of the fact that Christ had not yet taken upon Him our flesh.

And Robert Rollock observes: "Daniel saw one like the Son of Man, not the Son of Man Himself. When long ago (iam olim) Christ appeared in human form to the Fathers and Prophets He was not then clothed with true human flesh, but took on the form only and as a certain shadow of His future humanity. For the humanity of Christ was not already present from the beginning, but in time. But as Tertullian said, He at that time (olim) put on a specimen (prælusit) of His humanity." It may be that there is an element of truth in these interpretations, and, in so far as there is, the Figure does represent the *humanity* of the Messiah, who is to come.

What, precisely, is signified by this heavenly Being? According to Porphyry it referred to Judas Maccabaeus, whereupon Jerome very appositely asked how he came upon the clouds and how his kingdom was to be regarded as eternal.[3]

A common interpretation is to find the representation in the people of Israel. This view has been adopted by a long line of expositors of which M is one of the latest representatives. The principal argument employed in defence of this position is an appeal to vv. 18 and 27 where it is said that the kingdom is given to the saints of the Most High. It is further alleged that the symbolism of the vision supports this interpretation. To antiquity also appeal is made, for Ephraim of Syria had found the primary reference to be to the Jews, although he also believed that the prophecy was fulfilled in our Lord.

The earliest interpretation and the one adopted in this commentary is the Messianic. In Enoch (37-71) the phrase occurs 14 times, and this view has generally been adopted by the Rabbis. However, the conclusive proof that this view is correct is the application of the title to Himself by our Lord, e. g., Matt. 25:31; Mk. 10:45, Luke 17:24 etc. (See SDJ, pp. 228-256 for a discussion of our Lord's use of the title).

In recent times the Messianic interpretation has really found support in the appearance of what may be called the mythological view. In brief this position regards the heavenly Figure as belonging to tradition. The Figure stands for a person (the Divine conqueror), not for the people, who are called the saints. At least, therefore, this view has the merit of insisting upon the "individualistic" as over against the collectivistic interpretation of the passage.

In conclusion it may be said that the Figure like unto a Son of Man, represents a supernatural Person, for He comes with the clouds, is conducted to the throne of God, and a universal and eternal kingdom is given Him. In so far as the word "man" has reference to man as frail and weak, and in so far as the preposition "like" may indicate the pre-incarnate state of the heavenly Figure (I am not ready entirely to reject

---

3 "Docere debet quomodo cum nubibus coeli veniat, quasi Filius hominis,—et potestas eius aeterna sit."

the interpretation of Tertullian and others) the humanity of the Person is also indicated. It was in the state of His humiliation that our Lord spoke of Himself as Son of Man. Yet, thereby, He indicated, as strongly as could be desired, His Deity. The employment of this title by Jesus Christ is one of the strongest evidences that He attributed Deity to Himself. *He was brought*]—The idea is that He was brought near or presented. It is a royal audience. Those who bring Him near are evidently angels or ministering spirits. The tremendous majesty of the scene serves to bring to the fore the importance and dignity—yes, the Deity—of the Person Who comes with the clouds of heaven.

Vs. 14. *And to Him there was given dominion and honor and sovereignty; and all peoples, nations and tongues serving Him; His dominion an everlasting dominion that does not pass away, and His kingdom that is not destroyed.* The words dominion, honor and sovereignty, recall chs. 3:33; 4:31; 6:22. Zœckler suggests that upon this trilogy is based the doxology at the close of the Lord's Prayer, "For thine is the kingdom, and the power, and the glory forever. Amen." *And all peoples*]—The idea can perhaps best be expressed in English by means of the preposition "with." It is a kingdom with all people serving Him. It is a kingdom that is thus truly universal. *Serving*]—i. e., rendering religious service. It is true that this word is not always employed to designate religious worship, but surely the context shows that such is intended here. Cf. also vs. 27 and 3:12, 14, 17f.; Ezra. 7:19, 24. The eternity of the kingdom is stressed both in a positive and negative fashion. Attention should be called to the great commission, Matt. 28:18b-20, "All power is given unto me in heaven and in earth. Go ye therefore, and teach all nations, baptizing them in the name of the Father, and of the Son, and of the Holy Ghost: Teaching them to observe all things whatsoever I have commanded you: and, lo, I am with you alway, even unto the end of the world. Amen." When our Lord uttered these words, there can be no doubt but that He had in mind this passage in Dan. Herein is but further evidence that He regarded Himself as one with the supernatural Figure of the vision and therefore placed the imprimatur of His approval upon the Messianic interpretation of the passage.

b. vv. 15-28. The interpretation of the vision.

Vs. 15. *As for me Daniel, my spirit was anxious in the midst of my body, and the visions of my head were troubling me.* While yet in the vision Dan. brings forth his own person in order to show his reaction. His spirit, i. e., himself, is anxious and he is troubled because of the vision. It is not the sight of the various figures that troubled him, since, after the explanation in vs. 28 is given, he is still not at rest. It is, rather, the meaning symbolized by the figures which caused Dan. concern. *My body*]—lit., my sheath, the body being conceived as the sheath in which the spirit or soul is placed. By a slight change of the consonants M would read *on account of this*, but this change does not appear to me to have sufficient warrant.

Vs. 16. *I drew near to one of the attendants to ask him the certainty concerning all this; and he said to me that he would make me to know the interpretation of the things.* In order to learn the meaning of the vision, Dan. turns to one of the attendants, i. e., one of those standing by in attendance at the throne of God. *The certainty*]—i. e., the sure explanation. The translation—so he told me, and made me know (AV) is incorrect.

Vs. 17. *These great beasts that are four; four kings shall arise from the earth.* The thought, of the vs. may be paraphrased: As to these great beasts which, to be explicit, are four in number, the meaning is that four kings shall arise from the earth. *Kings*]—The concrete is used for the abstract *kingdoms*. The king embodies the characteristics of the kingdom which he represents. *From the earth*]—an explanation of the figure of the sea, vs. 3. From the words *shall arise* some expositors have concluded that the first empire must also be future. But this is unwarranted, for the Babylonian empire was already in existence at the time of this vision. The interpreter says little about the first three empires, but concentrates upon the fourth.

Vs. 18. *And the saints of the Most High shall receive the kingdom and shall possess the kingdom for ever, even for ever and ever.* The saints of God will receive from the Son of Man(to whom it was given) the eternal kingdom, and will hold it in possession for ever. *Saints*]—lit., the holy ones. The word is not of frequent occurrence, cf. also 8:24; Ps. 16:3; 34:9. Elsewhere a different word is employed. These saints are not the Jews in distinction from the heathen (Maurer), nor "the Godfearing Jews, who pass through the great tribulation and inherit the blessings and promises which God gave through their own prophets" (Gaebelein). This kingdom *cannot* be millennial, since it is clearly described as everlasting. The saints are the true members of the covenant nation, the elect of God "the congregation of the New Covenant, consisting of Israel and the faithful of all nations; for the kingdom which God gives to the Son of man will, according to vs. 14, comprehend those that are redeemed from among all the nations of the earth" (Keil). The word thus expresses the principle which God intended should characterize His chosen people, as in Ex. 19:6 "ye shall be to me a kingdom of priests, a holy nation"; also, Deut.

7:6. *Most High*]—i. e., God. A hebraizing pl. form is used, evidently to express majesty. *Shall receive*]—from the Son of Man. The word is used as in 6:1. They are not to establish or found the kingdom by their own power. *Shall possess*]—i.e., continued possession is indicated. *For ever*]—a superlative expression is used.

Vs. 19. *Then I desired to make sure concerning the fourth beast, that was diverse from all of them, exceeding dreadful, its teeth of iron and its claws of brass; it was devouring, crushing and stamping the residue with its feet.* Dan. is particularly interested in making sure (ascertaining) the meaning of the fourth beast. One detail is here added, namely, that the beast had claws of brass.

Vs. 20. *And concerning the ten horns which were on its head and another that came up and there fell from before it three; and (as for) that horn, it had eyes and a mouth speaking great things and its appearance was greater than its fellows.* Dan. here concentrates upon the little horn, describing its appearance as greater than that of its fellows. By this he may mean that the horn was actually larger in size. However, the fact that this horn is characterized as little seems to oppose the thought that it grows into great size, although this is certainly not conclusive. More likely, Dan. is referring to the haughty, swaggering appearance of the little horn.

Vs. 21. *I was beholding, and that horn was making war with the saints and prevailed over them.* The attention of Dan. is directed to the last phase of the beast's existence, the period of the little horn. If, therefore, the little horn has reference to the Anti-Christ, there is no point in referring these conflicts to the persecutions of the Caesars, as does Calvin. Rather the vs. directs our attention to the culmination of opposition to the people of God. Antiochus had afflicted the Church, and terrible persecution broke out at the time of our Lord's appearance upon earth. This persecution has never ceased, for it is stirred up by Satan himself. Wherever God's people have sought to carry forth His work and extend His kingdom, Satan has tried to interfere. Sometimes this antagonism has taken the form of bloody persecution; indeed, this has often been the case. But in the days of the little horn, this opposition will break forth as never before, as the Satanically inspired little horn, swaggering in its own pride and haughtiness, will make war with the Church. And, with respect to that Church, he will prevail, for the Church, in herself, cannot match the devices and power of those who employ Satan's methods in battle. Yet, against this Church the gates of hell shall not ultimately prevail, for the battle is the Lord's. Luther's hymn well expresses this truth:

"Did we in our own strength confide
Our striving would be losing,
Were not the right Man on our side,
The Man of God's own choosing.
Dost ask who that may be?
Christ Jesus, it is He!
Lord Sabaoth His Name,
From age to age the same,
And He must win the battle."

At the time of their greatest extremity God will intervene to deliver His people.

Vs. 22. *Until that the Ancient of Days came, and judgment was given for the saints of the Most High, and the time came and the saints possessed the kingdom.* The ultimate outcome is stated. The little horn prevails only until the time that the Ancient of Days comes and pronounces a judgment in favor of the saints, and the saints are in eternal and secure possession of the kingdom. It must be remembered that vv. 21, 22 are not an interpretation of the vision, but are part of the vision itself and serve the purpose merely of carrying on the history of the fourth beast and its relationship with the saints until the very end. The judgment here referred to is, I think, the final judgment, and not to be considered as identical with the judgments of vv. 11, 26 which latter refer to all judgment passed upon the world empires. *Judgment*]—not, as H suggested, a judgment made by the saints (cf. I Cor. 6:2), but a judgment rendered on behalf of the saints.

Vs. 23. *Thus he said, The fourth beast: A fourth kingdom shall be upon earth which shall be different from all the kingdoms, and shall devour all the earth, and shall stamp upon it and crush it.* The interpretation of the fourth beast now begins. This beast represents a kingdom (the fourth in the series represented by beasts in vv. 1-7). It is to be a kingdom different from all the preceding ones in that it shall conquer all the world (not merely Palestine, as Stuart argues, although the words are capable of this interpretation). The whole point of the ch. is to show that there is only one truly universal Kingdom, and that the others could be called such in name only. This kingdom, therefore, was mightier in its conquests than any which had preceded it.

Vs. 24. *And the ten horns, from the kingdom ten kings shall arise, and another shall arise after them, and he shall be different from the first ones and he shall bring low three kings.* From this very kingdom represented by the beast ten kings shall arise. As pointed out before (see on vs. 7) the number ten may be merely indicative of completeness and need not necessarily be taken as absolutely literal. "The symbolism of the description must be taken into account" (Allis). Furthermore, the kingdoms need not be regarded as strictly contemporary (who will maintain that they must all begin at the same time, as a strict interpretation of the symbolism would require?) These kingdoms, however, have this in common, that they exist during the second phase of the beast's history (See remarks on vs. 8).

According to Gaebelein, the ten horns correspond to the ten toes of the image of ch. 2. However, we must again remark that nowhere in Scripture is the image said to have ten toes. The Roman Empire, argues Gaebelein, is to be revived and divided into ten kingdoms. This, however, is to go contrary to the symbolism. The ten horns appear *on* the beast which is alive (cf. remarks on vs. 7 and note phrase *acting diversely*). The beast does not die and come to life again in its ten horns. Rather, these horns grow out of the *live* beast. They must, therefore, represent a second phase in its history, and not a revived form of the beast's existence. Gaebelein and other expositors of the same school are not at this point true to the symbolism. On the basis of Rev. 13:1-7 and 17:8 Gaebelein concludes that the Roman Empire which "ceased existing in 476 A. D." will "come into existence again when the times of the Gentiles come to their end." This revived Roman Empire will appear in the seven years (said to be the 70th week of ch. 9) which follow *after* the return of Christ for His saints, and the political revival will be "energized" by Satan himself. For the second 3½ years of this period Satan's power will be shown in this politically revived Roman Empire, in the appearance of the little horn of Dan. 7. At the end of the first 3½ years (the "middle of the week" of 9:27) this Gentile little horn will break the covenant which he has made with the Jews who have returned to Palestine. His true character now appears, since he is actually possessed of Satan. The refutation of this ingenious theory must be reserved until later. *Bring low*[—The third period of the beast's history is represented by the other horn, who will differ from the former ten horns in his aggressiveness and presumptuousness. He will bring low (i. e., put down) three of these kings. How this is to be accomplished is not stated, nor is sufficient revealed to enable us to identify with certainty this event when it transpires.

Vs. 25. *And words against the Most High will he speak; and the saints of the Most High he will wear out; and he shall think to change times and law; and they shall be given in his hand until a time and times and half a time.* The little horn will speak blasphemies against (lit., at the side of) the Highest. Speaking words, in itself, had an evil connotation (M), cf. Hos. 10:4. He will employ language in which he will endeavor to set God aside and will arrogate unto himself prerogatives which belong alone to

God, cf. 2 Thess. 2:4. Thus he will try to wear out (consume, afflict, humble) the saints of the Most High. His arrogance will be manifest in his intention to change times and law, "the foundations and main conditions, emanating from God, of the life and actions of men in the world" (Keil). *Times*]—not necessarily fixed times for religious observance, but times or seasons ordained by God (cf. Gen. 1:14; 17:21; 18:14). *Law*]—general laws or ordinances, as 2:13, 15; 6:6, 9; not necessarily religious law. The reference is not to Antiochus' edict to suppress the Jewish religion (I Macc. 1:41, 42), although Antiochus serves as one illustration of the manner in which the Antichrist will act. This act of Antichrist will affect all men, but specifically the people of God, and this tyranny will endure for a definite period, a time, times and the dividing of a time.

Those who regard the fourth beast as representing the Grecian Empire find the reference in Antiochus Epiphanes. Antiochus' persecution commenced with the mission of Apollonius against Jerusalem (June 168 B. C.) and the edict of Antiochus (I Macc. 1:20-53), and after a three year period of desecration, it ended with the rededication of the Temple on the 25th Chislev, 165 (I Macc. 4:52 ff. and GJV 1:200, n. 39; 208, n. 7 and M. M also calls attention to 2 Macc. 10:3 according to which the desecration lasted but two years). Assuming, however, that I Macc. is correct, we may ask, how is the half year to be accounted for? Some declare that it may have reference to the months preceding the actual profanation of the Temple. M suggests that it may be a current phrase for half a sabbatic lustrum as we say "half a decade," and thus the writer would be using a "cryptically expressed but fairly exact definition of time." But this does not do justice to the peculiar force of the expression —time, times and the dividing of a time.

Some equate this period with the 3½ years or 1260 days which are said to constitute the last half of Dan.'s 70th week, the period of the great tribulation. The refutation of this position must be reserved for the discussion of 9:24-27.

The purpose of these designations of time is to set forth more definitely the last stage of the power of the little horn as a period of time the length of which is measured by God. The word used is different from that in the first part of the vs. (seasons) and is in itself a chronologically indefinite expression. This fact shows that "'a chronological determination of the period is not in view, but that the designation of time is to be understood symbolically" (Keil). The view that the word means a year is based upon an appeal to Dan. 4:16; 12:7 and Rev. 13:5 and 11:2, 3 where the expressions 42 months and 1260 days are employed interchangeably. However, as the exposition has shown, the "seven times" of 4:16 need not represent seven years, and it is surely questionable whether in other passages periods of time are indicated which are to be taken chronologically. Hence, it seems best to take the present passage symbolically. What, however, is the meaning of the symbolism? Apparently the expression is intended to indicate the half of seven times, but, if so, what is the meaning of this half? This period, a time, times and half a time, apparently stands for a period of testing and judgment which for the sake of God's people, the elect, will be shortened (cf. Matt. 24:22). A "septenarius truncus" (Keil). This oppression appears for a time, then extends itself for two times. It would then seem that it should continue for double two times or four times (i. e., seven times all told). However, it does not thus extend itself longer and longer. Instead of the four times it breaks off—merely half a time. "The proper analysis of the three and a half times in that the periods first mount up by doubling them, and then suddenly decline, shows that the power of the horn and its oppression of the people of God would first quickly manifest itself, in order then to come to a sudden end by the interposition of the divine judgment" (Kliefoth in Keil).

Vs. 26. *And judgment was given, and there was taken away its power to destroy and to annihilate unto the end.* The judgment is here described only as it has reference to the destruction of the little horn, the Antichrist. The power of the little horn for evil was taken away. *Unto the end*]—i.e., for ever.

Vs. 27. *And the dominion and sovereignty and greatness of the kingdoms under all the heavens were given to the people of the saints of the Most High; their kingdom (is) an eternal kingdom, and all sovereignties shall serve and obey them.* This vs. describes the same thing as vs. 18. Thus, the history of the beast culminates in the destruction of the little horn in whom the beast character came to its strongest expression, but the people of the saints of the Most High will receive the kingdom eternally. *Their kingdom*]—the antecedent is *people,* not *Most High.* However, this vs. cannot be employed to identify the heavenly Figure like a Son of Man. That Figure is presented as a truly supernatural Being, whereas such is not the case with the saints. It is simply stated that the kingdom which is given them is eternal, and that all dominions will serve and obey them. Calvin rightly remarks, "hence, we are deservedly called kings, because he (Christ) reigns, and as I have already said, language which is exclusively appropriate to him, is transferred to us in consequence of the intimate communion existing between the head and the members." What is meant is the "empire of the Church" (Calvin). The antecedent is taken by many as the Most High, so e. g., AV, but this is incorrect grammatically. The conquest referred to is spiritual in nature, "—God's royal sceptre went forth from Jerusalem, and shone far and wide, while the

Lord was extending his hand and his authority over all the regions of the world" (Calvin).

* * * *

These vv. i.e., 15-27 appear to teach that toward the close of the present age the power of the little horn will be manifested. The Anti-Christ will prevail against the elect of God, becoming ever stronger and stronger. Against him God's people will not be able to stand. Suddenly however, his power will be cut off, and the Lord Jesus Christ shall return from heaven. The saints who have belonged to the kingdom of the Son of Man (i. e., all who are truly the elect) shall receive this kingdom and possess it eternally. May all who read these lines give diligence to make their calling and election sure.

* * * *

Vs. 28. *Unto this point (is) the end of the matter; as for me Daniel, my thoughts greatly troubled me, and my color changed upon me, and the matter I kept in my heart.* Here the entire vision and its interpretation ended. The thought may be paraphrased: thus far, or hitherto, or with this, the matter came to an end. The result upon Dan. is stated. His thoughts alarmed him, and the color of his countenance was changed, but he kept the matter in his heart. Cf. Luke 2:19,51. "Deep soul exercise followed from this vision for the prophet" (Gaebelein).

Of particular interest are the comments of Haller, who believes that we are here in the presence of ancient mythological tradition, and that traces of this ancient mythology appear in the ch. The kingdoms which follow one another, for example, correspond to the original mythological theory of periods. The lion stands for Babylonia, for which the composer had a predilection. The bear is the animal of the north in which one may perhaps discern an original embodiment of the north wind. Or possibly it has some relation with a constellation or with a prophetical passage (Isa. 11:7 ff.). The panther may possibly be regarded as a symbol of the south. Perhaps in the four wings there is some remembrance of a Babylonian demon form, whose four-fold character (Viergliedrigkeit) had some relation to the four corners of the world. These beasts arise from the sea, which causes one to think of the original sea that covered the earth. They are dragon figures, none of which belonged to the known animal kingdom, but, corresponding to the water, had the form of a fish (Fischnatur).

Haller is surprised that the division of Alexander's empire (represented, he thinks, by the fourth beast) is not mentioned in this ch., as in the corresponding vision (2:33ff.). Hence, he concludes that the author had not experienced this event but wrote just after the death of Alexander.

A later reader who knew the history of the Diadochi up to Antiochus IV, felt compelled to introduce the account of the ten horns and to stamp the fourth beast as a representative of the kingdom of the Seleucids. To a later editor Haller assigns vv. 7b, 8; 20-22; 24-25.

Haller thinks that Dan. is the first to carry through a scene of judgment in heaven. The condemnation of the fourth beast to fire is compared with Bertholet's statement that in Persian religion the serpent who represented evil would be burned in a flowing stream of metal. Persian thought concerned itself with the judgment, and Haller believes that the Jews had adapted certain Persian representations of judgment.

As to the heavenly Figure, Haller calls Him *Der Menschenæhnliche* Originally, this was a designation of an individual, but came in time to represent Judaism.

The subjective character of much of the above and the anti-theistic principles upon which it rests, must surely be apparent to a careful student. Once grant the unscientific assumption that the OT is to be treated just as any other book, and that Israel received no direct supernatural revelation, and we are compelled to discover the various features of Israel's religion among the religions of other people. This is precisely what Haller endeavors to do. He fails, because he is trying to explain the supernatural upon purely naturalistic grounds.

CHAPTER EIGHT

a. vv. 1-14. The vision of the ram and the he-goat.

1. vv. 1-2. *Introduction to the vision.*

Vs. 1. *In the third year of the kingdom of Belshazzar the king, a vision appeared unto me Daniel after that which had appeared to me in the beginning.* From this point until the end of the book the language is Hebrew. Gaebelein is in some error in asserting that the seventh ch. is in Hebrew (pp. 92, 9), although he does say, apparently unaware of the contradiction, that "chapters 2:4 — 7:28 are written in Aramaic" (p. 9). The reason for this change of language, it would seem, is that the author now intends to deal more in detail with the development of the kingdom of God. This ch., therefore, is not to be regarded as a mere appendage to ch. 7, for it brings forth information upon which ch. 7 had been silent. It treats of the second and third empires with a wealth of detail that was entirely missing in ch. 7. At the same time ch. 8 does stand in an integral relation to ch. 7. This is shown by the designation of time in vs. 1 and also by the discussion of the second and third empires which had already been introduced in ch. 7. *In the third year*]—i. e., two years after the vision of the night recorded in ch. 7. Hence, both chs. 7 and 8 are chronologically prior to the events recorded in ch. 5. Gaebelein suggests that this was the year in which the "feast of blasphemy was held and Babylon fell." At any rate, this vision occurred shortly before the events of the fatal night of ch. 5. *A vision*]—This vision was not a dream vision like that of ch. 7. "It is evident that the prophet was awake and conscious during this vision, from the language of the verses at the beginning and end of the section (vs. 2 and 27), and also from a comparison with the vision in chap. 10, which is analogous in form (see especially vs. 7-10)" (Zœckler). *Unto me Daniel*]—lit., *unto me I Daniel.* This idiom occurs both in the Hebrew and Aramaic portions of the book (cf. also 7:15). It does not serve to indicate that the writer wished to give himself out as Dan. (Ewald), but that Dan. continues to speak of himself in the 1st person (as in 7:15, 28—an incidental evidence for the unity of authorship of these two chs.). *In the beginning*]—At the first, as in 9:21, i.e., earlier. The reference is to the vision which appeared during the first year of Belshazzar's reign.

Vs. 2. *And I beheld in a vision; and it came to pass while I was seeing that I was in Shushan the fortress which is in Elam the province, and I beheld in a vision, and I was by the stream Ulai.* Was Dan. present in Susa in person or in spirit? Josephus (*Antiq.* X:11:7) relates (apparently ignoring the chronology of Dan.) that after his deliverance from the lion's den, Dan. built a fortress in Ecbatana in Media, which was a very attractive work and "wonderfully made" and which had existed even unto his own day. "In this fortress" he continues, "they bury the kings of Media, Persia, and Parthia even now, and the person to whose care it is entrusted is a Jewish priest; this custom is observed to this very day" (trans. by Marcus). The so-called Tomb of Dan. is standing even today "a little of W. of the mounds which mark the site of the ancient acropolis of Susa, on the opposite side of the Shaour" (Driver). Rosenmueller seems to assume, in connection with vs. 27 that Dan. was in Susa for the purpose of carrying on business for the king (ibique Belshazari regis in administrandis regni negotiis ministraret, ut infra Vs. 27. dicitur). But Dan. explicitly states that it was in a vision that he found himself in Susa, and hence we are to regard this as a presence in spirit. So the majority of expositors, e.g., Charles, Driver, Keil, etc., *Shushan*]—Cf. Neh. 1 and Esther. Susa was the chief capital of the Persian Empire. It "is the modern mound of Shush, 15 mi. S.W. of Dizful in Persia" (Paton). As early as the 3rd millennium B.C. Susa was capital of Elam and sanctuary of the goddess Shushinak. In 2280 B.C. it achieved independence from Babylonia. In the 12th century B.C. the king of Elam attacked Babylon and brought its spoil to Susa including the famous code of Hammurabi, which in 1901-02 was discovered in Susa by the French expedition. Later Susa formed alliances with Babylonia against Assyria, and about 625 B.C. was captured by Ashurbanipal. With the downfall of Assyria, Susa became again the capital of Elam, and c. 596 B.C. (when Dan. was in Babylon) was taken over by the Medo-Persian migration. Under Cyrus Susa again became the chief capital, and it continued to be inhabited until the Middle Ages. "The vast size of the mounds that now mark its site is a witness to its antiquity and former glory" (Paton). *The fortress*]—This word is in opposition to *Shushan* and does not designate a part of the city, e.g., the acropolis (Paton), but characterizes the city itself. This is the constant designation of Susa in the OT (Neh. 1:1; Esther 1:2, 5; 2:3, 5, 8; 3:15; 8:14; 9:6, 11, 12). It "denotes a castelated building or enclosure, a castle, citadel, or acropolis" (Driver). *Elam the province*]—This vs. is not in conflict with Ezra 4:9 (Charles) which distinguishes between Shushanchites and Elamites, for in Ezra the purpose is simply to distinguish between dwellers in the city (Shushan) and dwellers in the province (Elam). Some have questioned the accuracy of the description by arguing that at this time Elam was not a province of Babylonia. However, it has been capably argued that such was the case. At any rate, if it was not a province of Babylon it was one of Media, so that the designation in itself is not inaccurate. Also, the word need not be taken in a technical sense (cf. Dan. 3:2). *By the stream Ulai*]—The word translated *stream* is rare in the OT occurring only here and in vv. 3, 6. The Ulai (Ass. *U-la-a-a,* Classical *Eulaeus*) is the stream whose waters Ashurbanipal says he "colored with blood like wool" (KB II:183). According to Pliny, it flowed close by Susa. Apparently it was a large artificial canal (c. 900 feet in breadth) which connected two other rivers, the Choaspes and the Coprates and passed by Susa on the north east.

2. vv. 3-8. *The vision itself.*

Vs. 3. *And I lifted up mine eyes and beheld and lo! one ram was standing before the stream and he had two horns, and the two horns were high, the one was higher than the other, and the higher was coming up last.* While in the vision Dan. lifted his eyes, cf. 10:5 and Gen. 31:10; Zech. 1:18; 2:1; 5:1, 9; 6:1. *One ram*]—The numeral serves to emphasize the contrast. The *two* horns are on the *one* ram. Hence, the numeral should not be regarded as an indefinite article, although this would be grammatically possible. The ram is an emblem of princely power, cf. Ezek. 34:17; 39:18; and (vs. 20) is explained as representing the kings of Media and Persia. "In *Bundehesch* the guardian spirit of the Persian kingdom appears under the form of a ram with clean feet and sharp-pointed horns" (Keil). Amm. Mar. (19:1) states that the Persian king, standing at the head of his army, bore the head of a ram (ipse praeibat agminibus cunctis, aureum capitis arientini figmentum, interstinctum lapillis, pro diademate gestans). *Before*]—probably on the eastern bank. *The one*]—From the first Dan. saw the two horns, but afterwards one of the horns grew higher than the other. These two horns symbolize the people of the Medes and Persians. The horn which grew higher than the other represents the Persians, who under Cyrus, were raised above the Medes. This vs. refutes the notion that the author of Dan. believed in the existence of a separate Median kingdom.

Vs. 4. *I saw the ram pushing to the west and to the north and to the south, and no beasts could stand before him, and there was none to deliver from his hand, and he was doing according to his will and acting greatly.* Dan. beheld the ram pushing (i.e., butting), thus symbolizing the rapid conquests of Cyrus and Darius. The ram pushes to the west, north and south, but not to the east, for not until the time of Darius did the Persians make many conquests in the east and these were not of a permanent nature. Keil conceives of the ram as standing on the western bank of a river which flows to the west of Susa, else the ram would be pushing against his own city. But this conclusion does not necessarily follow. The directions are merely intended to indicate the directions in which the Persian Empire made her greatest conquests; to the west, Babylonia, Syria, and Asia Minor, to the north, Armenia and the regions about the Caspian Sea, to the south, Egypt, Ethiopia, etc. *Beasts*]—i.e., kingdoms. We are reminded of the command "Arise and devour much flesh" of ch. 7. *His will*]—i.e., he did exactly as he wished, indicating arbitrary, despotic behavior. *Acting greatly*]—i.e., was becoming great, powerful. "The verse describes the irresistible advances of the Persian arms, especially in the direction of Palestine, Asia Minor and Egypt, with particular allusion to the conquests of Cyrus and Cambyses" (Driver).

Vs. 5. *And I was perceiving, and lo! a he-goat was coming from the west over all the earth and it was not touching the earth, and as to the goat it had a conspicuous horn between the eyes.* As Dan. was considering (i.e., discerning, paying attention to) the ram, he saw an he-goat (lit., goat-buck) come from the west without touching the earth. *He-goat*]—This represents the Grecian empire (vs. 21). The animal is a fitting symbol of power, cf. Zech. 10:3. *Over all the earth*]—In 1 Macc. 1:3 Alexander's conquests are thus described, "He went through to the ends of the earth and took spoils of a multitude of nations; and the earth was quiet before him." Thus the *extent* of Alexander's conquests is noted. Cf. the four wings of the leopard in 7:6. *Not touching the earth*]—These words indicate the *rapidity* of the conquests. Cf. the similar description of Cyrus (?) in Isa. 41:2, 3, and *Aeneid*, 7:806 "Ferret iter, celeres nec tingeret aequore plantas." *Conspicuous horn*]—lit., a horn of sight. According to vs. 21 the horn represents the first king of Graecia, i.e., Alexander. The horn was between the eyes, or on the forehead, the center of strength. This vs. is a remarkable description of the rapid progress of Alexander's kingdom.

Vs. 6. *And he came to the ram which had two horns which I had seen standing before the stream, and he ran against him with the wrath of his strength.* The vs. refers to Alexander's conquest of Persia. With the greatest of fury the he-goat runs up to the two-horned ram and throws him down. In the vision this occurs by the river Ulai, the seat of the ram's power, and serves merely to indicate the complete subjugation and downfall of Persia. It, of course, does not pretend to indicate the actual course of historical events by which Alexander obtained his victories. Keil has a remark which is worthy of consideration, "This representation proves itself to be genuine prophecy, whilst an author writing *ex eventu* would have spoken of the horn representing the power of the Medes as assailed and overthrown earlier by that other horn."

Vs. 7. *And I saw him approaching near the ram, and he was enraged against him, and he smote the ram and he broke his two horns, and there was no strength in the ram to stand before him, and he cast him to the ground and trampled him, and there was none to deliver the ram from him.* A remarkable statement of the utter destruction of the Persian Empire. *Was enraged*]—lit., to be embittered, i.e., maddened. *None to deliver*]—As others had once been helpless before the ram, so now it was defenseless before the he-goat. Alexander came to be known as "he of the two horns," for he had himself represented with two horns to prove that he was a son of the ram headed Ammon of Libya. Zœckler comments, "The figurative description is especially defective in not containing any tolerably clear indication of the fact that *several* vigorous blows by the ram, which were inflicted at different points (the first at Granicus, the next at Issus, and the final one in the neighborhood of Susa and the Eulaeus river), were required to break and destroy the Persian power. A Maccabean pseudo-Daniel would hardly have escaped the temptation to introduce more tangible allusions to these features."

Vs. 8. *And the he-goat was acting exceeding greatly, and when he became powerful, the great horn was broken, and there came up conspicuously four in place of it, to the four winds of heaven.* Because of the enormity of its conquests, the he-goat is represented as acting greatly, i. e., presumptuously, arrogantly. *Exceeding*]—lit., *unto excess.* The breaking of the great horn symbolizes the death of Alexander. In the vision the manner of the great horn is not stated. When the "acting greatly" of the horn had reached its climax, then was the horn broken. Apparently we are to understand that Divine Providence permitted the great horn to continue for a time and then broke it. *Conspicuously*]—the same word as in vs. 5, nevertheless, its construction is difficult. M regards it as a gloss; others would take it as a noun, *conspicuousness*, but then the word *horns* would have to be understood, e. g., the conspicuousness (appearance) of four horns. The Greek versions would read *other* by a slight *change of the text.* While recognizing the difficulties involved, I take the word adverbially, to denote the manner in which the four horns appeared. It is true that they do not figure prominently in the subsequent narrative, but they do at first make their appearance conspicuously. *Four*]—These four horns represent four kingdoms into which Alexander's empire was broken up. These are 1) Macedonia under Cassander, 2) Thrace and Asia Minor under Lysimachus, 3) Syria under Seleucus and 4) Egypt under Ptolemy. Originally there were five of the Diadochi, but Antigonus was soon overthrown, so that in reality there became four kingdoms. *Four winds*]—The four kingdoms well correspond to the four points of the compass. Thus, the vast empire, founded by Alexander, was dispersed to the four winds.

3. vv. 9-14. *The interpretation of the vision.*

Vs. 9. *And from one of them went forth one horn from littleness, and it became exceeding great, unto the south and unto the east, and unto the Desire.* From one of the four horns (that of Seleucus, whose history and that of his immediate successors is passed over) there comes forth another horn. Unlike the little horn of ch. 7 which uproots three of the previously existing horns and grows in their place, this horn grows out of one of the four horns. *Littleness*]—The Hebrew is very difficult. As it stands it can probably best be translated, *there went forth one horn from* (*the state of being*) *little.* Stuart takes it in a partitive sense *of smallness.* By emending one letter we get the reading *a little horn,* and by emending two letters we get *another horn, a little one.* However, the very difficulty of the language is probably an argument in favor of its originality. The meaning then is that from small beginnings the horn grew to great power. *The Desire*]—a designation of the land of Canaan, the land flowing with milk and honey, Ezek. 20:6. The title is based upon Jer. 3:19, and appears in full form in Dan. 11:16, 41. It is not geographically absurd (M) to use such a designation, for it simply serves to point out that the horn waxes great toward the south and east and particularly toward the land of promise. There seems to be general agreement among expositors that the one horn which goes forth from smallness is Antiochus Epiphanes. Thus, *Antiq.* X:11:7, "And there would arise from their number a certain king who would make war on the Jewish nation and their laws, deprive them of the form of government based on these laws, spoil the temple and prevent the sacrifices from being offered for three years. And these misfortunes our nation did in fact come to experience under Antiochus Epiphanes, just as Daniel many years before saw and wrote that they would happen" (translation by Marcus). The *south* is Egypt (Dan. 11:5 and 1 Macc. 1:16ff.—And he entered into Egypt with a great host—and he took the spoils of Egypt). The *east* is Elymais and Armenia (1 Macc. 3:31, 37; 6:1-4). The third land, Canaan, lies in between, as in Isa. 19:23ff.

Zœckler would not restrict the reference of the horn to Antiochus, but prefers to include "the anti-theocratic or anti-Christian governing power in the empire of the Seleucidæ." But it was Antiochus himself who became the great persecutor of the people of God, and the description given in this and the subsequent vv. is too definite to be employed as Zœckler wishes.

Vs. 10. *And it became great even unto the host of heaven, and it caused to fall to the earth some of the host, and some of the stars it trampled.* In the vision the seer beholds the horn become great, not only toward the south and the east and the Desire, but also to the very host of heaven. Some of these it cast down and trampled. How this was accomplished in the vision is difficult to conceive. If one contemplate the details of casting down the stars and trampling upon them, the vision becomes extremely grotesque. And yet the central thought as depicted in the simple words of the text, is remarkably forceful. 2 Macc. 9:10 speaks of Antiochus as "the man that a short while before thought himself to touch the stars of heaven." (The text of 2 Macc. is, I think, a reflection of the language of Dan.). *Host of heaven*]—the stars, as in Jer. 33:22. The figure is used tropically of the people of God, the saints. Cf. Dan. 12:3 (The imagery of Rev. 12:4 is probably also based upon this passage). These saints are the true believers under the Old Dispensation, members of the holy nation (Ex. 19:6). The host, therefore, does not refer to any one particular group of the Jewish people such as the Levites, or the chief rulers. Ephraim e.g., had applied the passage to the priestly order; Jerome to the sons of Israel who were strengthened by the help of angels. Keil has, I think, set forth the idea as well as anyone. He argues that God, the king of Israel, is called the God of hosts, i. e., stars or angels. The tribes of Israel are also called the hosts of the LORD (Ex. 7:4; 12:41). "As sons of Israel from the host of God." "As God, the King of this people, has His throne in heaven, so there also Israel have their true home, and are in the eyes of God regarded as like unto the stars" (Keil). Thus it is seen that the deeds of Antiochus against the saints of God were in reality wickednesses against Heaven itself. The saints of God, although living in this present evil world, are nevertheless citizens of Heaven. They are "strangers and pilgrims on earth" who "desire a better country, that is, an heavenly" (Heb. 11:13b, 16a). "Hence we derive this useful lesson, that we should bear it patiently when we are thrown prostrate on the ground, and are despised by tyrants and contemners of God. In the meantime our seat is laid up in heaven, and God numbers us among the stars, although, as Paul says, we are as dung and the offscourings of all things" (Calvin).

SRB declares that this passage (vv. 10-14) is "confessedly the most difficult in prophecy." It refers the passage to Antiochus but asserts that "in a more intense and final sense Antiochus but adumbrates" the blasphemy of the little horn of Dan. 7. "In Daniel 8:10-14 the actions of both 'little horns' blend" (SRB). I can see no exegetical warrant for such an interpretation. The present passage is describing the action of a horn that came up from the Grecian Empire; Dan. 7 is describing a "little" horn that came up from the fourth beast, which, according to SRB, is Rome. There is no warrant for regarding the horn of ch. 8 as typical of the little horn of ch. 7.

Vs. 11. *And unto the Prince of the Host he acted greatly, and from him was taken away the Continual, and the place of his sanctuary was cast away.* This and the following vs. present many textual difficulties. I do not think that these two vv. offer a description of what was seen in the vision but constitute, rather, a further account of the impious actions of Antiochus. The height of his sinful course was his wicked defiance of God Himself. *The Prince*]—not Onias, the high priest, but God. Right up to God (so the force of the verb and prep.) did Antiochus magnify himself. The second half of the vs. relates wherein this "acting greatly" consisted. It was in the removal of the Temple sacrifices. The *Continual*]—The word is taken by M and others to refer to the daily morning and evening sacrifices. However, this technical abbreviation occurs only here and in vv. 12, 13; 11:31; 12:11. Elsewhere in the Bible it is not to be found, although it does occur with frequency in the Talmud. I think that it should not be restricted to the daily morning and evening sacrifice, but that it is intended to include all that is of continual, i. e., constant, permanent, use in the Temple services. Thus, 1 Macc. 1:44-47 describes the fulfillment of this prophecy, "And the king sent letters by the hand of messengers unto Jerusalem and the cities of Judah, that they should follow laws strange to the land, and should forbid whole burnt offerings and sacrifice and drink offerings in the sanctuary; and should profane the sabbaths and feasts, and pollute the sanctuary and them that were holy." *Place*]—lit., that which was set up, erected, cf. Ex. 15:17; 1 Macc. 1:39,46; 3:45. Apparently Antiochus did not actually tear down the temple, although evidently he desecrated it to such a point that it was hardly fit for use.

Vs. 12. *And a host was given upon the Continual in transgression, and it cast truth to the ground, and it wrought and prospered.* In giving the above translation, I am merely setting forth what the text seems to mean. The sequence of the verbs, as the text now stands, is extremely difficult. *A host*]—This word has occasioned much difficulty among commentators. "Strength was given to him" (Jerome, Luther); "a time" (Calvin); "a warlike expedition was made or conducted against the daily sacrifice with wickedness" (Hitzig); "a host placed against the daily sacrifice on account of sin." The language of the text is difficult, but I follow Maurer, Hævernick, Keil, von Lengerke and others in adopting the reading, "and an host was given up together with the daily sacrifice, because of transgression." Thus, an host (i. e., many of the Israelites), on account of transgression (i. e., apostasy from God), will be given up (delivered up in transgression) together with (i. e., thereon, at the same time) the Continual sacrifices.

Further, the horn cast down truth (i. e., the objective truth, manifested in the worship of God) to the ground, and prospered in his actions. Cf. 1 Macc. 1:43-52, 56, 60 for the historical fulfillments.

Vs. 13. *And I heard one Holy one speaking, and one Holy one said to the one who was speaking, How long is the vision? The Continual and the desolating Transgression, the giving of both the sanctuary and host to be trampled?* Dan. hears a holy one(i. e., an angel) speaking, i. e., relating the contents of vv. 10-12. The vision has passed from that which is seen to that which is heard; cf. also Zech. 1:12ff. A second angel addresses the first, lit., *and one holy one said to so-and-so who was speaking,* and asks the length of the vision. The thought may be paraphrased as follows: How long is to be the vision, the Continual and the Transgression which desolates, the giving up of both (lit., and) the sanctuary and the host for trampling?

Vs. 14. *And he said unto me; Unto evenings and mornings, two thousand and three hundred, and the sanctuary will be vindicated.* The principal versions have *unto him* instead of the *unto me* of the Hebrew. The reply of the second angel is stated in this vs. This angel had been addressed in vs. 13 as *so-and-so.* The word thus translated (palmoni) is said by Gaebelein to mean "the wonderful numberer." Calvin also takes it as an identification of Christ in His mysterious incomprehensible nature. However, such interpretations are not justifiable. It is merely a certain angel who speaks and says that the desolation will continue for 2300 evenings—mornings. There are two principal interpretations of this designation:

1. *It means* 1150 *days.* This interpretation, as far as I know, was first set forth clearly by Ephraim of Syria, although it appears to have been held also by Hippolytus. Those who adopt it argue that the prophecy is related to the sacrifice of the Continual, i.e., the morning and evening sacrifices. 2300 such sacrifices therefore, would be offered on 1150 days. Many also find support for this position in an appeal to 7:25 which, they assert, means 3½ years, and the 1150 days, they say, is nearly equivalent to the 3½ years. But it is obvious that 1150 days do not equal 3½ years, even when these years be regarded as comprising only 360 days each or a total of 1260 days. This discrepancy is of course recognized, and Zœckler, possibly the ablest advocate of this view, thinks that the 1150 days represent a designed narrowing of the period. Appeal is also made to the 1290 and 1325 days of 12:11, 12, and these are regarded as representing a designed extension of the period. Zœckler concludes, "*These prophetic limitations of time correspond generally* to the events of the primary historical fulfillment of this vision in the Maccabæan era of oppression and revolt, *without being chronologically covered by them.*" Zœckler believes that the

correspondence of these predicted periods with the actual history is remarkably close, but that it is merely general or approximate. In other words, "the *prophetically-ideal* value of the numbers in question must be recognized."

2. *It means* 2300 *days*. This interpretation appears in the Greek versions, Jerome, most Protestant expositors and AV, and appears to be correct. In the first place any appeal to 7:25 cannot be regarded as justifiable, since, as the exposition (see in loc.) has shown, the expression *time, times and the half of a time* does not mean 3½ years. Furthermore, the reference in 7:25 is to something entirely different from that of the present passage. 7:25 is speaking of the persecution caused by the Antichrist, whereas this vs. has reference to the abominations of Antiochus. In order to arrive at the correct interpretation, we must first examine the phrase itself. There is no exegetical support for the position that the phrase *evening-morning* means that the evenings and mornings are to be counted separately, thus 1150 evenings and 1150 days. Zœckler says that the phrase is an asyndeton and admits that it "occurs *only in this place* as a designation of time." But he presents no exegetical support for his position; it is based upon assumption. Now it is true that the phrase occurs only here and is very similar to 2 Cor. 11:25 (night-day-a full day). Probably it is derived from Gen. 1, where an evening and a morning are reckoned as a full day, e.g., "And there was evening and there was morning, day one" (Gen. 1:5). In the OT, an expression such as "40 days and 40 nights" (Gen. 7:4, 12; Ex. 24:18; I K. 19:8 etc.) does not mean 20 days, nor does 3 days and 3 nights (Jonah 1:17; Matt. 12:40) mean either 6 days or 1½ days; it means 3 days. As Keil correctly argues "A Hebrew reader could not possibly understand the period of time 2300 evening-mornings of 2300 half days or 1150 whole days, because evening and morning at the creation constituted not the half but the whole day." Hence, we must understand the phrase as meaning 2300 days.

How are the 2300 days to be applied to the history of Antiochus? It may be that the beginning of the period is to be placed in the year 171 B. C., c. one year before the return of Antiochus from his second expedition to Egypt. In this year began the laying waste of the sanctuary. The termination would then be the death of Antiochus (164 B.C.). The 2300 days cover a period of six years and about 4 months. Keil believes that the number (being a little short of 7 years) possesses a symbolical meaning, namely, not quite the full duration of a period of divine judgment. It does seem to be used to cover approximately the period of the persecution under Antiochus. It does not exactly fit this period, since it is intended, as Zœckler rightly remarked, to carry a "*prophetically-ideal* value." Keil in my opinion, rightly sums up the matter by saying, "While by the period 'evening-morning' every ambiguity of the expression, and every uncertainty thence arising regarding the actual length of the time of the affliction is excluded, yet the number 2300 shows that the period must be defined in round numbers, measuring only nearly the actual time, in conformity with all genuine prophecy, which never passes over into the mantic prediction of historico-chronological data."

2300 days—approximately 171 B.C. to 165 B.C. the period of Antiochus' abominations.
1290 days (Dan. 12:11)—the 3½ years (168-165 B.C.) during which the Temple was used for heathen sacrifices.

Will be vindicated]—lit., justified. The thought is that the sanctuary will be restored. The word *sanctuary* is broader than *temple*, which is used in Dan. 9:17 and 11:31 and in vs. 11 of this ch. Hence, the thought here comprehends more than the purification and re-consecration of the temple. The sanctuary will be vindicated in being restored, thus showing that its period of desolation was unjustifiable.

b. vv. 15-27. The interpretation of the vision.

1. vv. 15-18. *Gabriel is commanded to instruct Daniel as to the interpretation.*

Vs. 15. *And it came to pass while I, even I Daniel, was beholding the vision, that I sought the meaning, and behold! there was standing before me as the appearance of a man.* As Dan. was beholding the vision he sought for its explanation. This he did, not by addressing a question to the angel, nor by a silent prayer to God, but by seeking to understand the vision in his mind. Suddenly there stood before him an angel in the likeness of a man. In reality he was not a man, but assumed this form merely in the vision. The word for man, gabher, is evidently chosen because of the name Gabriel (vs. 16). It denotes one that is strong or powerful.

Vs. 16. *And I heard the voice of a man amidst the Ulai, and he called and said, Gabriel, cause this one to understand the vision.* Dan. heard a human voice of one who was between the two banks of the Ulai, apparently hovering in the air, as in 12:6, 7. *Of a man*]—i.e., a human voice. Since this voice issues commands to Gabriel, Calvin believes that the Speaker is Christ. Stuart thinks that it was an angel high in station. The voice, it seems to me, although speaking *more humano* that Dan. might hear it, is that of supreme authority. In other words, it is God who speaks. *Amidst the Ulai*]—not between the two branches of the Eulaeus (Zœckler), but between its two banks, hence, above the river itself. *Gabriel*]—

Here and in 9:21 Gabriel is named; in 10:13ff. Michael is named. The only OT book in which angels receive names is Dan., and Gabriel and Michael are the only two who are named. So, in the NT, Luke 1:19, 26, Jude 9. The name probably means "man of God". *This one*]—i.e., Dan. The word is rare in Hebrew. M brings out its force "yon one".

Vs. 17. *And he came near where I stood, and as he came I was panic stricken, and I fell down upon my face, and he said unto me, Understand, oh! son of man, for with the time of the end is the vision.* In obedience to the command, Gabriel approaches Dan. This causes Dan. to be filled with terror, for as a sinful creature he could not bear the perfect holiness which appeared before him in the angel. Hence he falls down on his face, an acknowledgment of his own unworthiness. The angel addresses him as son of man, a phrase common to Ezek., in order to emphasize the weakness of mankind, and to point out that, despite this weakness, he, Dan., is to receive the Divine interpretation. The vision, it is said, has to do with the time of the end, and must, therefore, be understood. *The time of the end*]—This phrase is very difficult, but the key to its interpretation is to be found in the phrase *in the latter part of the indignation* (vs. 19). Thus, it refers to the end of time when afflictions or indignation are to be permitted upon Israel. It is the end of the OT period and the ushering in of the New. This particular vision had reference to *the time of the end* in that it "reaches only to *the end* of those special afflictions that are to come on the people of the Jews *before* the Messianic period, and which are made the subject of prophecy because of their importance." (Stuart). The phrase therefore does not mean the final period of earthly history (Zœckler), nor does it mean that the prophet was under the impression that at the end of the 2300 days the Messiah would appear to set up his kingdom (Maurer, Hitzig). Likewise untenable is the view that the time of the end has reference to the great tribulation, which is supposed to occur during the latter half of the 70th week (Gaebelein). This position is utterly without exegetical support.

Vs. 18. *And while he was speaking with me, I swooned upon my face to the ground, and he touched me, and made me to stand upright.* For the translation *swooned*, I am indebted to M. Because of fear at the Angel's speaking, Dan. completely lost consciousness and fell upon his face. Whereupon Gabriel touched him (cf. 10:9; Rev. 1:17) and caused him to stand, lit., upon my standing, i.e., upright, where he had stood before.

2. vv. 19-26. *The angel's interpretation.*

Vs. 19. *And he said, Behold! I am about to cause thee to know that which shall be in the last time of the indignation; for a term is the end.* The angel announces that he is about to make Dan. know that which will be in the latter part of the indignation. The *indignation* amounts to being a technical term for designating the wrath of God and His displeasure; cf. Isa. 10:5, 25; 26:20. "It plainly means here the *season of indignation* on the part of God, who gives up his people to punishment, because they have sinned against him" (Stuart). The subject of the present vision is to take place in the last portion of this period of wrath. In other words, when the abominations of Antiochus occur, it will be an evidence that the last time of the period of wrath has appeared. Hence, the pl. does not refer to the ultimate issue of all things, but to the *last time* which follows the Wrath (as manifested particularly in the Babylonian Exile). This *last time* is the appearance of Antiochus, after which the Messianic kingdom is to be established. Stuart well puts it, "That which is to take place near the close of the indignation-period, is the most prominent thing in the prophetic vision, and that which Daniel and the Jewish people were most interested to know." *A term is the end*]—lit., *since for a term (is) an end.* These words are difficult, but the meaning seems to be that the end, i.e., the *last time* of the first part of the vs., is to endure for an appointed period, a term. Or, it may be that the end is to come *at* an appointed period (Stuart). Either of these two constructions is possible. But *end* is to be taken as subject. Hence, as the text now stands, it should not be read, "for (the vision) is for the term of the end" (thus Keil). The thought of the entire vs. may be paraphrased as follows: "I am about to explain to thee that which shall take place during the latter part of the period known as the Wrath, for at an appointed time the End will be."

A note in *SRB* declares that the word "end" has reference both to the end of the Grecian empire and "prophetically, the end of the times of the Gentiles (Lk. 21.24; Rev. 16.14), when the 'little horn' of Dan. 7. 8, 24-26, the Beast, will arise—Daniel's *final* time of the end (Dan. 12.4, *note*)." But this is to read into the vs. what is not found there. Gabriel explicitly states that the vision has reference to the *latter part* of the Wrath (not the end of the times of the Gentiles). With this phrase, *latter part* he equates the word *end,* by using the word *since.* The vision has to do with what will take place in the *latter part* of the Wrath, says Gabriel, *since* (or *because, for*) *the end* is at an appointed time. The whole point of his explanation would be lost, and the vs. would be rendered nearly meaningless, if the note in the *SRB* is correct. The force of the vs. (if *SRB* is correct) would be somewhat as follows; "I shall cause thee to know (i.e., by way of explanation of vv. 1-18) what will occur in the last time of the indignation (i.e., the period after the Exile) since at an appointed time the end (of the times of the Gentiles) will come." Such an interpretation does not make good sense. Vs. 19b is an explanation of 19a (however 19b be translated), and *SRB,* Gaebelein and others of that school ignore this fact.

Furthermore, this interpretation causes a mingling of the contents of chs. 7 and 8 that is not justifiable. The "little horn" of 7 is the Antichrist; the "horn" of 8 is Antiochus. Ch. 7 lays its emphasis upon the fourth world empire; ch. 8 upon the 3rd. McKee (*Searching the Scriptures,* p. 126) appeals to a law of double reference which permits "blended references, some of which apply to the Great Tribulation at the end of the present age." But one is warranted in discovering such a double reference only when the language of the text and the analogy of Scripture demand it. Such is not the case here.

Lastly, the he-goat is explicitly said to be the king of Greece (vs. 21). Hence, it is utterly unjustifiable to fly in the face of this Divine interpretation, and to discover any reference whatsoever to the Roman empire of the future. In the light of the interpretation which the Holy Spirit places upon this symbolism, we must reject the views of Scofield, Gaebelein, etc.

Vs. 20. *The ram which thou sawest, he of the two horns,—the kings of Media and Persia.* The Medo-Persian empire, i.e., the successive kings of this empire. Neither here or elsewhere does Dan. conceive of an independently existing Median empire.

Vs. 21. *And the he-goat is the king of Javan and the great horn which is between his eyes is the first king.* The he-goat represents Javan, i.e., Greece. This is the name (Ionian) by which the Greeks were known to the Hebrews, cf. Gen. 10:2, 4; Isa. 66:19; Ezek. 27:13. The first king is Alexander the Great, who "ruled first over Greece" (I Macc. 1:1).

Vs. 22. *And the broken one—and four stood up in its place, four kingdoms from the nation shall stand, but not in its strength.* The thought may be paraphrased: as concerns the horn that was broken and the four standing in its place, this means that four kingdoms shall arise from the nation. *Nation*]—lit., *a nation,* for the definite article is not employed. It means, from the nation over which the great horn once ruled. The word nation is used not in a restricted sense, but broadly, to indicate the territory over which the king had ruled. *In its strength*]—i.e., not equipped with the strength of the first king.

Vs. 23. *And in the latter part of their kingdom, when the transgressors are come to the full, there shall stand up a king strong of countenance, and understanding riddles.* In the latter part of the kingdom (sovereignty) of the four horns, there will arise a king, i.e., Antiochus Epiphanes. "It was then a matter of historical fact, that the dominion of Antiochus Epiphanes, commenced during the *latter part* of the Syrian dynasty, whether we have respect to time or to the declining state of the government, in computing such a period" (Stuart). *Transgressors*]—The word may be pointed to read transgressions, and for this M makes out a strong case. The thought is: "when they have completed their transgressions." The transgressors are not the heathen, but the apostate Jews who introduced heathen rites among the Jews and built in Jerusalem a heathen gymnasium for their games. *Strong of countenance*]—i.e., hard, determined, unyielding, adamant. The word is used in a derogatory sense. The expression seems to be taken from Deut. 28:50, "A nation of fierce countenance, which shall not regard the person of the old, nor show favour to the young." In Prov. 7:13 the same verb is used, lit., "she strengthened her face", i.e., was impudent. *Understanding riddles*]—i.e., one who practised deceit, "a master of dissimulation, able to conceal his meaning under ambigious words, and so disguising his real purposes" (Driver). The king is to be a master of cunning, but also one that can not easily be deceived. This is not a compliment, but a severe censure upon the king's nature. Who is this king? According to this vs. he is one who will arise in the latter time of the sovereignty of the four kingdoms (vs. 22) represented by the four horns which arise in place of the first broken horn (vv. 21, 22). Since the first broken horn is said to be the first king of Grecia (vs. 21) the king of strong countenance can only be Antiochus Epiphanes. Calvin thus correctly says, "Without the slightest doubt, he implies the iniquity of Antiochus by this phrase" (i.e., strong countenance). And surely the description herein given well applies to Antiochus, whom M has characterized as "... a master in Machiavellian arts, master-diplomatist, able to deceive 'the very elect'."

Hence, it is strange to find Gaebelein teaching that this king is not Antiochus; but rather "the Assyrian," "the king of the North." Now Gaebelein does not refer to the historical Assyrian, but to an alleged enemy of the Little Horn of Dan. 7 who, after the Jews have made a covenant in Palestine with the Little Horn of Dan. 7, "makes his appearance and rushes against the people and their cities." As a hater of Judah "he persecutes the nation, while the beast, the little horn of Daniel 7, persecutes the Saints." Gaebelein thinks that there are other references to this future "Assyrian," e.g., Isa. 8:7, 8; 10:5-34; 14:24, 25; 30:31-33; Micah 5:1-7; Joel 2; Ps. 74:1-10; 79. Gaebelein continues, "The prophecy in the chapter before us makes it plain that this desolator will arise from one of the divisions of the Grecian empire. That territory is held now by Turkey. When the time of the end comes the greatest upheavals will take place both in Asia Minor and in the surrounding countries. What changes will then take place, whether a great Russian Czar or some other one will accomplish the great eastern confederacy remains as a secret with God."

This strange view flies in the face of the express statements of Scripture.

1. Scripture explicitly says that the king of fierce countenance will arise in the latter time of the sovereignty of the four kingdoms (vs. 22). According to Gaebelein, he will arise long after the end of the sovereignty of these four kingdoms.

2. Gaebelein bases this view upon a misconstruction of the words "last end of the indignation". (See commentary upon vs. 19).

3. The other passages of Scripture to which he appeals do not bear the interpretation which he places upon them, as may be shown by a careful study of the passages in question.

Vs. 24. *And his power shall become strong but not by his power, and marvellously shall he destroy, and he shall prosper and accomplish, and he shall destroy powerful ones and the people of the Saints.* The vs. describes the tremendous power exhibited by Antiochus. *Not by his power*]—These words are regarded as a gloss by M, Charles, etc. and so are omitted. They do not appear in Th. and may not be original in the Greek. Yet they seem to have a proper force. They do not imply a contrast between the king's strength and cunning, as though to suggest that he became strong enough through cunning rather than strength, (Stuart), but rather indicate that his attainments were under the providence of God. Calvin refers the antecedent to Alexander. Yet, I think that if the words be allowed to stand, they refer to the king. *Marvelously shall he destroy*]—lit., in respect to wondrous things he shall destroy, i.e., to a remarkable, extraordinary degree. The word is here used as an adverb, as in Job 37:5. *Powerful ones*]—his rival claimants of the throne (Hitzig), warlike enemies over whom he triumphs (Zœckler), many Israelites (Kliefoth), elders of Israel, but the phrase probably has a general reference to all who are powerful, particularly political enemies. *People of the Saints*]—The nation Israel, cf. 7:25. This phrase is not epexegetical of *powerful ones,* but is perhaps used in direct contradistinction. Not only will he destroy powerful ones such as his political enemies, but also the Israelitish nation, the nation in which the Saints live.

Vs. 25. *And on his understanding he shall cause deceit to prosper through his hand, and in his heart he shall do greatly, and in security he shall destroy many; and against the Prince of princes shall he stand, and without hand shall he be broken.* Because of his cleverness or cunning, the king will cause deceit to prosper. *On his understanding*]—i.e., upon the basis of his understanding. The word is here used in a bad sense, cunning. Since he so well understands how to employ deceit, he can cause it to prosper. *In his heart*]—His heart was full of pride and so he devised plans which were presumptuous and self-glorifying. *In secur-*

ity]—i.e., false security, when men feel there is no need to be on guard. Upon the basis of a similar idiom in Aramaic, many render the words *unexpectedly*, and this at least serves to bring out the idea. While men are at ease, this king suddenly comes upon them. Cf. 1 Macc. 1:10 for the historical fulfillment. *Prince of princes*]—i.e., God Himself, Who is spoken of as Prince of the host in vs. 11. *Without hand*]—i.e., without human hand. He has risen up against God and by God he will be overthrown. These words are for the comfort of the saints who, being the meek, cannot in themselves contend with enemies such as Antiochus. Because of our sins God permits such tyrants to arise and harass His church. "It is therefore no matter of surprise, if, instead of one Antiochus, God should raise up many who are hardened and invincible in their obstinacy, and in their cruelty make many attempts with clandestine arts, and plot for the destruction of the Church" (Calvin). But when such things occur, let us trust in God. The battle is His, and the overthrow of the enemy will often be without hand. Tyrants like Antiochus cannot halt the working of the efficacious grace of God.

Vs. 26. *And the vision of the evening and the morning which has been told is true; and thou! seal up the vision, for (it is) for many days.* The vision was revealed to Dan. in words, i.e., it was told (spoken), rather than seen. Here it is solemnly declared that what has been told Dan. of the vision of the evening and morning is true. Hitzig thought that this confirmation was to make the book falsely appear as if it were old (Die Worte halten einfach den fingirten Standpunkt inne). Rather it "much more is fitted to serve the purpose of strengthening the weakness of the faithful, and giving them consolation in the hour of trial" (Keil). Cf. also 10:1; 12:1; Rev. 19:9; 21:5; 22:6.

Since the prophecy was for a long time (many days) Dan. was to shut up the prophecy. This does not mean that he was necessarily to keep it secret, but that he should preserve it. "Preserve the revelation, not because it is not yet to be understood, also not for the purpose of keeping it secret, but that it may remain preserved for distant times" (Kliefoth). The idea of some that these words are intended to explain why the prophecy had never been heard of until the days of Antiochus are certainly incorrect. This makes the author guilty of deliberate falsification and misrepresentation which cannot be excused on the basis of mere appeal to the nature of Apocalyptic. Furthermore, the idea that Dan. had never been heard of before the time of Antiochus is based upon the fact that today there are no known extant references to the book which come from before this time. This is not sufficient evidence upon which to base the assumption that the prophecy was not known until this time. If a Maccabean author inserted these words for the purpose of explaining why the book had not previously been known (as some critics maintain), he was a dishonest person, and the book he composed is of no value for the edification of the saints of God.

3. vs. 27. *Daniel's sickness.*

Vs. 27. *And I Daniel was done with, and I was sick for (several) days, and I arose and did the business of the king, and I was astonished at the vision and without understanding.* The psychological effect of the vision upon Dan. is stated. So overcome was he, that for some days he was sick before he could continue the king's business. *Done with*]—The verb is the same as that used in 2:1. It is a peculiar expression and apparently means exhausted, worn out. *Rose up*]—i. e., from the bed of sickness. *The business*]—What this business was is not stated. *Without understanding*]—It seems to me that this is intended to refer to Dan. himself, and not, as AV, *and none understood it.* The contents of the vision and its interpretation remained firmly fixed in Dan.'s mind and greatly perplexed him, for, as it was a vision that had to do with many days that were yet to come, he did not understand it. The AV rendering is grammatically possible, but since Dan. is the chief character, the reference here seems to be to him. This does not exclude the fact that when Dan. related the vision to others, they too did not understand. Cf. also 12:5 "I heard and could not understand," which seems to support the translation here adopted.

— — — — —

With one exception Haller's remarks upon ch. 8 do not call for particular comment. This exception is found in the assertion that the hatred of the author toward Antiochus is shown by the fact that every time he speaks of him, his pen runs away (Wie gluehend der Hass gegen ihn ist, zeigt der Umstand, dass dem Verfasser jedesmal, wenn er von ihm spricht, gleichsam die Feder durchgeht v. 9-12). This statement cannot be permitted to pass unchallenged, for it is utterly incorrect. The vv. to which Haller appeals merely relate the powerful growth of the horn, not only to the south, east and north, but also to the Prince of heaven, and indicate the defiant activity of Antiochus toward God. There is here a sober description of fact, and an utter absence of fanaticism or hatred. Nowhere does the unscientific character of Haller's commentary appear more clearly than at this point.

CHAPTER NINE

a. vv. 1-3. Introduction.

Vs. 1. *In the first year of Darius the son of Ahasuerus from the seed of the Medes, who was made king over the kingdom of the Chaldeans.* As to the indentity of Darius, see 6:1. *Ahasuerus*]—The name occurs elsewhere, in Ezra 4:6; Esther 1:1, etc. The word is based upon the Persian. Who this individual was, we do not know. *Seed of the Medes*]—This king was of Median ancestry. *Made king*]—Some would translate by the intransitive, became king, which may be correct, since it is supported by the versions. If the passive be retained, it may mean that Darius was made king by God, but more likely he received the office as a viceroy from Cyrus.

Vs. 2. *In the first year of his reign I Daniel perceived in the Books the number of the years that the word of the Lord was unto Jeremiah the prophet to complete with respect to the desolations of Jerusalem seventy years.* The mention of the date is deliberate in order to call attention to the time. Babylon was now fallen and the liberating country was in the first year of its sovereignty. The time had come in which to expect the end of the captivity. *Perceived*]—i. e., observed, marked. *The Books*]—The phrase does not indicate a private collection of sacred books, nor the canonical books of the Prophets. Stuart takes it to refer to the book of Jer. In 25:13 Jer. calls his prophecy of the 70 years "this book." These two, thinks Stuart, may be called "the books." But this is over refinement. It is better to take the word in its simple sense as referring merely to a group of writings among which the prophecies of Jer. were to be found. Probably the term applies broadly to the Scriptures, those sacred books which were recognized as authoritative. It should be noted that there is nothing whatsoever in this phrase which lends support to the idea that the canon was closed. These books, because they were regarded as inspired, were accepted as Divinely authoritative. (See the author's article "The Authority of the Old Testament" in *The Infallible Word,* Phila., 1946, pp. 53-87). *The number*]—object of I perceived. The reference is probably to Jer. 25: 9-11, "And this whole land shall be a desolation, and an astonishment; and these nations shall serve the king of Babylon seventy-years" (vs. 11), and also to Jer. 29. *That the word*]—lit., which the word. The antecedent is *number. To complete*]—The thought may be paraphrased: "With respect to the desolation of Jerusalem, 70 years must be completed." This desolation began with the captivity of Dan. and the first devastation of Jerusalem in 606 B. C., the third year of Jehoiakim. Hence, in the first year of Darius, the period of desolation would be almost expired. This seems to be the reckoning in 2 Chr. 36:21-23; Ezra 1:1 ff.

Many, however, regard the destruction of Jerusalem in 587 as the *terminus a quo*. But if this were correct Dan. would not now in the first year of Darius feel that the time was nearing its completion. This view would not explain why he gives himself over to prayer.

Vs. 3. *And I set my face unto the Lord God to seek with prayer and supplication in fasting and sackcloth and ashes.* As yet Dan. beheld no signs that liberty to return to Judah had come, he turned to earnest prayer. *I set my face*]—It may be, as M suggests, that these terms are reminiscent of old cultic usage. If so, however, they have entirely lost such connotations here. Dan. does not mean that he is directing his face toward Jerusalem (Stuart), but merely that he is turning his face toward the Lord God. The covenant name is not used in this vs., although Dan. prayed to the covenant God. He seeks the Lord, who is *the* God, i. e., the true God of heaven and earth. *In fasting*]—Thus Dan. exhibited his grief and mourning over sin and confessed his unworthiness of receiving Divine mercy. These are marks of contrition; cf. Jonah 3:5, 6; Ezra 8:23; Neh. 9:1; Esther 4:1, 3, 16; Job 2:12. "All these were outward signs of internal humiliation and penitence" (Stuart).

b. vv. 4-19. The prayer of Daniel.

Vs. 4. *And I prayed to the LORD my God and made confession, and I said, Ah! Lord, the great and dreadful God, who keepeth covenant and lovingkindness to those who love him and to those who keep his commandments.* Dan. has been meditating over the number of years of the desolation of Jerusalem. The predicted time is nearly at an end and there is in sight no hope of return to Jerusalem. Because he well knows that the exile has come upon the people in punishment for their sins, he turns to the LORD on behalf of himself and his people and engages in deep confession of sin and supplication for mercy. His main concern, therefore, is not to know the precise meaning of the number seventy; it is to implore the Divine pardon for his and the people's sins. This disposes of the objection that the theme of the prayer does not correspond to the context.

The prayer consists of two principal parts: 1) an acknowledgment of sin and guilt (vv. 4-14) and 2) a plea for mercy. The 1st part further divides itself into a) 4-10 a statement of sin and guilt, and b) 11-14 God's punishment because of sin and guilt. *The LORD*]—Dan. acknowledges the LORD to be his own God and thus declares the existence of a personal relationship. God only hears the prayers of those who truly know Him. *Great and dreadful*]—This language also occurs in Neh. 1:5 which has led some critics to think that Dan. borrows from Neh. and therefore must have been written at a much later time, namely, the Maccabean age. But the expression finds its roots, as Keil has indicated, in Deut. 7:9, 21. It also occurs in the prayer in Neh. 9:32 (cf. Deut. 10:17). It should be noted that since the prayer in Neh. 9 is more expanded in form than that of Dan. 9, the dependence, if any, is on the part of Neh. and not of Dan. By this expression, *great and dreadful,* the fact is brought out that God by mighty acts punishes sinful peoples. The thought probably comes to Dan.'s mind as he reflects upon the present condition of his people. *Keepeth covenant*]—God is faithful to remember His promises made toward His chosen ones. *Lovingkindness*]—By keeping the covenant God manifests lovingkindness to those who love Him. This love to God is exhibited by the keeping of His commandments.

Vs. 5. *We have sinned and done perversely and done wickedly, and we have rebelled and turned aside from thy commandments and thy judgments.* Dan. uses various words in order to acknowledge all kinds of sin. In I K. 8:47 Solomon had spoken of sin, iniquity and wrongdoing as "an exhaustive expression of a consciousness of sin and guilt" (Keil). *Sinned*]—i.e., we have wandered astray from the right. *Done perversely*]—i.e., unrighteously. *Done wickedly*]—in rebellion against God. To these words Dan. adds *we have rebelled.* His series reaches its climax in the phrase *we have turned aside,* a form of expression being used in the Hebrew which emphasizes the action. In all this confession of sin, Dan., who had lived most of his life in Babylon and was now an old man, by using the pronoun *we,* identified himself with his people. This is the more remarkable, when we consider how pure was his character.

"And they who fain would serve Thee best
Are conscious most of wrong within."

Vs. 6. *And we have not harkened unto thy servants the prophets who spake in Thy Name unto our kings, our princes and our fathers, and unto all the people of the land.* The guilt of the people becomes greater, since God had sent the prophets to them to reveal His will. In spite of their clear utterances, however, the people rebelled. This sin, therefore, is not one of ignorance, but of wilful disobedience. That Dan. has been meditating upon the book of Jer. is shown by the fact that the language of this vs. is reminiscent of Jer. 26:5; 44:17, 21. The same language is later used in Neh. 9:32, 34 and Ezra 9:7, with the addition of "our priests." This expansion shows that Ezra and Neh. are later than Dan., and characterizes the age when the priests were active, just as the omission is well suited to the time of the exile when the priestly office was suspended. *Who spake*]—These were true prophets who clearly indicated that they were from God. They did not carry on their work in a corner, but preached to all the people, high and low. Hence, the enormity of the nation's sin. All, without exception, are guilty.

Vs. 7. *To thee, oh! Lord, is righteousness, and to us shame of face, as at this day, to the men of Judah and to the inhabitants of Jerusalem, and to all Israel, those near and those far off, in all the lands whither thou hast driven them, because of the treachery wherein they have dealt unfaithfully against Thee.* To God belongs righteousness, i. e., perfect righteousness which is manifested in all His dealings with Israel. In sending to them His prophets, warning them of sin, and particularly, in sending the exile as a punishment, God is vindicated as right. To the sinful people, however, belongs shame of face, i. e., confusion, because of the consciousness of punishment which is well deserved. *As at this day*]—i. e., as present circumstances exemplify. *To us*]—i.e., the men of Judah, cf. 1:3, 6. *All Israel*]—not the ten tribes (Keil), for in 1:3, 6 Israel and Judah are used interchangeably, but all of God's people—members of the Israelitish nation—who were not in Babylonia but were scattered elsewhere throughout the world. The entire nation (northern and southern kingdom alike) has been guilty of faithless dealing toward God, hence, as the present day shows, whether it be in Babylon or far away it is a reproach to all the world, conscious that its punishment is well deserved. What a tragic confession when we consider that Israel was to be a light to all the world.

Vs. 8. *Oh! Lord, to us is shame of face, to our kings, to our princes and to our fathers who have sinned against thee.* Dan. repeats the thoughts of 7a in order to set out in bold relief the sinfulness of the people as over against the Divine compassion which he stresses in vs. 9.

Vs. 9. *To the Lord our God belong compassion and forgiveness, for we have rebelled against Him.* We have rebelled against God and therefore are thrown upon His mercy which we so desperately need. *Compassion*]—lit., the compassions and the forgivenesses. "The plur. form of these nouns denotes intensity in the manifestation, or the continued and extended exercise of these qualities or attributes" (Stuart). However, the words are probably best translated as above.

Vs. 10. *And we have not hearkened to the voice of the LORD our God, to walk in his laws, which he has set before us through the hand of his servants the prophets.* A further acknowledgement of guilt. The laws of God are those instructions which He has set forth before His people.

Vs. 11. *And all Israel have transgressed thy law and turned aside so as not to hearken to thy voice, and there has been poured out upon us the curse and the oath which is written in the law of Moses the servant of God, for we have sinned against him.* Not hearkening to God's voice and transgressing His law (here the Pentateuch) are equated. By transgressing the Law Israel has not hearkened to God's voice. Therefore, the curse, reinforced with an oath, has been poured out as from vials of wrath (cf. Rev. 16:1-4), like a rain of fire, cf. Nah. 1:6; Gen. 19:24; Jer. 7:20. *Curse and oath*]—Deut. 29:20; Lev. 26:14 ff.; Deut. 28:15 ff.

Vs. 12. *And he has established his words which he spake concerning us and concerning our judges who judged us that he would bring upon us a great evil, so that there has not been done under the whole heaven what has been done with Jerusalem.* God has established (lit., made to stand, i. e., confirmed) His word (cf. Neh. 9:8) by bringing about the exile (cf. Jer. 35:17; 36:31). *Judges*]—an expression which includes the leaders of the people and which sums up the officials of vv. 6 and 8. Jerusalem, the city of the great king, because of her unfaithfulness, has been made an example to all the world.

Vs. 13. *Even as it is written in the Law of Moses, all this evil has come upon us, and we have not mollified the face of the LORD our God by turning from our iniquities and having discernment in thy truth.* This vs. supports the statement of vs. 11 by a further appeal to the Pentateuch. *All this evil*]—i. e., the exile and its attendant evils. *Mollified*]—For this translation I acknowledge indebtedness to M. The verb means "to make the face sweet," used both with man (e. g., Ps. 45:12) and God (e. g., Jer. 26:19) as object. *By turning*]—Had we turned from our iniquities and given heed to God's Law, He would have removed these evils from us. The vs. does not teach that salvation is by works or that God is rendered propitious toward the sinner, because of human works of righteousness. But when God's people sin grievously, He must send upon them evils as chastisement. If they continue in their wicked way, the chastisement must also continue. But when they repent and turn from their sin, He will show His favor to them by removing the chastisement. This is in no sense inconsistent with the doctrine of salvation by grace. *Having discernment*]—i.e., acquiring insight into God's Law. The RV renders *deal wisely through*, which is also a possible translation. It would then mean that the wise dealing was shown by turning from sin to obey the truth.

Vs. 14. *And the LORD hath watched upon the evil and has brought it upon us, for righteous is the LORD our God in all his works which he has done, but we have not hearkened unto his voice.* The Lord watched (i. e., was vigilant) to bring the evil upon His people at the proper time. The idea is taken from Jer. 1:12; 31:28; 44:27; etc. *Righteous*]—lit., on the ground of all His works. God's works, which He has done (or doeth, as Zœckler) bear witness that He is righteous. Despite this fact, however, we have not hearkened unto Him, and our guilt, therefore, is all the greater.

Vs. 15. *And now, oh! Lord our God, who hast brought forth thy people from the land of Egypt with a strong hand, and hast made Thee a Name as this day; we have sinned; we have been wicked.* Dan. now makes the petition itself "in its intensity and importunity, which increase from sentence to sentence" (Zœckler). He bases his petition upon the great act of mercy accomplished by the LORD in the exodus from Egypt. It was this mighty act of deliverance by which the LORD made for Himself a name among the nations. Hence, Isa. and Jer., for example, could ground their pleas for favor upon the LORD'S Name, Isa. 63:11-15; Jer. 32:20ff. It was the historical act of redemption which distinguished the LORD from false gods, and gave Him a Name, as the covenant God of deliverance. Stuart well sums up the thought of the prayer, "O God, who in times past hast wrought wonderful deliverances for thy people, and thereby acquired a glorious name—repeat thy wonderous doings, and add to the glory which thou hast already acquired! As thou didst bring us out of exile in Egypt, so also bring us out of exile in Babylon."

Vs. 16. *Oh! Lord, according to all thy righteousness, let turn now thine anger and thy wrath from thy city Jerusalem, the mount of thy holiness, for by means of our sins and by means of the iniquities of our fathers, Jerusalem and thy people are become a reproach to all round about us.* God's righteousnesses are the acts which vindicate or justify Him and show Him to be righteous. Among these deeds of righteousness were the mighty acts which accompanied the deliverance from Egypt. It is to such that Dan. makes his appeal, as though to say, In accordance with the great deeds which Thou hast already performed, wilt Thou now save Thy city. *Jerusalem*]—Dan.'s great concern is that the wrath and anger of God be turned away from God's holy city. *The mount*]—i. e., Zion, upon which the Temple had stood, the center of God's kingdom. "The opposition is the more appropriate, as in Daniel's time nothing remained of Jerusalem but its site, its mountain" (Zœckler). The prayer is a tragic confession of guilt. Jerusalem should have been the mount unto which all nations would flow, and Israel should have been a light unto the Gentiles, but because of the people's sins, Jerusalem and Israel have become a reproach.

Vs. 17. *And now, hearken oh! God, unto the prayer of thy servant and* unto his supplications, and cause thy face to shine upon thy desolate *sanctuary for the Lord's sake.* The earnestness of this prayer is remarkable. To shine]—cf. Num. 6:25; Ps. 80:3. *For the Lord's sake*]—The text is difficult at this point, and some with reason, would read, *for thy sake, oh! Lord.*

Vs. 18. *Incline, oh! my God, thine ear, and hear, open thine eyes, and see our desolations and the city upon which thy name is called, for not on account of our righteousnesses do we lay our supplications before thee, but for thy great mercy's sake.* The city upon which God's name is called is a city which God has conquered and over which His name is named. Cf. 2 Sam. 12:28; Ps. 48:2 ff. *We lay*]—The thought is probably derived from the custom of falling down before God in prayer; lit., *we cause our supplications to fall,* cf. Jer. 38:26. When Dan. looks at his own and the people's righteousness, he realizes that there is no hope. He appeals, therefore, to the only source of hope, the mercy of God. Salvation in the Bible is consistently presented as by grace.

Vs. 19. *Oh! Lord, hear, oh! Lord, forgive, oh! Lord, attend and do, delay not for thy sake, oh! my God, for thy name is called upon thy city and thy people.* "The *Kyrie eleison,* of the O. T." (M). The intensity of conviction and importunity expressed in this prayer well serve as a model for the attitude in all true prayer.

c. vv. 20-23. The coming of the angel Gabriel to answer the prayer.

Vs. 20. *And while I was yet speaking and praying and making confession of my sin and the sin of my people Israel, and laying my supplication before the LORD my God for the holy mount of my God.* Gaebelein well calls this the "Interrupted Prayer." While Dan. is still engaged in prayer, the angel visits him. *For*]—i. e., on account of, for the sake of.

Vs. 21. *And while I was yet speaking in prayer, the man Gabriel, whom I had seen in the vision in the beginning, being made to fly in weariness, reached me about the time of the evening oblation.* Gabriel is called "the man," in order to identify him with the one whom Dan. had previously seen in the vision, 8:15, the one who had appeared in the form of a man. *Gabriel*]—see comments on 8:16. It has sometimes been held that the doctrine of angelology was derived from Persia. This may perhaps be true, to an extent, with regard to some phases of the later Jewish doctrine. It is certainly not true, as far as the teaching of the book of Dan. is concerned, cf. *SBD*, II, pp. 127-131. *To fly in weariness*]—This phrase, in the Hebrew, is very difficult to understand. The first word which I have rendered *to fly* may be derived from two different verbs, meaning respectively *to fly* and *to be weary*. Thus, there seem to be two possible translations, 1) *to be weary in weariness* (being sore wearied, RV margin), and this may refer either to Gabriel or to Dan.; 2) *to fly in weariness*, i.e., exhausted by the flight. I have adopted this rendering because it seems most faithfully to reflect the original. The translation *to fly swiftly* (AV and some of the ancient versions) gives a good sense but does not accurately represent the original. *Reached*]—not *touched* (AV). *The evening oblation*]—lit., the meat offering. This was the time of evening prayer, probably about 3-4 p.m.

Vs. 22. *And he made me to understand, and he spake with me, and he said, oh! Daniel, now am I come forth to make thee wise in understanding.* With the Greek and Syriac, M would change the first verb to read, *and he came*. However, this seems to be a needless repetition of the statement just made in vs. 21. Th. renders, *and he made me to understand*, which gives the proper sense. The verb as it stands is difficult, because it does not have a direct object. Yet, upon the basis of Th. I think it should be retained. It sums up at the beginning the thought of the vs. The vs. then proceeds to show how Gabriel gave this understanding. *Now*]—i.e., in consequence of the prayer. *I am come*]—from the very presence of God. *To make thee wise*]—i.e., to give thee skill in understanding, or, to impart to thee understanding.

Vs. 23. *At the beginning of thy supplications a word went forth, and I am come to make (it) known, for very precious art thou, so mark the word, and understand the vision.* When Dan. had begun to pray, a word (the interpretation given in vv. 24-27) went forth from God, and Gabriel has come to make this word known. The reason why God immediately sent forth the word (i.e., answered the prayer) is that Dan. was a man greatly beloved (lit., most desired). *For*]—to be construed with *went forth*, not with *I am come*. *The word*]—The word is the Divine revelation itself, and the vision is the form in which this revelation came, namely, the appearance of the angel, and the manner in which he communicates the revelation.

d. vv. 24-27. The revelation of the seventy sevens which Gabriel communicates to Daniel in answer to his prayer.

Introduction

In answer to his prayer Gabriel announces to Dan. that a period of seventy sevens (hebdomads) has been decreed with reference to Dan.'s people and holy city for the purpose of restraining the transgression, making an end of sins, making reconciliation for iniquity, bringing in everlasting righteousness, sealing up vision and prophet and anointing a holy of holies. Dan., therefore, should know and understand that from the going forth of a word to bring back and to build Jerusalem unto an anointed One, who is also a prince, is seven sevens and sixty and two sevens. The street and moat shall be built again in times of affliction. After the sixty and two sevens an anointed One shall be cut off and has nothing. And as to the city and the sanctuary, they shall be destroyed by the people of a prince who will come, and its end will be with an overflow, and unto the end is war, desolations which are determined. And he shall cause a covenant to prevail with respect to many for one seven, and in the midst of the seven he shall cause the sacrifice and oblation to cease, and upon the wing of abominations is one making desolate, even until a full end and that decreed shall be poured out upon the desolate.

This passage (the translation of which will follow later) is one of the most difficult in all the OT, and the interpretations which have been offered are almost legion. M remarks that "The history of the exegesis of the 70 Weeks is the Dismal Swamp of OT criticism." Those who are interested in studying the history of the interpretations of this passage should consult the following works:

The Patristic Period

1. L. Knowles, "The Interpretation of the Seventy Weeks of Daniel In the Early Fathers" in WThJ., Vol. VII, May, 1945, pp. 136-160.

The Middle Ages

1. Zœckler in his Commentary.

The Reformation and Later

1. Matthew Pole's Synopsis.
2. See Zœckler above.

Recent Commentaries

1. See *Bibliography*.

In order properly to approach the study of this passage, it will be necessary briefly to state the principal interpretations.

A

The Traditional Messianic Interpretation. This view was stated in its essentials by Augustine, and has been very fully expounded by Hævernick and H. It is also held by Pusey, Wright, Wilson, and is adopted in this commentary. Since it will be set forth in detail in the exposition, we need not now do more than mention it. It regards this passage as a prophecy of the first advent of Christ in the flesh, the central point of which is His death, and it speaks also of the destruction of Jerusalem by the Romans.

B

The second view is one which applies the passage to Antiochus Epiphanes. There is a passage in I Macc. (1:54) which is thought by some (without warrant, I believe) to apply this passage to the times of Antiochus, and the LXX also, by means of additions to the text, appears to interpret the passage in the same way. Josephus, however (*Antiq.* X:11:7) considers these vv. to refer to the destruction of the city by the Romans, and this interpretation seems to have been held by the Jews of Jerome's time.[1] Saadia Gaon and later Jews however modified this interpretation.[2]

Julius Hilarianus (toward the close of the 4th cent.) denied the Messianic character of the prophecy, and referred it to the desolation of Antiochus. He thinks that there are 62 weeks (i.e., 434 years) between the return under Zerubbabel and Antiochus, an obvious error (see *PL*: 13, col. 1102 f.).

The following are some of the principal presentations of this interpretation:

a) *Maurer* divided the prophecy as follows: The 7 sevens are from the destruction of Jerusalem (588) to Cyrus (538); the 62 sevens from Cyrus to Seleucus (176) and the last seven to Antiochus.

---

[1] Jerome, *Com.* in loc. Haec loquuntur Hebraei, non magnopere curantes a primo anno Darii regis Persarum, usque ad extremam subversionem Jerusalem, quae sub Hadriano eis accidit, supputari Olympiades centum septuaginta quattuor, id est, annos sexcentos nonaginta sex, qui faciunt haebdomadas Hebraicas nonaginta novem et annos tres; quando Cochebas dux Judaeorum oppressus est, et Jerusalem usque ad solum diruta est." Cf. also Nasir 5; Sanhedrin 11; Kelim 9.

[2] Thus Saadia and Rashi referred the anointed one to Cyrus.

b) *Hitzig* counts the 7 sevens from the destruction of Jerusalem (588) to Cyrus (539), the 62 sevens to Onias III (170) and the last seven to Antiochus.

c) *Behrmann* counts the 7 sevens from 606 B.C. to 558 (year of Cyrus' accession). He then allows the sevens to overlap, by referring the 62 sevens from 606 to 171, the year of Onias death, and the last seven from 171 to 165 (164), the year in which the services were reinstated in the temple. Thus the 7 sevens fall within the period of the 62 sevens, making a total, as far as the application to history is concerned, not of 70 but of 63 sevens.

d) *Prince* counts the 7 sevens from 586 to 537 and takes Messiah the Prince as possibly Joshua the son of Jozadak (Ezra 3:2). The 62 sevens begin in 537 and reach to c. 174, the error in chronology being due to the supposed Maccabean author's ignorance of the chronology of the Persian period. The last seven ends with the restoration of Temple worship in 164.

The four interpretations above mentioned are merely examples. Essentially this position is adopted by Driver, M, and by the conservative critics Zœckler and Stuart. The present writer believes that this non-Messianic interpretation is utterly inadequate, but must leave the refutation to the detailed study of the passage.

C

The Christian Church Exposition. Kliefoth, in his masterful commentary (1868) presents the following view: The sevens are not to be taken as designating weeks of years, but are merely symbolical numbers. After the expiration of the 70 years of exile, there is to follow a period of indefinite length during which the people of God will be brought to salvation, a period which will endure as long as the world and time, indeed, until the very consummation. This indefinite period is itself divided into three parts. The first of these, designated as 7 sevens, begins with the edict of Cyrus (Ezra 1), and extends to the appearance of a Person, an anointed one who is also a prince, namely Christ (. . . die ersten 7 unter diesen 70 Siebenheiten sich von da an bis auf die Erscheinung Eines, der Priester and Kœnig in Einer Person ist, bis auf Christum erstreken sollen). Following this is the period of 62 sevens. During this time there will be returning and rebuilding, figurative expressions for the preaching of the Gospel and the conversion of sinners. This is to occur in affliction of the times, which means the changes of fortune and hindrances of the times. This will continue until the anointed One is cut off. After this period of 62 sevens follows a third in which the Christ will be cut off, i.e., in His position as Messiah will be brought to naught so that He loses all that He could have. He has no longer any power over the world nor any influence in it. Then will appear a prince who, opposed to God, will take the position of the Messiah as prince. The people of this wicked prince will destroy God's city and sanctuary, and war and desolations will continue unto the end. This last seven comprises the period of the domination of this prince, the Antichrist. His domination is brought to a close by the absolute consummation. Thus, according to Kliefoth, this prophecy parallels that of chs. 2 and 7. Essentially this position is also adopted by Keil.

D

The Parenthesis Interpretation. The most recent exposition of this view is by Ironside (*The Great Parenthesis,* 1943). Ironside places the *terminus a quo* of the 70 sevens in the 20th year of Artaxerxes, i.e., c. 445 B.C. (Neh. 2). The period of 7 sevens refers to the 49 years during which Jerusalem was rebuilt, i.e., the restoration from the Exile. The 62 sevens begin immediately and bring us down to (most likely) the Triumphal Entry, after which, within less than a literal week, the Messiah was cut off. The promises made in v. 24, however, were not fulfilled at Christ's first advent, for "Israel did not recognize their Messiah. They do not know Him yet as their Sinbearer. Their transgression has not been finished" (Ironside).

The 70th seven is not to follow the 62 sevens immediately. "Between the sixty-ninth and the seventieth weeks we have a Great Parenthesis which has now lasted over nineteen hundred years. The seventieth week has been postponed by God Himself, who changes the times and the seasons because of the transgression of the people. As I have put it elsewhere, though some have objected to the expression, the moment Messiah died on the cross, the prophetic clock stopped. There has not been a tick upon that clock for nineteen centuries. It will not begin to go again until the entire present age has come to an end, and Israel will once more be taken up by God" (Ironside).

When the Parenthesis ends and the 70th seven begins, the great Roman leader appears, pretending at first to be a friend of the Jews. He will "make a covenant with the nation for seven years, promising them protection and liberty in religion as they return to their land." In the midst of the 70th week, i.e., at the end of 3½ years, he will seek to break the covenant and demand that the Jewish worship cease. For the remainder of the week will occur the Great Tribulation or time of Jacob's trouble. Such, in essence, is the parenthesis view of Ironside. Essentially this position is adopted by *SRB* and Gaebelein. This view is very popular today. It may be regarded as one form of the Messianic interpretation.

If the reader will carefully study the above interpretations he will be prepared for the discussion which follows. In the procedure which I have adopted, I am guided by Keil in an endeavor "—first of all to ascertain the meaning of the words of each clause and verse, and then, after determining exegetically the import of the words," to "take into consideration the historical references and calculations of the periods of time named" and finally, to present in summary form, that which seems to me to be the teaching of this remarkable prophecy.

1) vs. 24. *The announcement of the seventy sevens.*

Vs. 24. *Seventy sevens are decreed upon thy people and upon the city of thy holiness, for restraining the transgression, and completing sin, and covering iniquity, and for bringing in everlasting righteousness, and for sealing vision and prophet and anointing a holy of holies.* This vs. is a Divine revelation of the fact that a definite period of time has been decreed for the accomplishment of all that which is necessary for the true restoration of God's people from bondage. *Seventy sevens*]—lit., sevens seventy. the word *sevens*—usually translated *weeks*—is placed first for the sake of emphasis. It constitutes the great theme of the passage. For the same reason, the numeral here follows the noun, and does not precede it, as is usually the case. The thought of the author may then be paraphrased, "Sevens—and in fact seventy of them are decreed, etc." The word *sevens* here occurs in the m.pl., whereas it generally has a f.pl. This m.pl. also appears in Dan. 10:2, 3. The reason for this m. form is not that Dan. is a late writing (*BDB*), nor was it likely that the m. was chosen because it would sound like the word seventy (Rosenmueller—the two words are spelled with exactly the same consonants), nor is it to indicate that the usual weeks of seven days are not intended, nor is it to be regarded as an arbitrary correction (Ewald), since it has already appeared in Gen. 29:27 (in the s.). The form is really a participle meaning *besevened,* i.e., computed by sevens (so Stuart and H), and here gives evidence of the fact that the word was originally m. What led Dan. to employ the m. instead of the f. however, is not clear unless it was for the deliberate purpose of calling attention to the fact that the word *sevens* is employed in an unusual sense. The word means *divided into sevens,* and generally signifies the most common of such divisions, namely, the ordinary week of seven days, e.g., Gen. 29:27 f. and Dan. 10:2,3. In the expression itself there is no intimation as to the length of time intended. How long, then, is the seven? In Dan. 10:2, 3 an expression of time, *days,* is added, so that in this passage we are to understand ordinary weeks of 7 days each, or perhaps, three full weeks. Also in Dan. 8:14, where Dan. intends a definite period of time, he adds an expression "evenings-mornings."

How then are we to determine the length of that which is designated by the present word *sevens?* We can determine this, not from the word itself, but only from other considerations. It seems obvious that ordinnary weeks of 7 days are not intended. There does appear to be a reference to the "years" of Jer. which such an interpretation would not satisfy. Also, the prophecy, upon this view, would become practically meaningless. The brief period of 490 days would not serve to meet the needs of the prophecy, upon any view. Hence, as far as the present writer knows, this view is almost universally rejected.[3]

Most expositors find here a week of 7 years duration, a total of 490 years. To support this, various expedients are adopted, but the most convincing is an appeal to the years of Jer. "A reference to these is sufficient to show that seventy ordinary weeks cannot for a moment be thought of. For what comfort would it have afforded to Daniel, if he had been told that, as a compensation for the seventy years of desolation, the city would stand for seventy ordinary weeks, and then be destroyed again? Moreover Daniel himself must have been able to perceive, from the magnitude of the events, which were to take place during this period; that something more was intended than ordinary weeks" (H).

But this appeal to the years of Jer. does not prove that weeks of years are intended, and in fact, there is no satisfactory proof of this position.[4] Keil, therefore, correctly, I believe, follows Kliefoth in the assumption that the reference is to "an intentionally indefinite designation of a period of time measured by the number seven, whose chronological duration must be determined on other grounds."[5]

H would understand the word *time* before *seven,* thus, a time of 70 sevens. This, however, is unnecessary. The s. *is decreed* shows that the phrase is to be taken in a collective sense. We might paraphrase: "A

---

[3] An exception appears in Wieseler who wrote a dissertation on the 70 weeks in which he advocated the view that in v. 24 literal weeks were meant, but that in vs. 25 ff. periods of seven years each were intended.

In a mimeographed paper by J. Sladen, *The Seventy Weeks of Daniel's Prophecy,* London, 1925, the view is also advocated that the weeks are seven-days in length.

[4] Appeal is sometimes made to the sabbatical years (2 Chr. 36:21), but these are not called weeks.

[5] Aalders defends the position that the sevens are not sevens of years but definite periods (het woord *zevental* typeert die tijdruimten dan alleen also tijdvakken die in zichzelf een zekere eenheid vormen) upon the basis of the following: a) The signification week of years (*jaar*week) is not found in the O.T.; b) This particular prophecy contains no indication that the sevens are sevens of years; c) The total of 490 years does not fit the needs of the prophecy; d) It is questionable whether in this Divine revelation a precise chronological reckoning is to be expected (Ik acht het veel aannemelijker, dat de zeventallen te verstaan zijn van tijdruimten van niet nauwkeurig bepaalden duur) (op. cit. p. 201).

period of sevens—even 70 of them—is decreed." The 70 sevens are thus to be regarded as a unit.

Is decreed]—i.e., by judicial decision, hence the AV "determined" is a good rendering. It is God who has decreed this period of time for the accomplishment of His redemptive purposes. *Upon*]—or, concerning. Not that the decree was to lie like a burden upon the people, but that it was made upon them. M takes it to mean "against" in the sense of legal debt. But the meaning rather is: "As far as thy people are concerned, a period of 70 sevens has been decreed for accomplishing their salvation."

Thy people]—Dan. has just prayed for his people, and the angel tenderly acknowledges this love. Even though in ruins, Jerusalem, because of her past and her future, is the holy city. Gaebelein would restrict the reference, "Now it must be borne in mind that these things concern exclusively Daniel's people and not Gentiles but the holy city Jerusalem." It is true that the primary reference is to Israel after the flesh, and the historical Jerusalem, but since this very vs. describes the Messianic work, it also refers to the true people of God, those who will benefit because of the things herein described. *For restraining*]—These phrases express the purpose why the sevens have been decreed. We may paraphrase: "In order to finish the transgression, etc., a period of 70 sevens has been decreed." This means that the things described, e.g., finishing the transgression, etc., are to occur within and not after the period of 70 sevens. This latter view might be grammatically possible (so von Lengerke), but the sequel shows that it is not intended. The very purpose of decreeing the sevens is to finish the transgression, etc., and the contents of vs. 24 show that these things are to be accomplished before the expiry of the 70 sevens, although the blessings brought about thereby may continue for long after that expiry.

The 70 sevens are decreed for the purpose of accomplishing six results, and these six results comprise two groups of three members each, thus:

Negative	*Positive*
1. to *restrain* the transgression	4. to bring in everlasting righteousness
2. to complete sin	5. to seal vision and prophet
3. to cover iniquity	6. to anoint a holy of holies

The above arrangement is to be preferred to that of Maurer, Hitzig and the Massoretes, which finds three statements consisting of two members each. This arrangement rests upon a misunderstanding of the meaning of the separate members.

A. *The Negative Results to be Accomplished*

1. *For restraining the transgression*]—The interpretation to *finish* or *complete* does not seem justifiable. The original is difficult, but a good case can be made in defence of the present translation. The thought has well been expressed by H, "The sin, which has hitherto lain naked and open before the eyes of the righteous God, will now be shut in, sealed up and hidden by the God of mercy, so that it may be regarded as no longer existing; a biblical mode of describing the forgiveness of sins, analogous to the phrases, 'hiding the face from sin' 'putting away sin.'" The word *transgression* combines the ideas of apostasy and rebellion, which the prophet has already confessed in his prayer (vv. 5-11). The allusion is not merely to the apostasy and rebellion of the exile, but to all such apostasy and rebellion.

Gaebelein maintains that the phrase has a special meaning for Israel as a nation, and that the transgression of the Jewish nation has not yet been finished. This will not have been accomplished until after the expiry of the 70 weeks, and since, according to Gaebelein, the 70th week has not yet occurred, this particular blessing also has not appeared. According to him, it will appear during the millennium which is to follow the 70th week.

But, as we have pointed out, the period of 70 sevens is decreed in order to accomplish these blessings. They are to be introduced, then, during this period, not after it. Now, the work of shutting up sin can only be the work of God, which is to be performed with the introduction of the other blessings herein mentioned. This was done by Christ, the Great Deliverer. He shut up transgression by an act which He performed, namely, His atoning death. This is the only possible meaning of the words. And the transgression which He sealed up is, despite Gaebelein, not merely the transgression of Israel, but transgression generally. The definite article *the* means that we are to take the reference not to one particular transgression, but to transgression as such.

The phrase "upon thy people" etc., does not mean that the blessings described are for the benefit *only* of the literal nation Israel. Such a thought is utterly foreign to the universalistic nature of OT prophecy generally. Rather, the phrase "upon thy people" serves to indicate that as far as Israel is concerned, a period of 70 sevens has been decreed in order to bring about blessings which, while having a primary reference to Israel, do as a matter of fact, characterize the New Dispensation. The exegesis of the subsequent phrases will support this position.

2. *For completing sin*]—i.e., for making an end of sin. The word may be read *to seal up sin,* and then it is taken in the sense of *taking away* (so H), or *removed out of sight* (Kliefoth, Keil). However, as Bevan

points out, to seal up sin "elsewhere signifies 'to reserve it for punishment' (Job 14:17, cf. Deut. 32:34)". The word is difficult, but I here prefer the rendering of the AV. The thought is that an end will be made of sin as such.

3. *And covering iniquity*]—In what sense is this covering to be conceived? Not in a literal, but, as Driver rightly indicates, in a moral sense. Driver sums up the use of the word as follows. If the subject who covers is a priest, the meaning is to cover the sinner (usually) by means of a propitiatory sacrifice, hence, to make atonement or reconciliation. If God is the subject, it means to forgive, i.e., to regard as covered (cf. Jer. 18:23; Ps. 65:3). In this present instance, it is difficult to make this distinction, since no subject is mentioned. M in an endeavor to represent both the religious and legal implications of the verb, translates *absolve.* But the phrase may better be rendered, either, *to make reconciliation, to expiate iniquity,* or, *to pardon iniquity.* The thought seems to be either that the necessary propitiatory sacrifice will be offered and therefore sin is expiated, or that the necessary propitiatory sacrifice will be offered and therefore, sin is pardoned or forgiven. Perhaps the best translation, therefore, is "to make reconciliation for iniquity."

The iniquity referred to is not any particular iniquity, but iniquity in general.

To sum up; sin is here pictured as transgression, sins and iniquity. These three words well represent in its fulness the nature of that curse which has separated man from God. The first stated purpose of the decreeing of the period of 70 sevens is to abolish this curse. It is to be restrained, so shut up by God, that it may no longer be regarded as existing; it is to be brought to an end, that it may no longer be present to enslave; it is also to be done away, because the guilt which it involves has been expiated. How is this to be accomplished? The text does not say, but who, in the light of the NT revelation, can read these words without coming face to face with that one perfect Sacrifice which was offered by Him, who "appeared to put away sin by the sacrifice of Himself" (Heb. 9:26b)?

B. *The Positive Results to be Accomplished*

1. *For bringing in everlasting righteousness*]—Together with the taking away or removal of sin there is a positive unfolding of salvation. Righteousness is to be brought in from without. It is to be brought in by God through the Messiah. This righteousness is not mere prosperity, nor in any sense of a merely external nature. It is a righteousness that comes from God (Ps. 85:11-13; Isa. 51:5-8); it (as Keil reminds us) rises as a sun upon those who fear God (Mal. 4:2); it is similar to the everlasting

salvation of Isa. 45:17 and the eternal inheritance of the righteous of Isa. 60:21; and corresponds (in its heavenly character of everlasting) to the eternity of the Messianic kingdom (2:44; 7:18, 27).[6] It therefore comprises both external and internal righteousness. It is the righteousness of God which comes from God. More specifically, it is that state of rightness or right relationship with God which comes to the sinner through faith in Jesus Christ. It is the blessed condition of "being right" with God. Hence, this expression very properly corresponds to the first: "in the place of the absolutely removed transgression is the perfected righteousness" (Keil).

2. *For sealing vision and prophet*]—Many take this action to refer to the impression of a seal upon a writing so as to accredit it. Thus to seal up vision, etc., is said to mean that the prophecies are accredited. Some believe that the reference is to this particular prophecy of the 70 sevens.

This use of *to seal*, however, does not appear to be supported from the OT. The reference is not to accrediting the prophecy, but to sealing it up so that it will no longer appear. Its functions are finished, and it is not henceforth needed.

This is not done by way of punishment to Israel (Mauro) but because the period of prophecy is now at an end. Keil thinks that this extinction of prophecy is not to be sought in the period of Christ's first advent, since that concluded only OT prophecy. NT prophecy and its fulfillment are yet to be sealed up. Hence, Keil believes that this prophecy is to be fulfilled in the future.

However, the particular description herein chosen very clearly refers to the OT period. Vision was a technical name for revelation given to the OT prophets (cf. Isa. 1:1, Amos 1:1, etc.) The *prophet* was the one through whom this vision was revealed to the people. The two words, vision and prophet, therefore, serve to designate the prophetic revelation of the OT period. This revelation was of a temporary, preparatory, typical nature. It pointed forward to the coming of Him who was the great Prophet (Deut. 18:15). When Christ came, there was no further need of prophetic revelation in the OT sense.

This fifth clause seems to stand over against the second, *for completing sin*. When sin is brought to an end by the appearance of the Messiah, so prophecy, which had predicted His coming and His saving work, is no longer needed. It has fulfilled its task and is therefore sealed up.

3. *Anointing a holy of holies*]—lit., holiness of holinesses. The reference is not to the dedication of the temple which was built by Zerubbabel.

---

6 "This righteousness is called an eternal righteousness, both on account of its origin in the eternal counsel of the eternal God, and also because of its eternal duration, in contradistinction to the transitory gifts of righteousness and grace under the Old Testament, and to everything that is created and subject to decay" (H)

nor to the consecration of the altar of burnt offering which had been desecrated by Antiochus (I Macc. 4:54). Nor, with Keil and Kliefoth, can we apply it to the consummation, the holy city, the heavenly Jerusalem (Rev. 21:1-27).

The words refer to the anointing of the Messiah. Since the phrase occurs without the definite article, it means *a most holy thing.* In what sense, then, may this be applied to Christ? In the OT the anointing oil was a symbol of the Spirit of God (Zech. 4). Thus, in I Sam. 10:1ff. after anointing Saul, Samuel says to him, "—The Lord hath anointed thee"—"And the Spirit of the Lord comes upon thee—" Cf. Isa. 61:1, "—The Spirit of the Lord is upon me, because the Lord hath anointed me—." Hence, it may be concluded with H, "—the anointing of a Holy of Holies can only denote the communication of the Spirit to Christ, to which prominence is given in other prophecies of the Old Testament, as a distinguishing characteristic of the Messiah."

The six items presented in this vs. are all Messianic. This fact settles the *terminus ad quem* of the prophecy. The termination of the 70 sevens coincides then, not with the times of Antiochus, nor with the end of the present age, the 2nd Advent of our Lord, but with His 1st Advent. "For when our Lord ascended into heaven and the Holy Spirit descended, there remained not one of the six items of Daniel 9:24 that was not *fully accomplished*" (Mauro).

2. vv. 25-27. *The three divisions of the* 70 *sevens.*

Vs. 25. *And thou shalt know and understand, from the going forth of a word to restore and to build Jerusalem unto an anointed one, a prince (is) seven sevens and sixty two sevens; it shall be built again street and moat* (?) *and in affliction of the times.* Dan. is bid *to know and understand,* not to *mark well.* The phrase is similar in import to our Lord's "whoso readeth, let him understand," etc. Such expressions indicate that the message is difficult and requires a mind that is well acquainted in understanding spiritual truths. *From the going forth*]—This phrase has reference to the issuance of the word, not from a Persian ruler but from God.[7] God is the Author of this word; He has determined the length of the time until the things prophesied in vs. 24 shall be completed. In vs. 23 also this same phrase occurs to describe the issuance of a Divine word. It seems difficult, therefore to assume that here, two vv. later, another subject should be introduced without some mention of the fact. This issuance of the word is, in itself, an invisible event, yet as H correctly points out, the effects of such an issuance must have appeared upon this earth. "As

[7] The translation of the AV, "—the going forth of the commandment" is misleading. The text does not mention a commandment.

the covenant people were then subject to the Persian king, we naturally expect to find an echo of the word of God in the edict of a Persian monarch" (H).

When, therefore, do we find the people beginning to return and build Jerusalem? What, in other words, is the *terminus a quo* of this prophecy?

1) M. The word which was issued was that of the Lord to Jer. (vs. 2). There are here two interpretations of this prophecy. One regards it as 7 x 7 years in length and finds its fulfillment in the return from Exile. The other, a secondary interpretation, was adopted because Jer.'s prophecy had failed of fulfillment. Hence, Jer.'s 70 years were taken symbolically, as 70 year-weeks. This theory would then place the going forth of the word in 586 B.C.

However, it is perfectly clear that in 586 B.C. no word went forth to restore and to build Jerusalem.

2) Behrmann places the year as 606 B.C., but against this also it must be objected that no word went forth in that year such as that herein described.

3) H, followed by Gaebelein, Sir Robert Anderson and many others take the year 445 B.C. as that in which the word went forth. This is the 20th year of Artaxerxes (Neh. 2). To support this position H shows that the actual restoration of Jerusalem was not commenced before the time of Neh., but was begun by Neh. himself.

However, well elaborated as this theory is, there are certain fatal objections to it. For one thing, the prophet Haggai (about 70 years before 445 B.C.) spoke of the people dwelling in ceiled houses in Jerusalem (Haggai 1:2-4). Also, the Lord definitely prophecies of Cyrus that he will build the city (Isa. 45:1, 13; 44:28).

4) The word which went forth became evident in history during the first year of Cyrus. This seems to be the year (538-7 B. C.) in which the exile came to an end, and a new order of things appeared. Thus, in Dan. 1:21 we are told that Dan.—the great statesman at the Babylonian court, the court of that nation which oppressed Israel —continued until the first year of Cyrus. This was the year of the great change, as far as Israel was concerned. Also, it was in this year that the great edict of liberation was issued, the edict whch marked the formal termination of the exile (Ezra 1:1-4). This edict, furthermore, was issued in fulfillment of the prophecy of Jer., and it speaks expressly of going to Jerusalem and building there the temple—the first and most important step in the rebuilding of the city. In this connection also one should consider the prophecies of Isa. 44:28 in which Cyrus is described as "saying to Jerusalem, Thou shalt be built; and to the temple, Thy foundation shall be laid." Likewise Isa. 45:13 declares of Cyrus, "he shall build my city, and he shall let go my captives."

Lastly, it should be noted that the book of Ezra pictures Jerusalem as an existing city (cf. Ezra 4:12, 9:9).

It cannot be denied that this was the year in which the effects of the going forth of a word began to appear in history. Cyrus issued the decree which brought an end to the exile and again turned the Jews toward Jerusalem. It is not justifiable to distinguish too sharply between the building of the city and the building of the temple. Certainly, if the people had received permission to return to Jerusalem to rebuild the temple, there was also implied in this permission to build for themselves homes in which to dwell. There is no doubt whatever but that the people thus understood the decree (cf. Haggai 1:2-4). The edict of Cyrus mentions the temple specifically, because that was the religious center of the city, that which distinguished it as the holy city of the Jews. If, therefore, we are to discover in history the effects of the going forth of a Divine word we discover them first appearing during the first year of Cyrus the king, and this year is thus to be regarded as the *terminus a quo* of the 70 sevens. So Calvin, Kliefoth, Keil, and lately, Mauro also, has very ably presented this view. *To restore and to build Jerusalem*]—These words state the purpose for which the word went forth. Not, *to build again* M, for the words *to restore* should not be taken as an auxiliary verb meaning *again.* The words mean literally, to cause to bring back. The object of the verb is *Jerusalem,* thus, to cause to bring back (Jerusalem) and to build Jerusalem, i. e., to restore the city to its former condition. This does not necessarily include the complete restitution (as H argues) but merely the beginning of such restitution. The words *to build* in distinction from *to restore* "denotes the building after restoring, and includes the constant preservation in good building condition, as well as the carrying forward of the edifice beyond its former state" (Keil). *Unto an anointed one, a prince*]—These words set forth the *terminus ad quem* of the 7 and 62 sevens. The meaning is not *an anointed prince,* nor *till a prince is anointed* but *unto an anointed one* who is at the same time a *prince.* In the OT kings and priests were anointed, and hence we are to think of one who is not only a priest (anointed one) but also a king (prince).[8] The reference, therefore, is not to Cyrus (Driver) for he was not a theocratic king but a heathen. (It is true, as H says, that "there is only one heathen king to whom the expression is applied, namely Cyrus, who is called 'anointed' in Isa. 45:1, not as a king merely, but on account of the remarkable relation which he sustained to the church [a relation unparalleled in history],—on account of the gifts, with which he was endowed by

[8] There is no recorded instance in the OT of the anointing of a prophet. The only exception seems to be I K. 19:16. In this passage Elijah was commanded to anoint Elisha, but he seems never to have done so. Cf. also Ps. 105:15 and Isa. 61:1.

God for the good of the church,—on account of his possessing the first elements of the true knowledge of God, as his edict in the Book of Ezra clearly shows,—and lastly on account of the typical relation in which he stood to the author of a still higher deliverance, namely the Messiah himself"). However, the deliberate antithesis between the prince in this vs. and the heathen prince in vs. 26 shows that here a theocratic ruler is intended. Again, the reference is not to Onias III because he was not a prince. Stuart confesses inability to discover the reference, "That some distinguished personage is meant, can hardly be questioned. *Who* it is, or *when* he was to appear, are questions, as we have seen, which cannot easily be solved by any history known to us."

The fact is that there is only One in history who fully satisfies the two essential requisites of the theocratic king, Jesus who is the Messiah (see Zech. 6:13; Ps. 110:4; John 4:25). He was anointed and appointed a Prince as was required and this in a most perfect manner. "These requisites are here attributed to Him as predicates, and in such a manner that the being anointed goes before the being a prince, in order to make prominent the spiritual, priestly character of His royalty, and to designate Him, on the ground of the prophecies, Isa. 61:1-3 and 55:4, as the person by whom "the 'sure mercies of David' (Isa 55:3) shall be realized by the covenant people" (Keil).

Dan. therefore was to look for the one who at the same time was both an anointed one and a prince (the definite article is missing) and when such a one appeared, the prophecy would be fulfilled.

Seven sevens and sixty-two sevens]—the length of time between the *terminus a quo* of the prophecy and the appearance of an anointed one, a prince. The interpretation of these words is, to my mind, the most difficult point in this prophecy.

The Mas. pointing[9] separates between the two periods, and if this pointing is to be followed, the vs. should be translated thus:

"And thou shalt know and understand from the going forth of a word to restore and to build Jerusalem unto an anointed one, a prince, (is) seven sevens: and (for the space of) sixty and two sevens it shall be built again street and moat (?) and in affliction of the times." Thus we get the following:

Terminus a quo	————	*Terminus ad quem*
Going forth of a word	←⫷ 7 sevens ⫸→	an anointed one, a prince.

[9] The Masoretes were Jewish scholars who supplied the consonants of the Hebrew text with vowel points and accents, some of which had the force of marks of punctuation. After the word *sevens* they have placed an accent called Athnach, which often—not always—marks the principal break in a sentence.

Upon this construction are based the following interpretations:

1. That which would terminate the 7 sevens with Cyrus. The *terminus a quo* would then be the destruction of Jerusalem (c. 586 B. C. variously dated by different writers). However, the exegesis has already shown that c. 586 no word went forth to restore the city and Cyrus cannot rightly be described as an anointed one, a prince.

2. The view of Behrmann, that 606 B. C. is *terminus a quo* both of the 7 sevens and the 62 sevens. This also must be rejected for the same reasons as the preceding view. In addition it introduces an overlapping, which is not warranted. The 62 sevens are conceived of as *following*, not *coinciding with* or *overlapping* the 7 sevens.

3. The view of Keil and Kliefoth that the 7 sevens extend from Cyrus to Christ. There is nothing inherently objectionable in this except that vs. 25b is then made to extend from the 1st advent of Christ to the consummation, and this is contrary to the Messianic character of vs. 24.

— — — — —

If the Mas. pointing be retained, it may be regarded merely as serving to indicate, not the principal division of the sentence, but simply that the two phrases are not to be connected, thus

"seven sevens — and sixty and two sevens."

It may be that the Mas. pointing is in error, as I think it certainly is in vs. 24. At any rate, this violent separation of the two periods is out of harmony with the context. Furthermore, I question whether it is really in accord with the rules of Heb. syntax to render, "(for the space of) sixty-two sevens," i. e., as an acc. of duration (See, however, Kliefoth). It is best, therefore, to understand (although I am painfully aware of the difficulties) the text as stating that between the *terminus a quo* and the appearance of an anointed one, a prince, is a period of 69 sevens which is divided into two periods of unequal length, 7 sevens and 62 sevens. To what, then, do these two subdivisons have reference? The 7 sevens apparently has reference to the time which should elapse between the issuance of the word and the completion of the city and temple; roughly, to the end of the period of Ezra and Neh.[10] The 62 sevens follows this period. In vs. 25 these 62 sevens are not characterized, but in vs. 26 we are told what will happen after the expiry of the 62 sevens. The 62 sevens

---

10 H points out the suitableness of the 7 sevens to designate this period. "According to the Mosaic decrees, the year of praise or jubilee, the welcome period of restoration to all the wretched, returned at the end of every seven weeks of years" (cf. Lev. 25:8,10,13).

therefore have reference to the period which follows the age of Ezra and Neh. to the time of Christ.

It may be objected that 7 x 7 years or 49 years from the 1st year of Cyrus would not be long enough to include the days of Ezra and Nehemiah. True enough, but the burden of proof rests with those who insist that sevens of years are intended. Of this I am not convinced. If the sevens be regarded merely as a symbolical number, the difficulty disappears.

It shall be built again]—H would translate "restored and built is the street, and firmly determined." Behrmann thinks that the words street and moat are two proper names. The "street" was probably near the temple and the "moat" the Tyropoean valley, though why these two places should be mentioned, Behrmann does not know. Probably, however, the translation which we have given should stand. The word "moat" means a trench and the two words taken together present a picture of the complete restoration of the city.

In affliction of the times]—This was well illustrated by the oppression and opposition which God's people suffered during the times of Ezra and Nehemiah (Cf. Neh. 4:1 ff; 6:1 ff.; 9:36, 37). Kliefoth and Keil refer this to the spiritual building of the City of God.

Vs. 26. *And after the sixty and two sevens there will be cut off an anointed one, and there is naught for him; and the city and the sanctuary shall destroy (them) the people of a prince who will come, and its end (is) with an overflow, and unto the end (is) war, determined are desolations.* In vs. 25 Dan. set forth the distinguishing characteristic of the 7 sevens, namely, the rebuilding of the city. He now exhibits the distinguishing characteristic of the 62 sevens, namely, that it is the period which must intervene between the building of the city and the cutting off of an anointed one. *After* the 62 sevens, two events are to occur, 1) the cutting off of the Messiah and 2) the destruction of the city. This vs. does not state how long after the 62 sevens these things will take place but from vs. 27 we learn that the cutting off of the anointed one occurs in the middle of the 70th seven. The destruction of the city takes place after the expiry of the 70 sevens.

Cut off]—The word is used of the death penalty, Lev. 7:20; and refers to a violent death, unless some further explanation is given (e. g., cut off from the congregation of Israel). It is used, as H points out, of the fate of the ungodly, e. g., Ps. 37:9. Hence, in the present passage it means "cut off by death."

An anointed one]—The definite article is omitted, intentionally, it would seem, in order to show the identity of the anointed with that mentioned in vs. 25. The reference cannot possibly be to Onias III (e. g., M and Driver). Such an interpretation is based upon the erroneous assumption that the 7 sevens began either in 606 or 586 B. C., and both of these dates are untenable. Driver argues that the "Messiah" of vs. 26 cannot be the same as the one in vs. 25, because he lived 62 sevens after him. But such a statement rests upon the assumption that only 7 sevens elapsed between the going forth of a word and the anointed one, and this supposition, as we have sought to indicate, is incorrect.

In reading this description, we are reminded of the language of Isaiah —"he was cut off from the land of the living" (53:8). As H indicates, the word "anointed one" is unintelligible when taken by itself. It can be understood only in connection with "an anointed one, a prince" of vs. 25. The old evangelical interpretation is that which alone satisfies the requirements of the case. The "anointed one" is Jesus Christ, who is cut off by His death upon the Cross of Calvary. *And he has naught*]—lit., and there is not to him. These words are exceedingly difficult, but they seem to indicate that all which should properly belong to the Messiah, He does not have when He dies. This is a very forceful way of setting forth His utter rejection, both by God and man. "We have no king but Cæsar," cried the Jews. "My God, my God, why hast thou forsaken me?" were the words from the Cross. In that hour of blackness He had nothing, nothing but the guilt of sin of all those for whom He died. Utterly forsaken, He was cut off. Keil and Kliefoth, in accordance with their theory, think that the reference is to the time in the history of the Church, when wickedness shall become so strong that the Messiah will lose His influence over the world, even His place and function as Messiah. *And the city and sanctuary*]—These words are the objects of the verb and are placed first for the sake of emphasis. *People of a prince*]—In consequence of the cutting off of the Messiah the people of a coming prince will destroy the city and sanctuary. This prince is not Christ (Tertullian), nor is it Antiochus. For, in addition to the many objections which prevail against such an interpretation of the prophecy, it may be noted that the Greek armies did not completely destroy the city in a physical sense (cf. I Macc. 1:31 ff.). Keil and Kliefoth refer the words to the Antichrist. However, it seems most likely that the "people" are the Romans, and the prince who is to come is Titus Vespasianus. *Who will come*]—i. e., either in the future as a new person or, as is more likely, in a hostile sense, as an invader, as in 1:1. *Its end (is) with an overflow*]—The word *overflow* suggests an overwhelming flood. Cf. Nah. 1:8 where it is used of the outpouring of Divine wrath. What is the antecedent of *its?* Some refer it to the anointed one, others to the prince. Probably it is best taken as referring to the end of the destruction as such. Thus H translates, "and it will end in the flood." The destruction will be of such a nature that it will end in a mighty overflow. *Unto the end*]—The general sense seems to be clear;

although the precise relationship of the words one to another is difficult to determine. Unto the end of the destruction war and desolation will continue. Are we to read, however, "and unto the end (is) war, desolations are determined," or "and unto the end of war, determined with desolations"? Probably the first is to be preferred. Keil rightly expresses the thought, "Till the end war will be, for desolations are irrevocably determined by God," and H very justifiably remarks, "It is no passing hostile invasion that is here referred to, like that which occurred in the time of Antiochus Epiphanes; but one in which the city and the temple would be completely destroyed."

Vs. 27. *And he shall cause to prevail a covenant for the many one seven, and in the midst of the seven he shall cause sacrifice and oblation to cease, and upon the wing of abominations (is) one making desolate, and until end and that determined shall pour upon the desolate.* The final seven and the end. The first question to be answered is, Who causes the covenant to prevail? Several answers have been suggested:

1) The subject is indefinite, "it." (Fuller).

2) The prince of vs. 26 (Zoeckler, Maurer, Kliefoth, etc.) This prince is thought to be:

a) Antiochus—". . . the allusion will be to the manner in which Antiochus found apostate Jews ready to cooperate with him in his efforts to extirpate their religion" (Driver), and cf. I Macc. 1:11-15. "The clever diplomacy whereby Ant. made his bargain with the worldly majority, at least of the aristocracy, in Jerusalem" (M).

b) The prince is Antichrist who "shall impose on the mass of the people a strong covenant that they should follow him and give themselves to him as their God" (Keil).

c) The prince is the "little horn" of Dan. 7, who will make a covenant with the Jews at the beginning of the 70th week (Gaebelein, SRB).

3) The subject is "one week" (H. Hævernick, Th. Hitzig), i.e., "one week will confirm the covenant to the many."

4) The subject is Messiah, "and he, i. e., Messiah, will cause to prevail, etc." This is the view which seems to be most tenable. To construe "prince" as subject, does not appear to be the most natural reading, for the word occupies only a subordinate position even in vs. 26, where it is not even the subject of a sentence. The city and sanctuary are to be destroyed, not by a prince, but by the *people* of that prince. The *people* are in a more prominent position than is the *prince*. Furthermore, the phrase, *and its end* in vs. 26 need not refer to the prince but more likely to the end of the destruction as such. The phrase *of the prince* in vs. 26 is in such a subordinate position that it is extremely unlikely that we are to regard it as antecedent of "he will confirm."

Furthermore, this entire passage is Messianic in nature, and the Messiah is the leading character. The general theme of the passage, introduced in vs. 24, is surely Messianic. The blessings therein depicted were brought about by the Messiah and they form their climax in the "anointing" of a holy of holies. Furthermore, in vs. 25 the appearance of the Messiah is the great *terminus ad quem* of the 69 sevens. They lead up to Him, who is their goal. The exposition has shown how utterly impossible it is to refer this vs. (25) to Antiochus. In vs. 26 two principal themes are introduced: 1) the death of the Messiah and 2) the *consequent* destruction of the city and sanctuary by a people of a prince (not *the* prince) who will come. In this vs. therefore, the principal characters are the Messiah and the people—not the prince. As the exposition will endeavor to bring out, what is related in vs. 27 also has reference to the Messiah.

He shall cause to prevail a covenant]—The writer does not mean to say that he will make a covenant. The ordinary idiom to express such a thought is "to cut a covenant," and this idiom is not used here. Now, if the writer had wished to state that a covenant would be *made*, why did he not employ the ordinary Hebrew idiom for expressing such a thought? Why did he use this strange phrase "cause to prevail" which appears in only one other passage of the OT, Ps. 12:4? Hence, we must conclude with Allis, "It is a mistake to say that these words speak of the making of a seven-year covenant, and to infer that the maker of it cannot be the Messiah whose covenant is an everlasting covenant." The reference, therefore, is not to the making of a covenant but to a covenant which has already been made. The following interpretations are thereby excluded:

1) Any bargains which Antiochus may have made with the majority of the Jews. The facts are as follows:

> 11. "In those days came there forth out of Israel transgressors of the law, and persuaded many, saying, Let us go and make a covenant with the Gentiles that are round about us; for since we were parted from them many evils have befallen us.
>
> 12. And the saying was good in their eyes.
>
> 13. And certain of the people were forward herein and went to the king, and he gave them licence to do after the ordinances of the Gentiles.
>
> 14. And they built a place of exercise in Jerusalem according to the laws of the Gentiles; and they made themselves uncircumcised, and forsook the holy covenant, and joined themselves to the Gentiles, and sold themselves to do evil" (I Macc. 1:11-14).

The above passage teaches that certain transgressors suggested making a covenant with the nations round about. Their language is reminiscent of Judges 2:2 and may mean, not the formal ratification of some covenant, but simply a determination to follow the Gentile way of life.

Antiochus gave his royal permission for the Jews to do this, for without such permission they could not have introduced these heathen innovations. Antiochus, therefore, does not make any covenant, nor does he cause any covenant to prevail, unless his granting permission to the Jews to Hellenize be considered as causing a covenant to prevail. However, since the covenant of Dan. 9:27 is to be regarded as already in existence, how can it possibly apply to Antiochus? Without fear of successful contradiction it may be said that Antiochus did not cause any covenant to prevail. Those who caused the covenant (if it was a real covenant and not a mere intention to imitate the Greeks) with the nations to prevail were certain transgressors and not Antiochus. Furthermore, the covenant (even granting that the word may be used in this broad sense) could not have been said to prevail for one week. At first Antiochus used stratagem, but later abandoned this for force. The reference to him, therefore, must be rejected.

2) The view of Kliefoth that the Antichrist will make a pseudo-religious covenant with the mass whose love has grown cold. This he will accomplish, not through sacrifice but through power. This is to occur after the 62 sevens, i. e., toward the close of the present age. However, the emphasis in this position appears to be upon the making of a covenant. Basically, therefore, this view does not do justice to the language of the text. Furthermore, as the exposition has shown, it must be rejected also on other grounds.

3) The view that the prince is not Titus but the little horn of Dan. 7, a prince of the revived Roman empire. Thus:

"This covenant the Roman prince will make with the many, not with all the Jews" (Gaebelein). It is said to be a covenant with death and an agreement with hell, Isa. 28:15, 18.

"The one who makes the seven-year covenant is the Roman Prince, the one 'that shall come' " (McClain).

"If the events of Daniel's seventieth week are future, it is clear that the person who makes the covenant must be the wicked character who is the persecutor of all who will not worship him. The 'many' with whom the covenant is made can be, on the basis of the context, only Israel, still in unbelief" (Walvoord).

"Daniel's 'prince that shall come', our Lord's 'abomination', and Paul's 'man of sin,' all refer to the same person. He is a ruler, in political sovereignty over regions which include Jerusalem, for he makes a covenant with 'many', who can only be unbelieving Jews in Jerusalem, permitting the restoration of the temple service ('sacrifice and oblation', Dan. 9:27) for one 'week' " (Scofield).

"In the last days when God takes Israel up again and is about to bring them into fullness of blessing, a Roman prince will arise who will make a covenant with the nation for seven years, promising them protection and liberty in religion as they return to their land" (Ironside).

All of the above statements fall to the ground, because they read into the text what does not belong there. All speak of the making of a covenant, whereas the text says nothing whatsoever about this. Furthermore, vs. 26 states that the city and sanctuary will be destroyed by the people of a prince that will come. All of the above writers believe that the allusion is to the destruction of Jerusalem by the Romans. The destroying people are the Romans, but the prince is not Titus, not a prince of the historical Roman empire but of a future, revived Roman empire. It therefore follows, upon this view, that the people belong to a prince who will not appear for years (nearly 2000 have already elapsed) after they themselves have perished. But how can this be? How can the Roman armies of Titus possibly be regarded as belonging to a prince who has not even yet appeared? This interpretation can be adopted only because of extreme exegetical necessity.

As may be seen from the following quotations, various methods are used to escape the difficulty. Thus:

"Now the people who are here in view are the Romans. Out of the Roman empire there shall arise in the future a prince" (Gaebelein).

"And since it is now a matter of history that Jerusalem was destroyed in A.D. 70 by the *Roman* people, not by the Jewish people, it follows that 'the prince that shall come' cannot be the Jewish Messiah but is some great prince who will arise out of the Roman Empire" (McClain).

"The people represented here can be none other than those of Rome. The 'prince of the people' is accordingly a Roman prince" (Walvoord).

"And now we know from whence he will come, for it was his 'people', the Romans, who were the destroyers" (Scofield).

"He however (i.e., the prince) has not appeared yet, but his people, that is, the Roman people were used as the scourge of God to punish Israel for their sins, and they destroyed Jerusalem and the Temple of Jehovah" (Ironside).

These quotations will serve to give a good idea of the relation in which the prince and the people, are conceived (by the advocates of this hypothesis) as standing. Most of these statements appear to be based upon the assumption that since the prince will arise out of the Roman empire he will therefore be a Roman. In other words, he is, as Walvoord puts it "prince of the people". But the emphasis in vs. 26 is *not* upon a prince from the people, but upon the people who belong to the prince. This prince, therefore, must be one who rules over these people, who can truly say that they are his. In other words, he must be their contemporary, alive when they are alive. We cannot, by any stretch of the imagination, legitimately call the army of George Washington the army of a general, and by that general have reference to Eisenhower. The armies of Washington are in no sense Eisenhower's armies. And the fact that Eisenhower was born in America many years after the time of Washington's armies does not in the least permit us to say that they are his armies. The people who destroyed the city and the prince that should come (if *should come* is future, it is future from the standpoint of Dan., not of the destroying people) are contemporaries. Otherwise, the language makes no sense. And if the prince is a contemporary of his people, then the antecedent of "he shall cause to prevail" cannot be some prınce other than that mentioned in vs. 26.

This view, therefore, that a future Roman prince is to make a covenant with the Jews must be abandoned.

In what sense, however, may it be said that the Messiah causes a covenant to prevail for many? The answer to this question, it would seem, is to be found in the fact that the Messiah during His earthly ministry and by means of His active and passive obedience to the Law of God, did fulfill the terms of that covenant which was in olden times made with Abraham and his seed. Romans 15:8 speaks of this covenant as "the promises made unto the fathers."

This covenant which was made with the fathers is generally called the Covenant of Grace. Thus, the Westminster Confession rightly says (7:3), "Man by his fall having made himself incapable of life by that covenant (i.e., the Covenant of Works), the Lord was pleased to make a second,[11] commonly called the Covenant of Grace: whereby he freely offereth unto sinners life and salvation by Jesus Christ, requiring of them faith in him, that they may be saved;[12] and promising to give unto all those that are ordained unto life his Holy Spirit, to make them willing and able to believe.[13]

5) "This covenant was differently administered in the time of the law, and in the time of the gospel; under the law it was administered by promises, prophecies, sacrifices, circumcision, the paschal lamb, and other types and ordinances delivered to the people of the Jews, all foresignifying Christ to come, which were for that time sufficient and efficacious through the operation of the Spirit, to instruct and build up the elect in

---

[11] Gal. 3:21; Romans 3:20, 21; 8:3; Gen. 3:15; See Isa. 42:6.

[12] John 3:16; Romans 10:6, 9; Rev. 22:17.

[13] Acts 13:48; Ezek. 36:26, 27; John 6:37, 44, 45; I Cor. 12:3.

faith in the promised Messiah, by whom they had full remission of sins, and eternal salvation; and is called the Old Testament."

Thus, our Lord fulfilled the terms of this Covenant of Grace, that upon the basis of His finished work, life and salvation might be freely offered to sinners. This explanation, and this alone, fits the Heb. text. The language here employed is obviously based upon the ordinary Heb. idiom which is used to describe the making of a covenant. Thus:

To Cut A Covenant With (For) = To Make A Covenant
To Cause A Covenant To Prevail For = To Make A Covenant Efficacious

This covenant is caused to prevail *for the many.* Thus a contrast is introduced between *He* and the *Many,* a contrast which appears to reflect upon the great Messianic passage, Isa. 52:13-53:12 and particularly 53:11. Although the entire nation will not receive salvation, the many will receive it. Here, the particular reference appears to be to the Israelitish believers "for the period up to the stoning of Stephen, or perhaps, in mercy, until the time of the destruction of Jerusalem, at which time the 'new covenant', which was in fact only the full unfolding of the old covenant and made no distinction between Jew and Gentile, went fully into effect through the destruction of the temple and of Jewish national existence" (Allis).

When Do the Events of the Seventieth Seven Occur?

According to McClain, "—the Seventieth Week does not immediately follow the Sixty-ninth Week, but there is a great parenthesis of time between these two which has already lasted for over nineteen hundred years, and therefore the Seventieth Week still lies in the future."

"Between the sixty-ninth and the seventieth weeks we have a Great Parenthesis which has now lasted over nineteen hundred years" (Ironside).

"Between the sixty-ninth week, after which Messiah was cut off, and the seventieth week, within which the 'little horn' of Dan. 7, will run his awful course, intervenes this entire Church-age" (*SRB*).

"With this event (i.e., the rejection of the Messiah), as we have seen, the 69th week closed and an indefinite period of unreckoned time follows; when that is expired the last prophetic week of seven years will begin and run its appointed course" (Gaebelein).

According to the "Parenthesis" or "Gap" theory, therefore, the 69 weeks came to a close at some point during the earthly ministry of Christ. This point is often regarded, particularly since the appearance of Sir Robert Anderson's work, as the Triumphal Entry of our Lord (thus,

Gaebelein, Walvoord, McClain). Ironside is not dogmatic on the subject, and *SRB* merely says "—we are brought to the time of Christ. Prophetic time is invariably so near as to give full warning, so indeterminate as to give no satisfaction to mere curiosity (cf. Mt. 24:36; Acts 1:7)."

The arguments which are generally employed to support this position are the following:

1) The events of vs. 26 are said to take place *after* the sixty and two sevens of vs. 25. These events however (the cutting off of the Messiah and the destruction of the city and sanctuary) do not occur during the 70th seven but before it. It is the mention of these events of vs. 26 which is said to demand the presence of a gap or parenthesis between the 69th and 70th seven. Thus:

vs. 25	vs. 26	vs. 27
7 sevens and 62 sevens	Messiah cut off Destruction of city and sanctuary	Confirming of covenant
69 sevens	*Parenthesis*	*70th seven*

2) the events of vs. 24 have not yet been fulfilled. The 70 sevens, therefore, cannot yet have run their course and the 70th seven must be in the future.

3) "An unseen gap in prophetic time is not at all an unusual phenomenon in Old Testament prophecy" (McClain). McClain appeals to Isa. 9:6; Zech. 9:9-10; Isa. 61:1, 2.

4) Christ, by speaking of the abomination of desolation (Matt. 24:15), showed that the 70th seven was yet future.

These arguments are taken from McClain who has written one of the most attractive and cogent expositions of the Parenthesis Theory. In reply it may be said:

At first sight, the theory that a gap which already is nearly 2000 years in length (i.e., four times the length of the entire prophecy itself) should intervene between the last two sevens is surely surprising. Its startling character appears the more clearly when it is represented by a diagram

49 years | 440 years [GAP—2000 years] 1 year
|———————— THE SEVENTY SEVENS ————————|

Secondly, since there is no gap between the 1st period (7 sevens) and the 2nd (62 sevens), it comes as somewhat of a shock to learn that such a tremendously long gap must occur between the last two sevens.

These, however, are but general impressions. They have their place, certainly, but the question must finally be resolved upon the basis of exegesis alone.

1. It is true that the two events of vs. 26 are said to take place after the sixty and two sevens. However, *it is not said* that the events of vs. 27 occur *after* those of vs. 26. This is mere assumption. The exposition has already shown that the whole picture of a coming Roman prince who makes a covenant for one week with the Jews is based upon an incorrect interpretation of the Heb. Since vs. 26 declares that the Messiah is cut off (i.e., by death), He must cause the covenant to prevail *before* he dies or at least at the same time that He dies. The action of causing the covenant to prevail, therefore, belongs to the 70th seven and is contemporaneous with the death of the Messiah (vs. 26); which is to be placed in that 70th seven. If this be so, there certainly is no reason for assuming that the 70th seven does not immediately follow the sixty-two.

The destruction of the city and the sanctuary also follows the sixty and two sevens. However, it does not occur within the compass of the last seven. It is a detail of information which is added that the Jews may know what will befall their city *consequent* upon the death of the Messiah. Two events, therefore, are mentioned in vs. 26. One of these, as vs. 27 shows, belongs to the 70th seven; the other does not.

2) As the exposition has already shown, the events of vs. 24 have been fulfilled. The dispensationalists, however, press upon the language of this vs. a literal interpretation which the words were not intended to bear. Thus, e.g., the phrase "for restraining transgression" would have to mean the complete eradication of transgression. This, however, would be strange, for the dispensationalists insist that following the 70th seven there is to be the millennium when sin, although held down, will nevertheless be present.

3) Even if the passages to which McClain appealed did contain a gap—and they do not—this would not in itself prove that there was a similar gap in this present prophecy of Dan.[14]

4) It is assumed that when Christ spoke of the abomination of desolation, He had in mind this present passage of Dan. Since, therefore, He regarded the abomination as future, the 70th seven in which the abomination is to occur, must also be future. The NT references are Matt. 24:15, 16; Mk. 13:14; Luke 21:20, 21). A detailed discussion of Dan's language will be presented at the proper place (p. 218). It may at this point, however, be said, that the desolations depicted by Dan. in 9:27b are to be considered as *consequent* upon the causing the sacrifices and oblation to cease and not as necessarily falling within the compass of the 70 sevens. By this reference, our Lord had in mind, as the exposition will

[14] A careful study of the passages in question will make it clear that the gap which some profess to find is in reality not present. For a thorough study of the entire system of dispensational teaching see Allis.

endeavor to make clear, the encompassing of the city of Jerusalem by the armies of Titus. Calvin says, "Without the slightest doubt, this prophecy was fulfilled when the city was captured and overthrown, and the temple utterly destroyed by Titus the son of Vespasian. This satisfactorily explains the events here predicted."

In addition to the foregoing replies it should be clearly noted that the "parenthesis" view is not the natural interpretation of the prophecy. As vs. 24 shows, it is a period of 70 sevens which is determined. Mauro well remarks, "They (i. e., the language of vs. 24) are just the words which would be used by one who wished to be understood as saying that, within the measure of 70 weeks, the six things specified in Daniel 9:24 would happen." The 70 sevens are presented as a unit, just as are the 70 years of Jer. the study of which led Dan. to *understand* the years of the captivity. If there is no warrant for inserting a gap in Jer.'s prophecy, what warrant is there for doing so in the prophecy of the 70 sevens? Had there been a gap in Jer.'s prophecy (Jer. 29:10). Dan. could never have understood the years of the captivity. The prophecy would have deceived him. The same is true in the present case.

In this connection, it should be noted, as Mauro has ably pointed out, that when the measure of time in which an event is to occur is designated, the measure is intended in its plain and ordinary sense. Mauro gives the following examples:

a) Gen. 15:13; Ex. 12:40; Gal. 3:17—these were 430 *consecutive* years.

b) Gen. 45:6—the seven years of plenty and of famine were respectively *consecutive* years.

c) Nu. 14:34—the 40 years of the wandering were *consecutive* years.

d) The three days after which our Lord was to arise were three *consecutive* days.

Mauro concludes, and I can find no reason for disagreement, "We are bold, therefore, to lay it down as an absolute rule, admitting of no exceptions, that when a definite measure of time or space is specified by the number of units composing it, within which a certain event is to happen or a certain thing is to be found, the units of time or space which make up that measure are to be understood as running continuously and successively." The natural presumption, therefore, is that the prophecy is speaking of 70 *consecutive* sevens.

— — — — —

And in the midst of the seven]—The phrase does not mean "and during half of the week" (Stuart), but in the middle of the seven, at the time when half of the seven has run its course. Stuart maintains that for half a week ($3\frac{1}{2}$ years) Antiochus suspended the temple rites. If the translation half, be insisted upon, Stuart would be correct. But, it should be noted that the word means *midst* as well as *half*, and such is the meaning here. The thought is not that for half of the seven, the sacrifice ceases, but at the midst of the seven.

He shall cause sacrifice and oblation to cease]—The subject of this verb is the same as that of the preceding. It is not Antiochus who suspended the temple rites. Nor must the phrase mean, as Stuart suggests, "remove them by violence, forcibly suspend them." As the exposition has endeavored to show, this passage makes no reference to Antiochus. Nor is the subject a prince of the revived Roman Empire. Thus "—in the midst of the week he will violate the covenant and demand that all worship to Jehovah cease, and the Antichrist will be manifested in his true character" (Ironside). However, this statement is untenable. The subject is the Messiah, who by His death causes sacrifice and oblation to cease. The two words are intended to represent bloody and unbloody offerings, i. e., the entirety of worship by sacrifice.

It has been objected that the death of the Messiah did not bring to an end the Jewish sacrifices. The Epistle to the Hebrews, however, argues that Christ by His death, did abolish the sacrifices of the Old Covenant. Note the following:

"If therefore perfection were by the Levitical priesthood (for under it the people received the law) what further need was there that another priest should rise after the order of Melchisedec, and not be called after the order of Aaron?" (Heb. 7:11)

"In that he saith, A new covenant, he hath made the first old. Now that which decayeth and waxeth old is ready to vanish away" (Heb. 8:13).

"Nor yet that he should offer himself often, as the high priest entereth into the holy place every year with the blood of others;

"For then must he often have suffered since the foundation of the world: but now once in the end of the world hath he appeared to put away sin by the sacrifice of himself" (Heb. 9:25, 26).

"Above when he said, Sacrifice and offering and burnt offerings and offering for sin Thou wouldst not, neither hadst pleasure therein; which are offered by the law; then said he, Lo, I come to do thy will, O God, He taketh away the first, that He may establish the second" (Heb. 10:8, 9).

It is true that immediately after Christ's death the sacrifices did not cease. Nevertheless, at His death, the veil of the Temple was rent in twain; the way into the Holy of Holies was opened, the Gospel was preached, and the sacrifices of the Jews could not longer be regarded as legitimate. "When Christ was put to death, Jerusalem ceased to be the holy city, and the temple was no longer the house of God, but an abomination" (H). After Christ's death the sacrifices continued for a time, until the destruction of the city by Titus. However, this actual cessation was in reality but the outward manifestation of that which had already been put into effect by our Lord's death.

And upon the wing of abomination (*is*) *one making desolate*]—The language of this passage is extremely difficult. In the first place it is necessary to determine the meaning of *wing*. The word is not to be changed so as to read *in its place* (Bevan, Prince). Nor does it mean *on wings*, i. e., that the desolator (the prince) will be carried on the wings of abominations (Keil, Kliefoth).[15] Nor is the reference to the wings of an army (Rosenmueller—exercitui detestando vastator dux praeerit). Nor does it mean *winged-fowl* (Stuart), i. e., over an abominable winged-fowl is a desolator, the reference being to the statue of Jupiter Olympius, which stood over an eagle with outspread wings. There is no point in adducing other views. The word apparently refers to the pinnacle of the temple which has become so desecrated that it no longer can be regarded as the temple of the Lord, but as an idol temple. The word *wing* is used of the extremity of the upper garment (I Sam. 15:27; 24:5) and of the uttermost part of the earth (Isa. 24:16) and (in the pl.) of the ends of the earth. It is true, as Keil indicates, that it is elsewhere never used of the highest point or peak of an object. However, that is precisely the sense in which it is *here* used. The wing of the temple (Matt. 4:5; Luke 4:9) is the summit of the temple itself. By the phrase *wing of abominations*, therefore, reference is made, it would seem, to the pinnacle of the temple. In what sense, however, may the temple be described as *abominations?* The word has a primary reference to idols. Now, at the time of Titus, actual idols were not erected in the Temple. Therefore, the word must be used figuratively to describe the worship of the Temple after the veil had been rent in twain. No longer was this the house of the Lord, but a house of abominations, for the true worship of Jehovah had ceased. The *one making desolate* is said to be over or upon the wing of abominations, i. e., he comes over the summit or highest pinnacle of the Temple, thus signifying its utter destruction, ". . . . inasmuch as the capture of the highest part presupposes the possession of all the rest" (H). The historical reference, I believe, is found in the destruction of the Temple by Titus. This event must be regarded, not as necessarily falling within the 70th seven, but as *consequent* upon the action of the

[15] The word is s. and construct and is introduced by the prep. 'al. It can only mean *upon the wing of*. The examples which Keil adduces are not really parallel since in these passages the pl. *wings of* is used. Isa. 24:16 does not mean from the ends of the earth, but from the end (wing) of the earth.

Messiah in causing the sacrifice and oblation to cease. *And until end and that determined shall pour upon the desolate*]—The rendering "even until the consummation" (AV) does not appear faithfully to represent the Heb. (See M for philological discussion). The word *end* means *full end*, and with the phrase *that determined* should be regarded as the subject of *shall pour*. In my opinion the phrase *that determined* has reference to the *full end*, so that we might paraphrase as follows, "and until the full end which has been determined shall pour upon the desolate." It is "a determined end," cf. Isa. 10:23; 28:22, from which the words appear to be taken. The *desolate* is not Titus, i. e., one who is made desolate, but rather is impersonal, that which is desolate, i. e., the ruins of the Temple and city. (See H for the philological discussion). Thus, since the Messiah has caused sacrifices and oblation to cease, there comes a desolator over the temple, and devastation continues until a full, determined end pours forth upon the desolation.

According to Gaebelein, the wing of abominations has reference to the protection of the idols which the apostate masses (during the latter half of the 70th seven) will seek. On account of this abomination there will be a desolator (from outside the land) who will "devastate the land and conquer Jerusalem till the consummation is reached. The consummation is the close of the seven years. When that is reached the desolator himself will be dealt with in judgment as well as the two beasts." This desolator is said to be the King of the North.

There are several considerations which conclusively demonstrate the untenableness of this position:

1) The word *wing* (s. not pl.) does not mean protection, but the extreme point, see the exposition above.

2) The Heb. word upon which Gaebelein bases his conclusion "on account of," means "upon." The translation "on account of" does not here faithfully reflect the Heb.

3) The rendering "until the consummation" is, as the exposition has endeavored to indicate, inaccurate.

4) The end determined will pour out, not upon a desolator, but upon the desolate.

Gaebelein's interpretation appears to be based upon the English Bible alone. The Heb. text will not allow such a view.

The last half of vs. 27 presents one of the principal stumbling-blocks in the way of the dispensational interpretation, and many of the representatives of this school pass over these words in comparative silence. To Gaebelein belongs the credit of having at least made an endeavor to do some justice to the language of the text.

Summary

In response to his prayer, Gabriel announces to Dan. that a period of sevens—the exact length of the seven is not stated—in fact, seventy of them, has been decreed for the purpose of accomplishing the Messianic work. This Messianic work is described both in negative and positive terms; negative—restraining the transgression, completing sin and covering iniquity; positive—bringing in everlasting righteousness, sealing vision and prophet and anointing a holy of holies.

Dan. therefore is to know and understand that from the going forth of a word to restore and build Jerusalem unto an anointed one who is also a prince (i.e., a royal priest) is seven sevens and sixty and two sevens. We are not told when this word went forth from the Lord but the effects of its issuance first appear in the return from bondage during the first year of Cyrus. This period is divided into two. The first period of seven sevens is evidently intended to include the time from the first year of Cyrus to the completion of the work of Ezra and Nehemiah, and the second that from the completion of the work of Ezra and Nehemiah unto the first advent of Christ who alone can be described as an anointed one a prince. During this entire period the city will be completely rebuilt although this will be accomplished during times of distress and affliction.

After the expiration of these two periods, two events are to occur Whether or not these two events fall within the 70th seven is not imme diately stated. One of them is the death of the Messiah and the other fol lows as a consequent, the destruction of Jerusalem and the Temple by th Roman armies of Titus.

For the period of the 70th seven the Messiah causes a covenant to pre vail for many, and in the half of this seven by His death He causes th Jewish sacrifices and oblation to cease. His death is thus seen to belon within the 70th seven. Consequent upon this causing the sacrifices an oblation to cease is the appearance of a desolator over the pinnacle (the Temple, which has now become an abomination. Upon the ruins determined full end pours out. This event, the destruction of the cit does not, therefore, take place within the 70 sevens, but follows as a co sequent upon the cutting off of the Messiah in the 70th seven.

The question naturally arises, What marks the termination of the 7 sevens? In answer it should be noted that the text does not say a wo about the termination. The *terminus ad quem* of the 69 sevens is clear stated, namely, an anointed one, a prince. No such *terminus ad quer* however, is given for the 70 sevens themselves. It would seem, therefor that the *terminus ad quem* was not regarded as possessing particul importance or significance. No important event is singled out as marki the termination. All schools of interpretation, therefore, are faced wi the difficulty of determining what marked the close of the 70 sevens. And all schools discover this event upon the basis of considerations other than those presented in the text. The text says nothing upon the subject. Therefore, we may safely follow the text. When the 70 sevens come to a conclusion, we do not know.

For that matter, the text is somewhat vague about the *terminus a quo* of the 70 sevens. It speaks merely of the going forth of a word. It appears that the principal emphasis is not upon the beginning and ending of this remarkable period but upon the mighty events which were to transpire therein, events which have wrought our peace with God. The passage is Messianic through and through. Well will it be for us, if we too, in our study of this supremely important prophecy, place our emphasis, not upon dates and mathematical calculations, but upon that central Figure who was both anointed and a prince, who by being cut off has made reconciliation for iniquity and brought in the only righteousness that is acceptable with God, even His own eternal righteousness.

CHAPTER TEN

Chs. 10-12. The Vision in the Third Year of Cyrus

a. vv. 1-3. Introduction to the manifestation of God.

Vs. 1. *In the third year of Cyrus king of Persia a word was revealed to Daniel whose name was called Belteshazzar. And true was the word and a great warfare and he understood the word and there was understanding to him in the vision.* There is no conflict between this date and that given in 1:21 (see exposition of that passage). It is evident, therefore, that Dan. did not return to Palestine with the first deportation under Zerubbabel but remained in Babylon. He was now an old man, and God had yet a further revelation to give him. His work in Babylon, therefore, was not yet complete. Bevan shows the low view of the book which he holds by remarking, "Some commentators have spent much time in discussing why Daniel remained in Babylonia until the third year of Cyrus instead of availing himself of the opportunity to return to Palestine. If we regarded the narrative of Daniel as historical it might be worthwhile to seek for an explanation of the fact, but for those who believe Daniel to be an ideal figure no explanation is needed." But if Dan. were merely an ideal figure, the creation of a Judaistic writer of the Maccabean age, why does not he conform to the image of Judaism and be made to return to Palestine? The fact that Dan. does not return to Palestine is a strong argument against the view that the book is a product of the Maccabean age. *King of Persia*] —This designation of Cyrus was contemporary usage (despite M). For the use of the titles of Persian kings the reader should consult R. D. Wilson, "The Title 'King of Persia' in the Scriptures, *PTR,* Vol. XV, 1917, pp. 90-145 and "Royal Titles in Antiquity: An Essay in Criticism," *PTR,* Vol. II. 1904, pp. 257-282; 465-497; 618-664; Vol. III, 1905, pp. 55-80; 238-267; 422-440; 558-572. *A word was revealed*]—The word is the Divine utterance, the content of which is to be found in the following revelation, which was vouchsafed to Dan. in an appearance of God, given in simple human speech. *Belteshazzar*]—Dan. speaks of himself here in the third person since this vs. forms a general statement of introduction to the revelation. He adds his Babylonian name, it would seem, because the Babylonian empire is now overthrown and he would preserve his identity among the people. He thus attests that he is the same person who was carried into captivity over seventy years previously and that he is the one concerning whom the previous portions of the book relate. *True*] —lit., *true was the word, true* being placed first and so emphacized. The reason for this assertion is that the message is difficult (cf. Rev. 19:9; 21:5; 22:6). *Warfare*]—These words are intended to show in what respect the revelation is difficult. They thus refer to what precedes, not (as in the Vss.) to what follows. The Vss. translate, *army* or *force;* some of the Jews *an appointed time,* Calvin, *the time will be long.* But the idea seems to be that the "warfare" is in the revelation itself, and that with this revelation the prophet must struggle (cf. vs. 2). Hence, M well translates "task"; Luther, "a great struggle." *He understood*]—in contrast to 8:27. Here the reference is to the vision which follows. ". . . by this assertion he confirms the prophecy which he is about to explain, and thus assures us of his not uttering anything either perplexed or obscure" (Calvin). *There was understanding*]—i. e., by means of the vision understanding came to him. "What he means to say is, that the manner of the vision which follows was such, that he attained to a satisfactory understanding of it—such an understanding as he had not had in respect to either of the three preceding visions; see 7:15, 28, 8:27, 10:12" (Stuart).

Vs. 2. *In those days I Daniel was mourning three full weeks.* Dan. now speaks in the 1st person. *In those days* refers back to the date given in vs. 1. The mourning in which Dan. engaged expressed itself in fasting. (cf. Matt. 9:14ff.) It may have been occasioned because he had heard that all was not going well with the rebuilding of the temple in Jerusalem (Calvin). On the other hand it may have been occasioned by reflection upon the sins of his people. *Three full weeks*]—lit., *three weeks, days.* The word *days* is added, not to indicate that these were weeks of ordinary days as distinguished from the weeks of Dan. 9:24-27, but to bring out the idea of duration, *three weeks long, three entire weeks.*

Vs. 3. *Pleasant food I did not eat, and flesh and wine did not enter my mouth, nor did I at all anoint myself, until the completing of three full weeks.* Dan. abstrained from delicacies (pleasant food) and also ordinary food and drink. During a period of sorrow or mourning, the anointing with oil, a sign of joy (cf. Amos 6:6), was omitted (2 Sam. 14:2). The length of this fast gives evidence of deep and sincere humiliation.

b. vv. 4-8. The vision of God.

Vs. 4. *And in the twenty-fourth day of the first month, as I was beside the great river, namely, the Tigris.* This period would include the Passover and Feast of Unleavened Bread. Passover fell on the 14th of the month Abib, Ex. 23:15, (later called Nisan, Neh. 2:1), and the Feast of Unleavened Bread, on the 15th to 21st. The date herein mentioned would be three days after the conclusion of the Feast. Dan. is present in body beside the river, not in a vision, as in 8:2.

Vs. 5. *That I lifted up mine eyes, and I saw, and behold! a man clothed in linen, and his loins girded with gold of Uphaz.* The linen clothing indicates a celestial visitant (cf. Ezek. 9:2, 3, 11; 10:2, 6, 7; Mark 16:5). *Gold*]—i. e., fine gold. The word chosen is poetical, and occurs in the expression, gold of Ophir (Isa. 13:12). *Uphaz* is taken by many as indicating a place. No such place, however, is known. M makes out a strong case for translating "gold and fine gold."

Vs. 6. *And his body as beryl and his countenance as the appearance of lightning, and his eyes as torches of fire, and his arms and his feet as the appearance of polished bronze, and the voice of his words as the voice of a multitude.* "In a word, he appeared in dazzling splendor and magnificence throughout" (Stuart). This remarkable description is in many respects reminiscent of Ezek. 1. The Jews were wont to identify this figure with an angel. H considers him to be Michael. However, the description seems to indicate that the majestic Person here presented is none other than the Lord Himself. The revelation therefore is a theophany, a preincarnate appearance of the eternal Son. This is proved by the very similar description (Rev. 1:13-15) of the One whom John sees walking in the midst of the seven golden candlesticks. *Beryl*]—lit., Tarshish, i. e., a Tarshish stone, chrysolith. Pliny describes this stone as "a transparent stone brought from Tarshish." "—said to be the topaz of the moderns" (Driver). Cf. also Ezek. 1:16; 10:9. *Torches of fire*]—This same description appears in Ezek. 1:13 "like the appearance of torches." *Appearance of polished bronze*]—lit., *the eye.* Cf. again Ezek. 1:7. *Voice of his words*]—i. e., the sound. "An impressive, but inarticulate, sound seems to be what the comparison is intended to suggest" (Driver).

Vs. 7. *And I Daniel alone saw the vision, and the men who were with me did not see the vision, but great trembling fell upon them, and they fled, for they hid themselves.* Trembling came upon the companions of Dan., not because of thunder and lightning, nor because they heard a voice, but because of the nearness (invisible to them but visible to Dan.) of the heavenly Being. Cf. Acts 9:3ff, where Paul's companions hear a voice but see no one. AV "they fled to hide themselves" is not accurate. Rather, by hiding themselves they reveal that they have fled.

Vs. 8. *And I was left alone, and I saw this great vision and there was not left in me strength, and my comeliness was changed upon me to disfigurement, and not did I retain strength.* Dan. was left alone, his companions having fled, and then he saw the vision. *Great*]—i. e., grand, majestic, such as he had not seen before. *Comeliness*]—i. e., "the natural beauty of a living thing, its appropriate strength and grace" (M).

c. vv. 9-14. The introductory words of the heavenly Being.

Vs. 9. *And I heard the voice of his words, and as I heard the voice of his words, then I was in a deep sleep upon my face, and my face was on the ground.* Upon hearing the sound of the Speaker's words, Dan. fell into a deep sleep or swoon upon the ground.

Vs. 10. *And behold! a hand touched me and it shook me upon my knees, and the palms of my hands.* Gradually Dan. is restored to consciousness. The hand shakes him, i. e., by way of rousing him, so that he is upon his knees. Only after he hears the words of comfort is he enabled to stand upright.

Vs. 11. *And he said unto me, Daniel, a man greatly beloved, give heed to the words which I am about to speak unto thee and stand upright, for now have I been sent unto thee, and while he was speaking with me this word, I stood trembling.* The Messenger encourages Dan. by assuring him that he is beloved to God, and by urging him to give heed to the message and to stand upright, since now, at last, He has been sent to Dan. As the Messenger speaks, Dan. stands upright, although in trepidation at the word to be revealed.

Vs. 12. *And he said unto me, Fear not Daniel, for from the first day when thou didst set thy heart to understand and to afflict thyself before thy God, thy words were heard, and I have come because of thy words.* From the time when Dan. first applied himself to understand the future of his people and to humble himself through fasting and sorrow before God, his words were heard, and because of his prayer, the present revelation was granted.

Vs. 13. *And the Prince of the kingdom of Persia was standing before me twenty one days, and behold! Michael, one of the chief princes, came to help me, and I was left there near the kings of Persia.* The coming of the Messenger to Dan. was hindered for twenty one days, the period of Dan.'s fasting, by the Prince of the kingdom of Persia. The Prince is not the king of Persia (Calvin, Hævernick), for the thought here is that of spiritual warfare, cf. Rev. 12:7. Furthermore, the earthly kings of Persia are designated by the words *kings of Persia;* Israel has an angelic "prince", Michael, hence, it is to be expected that the prince of Persia should also be an angel. The prince here is the guardian angel of Persia (cf. Isa. 24:21; 46:2; Jer. 46:25; I Cor. 8:5; 10:20), i. e., the "supernatural spiritual power standing behind the national gods, which we may properly call the guardian spirit of this kingdom" (Keil). *Standing before me*]— This spirit influenced the kings of Persia to support the Samaritans against Israel. In such a manner the "prince" stood before the Speaker. For twenty one days he continued until Michael came to aid. Then, the Speaker prevailed and was left near the kings of Persia (i. e., victorious), the Prince having been worsted. The Speaker is the "Angel of the Lord" (i. e., the Lord Himself) who here makes war on behalf of His own against the hostile spirit of the heathen world powers. To the aid of the Speaker came Michael, the prince of Israel, as a servant to aid his Master in obtaining the victory. (cf. Jude 9 and Rev. 12:7). The designation, *one of the chief princes,* seems to indicate an arrangement of degrees among the angels, and among these Michael was an archangel.

Vs. 14. *And I am come to cause thee to understand that which shall happen to thy people in the latter days, for there is still a vision for the days.* The fact that the Angel has come, i. e., from God, is no argument against His deity. (Cf. the similar expressions in Gen. 16:13; 18; 19; 31:11ff.; 32:24; 48:15, 16). *In the latter days*]—not the days of Antiochus (Driver) but the Messianic age (see note on 2:28). So Jerome "non in vicino tempore, sed in novissimis diebus, id est, in consummatione saeculi." Gaebelein applies the phrase to the last three and one half years of the 70th seven. However, it never has this meaning in the O. T. The language is taken from Gen. 49:1. *A vision*]—This vision is the word of vs. 1, the revelation given in ch. 11 which has to do with *the days,* i. e., the Messianic days. Thus, the central purport of this revelation is concerned with the Messianic age. This, however, does not preclude reference to Antiochus.

d. vv. 15-11:1. Daniel is made capable of receiving the full revelation from the Messenger.

Vs. 15. *And while he was speaking with me according to these words, I set my face toward the ground and was dumb.* In spite of the Angel's previous assurance, Dan. does not regain his composure. "As yet, he stood with his eyes fixed on the ground, dreading to look up and speechless" (Driver). "By becoming prostrate on the ground, he manifested his reverence, and by becoming dumb displayed his astonishment" (Calvin). Vs. 16. *And behold, as the likeness of the sons of men was touching upon my lips, and I opened my mouth and I spake and I said unto him who stood before me, My Lord, by the vision my pangs are changed upon me, and I have not retained strength.* One in human form touched Dan.'s lips in order that he might speak. Thus his power of speech was restored and he immediately explained the reason for his continued silence. *My pangs*] —Thus I translate, following M, who presents the philological evidence in support of the rendering. It is a figure of "extreme desperation" (M).

Vs. 17. *And how is the servant of my Lord here able to speak with that my Lord, since for me now no strength remains in me, and no breath is left in me.* The usual form of address employed among the Hebrews by a servant in speaking to a superior. *Now*]—i.e., at present.

Vs. 18. *And there touched me again as the appearance of a man and he strengthened me.* Dan.'s recovery is by degrees. He is again touched and strengthened in spirit. The word *appearance* is a different one from that translated *likeness* in vs. 16. The previous touch (vs. 16) restores the power of speech, this one completes Dan.'s recovery.

Vs. 19. *And he said, Fear not, man beloved, peace be to thee, be strong and take courage, and while he was speaking with me, I was strengthened, and I said, Let my Lord speak, for thou hast strengthened me.* The Speaker greets Dan. with the common greeting, peace be to thee. The imperative is repeated, lit., *be strong and be strong,* i. e., be very strong or take good courage. This repetition adds to the intensity of the expression. Stuart points out that the expression *I was strengthened* has somewhat of the reflexive idea in it, and he translates, *I felt myself strengthened.* "It is very useful to us to take due notice of this mental tranquility, because the Prophet ought first to become a diligent scholar to enable him afterwards to discharge for us the office of a faithful teacher" (Calvin).

Vs. 20. *And he said, Dost thou know why I have come unto thee, and now, I shall return to fight with the Prince of Persia and I shall go out, and behold! the Prince of Greece comes.* The question addressed to Dan. is not intended to elicit information, but rather to call Dan.'s attention to what has already been said (vv. 12-14). The words of the Speaker are difficult, and many interpretations have been offered. It seems to me that the meaning is as follows: "I go now to continue my warfare with the Prince of Persia in order that I may maintain the position already gained" (vs. 13). This would have reference to the hindrances and difficulties which the Jews would experience under the Persian rule in the rebuilding of their city walls and Temple. *I shall go out*]—i. e., from the struggle with the Prince of Persia, and another struggle will begin, that with the Prince of Greece.

Vs. 21. *But I shall make known to thee what is inscribed in the writing of truth, and there is no one putting forth strength with me against these except Michael your prince.* The chiastic order of these vv. has caused some to suggest a rearrangement. But 21a is evidently introduced to interrupt the train of thought and may be regarded as parenthetical. The Speaker has already declared that the people of God must experience the opposition of Persia and Greece. However, this opposition cannot exceed the limits of what has been decreed by God, it is inscribed in the writing of truth. The future, therefore, is pre-determined by God. These words, although they appear to break the train of thought, serve a very useful purpose in the consolation which they would bring to Dan., and should be allowed to stand where they are. Against these foes, i, e., Persia and Greece, there is none to help the Speaker, except Michael. This would seem to imply that severe trials are in store for the people of God. The *writing of truth* is not the book of Dan. itself (Gaebelein) but simply the writing in which the truth of what God has determined is recorded. It is, of course, a figurative expression, cf. Ps. 139:16; Mal. 3:16 and Rev. 5:1.

CHAPTER ELEVEN

Vs. 1. *And I, in the first year of Darius the Mede, I stood up to be a supporter and a stronghold unto him.* This vs. really belongs with the preceding. The Speaker now relates how He had previously been a help to Michael. During the first year of Darius, when the overthrow of Babylonia by Medio-Persia was effected, the Speaker had furnished to Michael the aid and support which he needed. *I stood up*]—lit., my standing up, *Unto him*]—not unto Darius (H) but unto Michael. Thus we learn that the overthrow of Babylon was accomplished by the Lord working through His archangel.

11:2 - 12:3. *The revelation of the future.*

a. vs. 2. The kings of Persia.

Vs. 2. *And now shall I make known to thee the truth, behold! yet three kings are to stand for Persia, and the fourth shall be abundantly rich above all, and when he has grown strong through his riches, he will arouse all the kingdom of Greece.* The Messenger again assures Dan. of the veracity of His message. Perhaps the word *truth* reflects upon the "writing of truth" mentioned in 10:21. This *truth* has to do with the future order of events in Persia, as Jerome early indicated. It is that there will be yet three kings over Persia, and after them a fourth, who will be very rich. The interpretations fall into two principal classes:

1) That which regards the third as the last king, i. e., the third after Cyrus, Calvin, e.g., identifies, 1. Cyrus, 2. Cambyses, 3. Darius Hystaspis, 4. Xerxes. Thus Xerxes is the third of the kings yet to arise, but if Cyrus be reckoned as first, he would be fourth. Calvin regards Smerdis as an impostor and does not include him for that reason. Polychronius[1] adopted

---

[1] Concerning the life of Polychronius, bishop of Aparnea, very little is known. He was bishop about 428 A.D. and a brother of Theodore of Mopsuestia. Some fragments of his commentary on Dan. are extant, in which he adopts an historical interpretation, applying passages to Antiochus instead of to Antichrist. He regarded the 4th kingdom as Macedonian, and is considered to have been one of the best interpreters of the Bible of the Antiochene school.

the order, Cyrus, Cambyses, Pseudo-Smerdis. Hitzig and Maurer take Cyrus, Darius, Xerxes.[2]

2) The second interpretation considers the words of the text to have been written *during* the reign of the first king, Cyrus. When, therefore, it is stated that there are *yet* three kings to arise, the meaning must be: that these kings will arise *after* Cyrus. The four kings would then be: 1. Cambyses. 2. Smerdis. 3. Darius Hystaspis, 4. Xerxes. This view is adopted by Jerome, Theodoret, Rosenmueller, Hævernick, Keil. It is probable that these four kings are intended, although it may be that the author wished merely to lay stress upon four historical epochs rather than upon the kings as such. It is perfectly true that there were more than four kings after Cyrus. The fact that the writer mentions but four kings is not that he knew only four (Hitzig) but apparently because he wishes to lay stress upon four important epochs which will follow that of Cyrus.[3] *The fourth*]—i. e., beginning with Cyrus, there were *five* kings all told, and the one designated *the fourth* is the last of these.

1.			Cyrus.
2.	1	YET	Cambyses.
3.	2	TO	Smerdis.
4.	3	STAND.	Darius Hystaspis.
5.	The 4th.		Xerxes.

At any rate the reference appears to be to Xerxes, whom Jerome calls "potentissimus rex et ditissimus, adversum Graeciam innumerabilem duxit exercitum, et ea gessit quae Græcorum narrant historiae." Cf. Her. 3:96; 7:27-29; DS 11:3. *Grown strong through his riches*]—The king spent his treasures for the raising and maintaining of a great army. *All*]—The last words of this vs. are extremely difficult. Possibly the phrase the *kingdom of Greece* is to be taken in apposition to *all. All* would then be used in a hyperbolical sense as denoting an extensive nation.

---

[2] M identifies Cyrus and the three yet to come, Xerxes, Artaxerxes, Darius III Codomannus, "the four Persian kings named in the Bible." Charles argues that since Cyrus is yet reigning, he must be included in the four. He thus finds Cyrus and Xerxes as 1st and last, and says that Cambyses and Darius Hystaspis should rightly be 2nd and 3rd. However, he is inclined to follow Bevan in thinking that the four kings of Ezra 4:5-7 are intended, but in the order Cyrus, Darius Hystaspis, Artaxerxes, Xerxes. Then he concludes, "If this is right, the reckoning of Xerxes as the successor of Artaxerxes would be one of the historical errors of the book." But Charles is incorrect.

b. vv. 3, 4. Alexander and the divisions of his kingdom.

Vs. 3. *And there shall stand up a mighty king and shall rule with a great rule and shall do according to his will.* The reference is to Alexander the Great, who is well characterized by the adjective *mighty.* Commentators point out that in describing Alexander, Q. Cur. employs the same language as does the Messenger in this passage. "By the aid of his good fortune, he seemed to the nations to do whatsoever he pleased (agere-quidquid placebat)" (10:5:35). Cf. also Dan. 8:5ff.

Vs. 4. *And when he shall stand up his kingdom shall be broken, and shall be divided to the four winds of heaven, and not to his posterity, and not according to his rule which he ruled, for his kingdom shall be plucked up, even for others apart from these.* "This language is concise, but there is no ambiguity in the sense" (Calvin). The framework of the vs. in some respects reflects upon 8:8. *When he shall stand up*]—lit., *and according to his standing up,* i.e., when the king has come to power. The expression suggests the brevity of his power. As is well known, Alexander was but 32 years of age at his death in Babylon. *Shall be divided*]—This division did not occur immediately upon the death of Alexander, but a few years thereafter. The *four winds of heaven* are mentioned merely to indicate that a four-fold division of the kingdom occurred. The direction or cardinal point is not the chief concern of the writer. *His posterity*]—The kingdom does not pass over to the actual children of Alexander. "Alexander had two sons; one named Hercules, by Barsine the daughter of Darius, who was assassinated soon after his father's death by Polysperchon; the other, by Roxana, who was named Alexander, and with his guardian Philip Aridæus was shortly cut off in the same manner" (Stuart). *Not according to his rule*]—None of the subsequent kingdoms shall be as great as was that of Alexander. On the contrary they shall be far inferior. *Apart from these*]—In itself this phrase is ambiguous. Does it mean, in addition to these, or, in exclusion to these? This latter view finds the antecedent in *Posterity* and asserts that the kingdom will belong, not to Alexander's posterity, but to others, namely, the four generals. So, Stuart. But, the meaning of the text probably is that in addition to the four-fold division, the kingdom shall belong also to others, namely, the petty dynasties which arose after the death of Alexander.

This prophecy was remarkably fulfilled. At the death of Alexander, the kingdom did not pass into the hands of his sons. His twelve generals divided the spoils of empire among themselves. At first Aridæus was

---

[3] Jerome preserves an interesting comment upon this point, "Non enim curae fuit spiritui prophetali historiae ordinem sequi, sed praeclara quaeque perstringere."

made king, but finally the four-fold division, already described in Dan. 8:8ff. emerged, and these four kingdoms were established. Thus was the great empire of Alexander "plucked up" and "broken." For the historical sources, see: D.S. 19:105; 20:28; Pausanias 9:7; Appian's *Syria* 51.

c. vv. 5-20. The wars between the kings of the South and of the North for dominion over the Holy Land.

Vs. 5. *And the king of the South shall be strong, and one of his princes, and he shall be strong above him and will rule; a great rule is his rule.* In the OT the word "south" usually applies to the Negeb, the land south of Palestine, but in this ch. it refers to Egypt, as is shown by vs. 8 where the North is placed in opposition to Egypt. *One of his princes*]—i.e.,one from among the princes of the king of the South. It is also possible to translate this phrase, *and one of his princes shall be stronger than he.* This translation requires no change of the text, and is adopted by some of the versions. However, it is contrary to the Mass. punctuation. The thought is that one of the princes of the king will prevail in strength above the king himself. The meaning is not that he will conquer the king, but that his rule will be far greater than that of the king. Rosenmueller adopts the strange view that the prince is one of Alexander's princes, (namely Ptolemy) but this would require that Ptolemy become greater than Alexander which is contrary to historical fact.

The king of the South is Ptolemy Soter, the son of Lagus, a Macedonian, an extremely capable and able general of Alexander who, after Alexander's death, obtained Egypt and ruled as satrap from 322 to 305 B.C. He died in 285 B.C. The prince of Ptolemy is Seleucus, also an officer of Alexander's who received the satrapy of Babylonia at the meeting in Triparadisus 321. When he was forced to flee, because Antigonus had taken Babylonia from him, he came to Ptolemy who appointed him a general and so recovered Babylonia in 312 B.C. the date from which the Seleucid's era is reckoned.

As a matter of actual historical fact, the dominion of the Seleucids did greatly exceed that of the Ptolemies. It reached from Phrygia in the west to the Indus on the east. For the sources, see DS 19:55,58; Appian 55; Arrian, *Anabasis* 7:22.

Zoeckler, who is a staunch defender of the integrity of the book of Dan., believes that in ch. 11 the work of a later redactor is present. He reasons as follows, "We believe ourselves warranted in holding a different view respecting this chapter, which is the chief support for the assumption of a continued series of the most special predictions, and therefore prefer to accept a revision in the time of Antiochus Epiphanes, by a pious apocalyptic investigator. Hence we charge the thorough description of the kingdoms of the Seleucidæ down to that tyrant, to the account of the modifying agency of this interpolator. We are not led to this view, either by a preconceived opinion that the Spirit of prophecy is incapable of producing such special predictions, or by a one-sided reference to the analogy of the remaining prophetical books of the Old Testament, which contain no such detailed descriptions of the future; but the decisive circumstance which arouses our suspicion concerning the assumption that Dan. XI is throughout and in all its details a proper prediction, and which even directly forbids it, is the fact that the Revelation of St. John, besides our book the only independent and more comprehensive production of the canonical apocalypse, *everywhere presents only ideal pictures of the future*" (translated by James Strong).

Zoeckler's position is thus set forth in order that the reader may more properly understand his comments upon the individual vv. The present writer cannot accept Zoeckler's position for the following reasons:

1. It amounts to the assumption of a pious fraud. The book of Dan. is a unit, and, as Green says, "—its eleventh chapter must share the fate of all the rest. If they are genuine, it is. If it is interpolated, there is no security that the others are not interpolated too."[4]

2. If ch. 11, particularly vv. 5-39, is attributed to an interpolator, the very heart or gist of the prophecy is removed and an irreparable hiatus is left. In other words all that remains is introduction and sequel. It is inconceivable that the original form of the prophecy should not have contained these vv. which form the message itself.

3. Zœckler's theory is subjective. It is not the business of the expositor to decide or to prescribe what methods God may use in revealing His Word. The duty of the expositor is to expound that Word as best he can.

Vs. 6. *And at the end of some years they shall join themselves together and the daughter of the king of the South shall come unto the king of the North to make an agreement, but she will not retain the strength of the arm, and neither will he stand nor his arm, and she shall be given up, and they that brought her and he that begat her and he that strengthened her in (those) times.* After the expiration of a course of years (cf. 2 Chr. 18:2) alliances will be formed. The subject is not "others" of vs. 4 (Kranichfeld) nor the king of the South and his prince (Keil) but the kings of the North and South after some time (Stuart). The verb may be taken impersonally in order to bring out its force. The reference, therefore is not

[4] William Henry Green, "Recent Expositions of Daniel" in *The Biblical Repertory and Princeton Review*, Vol. XLIII, New York, 1871, p. 398.

to Ptolemy Lagi and Seleucus Nicator (as in vs. 5) but probably to Ptolemy Philadelphus and Antiochus II (Theos), and the alliances described occurred 35 years after the death of Seleucus. *Agreement*]—lit., *uprightnesses*. The daughter of Ptolemy, Berenice, will go to Antiochus II as his wife, thus carrying out the terms of the agreement. Thus, she will *right* things. *She will not retain*]—Berenice, by means of this marriage, will not be able to maintain herself against her rival (See below for historical background). For that matter the king himself, i.e., Antiochus, will also not be able to stand, and *his arm*, i.e., his power and strength, will come to an end. *She shall be given up*]—Berenice shall be given up to death by her rival Laodice. *They that brought her*]—i.e., those who brought her to the Syrian king. The reference is not to her begetter nor to the one that led her home, but, apparently to those who brought her into the marriage. "The plural will designate the court of Ptolemy, who were doubtless concerned with the negotiation of the marriage" (Stuart) *And he that begat her etc.*]—Some believe that both references are to Ptolemy Philadelphus; others that the one who begat her is Ptolemy and the one who strengthened her is Antiochus. The text is difficult.

Antiochus II, called Theos (God), the grandson of Seleucus I, fo political purposes, married Berenice, the daughter of Ptolemy Philadel phus. But Antiochus was already married to Laodice, who had given hin two sons, Seleucus Callinicus and Antiochus. Berenice was brought t Antiochus in great pomp. Two years later Ptolemy died, and Antiochu divorced Berenice, taking back Laodice, from whom he had been separatec Laodice, fearing lest her husband might again turn to Berenice,[5] had hir poisoned and encouraged her son Seleucus to murder both Berenice an her infant, thus obtaining the throne for himself.

Vs. 7. *And there shall stand (one) from the branch of his roots (in) h place, and he shall come unto the army and shall come in the stronghol of the king of the North and shall deal with them and shall shew strengt* One of the shoots from Berenice's roots, i.e., from her ancestry, will stan in the place of Ptolemy Philadelphus. The reference is to the brother Berenice, Ptolemy Euergetes, the third Ptolemy in Egypt. He comes un the army, i.e., *against* the army of the North (not *to* power Haevernic nor *to his own* army Hitzig, Kliefoth), and enters even the strongho (i.e., the fortresses and territory) of the king of the North. In this exp dition he does according to his will against his enemy's subjects and su ceeds in putting to death Laodice, the murderess of his sister.

Vs. 8. *And also their gods with their molten images and with their pr cious vessels of silver and gold he will bring into captivity to Egypt, a*

5 "Since her husband was of unstable mind (ambiguum viri animum") (Jerom

he shall stand (some) years from the king of the North. This vs. describes the vast successes of Ptolemy. The Egyptians were so elated with the outcome that they gave to their ruler the name Euergetes (i.e., well-doer). The conquest of the gods would indicate a great victory, for the gods were thought to be the protectors of the land. Stuart refers to I Sam. 5:1ff. as an illustration. *Precious vessels*]—lit., the vessels of their desire. *He shall stand*]—Jerome, followed by many, take these words to mean that the Ptolemy will maintain himself, i.e., preserve his superiority, over the northern king. However, the idiom is better rendered by the RV, *he shall refrain some years from* (attacking) *the king of the North.*

Vs. 9. *And he shall come into the kingdom of the king of the South, and shall return unto his land.* The subject is the king of the North, Seleucus Callinicus, who after two years, succeeded in regaining his power. He then proceeded to march against Ptolemy c. 240 in which he was completely defeated.

Vs. 10. *And his sons shall be stirred up, and shall gather a multitude of great forces, and he shall certainly come and shall flood and pass over, and he shall return and shall stir himself up, even to his fortress.* The sons of the king of the North will stir themselves up for battle. These sons are Seleucus Ceraunus and Antiochus the Great. The reference "stirred up" is not merely to an expedition against Egypt, but probably is used in a broader and more comprehensive sense. *He shall certainly come*]—lit., *and he will come coming,* "—a strong description of the protracted but irresistible advance, followed by a portrayal of the overflowing masses of warriors that recalls the similar description in Isa. 8:8" (Zoeckler). It should be noted that the subject of the verb is here s., referring alone to Antiochus. Seleucus Ceraunus had perished in battle in Asia Minor. *He shall return*]—M and others would translate *and he shall again be stirred up even unto his stronghold.* This translation, taking the verb *return* as an auxiliary in the sense of *again,* is justifiable. Or, the text may mean that Antiochus returned to renew operations against Egypt and, having taken Phœnicia and Palestine, established himself in Gaza. The rendering *and they shall stir themselves up as far as his stronghold* (Driver) is based upon the assumption that the verb is pl. The s. however, is to be preferred, and is adopted by most expositors. *His fortress*]—either Gaza (Zoeckler, Driver) or possibly Raphia. The suffix appears to refer to the Egyptian king.

Vs. 11. *And the king of the South shall be enraged and shall go forth and fight with him, (even) the king of the North and he shall raise a great multitude, and the multitude shall be given in his hand.* The reference is to Ptolemy Philopator who, enraged at the approach of Antiochus goes forth to fight with him. It is said that he assembled 70,000 infantry, 5,000 cavalry and 73 elephants. *He shall raise a multitude*]—Zoeckler refers this to Ptolemy, but M to Antiochus. As Driver points out, there are objections to both of these views. However, on the whole, the latter seems to have the most in its favor. Antiochus raises the multitude, but it is taken from him and given into the hand of Ptolemy.

Vs. 12. *And the multitude shall be carried away, his heart will be lifted up, and he shall cause thousands to fall, but will not be strong.* The multitude of Antiochus shall be *carried away* by Ptolemy. (For this rendering, which is permissable, see RV margin, cf. Isa. 8:4; 40:24; 41:16). The heart of Ptolemy will be lifted up in pride over the victory. He, Ptolemy, will cause thousands to fall. This was fulfilled in the defeat at Raphia which he inflicted upon Antiochus, in which, according to Polybius (V:86) the Syrians lost 10,000 infantry, 300 cavalry, 5 elephants and 4,000 prisoners.[6] *He shall not be strong*]—He gained no lasting advantage. Apparently Ptolemy was a man of dissolute life, who did not press the advantages gained in battle, but soon resumed his easy life.

Vs. 13. *And the king of the North shall again raise a multitude, greater than the first, and at the end of some years he will certainly come with a great army and with great substance.* It might be well at this point to remind the reader that this entire account is described as something that will occur in the future. It purports, therefore, to be *prophecy.* If it was written *after* the occurrence of the events described, it must be regarded as a deception for its purpose is to set forth these events as *yet future* (cf. particularly 10:14, 21, and 11:2, *And now I will show thee the truth*).

Antiochus had managed to gather a large army because of his successes in the East and now returned to battle against Egypt. This occurred about 13 years after the battle at Raphia. Ptolemy Philopator was dead and his son was only a child of but four years. *Substance*]—The word has reference to the weapons of war and equipment of the army, as in I Chr. 27:31.

Vs. 14. *And in those times many shall stand against the king of the South, and the sons of the transgressors of thy people shall lift themselves up to cause the vision to stand, and they shall stumble.* The "many" are evidently Antiochus who had made a league with Philip of Macedon and probably also rebels who appeared in Egypt. *Sons of the transgressors*] —lit., of those who make a breach. To what, however, is the reference? Calvin refers it to factious men who betrayed the unity of Judea by

---

[6] Polybius (2nd cent. B.C.) was a Greek historian who wrote a work in 40 books, 5 of which are now extant.

aligning themselves with foreign monarchs. Zoeckler takes essentially the same position, finding the references to be to those of the Jews who made a league with Antiochus against Egypt. The reference is to those who break the law (cf. Ezek. 18:10). Jerome's application to Onias is interesting and illustrative, but this event occurred later after 164 B. C. (See M). The Law was broken in that certain factious ones evidently thinking that they were fulfilling prophecies, took the side of Antiochus against Egypt. M would compare Ezek. 13:6. In this however, they fall or stumble, i.e., they shall fail in their attempts to establish the vision.

Zoeckler thinks that certain ones revolt to establish the visions of Dan. 8 and 9 concerning the afflictions under Antiochus, but they shall fall in war. Then he remarks, "It is not to be denied that at any rate this particular passage presents a somewhat considerable discrepancy between the prophetic text of the section and the corresponding historical events." This is strange; if, as Zoeckler thinks, this passage is a late interpolation, surely the interpolator would have been at pains to remove any "discrepancy." The very appearance of "discrepancy"—if the words *they shall fall* are to be referred to a fall in battle—is an evidence of the genuineness of the text.

Vs. 15. *And the king of the North shall come, and shall cast up an entrenchment and shall take a fortified city, and the arms of the South shall not stand and the people of his choice, and there is no power to stand.* Most commentators see in this vs. an allusion to the capture of Sidon (M refers it to Gaza), but Ptolemy had sent one of his ablest warriors, Scopas, to take back his lost territory. Near the headwaters of the Jordan, Antiochus met and worsted him. Finally at Sidon, Antiochus brought about his surrender. *Cast up*]—lit., pour out siege-works. *A fortified city*]—lit., *a city of fortifications. Arms*—The arms of the body are employed figuratively for strength (cf. Ps. 71:18). Here the reference is to the armies of the South. *People of his choice*]—i.e., his chosen warriors.

Vs. 16. *And he that cometh against him will do according to his will, and there is none standing before him, and he shall stand in the land of Desire, and destruction (shall be) in his hand.* The reference is to Antiochus, "Having reached the height of victory, he falls under the dominion of pride and haughtiness by which he hastens on his ruin and overthrow" (Keil). His approach is irresistible. The land of *Desire* is the Holy Land. *Destruction*]—lit., *completeness, finishing,* for the Holy Land.

Vs. 17. *And he shall set his face to come with the power of all his kingdom and an agreement is with him, and he shall make (it) and he will give him the daughter of women to destroy it, but she will not stand, neither be for him.* The idiom "set one's face" means "to determine," as in 2 K. 12:8. *Agreement*]—lit., upright ones. The reference is to the treaty in which Antiochus betrothed his daughter Cleopatra to Ptolemy. The marriage, however, was not consummated until five years later. *Daughter of women*]—The pl. gives somewhat of a superlative force, i. e., to indicate her youth or possibly beauty. When the agreement was made, Ptolemy was but seven years of age. *To destroy it*]—The suffix is f. and some refer it to Cleopatra. However, this does not yield a good sense. Probably it has reference to the alliance itself. The marriage, in other words, was a stratagem by which Antiochus hoped to destroy his enemy. *She will not stand*]—In this stratagem, however, Antiochus fails, because Cleopatra constantly sides with her husband over against her father. These words might also be translated, *But it shall not stand nor be for him,* i. e., to his advantage.

Vs. 18. *And he shall turn his face to the isles and shall take many, and a magistrate shall cause his reproach to cease for him except that his reproach shall return to him.* The isles are the islands and coastlands of the Mediterranean, probably of Asia Minor particularly. *The magistrate* (judge) was Lucius Scipio Asiaticus, who brought about the defeat of Antiochus. *Reproach*]—Doubtless this word has reference to the high-handed and haughty dealings of Antiochus with the Romans. This reproach comes back upon Antiochus' head, in that he is greatly humiliated by defeat.

Vs. 19. *And he shall turn his face to the fortresses of his land, and shall stumble and fall and will not be found.* These words are evidently intended to indicate the enormity of Antiochus' defeat. No longer can he attack the strongholds of foreign lands, but must turn his attention to those of his own. His end is ignominious. He stumbles and falls and is found no more.

Vs. 20. *And there shall stand in his place one who causes an exactor to pass through for the glory of the kingdom, and in a few days he shall be broken, but not in rage nor in war.* In the place of Antiochus the Great will appear another king Seleucus Philopator. He will cause an exactor, i. e., one who collects money, to pass through the land for the sake of the kingdom. This one is Heliodorus, the prime minister, who was sent to seize the funds of the temple treasury. However, a divine apparition is supposed to have frustrated him. M shows that the position of Heliodorus as prime minister has been supported by archaeological evidence. The text is historically accurate, for after a short time Seleucus was suddenly and mysteriously removed, possibly through poisoning administered by Heliodorus.

d. vv. 21-12:3. The revelation concerning Antiochus Epiphanes and the future.

1. vv. 21-24. *The rise of Antiochus Epiphanes.*

Vs. 21. *And there shall stand in his place a despised one, and they have not placed upon him the glory of the kingdom, and he shall come in unawares and shall take hold of the kingdom by intrigues.* At this point Jerome finds a double reference in the prophecy. Antiochus appears here merely as a type of the Antichrist. Jerome takes issue with his opponent Porphyry who sees only a reference to Antiochus. Chrysostom agreed with Jerome in this respect and others have followed suit. Hippolytus introduced the Antichrist at v. 36 but Ephraim of Syria apparently referred everything to Antiochus.

The prophecy is confessedly difficult, and the present writer believes that it cannot in its entirety be applied to Antiochus. He adopts the view that Antiochus is portrayed as a type of the Antichrist, but that such portrayal begins only at v. 36.

The present vs. introduces Antiochus Epiphanes. For the historical background of his reign see App. VI and VII. The following estimate is by Stuart: ". . . one of the most extraordinary characters exhibited on the pages of history. He was both avaricious and prodigal, excessive in his indulgences and prone to violent passions, a compound of the veriest folly and weakness in some respects, and of great cunning and dexterity in some others, especially in regard to flattery. At one period of his reign, there was a prospect of his becoming quite powerful. But reverses came upon him, and he died at last nearly as his father had done before him, and on the like occasion. Indeed his extravagances and follies and cruelty were so great, that his contemporaries gave him the nickname of "epimanes" (madman), instead of the title which he assumed, viz., "epiphanes" (illustrious)."

Antiochus is introduced as a *despised* person, to whom the regal dignity did not belong, since it would naturally have passed to Demetrius Soter, the son of Seleucus Philopator. However, Antiochus determined to take the kingdom for himself. By flattery he won over the kings of Pergamus to his cause, and the Syrians gave in peaceably. In the attainment of this end, Antiochus, like all such dishonest persons, doubtless employed cunning flatteries and secret maneuverings. He was a master of intrigue.

Vs. 22. *And the arms of the overflow will overflow from before him, and they will be broken, and also the prince of the covenant.* The first clause may be translated, *and forces shall be completely overflooded before him* (See M). The arms are the forces, not of the auxiliaries which should aid in the restoration of the son of Seleucus (Calvin), but the forces of

Egypt, whom Antiochus routed between Pelusium and the Casian mountain. *They will be broken*]—as a vessel of pottery is broken. *The prince*] —Some identify the prince with Ptolemy Philometor, in the sense of an allied or confederate prince. But this does not seem adequately to describe the relations between Antiochus and Ptolemy. Furthermore, we should expect Ptolemy to be called the king of the South. Others refer it to Onias III, whom Antiochus deposed. But if the reference were to Onias, the Jewish priest, we should expect the definite article, *the covenant.* This view is at least as old as Theodoret, and may be correct. However, one cannot be dogmatic. I do not know to what the reference is. It apparently refers to some prince who had been in covenant relation with Antiochus. Hence, Stuart translates, *a covenanted prince.*

Vs. 23. *And from the time when he joins himself unto them, he will practice deceit, and he will go up, and will prevail with a small nation.* As Jerome points out, Antiochus manifested friendliness toward the Egyptians, thus winning their hearts. This policy seemed to prove of later advantage to him. *Go up*]—not to Palestine and Syria, nor up the Nile to Memphis but rather a general statement of the king's rise to power. *Small nation*]—Bevan refers these words to the partisans who helped Antiochus rise to power, but more probably we have here a description of the size of the Syrian nation itself.

Vs. 24. *And unawares and into the fattest of the provinces will he come and he will do that which his fathers had not done and his fathers' fathers; spoil and booty and possessions will he scatter upon them, and against fortresses will he plan his devices, and unto a time.* Antiochus will come unawares, lit., *in security.* When men think that all is secure and safe, he will slip in. It may be that a copyist has inserted the word in the wrong place, and that it should be placed with the verb, thus, *and into the fattest of the provinces will he come unawares.* The fattest provinces are the richest. *To them*]—Possibly this refers to Antiochus' followers, but more likely to the people generally. The historical sources represent Antiochus as a man who was lavish in his prodigality, cf. Livy 41:20; I Macc. 3:30; Poly. 26:10:9-10. *Fortresses*]—These are the fortresses or strongholds in Egypt against which Antiochus set his face. *Time*]—i. e., the time decreed by God.

2. vv. 25-28. *The first Egyptian campaign.*

Vs. 25. *And he shall stir up his strength and his heart against the king of the South with a great army, and the king of the South shall arouse himself for battle with a great and exceedingly powerful army, but he will not stand, for they shall devise devices against him.* This vs. refers to the first formal campaign into Egypt. Zoeckler is not incorrect in labelling these vv. *The second Egyptian campaign of Antiochus Epiphanes,* for Antiochus had already invaded Egypt. Driver remarks that we have no "independent evidence as to the relative size of the armies." He then says, "There is however, no reason to suppose that the author would not represent correctly what had taken place only two or three years before he wrote." However, let the reader remember that this account is told in terms of the future. It is the writer's intention to make it appear as though these events had not yet occurred. If the events *had* occurred when these words were written, it follows that the writer was a deceiver.

The king of the South, whether he be Ptolemy Physcon (Zoeckler) or more likely, Ptolemy Philometor, could not stand, because of the treachery of those who claimed to support him.

Vs. 26. *And they who eat his assignment shall break him, and his army shall overflow and many shall fall down slain.* It is true that some of those who supported Ptolemy did later desert. *Assignment*]—cf. note on 1:5. *Overflow*]—possibly the passive is better, *and his* (i. e., Ptolemy's) *army shall be overflowed,* i. e., swept away. *Many*]—I Macc. 1:18, "and many fell wounded to death."

Vs. 27. *And the two kings, their heart is for evil, and at one table they will speak lies, but it will not prosper, for there is yet an end to the appointed time.* The king of Egypt and Antiochus will plot evil against one another. Antiochus will show hospitality toward his enemy, yet will violate the customs of Oriental hospitality by lying words. Together, Philometor and Antiochus professed friendship and plotted to take Egypt. Antiochus pretended that he was showing friendship to Philometor, in planning to conquer Egypt for him. Philometor pretended to believe him. Their common plan, however, would fail, for God's appointed time for the end of the wars between Syria and Egypt had not yet come.

Vs. 28. *And he shall return to his land with great substance, and his heart shall be against the holy covenant, and he shall do and return to his land.* Antiochus returned from Egypt with great spoil, cf. I Macc. 1:19, 20. *Holy covenant*]—the holy land and its inhabitants. The term is used in I Macc. 1:15. The theocracy as represented in the people and land was thus the object of Antiochus' enmity. A description of his depradations in Judea is given in I Macc. 1:20-28. *He shall do*]—i.e., he shall accomplish the design of his heart.

3. vs. 29. *The next Egyptian expedition.*

Vs. 29. *At the appointed time will he come again to the South, and it shall not be as at the first so at the last.* This expedition is apparently the third,

168 B. C. In 169 he had made another expedition, concerning which the book of Dan. is silent. *At the appointed time*]—i. e., the time determined by God. The writer is conscious of the fact that all the movements of Antiochus are determined by God. He is evidently a man whose thoughts are filled with God. But if this is so, how could he also be a forger, as he would have to be if he wrote after these events had transpired? *At the first*]—The idiom means, it shall not be at the last as at the first. This last expedition will not have the same successful outcome as did the first.

4. vv. 30-35. *The persecution of the Theocracy by Antiochus.*

Vs. 30. *And there will come against him ships of Chittim and he will be disheartened, and shall return and rage against the holy covenant, and he will do and will fix his attention upon those who abandon the holy covenant.* The LXX reads, *and the Romans* will come. The expression *ships of Chittim* is based upon Balaam's prophecy, Num. 24:24. Jerome seems to have discovered the correct meaning by his translation *triremes*, for the reference appears to be to the Roman ships of Popilius Laenas which, according to Livy (45:10; also Poly. 29:1) sailed to Egypt in order to prevent Syria from taking that country. *Chittim* in the OT denotes the inhabitants of Cyprus. Because of the presence of the Romans (see Jerome), Antiochus became disheartened. Livy says that he was stupified (obstupefactus), and Poly. describes him as "weighed down and groaning in spirit." *Rage against*]—"The rage which he was unable to vent on Egypt is now turned against the holy covenant; in his displeasure he turns against Israel, without being hindered" (Fuller). After his return Antiochus will turn his attention to those Jews who apostatize and will find them suitable to carry out his designs. Cf. I Macc. 1:11-15; 2 Macc. 4:4-17.

Vs. 31. *And arms from him will stand and they will profane the Sanctuary, the Citadel, and remove the Continual and set up the Abomination, the Desolating.* "This brings us to the climax of the horrors under Antiochus Epiphanes" (Gaebelein). Armed forces, which belong to Antiochus, will stand as guards in the Temple at Jerusalem. *They will profane*]—On the Sabbath day the city was attacked, women and children were taken prisoner, many houses were overthrown and the citadel overlooking the temple was occupied. An endeavor was made to obliterate every trace of the Jewish religion and to introduce Hellenic culture. *Abomination*]—lit., the abomination that appalleth, causeth appallment. This is the heathen altar which was erected on the altar of burnt offering.

Vs. 32: *And those who act wickedly with the covenant will he pervert in intrigue, but the people who knows its God will be strong and will do.*

The apostate Jews who have forsaken the Law of their God will be perverted by Antiochus, in that he will aid and abet them in their designs. This he will do by flattery and intrigues. Those, however, who remain loyal to God will show themselves valiant and will accomplish much in their cause. I Macc. 1:62 reads, "And many in Israel were strong, and were fortified in themselves, not to eat unclean things. And they chose to die, that they might not be defiled with the meats, nor profane the holy covenant; and they died." Thus, the expression *the people who knows its God* refers to the elect, that portion of the outward Israel which is the true Israel, the Church, which knows its God and walks by faith and not by sight. Such people, united to God by a living faith, will not succumb to the subtle blandishments of a man of the character of Antiochus, but will exhibit constancy and firmness, refusing to yield to temptation, and will overcome (cf. I Macc. 2:42; 7:13; 2 Macc. 14:6). The vs. is a remarkable illustration of the truth, "This is the victory which overcometh the world, even our faith" (I John 5:4).

Vs. 33. *And they that understand among the people shall cause many to perceive, but they shall stumble through the sword and through flame, through captivity and through despoilment for many days.* M translates *the learned*, but the word seems to refer to those who show discernment or understanding. These understanding ones are the true members of the Theocracy who, since they themselves understand, cause others also to understand. In the book of Macc. the ones who were true to the Law were called "godly ones" (Hasidæans); "Then were gathered together unto them a company of Hasidæans, mighty men out of Israel, every one that offered himself willingly for the law. And all they that fled from the evils were added to them, and became a stay unto them" (I Macc. 2:42). It may be that such an outward party was in Dan.'s mind, but the *understanding* referred to is of a spiritual nature. Men of true faith will be enabled to point out to others the path of wisdom. Such a course, however, will result in much suffering until finally the time of deliverance arrives.

Vs. 34. *And when they stumble, they shall be helped with a little help, and many shall join themselves unto them in intrigue.* Apparently this prophecy (note that it is related in the future tense) was fulfilled in the appearance of Judas Maccabæus who, however, was unable to put an end to all the distresses of the people (cf. I Macc. 3:11ff.; 4:14ff.). Many hypocrites will associate themselves with the faithful who oppose Antiochus. This hypocritical association was doubtless due in part at least to the severity with which apostates were treated.

Vs. 35. *And some of the wise will stumble, to refine among them, and to purify and to make white, unto the time of the end, for it is yet to an appointed time.* Among those who may be described as wise, i.e., who have understanding, persecution will prove a testing time, and some will fall. Such falling away however will be for the purpose of separating the chaff from the true grain. "Such has been the experience in all periods of the church's history" (Keil). Such sifting must continue until the time of the end, which will come at the time appointed by God.

5. vv. 36-39. *The great arrogance of the enemy of God.*

Vs. 36. *And the king will do according to his will, and he will exalt and magnify himself against every god, and against the God of gods will he speak monstrous things; and he will prosper until the wrath is ended, for the determined thing has been made.* Driver remarks that "—it is contrary to all sound principles of exegesis to suppose that, in a *continuous* description, with no indication whatever of a change of subject, part should refer to one person, and part to another, and that 'the king' of *v.* 36, and 'the king of the south' of *v.* 45 should be a different king from the one whose doings are described in *vv.* 21-35." The matter cannot, however, be thus easily dismissed. It is by no means clear that the description is continuous, and because it is by no means clear, many commentators believe that there is a change in the subject. Again, when Driver asserts that there is no indication of a change of subject, it may be replied that the very fact that the description seems to transcend in large measure what might be applied to Antiochus appears to many earnest expositors to be a very sufficient indication of such a change. At any rate, the application of this and the following vv. exclusively to Antiochus is by no means universally accepted.

The following are the principal interpretations:

1) Antiochus Epiphanes. This, according to Jerome was the view of Porphyry, who is followed by Stuart, Zoeckler, M. Driver, etc.
2) Constantine the Great (Ibn Ezra—see the comments of Jerome as to the interpretations of the Jews).
3) Omar ibn El-Khattab (Ibn Ali, who finds in this ch. a description of the wars between the Caliphs and the Romans).
4) The Roman empire (Calvin).
5) The Dispensationalist Interpretations.
   a) The king (vs. 36) is the little horn of Dan. 7, who is an apostate, not from Judaism but from Christianity. He establishes his palace in Jerusalem, from which time runs the Great Tribulation, the last 3½ years of Dan.'s 70th week (*SRB*).

b) He is the Antichrist, not to be identified either with the little horn of ch. 7 or with that of ch. 8. This wilful king will be a Jew who in the midst of the Jewish people will assume kingly honors, being recognized by the Jewish apostates as the Messiah-King, and by the Christian apostates as the Antichrist. In the middle of the 70th week he will come and take his seat in the Jerusalem temple and will claim divine worship (Gaebelein).

6) The pope of Rome and the Papal System.

7) Herod the Great (Mauro).

8) The Antichrist. This may be called the traditional interpretation in the Christian Church. It was advocated by Jerome, and in this he has been followed by many.

It will be our purpose to study the text as we proceed, reserving the identification until later.

The first statement made about this king is that he will do *according to his will.* This had previously been related of Antiochus, 11:16, cf. also 8:4 and 11:3. Mauro finds it to be an apt description of Herod, both in that he was self-willed—"it would be difficult to find in history one who so ruthlessly executed the designs of his own tyrannical and cruel heart, even upon those of his own flesh and blood"—and also in the fact that he possessed the power to accomplish what he wished to do. Cf. *Antiq.* 12:9:4. Some (e.g., Haevernick) find a typical reference to Antichrist, whereas others discover a direct prophecy of him. *Exalt*]—The proud and presumptuous dealing of the king is stressed. Does this description apply to Antiochus? From the Israelitish point of view, thinks Driver, he might have been said to have set himself above all deities, by the manner in which he patronized and honored particular gods. This is questionable, however. Even though Antiochus himself assumed divinity, as the inscriptions upon his coins show, such assumption of deity was common upon the part of ancient kings. In what precise way did *this* king magnify himself not only above the true God, but also against every god? That is the question that must be answered and the available evidence does not reveal that this is a correct description of Antiochus. It is true that such an inscription as "Of King Antiochus, God. Manifest, Victory-bearer" shows that the king "took his godhead very seriously" (M), but it nevertheless does not do justice to the description given in Dan. Mauro takes the words to mean "every ruler and authority in Israel." Herod "did successfully aspire to the lordship over every authority in the land, whether priests or rulers" (Mauro). This may be true, but the interpretation is forced. The Romans passed "an opinion upon the right of each deity to be worshipped," says Calvin. But this could also have been said of Antiochus. The correct interpretation is given in 2 Thess. 2:4. Only of the Antichrist may the language of Dan. be predicated. *God of gods*]—i.e., against the true God who is above all other gods. Antiochus surely did speak against the true God, and thus may appear as a type of the Antichrist. So also the Romans; "—Cicero in his oration for Flaccus, tears most contemptuously to pieces the name of the true God; and that impure slanderer—for he deserves the name—so blurts out his calumnies, as if the God who had revealed himself to his elect people by his law, was unworthy of being reckoned with Venus or Bacchus, or their other idols" (Calvin). Mauro refers the words largely to the slaughter of the babes in Bethlehem which was an attempt to do away with Immanuel. The NT plainly says that the Antichrist "as God sitteth in the temple of God" (2 Thess. 2:4). *Monstrous things*]—things which, because of their blasphemous character will cause astonishment. *He will prosper*]—He will be successful in his impious course only until the anger of God towards His people has come to an end. "This anger of God is irrevocably determined, that His people may be wholly purified for the consummation of His kingdom in glory" (Keil).

Vs. 37. *And unto the gods of his fathers will he show no regard, nor unto the desire of women nor unto any god will he shew regard, for he will magnify himself above all.* The expression *gods of his fathers* has reference to the gods who were worshipped by his fathers, i.e., the gods whom his fathers worshipped—he did not regard. Mauro makes out a plausible case for the application of this passage to Herod. In speaking to the Jews, Herod did employ the expression "our fathers," (*Antiq.* 15:11:1). Also, some of the Herodians regarded him as a Messiah. In introducing the worship of Cæsar, thinks Mauro, Herod showed a definite antipathy toward the Jewish religion. But, as Mauro of course acknowledges, Herod was originally an Idumean. Calvin finds the reference in the fact that "—the Romans dared to insult all religions with freedom and petulance, and to promote atheism as far as they possibly could." The embarrassment of those commentators who would apply these words to Antiochus is obvious. Bevan admits that we are not told the manner in which Antiochus showed disrespect for the gods of his fathers but thinks that it may be in his abolition of local usages for the sake of centralizing his empire. He appeals to I Macc. 1:41,42. Driver thinks that by paying honor to foreign deities such as Jupiter Capitolinus there was implied a depreciation of the gods of his own country. Zoeckler is more convincing in suggesting that he will manifest his impiety by the robbing of temples and tear down religious systems. All of these are makeshifts, however, which do not do justice to the language of the text. The fact is that these words do not apply to Antiochus. The phrase has a Jewish emphasis and has reference to the Jewish religion. The one who has no regard for this Jewish religion is himself a Jew, the Antichrist. I fully agree with Gaebelein's statement, "Here his Jewish descent becomes evident." *No regard*] —lit., he will not perceive, i.e., will pay no regard to. *Desire of Women*] —that which women possess which is desirable, cf. I Sam. 9:20. This was first interpreted of love, but it has also been referred to some object of worship. According to Ephraim of Syria this was the goddess Nanaia, whose temple was at Elymais. But why would Nanaia be called the desire of women? Ewald suggested that it was Adonis, who was worshipped particularly by women, cf. Ezek. 8:14. Mauro applies the reference to Christ as the One upon whom the women of Israel had set their desire. Since, however, these identifications are based upon the assumption that the phrase *desire of women* has reference to something which women desire, we must reject them. The desire is human love, and "is named as an example selected from the sphere of human piety, as that affection of human love and attachment for which even the most selfish and most savage of men feel some sensibility" (Keil). Cf. the phrase, the love of women, in 2 Sam. 1:26. "This king, then, should cultivate neither piety nor humanity" (Calvin). *Any god*]—He has no piety nor reverence toward any god whatsoever. This was certainly not true of Antiochus, nor was it true of Herod. The reason why this king has no regard for any god is that he magnifies himself above them all.

Vs. 38. *But the god of fortresses in his place will he honor, and the god which his fathers have not known will he honor with gold and silver and precious stones and with things desired.* The king will show no regard to any god, but he will honor the god of fortresses. This designation is difficult to understand. It is not a proper name, e. g., MAOZIM (Jerome) nor Mars, the god of war, nor Jupiter, etc. If the reference is to some known deity then all that is said in vs. 37 about the king not regarding any god is nullified. What then is the meaning? In answer to this question, it must be replied that the reference is not to any particular god or cult. This seems to be stressed by saying that the god is one whom the fathers have not known. He is a god who is characterized by fortresses or strongholds. In other words he is the personification of war. The Jews had known of war, of course, but they had never deified it. Thus, *in the place* of any god he will honor war as his god. For religion he will substitute war, and war he will support with all that he has. This thought is figuratively expressed by the words, *with gold and silver, etc.* This vs. does not apply to Antiochus. A far more convincing case can be made out for Herod (see Mauro), but the words best apply to the activities of the Antichrist.

Vs. 39. *And he will do to the fortresses of the strongholds with (the help of) a foreign god whom he recognizes, he will increase glory, and he will cause them to rule over many, and the land will he divide for a price.* "With the help of this god, who was unknown to his fathers, he will so proceed against the strong fortresses that he rewards with honour, might, and wealth those who acknowledge him" (Keil). The mighty conqueror rewards those who have sided with him. This was true of Antiochus, but it is also true of all conquerors.

6. vv. 40-45. *The final conflict.*

Vs. 40. *And at the time of the end, there will butt against him the king of the South, and there will storm against him the king of the North with chariots and horsemen and with many ships, and he will come into the lands and will overflow and pass over.* The interpretation of this and the following vv. is extremely difficult.

I. *Views Which Find Antiochus Epiphanes As The Subject of This Passage.*

a) Stuart, e. g., holds that these vv. relate a later campaign of Antiochus and appeals to Porphyry's testimony (given in Jerome) for evi. dence. If Porphyry were inaccurate, thinks Stuart, Jerome would certainly have taken the opportunity to refute him.

b) Hitzig maintains that the author now goes back to describe events preceding 168 BC., i.e., previous to the invasion described in vs. 29.

c) The vv., according to Driver, relate the course of events unto the death of Antiochus.

d) The vv. relate merely the expectation of the author and not real facts (Bevan, M).

It will become apparent that the expositors who apply these vv. to Antiochus are faced with grave difficulty. Thus, Driver says, "How far the events here described correspond to the reality is a very doubtful point." The actual fact is that they do not correspond with what is known of Antiochus' death. We know that Antiochus, upon learning of the successful revolt of the Maccabees left half the army with Lysias his governor to destroy Israel. With the other half he himself set out toward Persia where he attempted to take the treasures of a rich city, but was frustrated by its forewarned inhabitants. Hence he set out for Babylon without the treasure which he needed for the prosecution of his wars against Israel. Word came to him that Lysias had been overthrown and the altar of the Lord re-erected in Jerusalem, whereupon in terror and dismay he fell sick and died (See I Macc. 3:27-37; 6:1-16; Poly. 31:11). Thus, it is impossible to agree with Porphyry that in his eleventh year Antiochus made an expedition against Egypt.

The only historical support for the view that there was such an expedition is furnished by Porphyry. However, Porphyry's testimony must be rejected, and that for the following reasons:

1) Porphyry describes the campaign as initiated by Antiochus, whereas Dan. says that the king of the South initiated it.

2) Egypt would now be under Roman protection, and an attack upon Egypt would have involved Antiochus in a war with Rome. Of such a war all history is silent.

3) At this time, according to all the historical sources Antiochus was in serious financial difficulty. This ill-accords with the words of Dan. 11:43—"he shall have power over the treasures of gold and silver."

4) The mention of Apedno as the place where Antiochus pitched his tent, is obviously based upon a misunderstanding of the Heb. word in vs. 45.

Nor can it be said that these vv. merely represent the hopes and expectations of the author. Their value as a prophecy would then be worthless, for they would then be presenting expectations which in large measure, were contrary to fact. The language purports to be that of true prophecy, and as true prophecy it must be regarded.

II. Those interpreters who do not apply these vv. to Antiochus, refer them to the Romans or to the Antichrist. See the note to vs. 36.

— — — — —

At the time of the end—These words mark the time when the events are to occur. *The end* is not the end of Antiochus' reign, nor is it a general reference to the final pre-Messianic days. Nor is there warrant for Mauro's view, that the words mean "the last stage of the national existence of Daniel's people, that is to say, the era of the Herods." There is no intrinsic objection to such an interpretation, but the general context does not warrant it. Nor do the words refer to the last-half of the 70th week, but rather, to the end of the present age or world-period. *King of the South*]—not Ptolemy Philometor (Driver), nor Cleopatra, aided by Mark Anthony (Mauro). He is a king to come, typified by the historical Ptolemies, for the battles between the South and the North evidently point forward to this great battle in the end of the age. The two opponents are the Antichrist and the king of the South who begins the battle by pushing or butting (cf. 8:4) against his enemy. *Storm against*]—Like a whirlwind the northern king will come in retaliation (cf. Hab. 3:14). His mighty forces are represented by the chariots, horsemen and ships. The description is probably intended merely to stress the great power of the king. Since it is said that he comes into the *lands* and overflows and passes over, it seems clear that the reference is to a land battle. Hence, it it is not necessary to press too literally the words chariots, horsemen and ships.

Vs. 41. *And he will come into the land of the Delight, and many will stumble, and these shall escape from his hand, Edom, and Moab and the chief of the children of Ammon.* The enemy king of the North comes into the Delightsome Land, i. e., Palestine. As a result, many (lands) will be overthrown. Three lands, however, will be delivered. It should be noted that, at the time of Antiochus, Moab no longer existed as a nation. These three nations were ancient enemies of God's people, the Israelites. They are mentioned here as symbolical representatives of nations which are enemies of God's people and who will escape the wrath of the king of the North. "Edom, Moab, and Ammon, related with Israel by descent, are the old hereditary and chief enemies of this people, who have become by name representatives of all the hereditary and chief enemies of the people of God. These enemies escape the overthrow when the other nations sink under the power of the Antichrist" (Keil). *Many will stumble*]—By the change of a vowel, the word *many* may be translated *myriads.* It would then refer to individuals, not to nations. *Chief*]—lit., *beginning,* the same word that is employed in Gen. 1:1. It refers to the foremost, the best of the people. These are spared because of their enmity to God's people.

Vs. 42. *And he shall send his hand upon lands; and the land of Egypt shall not escape.* He shall lay his hand upon countries in order to seize them. The principal object of his attack, Egypt, shall not escape, lit., *shall not become an escaped body.* Egypt probably stands as a representative of the powers which will resist the Antichrist.

Vs. 43. *And he will rule over the deposits of gold and silver and over all the desired things of Egypt; and the Libyans and Cushites will be at his steps.* These words represent the complete nature of the king's conquest. The inhabitants of Libya and Cush (Ethiopia, see Nah. 3:9; Ezek. 30:5) who are the allies of Egypt, will follow at his steps, i. e., in his train. Thus, they join the army of the conquering invader.

Vs. 44. *And reports shall trouble him from the East and from the North, and he shall go out in great fury to destroy and to annihilate many.* After the king has conquered Egypt with Libya and Cush, rumors come from the East and North which alarm him and inspire him with terror. These tidings are apparently to the effect that some of his peoples in the East and North are in rebellion against him. At any rate, the king is angered by these reports and because of them sets out to destroy the rebels. It should be noted that when these tidings reach the king, he is still in Egypt, and from Egypt sets out to destroy. These facts do not fit the life of Antiochus.

Vs. 45. *And he will plant the tents of his pavilion between the sea and the mountain of the delight of holiness, and he will come unto his end, and there is none to help him.* The *tents of his pavilion* is about equivalent to *his royal pavilion.* This he will plant (note that the future is employed. We are dealing with the language of predictive prophecy) as one plants a tree, i. e., he will establish between the sea and the holy mountain of Delight (lit., between seas to the mountain of the delight of holiness). The pl. *seas* is poetic (cf. Deut. 33:19) and the reference is to the Mediterranean Sea. The *glorious holy mountain* is Jerusalem or Zion. Hence, the king is to make his final stand between the Mediterranean Sea and Jerusalem. This statement cannot possibly apply to Antiochus, since he died at Tabae in Persia. It should be noted that in placing the destruction of the great world power which opposes the people of God near to Jerusalem, Dan. is in harmony with other similar OT references (cf. Joel 3:2, 12ff.; Zech 14:2). However, inasmuch as such names as Egypt, Moab, Edom, Ammon, etc., are employed in these vv. in a symbolical sense, so also is this present description employed. Precisely what is signified it is difficult to determine. At any rate, the great final enemy of the people of God, the Antichrist, will make his last stand and will come to his end in territory which is sacred and holy (peculiarly delighted in by the people of God—note the expression *mountain of the delight of holiness*—does this have reference to the church?) His end will be complete, apparently brought about by the glorious return of the Son of God from heaven.

— — — — —

"And then shall that Wicked be revealed, whom the Lord shall consume with the spirit of his mouth, and shall destroy with the brightness of his coming" (2 Thess. 2:8).

— — — — —

"Therefore, brethren, stand fast, and hold the traditions which ye have been taught, whether by word or our epistle" (2 Thess. 2:15).

CHAPTER TWELVE

7. vv. 1-3. *The final deliverance of Israel and the consummation.*

Vs. 1. *And at that time shall Michael stand, the great prince, who stands over the sons of thy people, and it shall be a time of distress, such as has not been from the existence of a nation until that time, and in that time thy people shall be delivered, everyone who is found written in the Book.* The words *at that time* refer back to the *time of the end* (11:40). The thought may be paraphrased, "At the time when the events of 11:40-45 take place, Michael will stand." The phrase does not refer to the last days of Antiochus. Apart from the general objections which preclude a reference to Antiochus, it should be noted that the greatness of distress herein described is far too strong a description for the time of Antiochus. *The great prince*]—Calvin believes that the reference is to Christ. However, Michael, as the representative of Christ, is the valiant warrior, who comes to protect God's elect from the fierce persecution of the king of the North. *Stands over*]—i.e., in the sense that he comes to protect God's people (cf. Esther 8:11; 9:16). *Time of distress*]—because of the activity of the king of the North. The phrase is evidently taken from Jer. 30:7. *Existence of a nation*]—No nation has ever witnessed distress such as this. How could such a phrase be applied to the days of Antiochus? The forces of evil will unleash themselves in desperate fury against the saints. This period of severe affliction is the time, times and half a time of Dan. 7:25. However, God's true people will be delivered. *Written in the Book*] —i.e., the book of Life. These are the elect, the true people of God, whom Satan can never destroy. "His book is that eternal counsel which predestinates us to himself, and elects us to the hope of eternal salvation. We now understand the full sense of this instruction, as the Church shall remain in safety amidst many deaths, and even in the last stage of despair it shall escape through the mercy and help of God. We must also remember this definition of a church, because many boast of being God's sons, who are complete strangers to him. This leads us to consider the subject of election, as our salvation flows from that fountain. Our calling, which is his outward testimony of it, follows that gratuitous adoption which is hidden within himself; and thus God when regenerating us by His Spirit, inscribes upon us his marks and signs, whence he is able to acknowledge us as his real children" (Calvin). These words bring out the deep, true meaning of the prophet.

Vs. 2. *And many of those who sleep in the ground of dust shall awake; some to life everlasting and some to reproaches to the abhorrence of eternity.* This vs. emphasizes further the deliverance of God's people. With respect to those who sleep, i. e., those who are dead (cf. John 11:11; Acts 7:60; I Thess. 5:10) there is to be a resurrection unto life and a resurrection unto death. *Ground of dust*]—This is a figurative expression for the grave, cf. Job 20:11. The thought is based upon Gen. 3:19. It means *dusty earth,* not *dust of the earth. Many*]—We should expect the text to say *all.* In order to escape the difficulty, some expositors have taken the word *many* in the sense of *all.* However, this is forced and unnatural. The correct solution appears to be found in the fact that the Scripture at this point is not speaking of a general resurrection, but rather is setting forth the thought that the salvation which is to occur at this time will no be limited to those who were alive but will extend also to those who ha lost their lives. We may paraphrase: "At the time of this persecutio many shall fall, but thy people, who are written in the book, shall b delivered. Likewise, from the numbers of those who are asleep in th grave many (i. e., those who died during the tribulation) shall arise. O these, some shall arise to life and some to reproach." The words, o course, do not exclude the general resurrection, but rather imply it. Thei emphasis, however, is upon the resurrection of those who died during th period of great distress. *Life everlasting*]—This is the first occurrenc of this expression in the OT. *Reproaches*]—The pl. expresses intensit and fullness. *Contempt*]—i. e., that which is an object of aversion, c Isa. 66:24. Cf. also Matt. 25:46; John 5:29. This doctrine of the resu rection was not derived from the Persians, but was revealed by God Dan. See *SBD*, II, p. 117ff. Porphyry believed that the vs. was speakin of the doctors of the law at the time of Antiochus. These would arise eternal life, but the transgressors (prævaricatores) to everlasting reproac According to Jerome, Porphyry applied this entire ch. to Antiochus.

Vs. 3. *And those who are wise shall shine as the brightness of the firm ment, and those who turn many to righteousness as the stars for ever a ever.* Those who during the period of persecution have dealt prudent and wisely in that they by their instruction have pointed many to the w of righteousness shall receive the glorious reward of their labors in th they shall shine eternally as the brightness of the firmament and as t stars. Although the immediate reference of this vs. is to 11:33-45, nevertheless sets forth the general truth that those who instruct others the way of truth are wise. *Those who are wise*]—"the intelligent who, instructing their contemporaries by means of word and deed, have awa ened them to steadfastness and fidelity to their confession in the times of tribulation and have strengthened their faith. and some of whom have in war sealed their testimony with their blood" (Keil). These "wise ones" therefore, are not limited to those mentioned in 11:33-35. *Shine*]—the heavenly and eternal reward. M well translates, *like the sheen of the sky*. Cf. Ex. 24:10, and Matt. 13:43; I Cor. 15:40ff.; Rev. 2:28. The reference is to the shining vault of heaven with all its suns and stars. *Turn many*]—not to justify, in the sense of a forensic justification, but, lit., *those who make many righteous*, i. e., those who, by their own righteousness point many to the way of righteousness.

Keil well sums up the thought of these vv.: "The salvation of the people, which the end shall bring in, consists accordingly in the consummation of the people of God by the resurrection of the dead and the judgment dividing the pious from the godless, according to which the pious shall be raised to eternal life, and the godless shall be given up to everlasting shame and contempt. But the leaders of the people who amid the wars and conflicts of this life, have turned many to righteousness, shall shine in the imperishable glory of heaven."

e. vs. 4. The final command to seal up the Book.

Vs. 4. *And thou Daniel, shut up the words and seal the book until the time of the end, many shall run to and fro, that knowledge may be increased.* To Dan. is given the injunction to shut up (i. e., guard, preserve, protect, as in 8:26) the words which have just been revealed to him (i. e., 10:2-12:3) and to seal (for the sake of preserving) the book (the book in which these words are found). Kliefoth has well brought out the force of the words "A document is sealed up in the original text, and laid up in the archives (shut up), that it may remain preserved for remote times, but not that it may remain secret, while copies of it remain in public use." The words, therefore, are the words which have just been revealed and which Dan. has just written down, but the "book" evidently includes more than these words. Else, why should this designation have been chosen? Evidently Dan. had written down his revelations, as he received them. This last revelation formed a conclusion, and the entire body, i. e., the book was now to be sealed. *Until the time*]—Dan. is to seal the book until the time of the end. He himself has now completed his prophetic ministry and is, as one of his last acts, to lay away the book that it may be preserved. The time of the end is the consummation, when the Lord shall return from heaven. The "words" which Dan. was to shut up contained revelations which extend to the "end." The "end," therefore, is *not* the terminus of the reign of Antiochus. *Many shall run*]—This phrase is extremely difficult to interpret. Th. renders *until many are taught and knowledge is fulfilled.* The LXX has *until many are left behind and the earth is filled with unrighteousness.* Calvin translates *many shall investigate,* and Jerome, followed by many excellent interpreters, refers the action to the study of the book itself (percurri librum). Thus, Kliefoth, "Daniel is to put away safely the prophecies which he has received until the time of the end, so that through all times many men may be able to read them and gain understanding from them." However, I find myself unable to accept any of these views, because they do not seem faithfully to reflect the force of the Heb. verb. This verb means "to go," "to rove about." Thus, Satan speaks to the Lord, and says that he has come from "going to and fro in the earth" (Job 1:7b). The present occurrence seems to reflect upon Amos 8:12, "And they shall wander from sea to sea, and from the north even to the east, they shall run to and fro to seek the word of the Lord, and shall not find it." The verb appears to describe a vain travelling about in order to discover knowledge. *That knowledge*]—These words state the purpose of the going to and fro. It is for the sake of increasing knowledge. This phenomenon is not a characteristic of the end, but simply of the period which lay ahead of Dan. We may paraphrase: "Preserve the book until the end, for it contains the truth as to the future. Many shall go to and fro in search of knowledge, but they shall not find it."

Thus, it is unwarranted to consider the modern increase in travel and in education as specific fulfillments of this prophecy. There is a strain of sadness in these words. The written revelation of God is in the world, but men heed it not. Instead, they look for knowledge where it is not to be found.

f. vv. 5-13. The conclusion of the prophecy.

Vs. 5. *And I Daniel saw, and behold, two others were standing, the one on this side of the bank of the stream, and the other on the other side of the bank of the stream.* A new scene in the vision appears. Two others, in addition to the glorious One who had been giving the revelation to Dan. now appear, one on each side of the stream. *The stream*]—This word is generally used of the Nile, but here it must have a broader sense, *a stream.* The stream was the Tigris.

Vs. 6. *And (one) said to the man clothed in fine linen who was above the waters of the stream, until how long is the end of wondrous things?* The identity of the speaker is not clear, for the text merely says, *and he said.* The subject is not mentioned. Doubtless, however, it was one of the two angels. The One addressed is the One who has given the previous revelation (cf. 10:5 ff). This One, clothed in fine linen, had alone been visible to Dan. His position above the waters, and the fact that He is questioned by the angel seem to indicate a superiority. *Wondrous things*]—The reference is to the extraordinary events which have just been revealed. It must be noted that the question is not, how long shall these wondrous things continue? but, how long is *the end* of these wondrous things? The end is that period upon which the revelation has placed its stress, namely, the events recorded in 11:40-12:3. The question, therefore, concerns the duration of the events concerned with the king of the North.

The two angels are probably present as witnesses to the oath uttered in vs. 7.

There must be a reason for the choice of the word translated *stream*. As already indicated, it is the common designation for the Nile river. Possibly it is deliberately employed here to remind Dan. that just as the Lord had once stood over Egypt, the world-nation which was hostile to God's people, so now does He stand over the world kingdom, represented symbolically by the Nile stream, actually the Tigris, ready again to deliver His people. On vv. 5 and 6 Jerome comments that whereas he interprets them of Antichrist, Porphyry, according to his custom (more suo) interprets of Antiochus.

Vs. 7. *And I heard the man clothed in fine linen who was above the waters of the stream, and he lifted his right (hand) and his left unto the heaven, and he swore, By the One who lives forever, (it is) for a time, times and a half, and when there is an end of breaking in pieces the hand of the people of Holiness, all these things shall come to an end.* The language of this vs. is majestic. Dan.'s attention is directed to the central Figure who, in most solemn fashion, utters an oath. Ordinarily, when an oath was taken, only one hand was raised. Cf. Gen. 14:22; Deut. 32:40. The solemnity of this oath, therefore, is emphasized by the fact that both hands are raised. The man clothed in fine linen swears by Him who lives forever, i. e., the true God. This designation had already been employed by Neb. but the present passage evidently reflects Deut. 32:40, "For I lift up my hand to heaven, and say, I live for ever." In this passage it is God who swears and who swears by Himself. This is also the case here in Dan.

Since, therefore, the oath is of so extremely solemn a nature, we cannot apply the passage to Antiochus, as does Porphyry. It must, rather, apply to that arch-enemy of the Lord, known as Antichrist. Furthermore, the description does not well fit Antiochus. *Time, times and a half*]—This is the exact Heb. equivalent of the Aramaic expression used in 7:25, and its meaning here is the same as in that passage. The word means a set or appointed time, and there is no warrant whatsoever for the assertion that it means a year. Not only must the application to Antiochus be rejected, therefore, but also the reference to the latter half (3½ years) of the 70th seven (Gaebelein). *When there is an end of breaking*]—At the time when the power of the holy people is shattered (broken in pieces) these things will come to an end. The Antichrist will practically have destroyed God's people, when Antichrist himself will be destroyed. In the time of deepest need, God works on behalf of His elect. The word translated *breaking* has sometimes been rendered *to scatter.* It means rather *to shatter, to beat in pieces,* as e. g., "thou shalt dash them in pieces like a potter's vessel" (Ps. 2:9b). When this terrible work has been completed, the end of these wondrous things will occur. *The hand of the people of holiness*]—The hand is a symbol of power. The people of holiness are those who are characterized by holiness, the holy people. This is not a mere designation of Israel after the flesh, but refers to the elect of God, who are renewed in holiness.

Vs. 8. *And I heard, but I did not understand, and I said, O my lord, what shall be the end of these things?* The specific question of the angel has been answered and, although Dan. heard the answer, he did not understand it. Of what, particularly, was Dan. ignorant? The answer is stated in the question, what shall be the end of these things? By the words, *these things,* he refers not to the *all these things* of vs. 7. Rather this phrase is to be taken in a broader sense, *these things generally,* which have been revealed to him, i. e., the revelation of ch. 11. The angel's questions concerning the end of the wondrous things has been answered. However, Dan. professes that he has not understood the matter. He wants therefore to know how the final issue of this revelation will turn out. What will be its end? He uses a word different from the *end* of vs. 8; here he speaks more of the *last part* or *closing stage* of these events.

Vs. 9. *And he said, Go! Daniel, for closed and sealed are the words until the time of the end.* "Although Daniel was not induced by any foolish curiosity to inquire of the angel the issue of these wonderful events, yet he did not obtain his request. God wished some of His predictions to be partially understood, and the rest to remain concealed until the full period of the complete revelation should arrive" (Calvin). *Go!*]—i. e., inquire no further, leave this matter alone. The reason for this command is stated in the fact that the words are preserved in security against destruction so that they may be read and understood at the time of their fulfillment. It is not necessary that Dan. himself should understand the answer to his question, for it does not have immediate application to him. There will come a time, however, when the words are needed and then they will be understood. Therefore, they are shut up and sealed until the time of the end. The vs. well illustrates the practical character of Holy Scripture. God in His infinite wisdom has revealed to us only that which it is needful for us to have in order that we may know what He requires of us. He does not reveal that which does not directly contribute toward this end. Scripture is not a body of esoteric mystery given to satisfy idle curiosity. It is given that we "might not sin against Thee" (Ps. 119:11b). It is a thoroughly practical Book. The present vs. should be pondered carefully by those who are constantly setting dates for the return of Christ or seeking to find specific fulfillments of prophecy in the events of modern history.

Vs. 10. *Many shall be purified and made white and refined; and the wicked shall do wickedly, and none of the wicked shall understand, but those who are wise shall understand.* This vs. presents a general description of the future. It is not a characterization merely of the time of the end (Driver). The thought seems to be: "Fear not, Dan., for although thou thyself dost not understand the words, many will understand them. The words, kept and sealed unto the time of the end, will prove to be a source of true blessing to the people of God even unto the end. For persecutions, trials and afflictions will come, and when they come, many will be purified and made white and refined. They will understand the words of the prophecy. The reprobate, however, will continue in their wickedness and will not understand. They show no insight into spiritual truth and so they act without understanding." This use of the word *understand* is obviously based upon Dan.'s statement in vs. 9.

Vs. 11. *And from the time of the turning aside of the Continual and to the giving of an abomination desolating is one thousand, two hundred and ninety days.* The words of this vs. are surprising; they come as one further bit of revelation before the book closes. Various interpretations have been offered, of which the following may be noted:

a) Some dispensationalists allege that the 1290 days are literal, and apply to the latter half of Dan.'s 70th week, supposedly a period of 3½ years (see *com.* in loc.). If, however, we reckon 30 days to a month,[1] we find that 1290 days amounts to 43 months or 3½ years plus an extra month. What is to be done with this extra month? According to Gæbelein, "The extra month will in all probability be needed to make possible certain judgment events especially with the overthrow of the nations, which came against Jerusalem and the judgment of nations as given in Matthew 25:31." SRB suggests that at the expiration of 1260 days the Stone smites the image and brings Gentile world dominion to an end, but before full blessing comes in the debris of the image must be carried away (p. 920). It has already been shown that this position is untenable.

[1] The Jewish calendar year apparently consisted of months of 29 and 30 days in length.

The difficulty of accounting for the 1290 days (the extra 30 days) simply adds to the weakness of this position.

b) Mauro says that it was exactly 43 months between the taking away of the daily sacrifice during the siege of Jerusalem and the appearance of the Roman army (the abomination), if the days of the month in which the two events occurred be not reckoned. Thus:

A.D. 66. Coming of the Romans under Cestius.
A.D. 70. Taking away of the Daily Sacrifice.

It must be noted, however, that upon this scheme the two events are reversed. If this were correct, we should expect the text to read, *from the abomination to the taking away of the continual sacrifice is* 1290 *days.* Hence, this construction does not do adequate justice to the text. Furthermore, the period between these two events is not 1290 days, but possibly 60 days more. The coming of the Romans took place about the 15-22 of Tishri (i.e., October, 66) and on the 30th of Hyperberetæus (i.e., c. 17th November, 66) Cestius led his troops into Jerusalem. On the 17th of Panemus 70 AD., (i.e., Tammuz in the Jewish calendar—our August) Titus learned that the continual sacrifice had ceased to be offered (See Josephus, *The Jewish Wars* II:19:1ff. and VI:2:1). Now the interval between these two events was not 1290 days or 43 months but about 1350 days. Note that 1290 days would carry us from November 17, 66 to June 17, 70. There still remains the interval (at least more than a month) up to August 17, 70. This view, therefore, must be rejected.

c) Most commentators consider these numbers to have reference to literal days and apply them to the times of Antiochus Epiphanes. They therefore look for a *terminus a quo* and find it in the removal of the daily sacrifice by Antiochus, in 168 B.C. What however, would be the *terminus ad quem?* According to Stuart, it is the purification of the temple by Judas in 165 B.C. He says that the time in question is made "as nearly as history will enable us to compute it." Driver finds the *terminus ad quem* in the death of Antiochus. Now, these views proceed upon the assumption that the days are literal, yet none of them presents a satisfactory explanation. The 1290 days do not fit. There must have been a special reason for the choice of 1290 days, which equals a period of one month over 3½ years, or, in other words, is just a month longer than half of seven years.[2] None of these views, which assume that the days are literal, is able to explain precisely why this figure was chosen. Prince (following Behrmann) comes closest to a satisfactory explanation by pointing out that every third year it was customary to add an extra month, and thus

[2] i.e.. reckoning 30 days to the month.

we would get 3 years 7 months, or 1290 days. But, if this were so, why do we have the expression time, times and half a time in vs. 7 and ch. 7:25 which, according to Prince, equals 3½ years? If it was customary to add this month, why was it not also added in vs. 11 and in 7:25, passages which according to Prince, are speaking of the same subject? The addition of this extra month must be accounted for upon the basis of other grounds than those which Prince has adduced.

d) The position which alone appears to be tenable is that offered by Keil. It is that these numbers are to be interpreted symbolically. They do refer to the times of Antiochus, that period of Israel's sore trial. The turning aside of the continual sacrifice and the abomination clearly seem to indicate this. This period, represented by the 1290 days, is to be one of severe persecution. But why the mention of "days" instead of "times"? Keil has well answered this question, "By the naming of 'days' instead of 'times' the idea of an immeasureable duration of the tribulation is set aside, and the time of it is limited to a period of moderate duration which is exactly measured out by God." This period is then lengthened by 45 days (see vs. 12) making a total of 1335. When these 1335 days have expired complete blessing will come. The 1335 days, therefore, have reference to the entire period of persecution, not only that under Antiochus, but the whole period of opposition to God's kingdom unto the consummation. The 1290 days, however, have reference not to the entire period of persecution, but only to the most severe phase of this period, namely, the persecution under Antiochus and its antitype, that under the Antichrist. The 1290 days are little more than ½ of 7 years and 7 appears to be a figure denoting completeness. The lesson which we are to learn therefore is that the most severe period of persecution will last but a little more than half the whole period. Even the full period, the 1335 days is not a completeness of persecution, but apparently a period fore-shortened, both in duration and intensity, so that it also is little more than half (45 days more than the severest period) of 7, the symbolical number of perfection and completion.

That the persecution under Antiochus is here regarded as typical of the later and more severe persecution under Antichrist is evident from the fact that the typical relationship of these two periods has been so clearly set forth in ch. 11. The wars between Antiochus and Egypt and the description of his persecution of God's people leads easily and naturally into the account of the wars of the future king of the North. The description of the work of Antiochus "shows in a figure how the Antichrist at the time of the end shall take away the worship of the true God, renounce the God of his fathers, and make war his god, and thereby bring affliction upon the church of God, of which the oppression which Antiochus brought upon the theocracy furnished a historical pattern" (Keil). And may we remember that as the persecution under Antiochus was cut short (3 years and 10 days—not fully 3½ years) so also will the final period, for the sake of God's elect, be shortened.

Vs. 12. *Blessed is he who waits and attains to the thousand, three hundred and thirty five days.* "He that endureth to the end shall be saved" (Matt. 24:13). These words may be said to form a Divine commentary upon this passage. So also the statement of our Lord, "Blessed is that servant, whom his lord when he cometh shall find so doing" (Matt. 24:46). The lit. rendering is, *O the blessings of the one who waits.* A Divine benediction falls upon the faithful who endure suffering and oppression and abide true to their Lord.

Vs. 13. *And thou, go to the end, and thou shalt rest and thou shalt stand to thy lot at the end of the days.* The final word of comfort and assurance is given to the prophet. *Go*]—i.e., not, go thy way, but rather, go on as thou art until the end of life. *Thou shalt rest*]—i. e., in the grave,[3] and thou shalt arise to receive thy appointed portion at the *end* (the consummation.) *The end of the days* is the final period, the consummation. Thus the salvation of Dan. is announced; his part or lot is to be that of the wise who turn many unto righteousness. Keil very aptly closes his great work with the words, "Well shall it be for us if in the end of our days we too are able to depart hence with such consolation of hope."

Prayer of John Calvin

"Grant, Almighty God, since thou proposest to us no other end than that of constant warfare during our whole life, and subjectest us to many cares until we arrive at the goal of this temporary race-course: Grant, I pray thee, that we may never grow fatigued. May we ever be armed and equipped for battle, and whatever the trials by which thou dost prove us, may we never be found deficient. May we always aspire towards heaven with upright souls, and strive with all our endeavors to attain that blessed rest which is laid up for us in heaven, in Jesus Christ our Lord.—Amen."

[3] The idea of "soul sleep" is not at all to be found in these words.

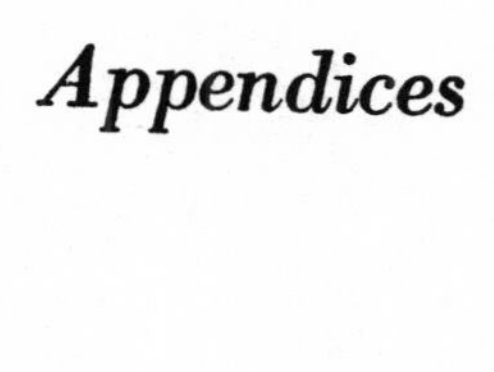

Appendices

I

The Third Year of Jehoiakim

In Prince's *Commentary* there appears the following statement (p. 18), "The chronological error in C. i that Nebuchadnezzar took Jerusalem as king of Babylon in the third year of Jehoiakim should be considered first." In their *Introduction to the Old Testament* (London, 1934) Oesterley and Robinson say ". . . in the opening verse of the book Nebuchadnezzar is said to have besieged Jerusalem and to have captured the city in the third year of Jehoiakim, i.e., 605 B. C. But this did not happen until 597 B. C. when Jehoiachin was king" (p. 335). Essentially similar statements may be found in many recent *Introductions* and *Commentaries* on Daniel.

In reply it should be pointed out first of all that the book of Daniel does not state that Nebuchadnezzar took the city of Jerusalem in the third year of Jehoiakim. All that Daniel asserts is that in Jehoiakim's third year Nebuchadnezzar came to Jerusalem and laid siege against it. God gave into his hands the king and a part of the temple vessels, and these alone are mentioned as the spoil which the Babylonian king received. There is a strange silence in the verse. The reader would expect a statement to the effect that the entire city had fallen, but such a statement *is not given.* Apparently Nebuchadnezzar had to give up the siege before taking the city. If we can believe Berossus, such must have been the case. The Babylonian king, hearing of the death of his father, hastened to Babylon to take up the kingdom (*Antiq.* X:11:1 and *CA* 1:19). At any rate, it is time that critics cease attributing to Daniel a statement which he does not make.

Secondly, Prince asserts that Daniel teaches that *as king of Babylon* Nebuchadnezzar took the city. But this is to attribute to the words a force which they need not possess. As the exegesis has shown (see under 1:1) the word king is here used proleptically and does not at all indicate ignorance or error upon the part of the author. This view has been widely held by commentators representing various schools of thought, e.g., Stuart, Pusey, Zoeckler, Wilson, Charles, Driver, etc.

The crux of the difficulty is to be found in Daniel's mention of the *third* year of Jehoiakim, since Jer. 25:1 equates the *fourth* year of Jehoiakim with the *first* year of Nebuchadnezzar, and Jer. 46:2 states that in the *fourth* year of Jehoiakim Nebuchadnezzar smote the army of Pharaoh-

Necho at Carchemish, and Jeremiah (25:8-14) in the *fourth* year of Jehoiakim speaks of the Chaldeans as though they had not yet come to Palestine.

Is there, however, a contradiction between the dates as given respectively by Daniel and by Jeremiah? According to some critics there is such a contradiction, but this is an assumption for which there is no real warrant. Various attempts have been made to resolve the difficulty. 1. Some of the older commentators advanced the theory that in reckoning the years of Jehoiakim and those of Nebuchadnezzar, a different method was employed. This view was thoroughly refuted by Hengstenberg (*Authentie* p. 53) and since, as far as I know, it is no longer held, no further attention need be paid to it. 2. Haevernick, Pusey. et al. have suggested that the expedition against Jerusalem actually preceded the battle at Carchemish. But such a supposition appears to be at variance with Jer. 25 where Jeremiah is represented as saying in the fourth year of Jehoiakim, "Behold, I will send and take all the families of the north, saith Jehovah, and I *will send* unto Nebuchadnezzar the king of Babylon, my servant, and will bring them against this land, and against the inhabitants thereof, and against these nations round about; and I will utterly destroy them, and make them an astonishment, and a hissing, and perpetual desolations" (Jer. 25:9). It is very unlikely that the prophet would thus speak if in the previous year Nebuchadnezzar had already attacked Jerusalem. Furthermore, there are strategical considerations which make this course of procedure improbable.

3. Aalders (*The Evangelical Quarterly*, Vol. 2, No. 3) suggests that in the Hebrew manuscripts, since numerals were represented merely by letters of the alphabet, a mistake was made by substituting a *gimel* (3) for *waw* (6). Thus, according to Aalders, the expedition described took place in the sixth year of Jehoiakim, probably the year in which, according to 2. K. 24:1, Jehoiakim rebelled, and bands of invaders came against him. This suggestion is not impossible, but the error, if such it was, must have been very ancient, since all the versions support the date offered by the present Hebrew text. Furthermore, the assumption of an error in the manuscript is not necessary to a solution of the difficulty.

4. Keil adopts the position and develops it with characteristic thoroughness and ability that the Hebrew word translated *came* in 1:1 may also mean *set out.* Thus, it is not at all necessary to assume that 1:1 teaches that Nebuchadnezzar actually arrived at Jerusalem and laid siege to it in Jehoiakim's third year, 1:1 may merely mean that in this third year the king set out for Jerusalem, whereas the actual arrival and siege may have taken place during the fourth year, as Jeremiah indicates. Such a translation, despite Driver's strictures, is perfectly possible and perfectly in accord with Hebrew usage. Keil adduces the following examples,

Gen. 45:17; Ex. 6:11; 7:26; 9:1; 10:1; Num. 32:6; I Sam. 20:19; 2 K. 5:5; Jonah 1:3.

It may very well be that this solution is correct, but the presence of the statement *and besieged it* in such close connection with the first verb of the sentence (*came*), together with the mention of the date, gives the impression that the siege also occurred in the third year. At least, that seems to be the natural impression which the verse conveys. This in itself is not decisive against Keil's rendering, but it is a weighty consideration.

5. The correct solution, it would seem, is to be found in the fact that in the book of Daniel the years are reckoned according to the Babylonian method, whereas in Jeremiah they are reckoned according to the Palestinian method. This view has been set forth fully by Wilson (*SBD*, I, pp. 43ff.) and recently it has been given expression in an admirable article by Pieters *The Third Year of Jehoiakim* in *From the Pyramids to Paul*, 1935.

According to the Babylonian system only the first *full year* of reign was called the first year of a king's reign. The year in which the king ascended the throne was not designated his *first* year, but "the year of the accession to the kingdom." Thus, when Daniel speaks of Jehoiakim's third year, he has reference to the same year as does Jeremiah in mentioning the *fourth* year. A table will make the point clear.

Babylonian		*Palestinian*
Year of Accession	....	First Year
First Year	....	Second Year
Second Year	....	Third Year
Third Year	....	Fourth Year

Pieters adduces evidence to show that the Babylonian method of reckoning the years is employed elsewhere in the Old Testament. He appeals to 2 K. 25:27 which speaks of "Evil-merodach King of Babylon *in the year that he began to reign . . .*", and to Jer. 52:28-30 which should be compared with 2 K. 24:18-25:30. The passage in 2 K speaks of the eighth and nineteenth years of a reign, whereas the corresponding passages in Jeremiah mention the *seventh* and *eighteenth* years. Further evidence is presented by Wilson.

If this assumption be adopted it removes entirely the difficulty which is supposed to be created by the reference to the third year in 1:1. It may be noted in passing that the mention of the third year seems on the face of it to be an indication of trustworthiness. Had this verse been composed by a later editor, he doubtless would have made the deportation accord with one of the two principal deportations, either that of 598 B. C. (2 K. 24:14-16), or of 587 B. C. (2 K. 25:2-21).

It remains to suggest what was the actual background of the events recorded in Daniel 1:1. In recent times Pieters has probably given as good a reconstruction as any, and we shall list the points which he mentions:

1. Early in 605 B. C. Jeremiah delivers the address recorded in Jer. 25.

2. Also early in this year Nebuchadnezzar, the crown prince, defeats the Egyptians at Carchemish (Jer. 46:2).

3. Nebuchadnezzar then appears in Palestine.

4. Then occurs the siege of Dan. 1:1, also recorded in 2 K. 24:1 and 2 Chr. 36:6, 7.

5. Something caused Nebuchadnezzar to hasten to Babylon. Apparently this was the news that his father Nabopolassar had died (see *supra*).

II

The Treasures of the Temple

Dan. 1:1 records Nebuchadnezzar's first invasion of Jerusalem, at which time he took away but a part of the sacred vessels of the temple. According to Stuart, there was a second invasion during Jehoiakim's reign, at which time another portion of the temple vessels was taken away (2 Chr. 36:7). However, it should be noted that the passage in Chronicles does not give the year in which this invasion occurred. The principal emphasis of the Chronicles' passage is to the effect that during the reign of the wicked Jehoiakim Nebuchadnezzar was enabled to despoil the temple of some of its sacred vessels. In the light of the discussion in App. I, it seems best to identify this invasion with that of Dan. 1:1, rather than to regard it as a distinct expedition upon the part of the Babylonian king (Cf. also Keil's discussion).

A second invasion, under the reign of Jehoiachin, is recorded in 2 K. 24:13. (Stuart considers this the third). A more thorough despoiling of the temple now occurred. "And he carried out thence all the treasures of the house of the LORD, and the treasures of the king's house, and cut in pieces all the vessels of gold which Solomon king of Israel had made in the temple of the LORD, as the LORD had said."

Under Zedekiah, the invader destroyed the temple and took away all the treasures (Cf. 2 K. 25:6-20). Part of these were brought back under Cyrus (Ezra 1:7), and the remainder under Darius (Ezra 6:5).

III

The Chaldeans

In the Old Testament generally, the term *Chaldean* is used in an ethnic sense, i.e., as the name of a race of people. In the book of Daniel it is also employed to denote a class of wise men. In this latter, more restricted, meaning it occurs in 2:2, 4, 5, 10; 3:8 (?); 4:7; 5:7, 11. (1:4 possibly uses the word in the ethnic sense). This latter usage does not occur elsewhere in the Old Testament, nor does it appear upon any of the inscriptions. The first extra-Biblical employment of the word to denote a caste, occurs, as far as I know, in Herodotus (c. 440 B. C.), and then appears in the Greek writers.[1] Because of this some critics assert that the mention in Daniel of the Chaldeans as a distinct class of wise men is inaccurate and indicative of a later date. Had the book been composed in Babylon during the sixth century B. C., so the argument runs, this error would not have been made.

In answer to this Wilson (*SBD*, I, p. 337ff.) believes that the term *galdu* of the monuments is a designation of the astrologers and may be the equivalent of *Chaldean*. In this he is followed by Aalders (*op. cit.*). However, this derivation is seriously questioned by Baumgartner (TR., 11, 1939. p. 72) ". . . ein angebliches (*amelu*) *galdu*, das einer laengst aufgedeckten Falschlesung von Pinches sein Dasein verdankt." At this point, I follow Baumgartner, and believe that appeal to the reading *galdu* should probably be abandoned.

In recent times perhaps the fullest and most adequate statement of the critical position has been given by H. H. Rowley, ('The Chaldeans' in the Book of Daniel, *The Expository Times* XXXVIII, 1926-27, pp. 423-428). Rowley's first conclusion is "That there is no evidence that the term 'Chaldeans' was used in any other than an ethnic sense in the sixth century B. C., and that any other use under a Chaldean dynasty is almost inconceivable" (p. 428). With the first part of this statement I find myself in agreement. However, it is necessary to consider the evidence adduced in support of the latter part of the statement. Why is it almost inconceivable that, under a Chaldean dynasty, the term Chaldean should be employed in other than an ethnic sense? If I understand Rowley aright, his argument to support this proposition is as follows. When the Chaldeans were at the height of their power and pride (i.e., at the time of Nebuchadnezzar), and when they were dwelling in their own capital, "it can hardly be supposed" that they would use their racial name in any but an ethnic sense. Later, at the time of Herodotus, when an important

[1] Cf. Strabo XVI: 1:6, DS II:29.

change in the status of the race had occurred, and the Chaldeans were "racially insignificant" the other significance of the term might have developed (p. 424).

We may agree with Rowley that, other things being equal, it is not natural to expect the term Chaldean to have any but an ethnic sense when the Chaldeans were at the height of their power. But for what reason would the second meaning of the word appear at a later time? At the time of Herodotus, the Chaldeans were under the dominion of Persia. Would they not then commonly be called "Chaldeans" in the ethnic sense, just as we today in the United States of America speak of Indians, using the word to refer to the descendants of the early American Indians? Surely the American Indian is today "racially insignificant," but the term *Indian* as applied to him, has never, so far as I know, been employed in any but an ethnic sense. Why, then, should the mere change in racial significance give rise to a new usage of the term?

Furthermore, it is necessary to consider Herodotus' employment of the word. He says (I:181), "as the Chaldeans, being priests of this god, say." Here he is describing the ziggurat of Bel (Marduk). Again (I:183), "In the greater altar the Chaldeans burn also 1000 talents of frankincense every year, when they celebrate the festival of this god." In the same chapter occur the phrases, "as the Chaldeans said, "and "I did not see it, but I say what is said by the Chaldeans."

It is obvious that Herodotus considers the Chaldeans to be priests. Furthermore, it should be pointed out that the festival which the Chaldeans celebrate, is, according to Herodotus, observed every year. It is not an innovation, but a long established practice. How long, then, had this practice been in existence when Herodotus wrote? There are certain clues in his paragraph which indicate that the practice had been established for a very long time indeed. The historian is describing a Babylonian temple in which is to be found a golden statue of the god. In this temple the Chaldean priests minister. These Chaldeans had told Herodotus that in the time of Cyrus the temple had also contained a huge golden statue of a man. Xerxes, the son of Darius, (486-465 B. C.) wanted this statue and killed a priest who forbade him to remove it.

The natural impression which is given by a reading of Herodotus' paragraph is that the order of things described had been in existence at least since the time of Cyrus. The sanctuary had been standing since that time, and one might be quite warranted in drawing the inference that the sanctuary priests—the Chaldeans—had also been in existence since that time. And, in the context of this paragraph, is it not most justifiable to infer that the priest who opposed Xerxes was of the same order as the priests whom Herodotus met, namely, a Chaldean? I do not say that the paragraph in question proves that this employment of the term "Chaldean" to denote a class of priests was much older than the time of Herodotus, but it certainly lends its weight in support of the view that such was the case. In fact, in the light of this paragraph from the Greek historian, it may almost with confidence be asserted that, if the change in the use of the term "Chaldean" occurred after the downfall of Babylon, the change in the racial significance of the Chaldeans had nothing to do with it.

We may agree, therefore, with Rowley that Daniel alone employs the term "Chaldean" in two senses, but should differ from him in our conclusions. We do not know how the term came to be employed in a restricted sense, but the mere fact that *to date* no extra-Biblical material of the sixth century B. C. employs the term in this restricted sense does not seem to be sufficient warrant for regarding Daniel's usage as indicative of a later age.

Rowley also asserts as one of his conclusions "That it is impossible to suppose that a faithful Hebrew should become a heathen priest, but that we have here the mark of a non-contemporary hand" (p. 428). In answer to this conclusion, which Rowley apparently bases upon Dan. 2:48, it may be replied that there is not a word in the book of Daniel to support the position that Daniel became a heathen priest.

Again, Rowley concludes, "That we cannot suppose that a close caste, like the Babylonian priesthood, would have admitted Daniel, or that Nebuchadnezzar would have dared to appoint him to the headship of the order" (p. 428). Nowhere in the book is it stated that Daniel was admitted into the Babylonian priesthood, or that he was appointed to the headship of any order. A reply to Rowley was issued by Mr. Geo. B. Michell of Cairo (*The Expository Times*, Vol. XXXIX, 1927-28, p. 45), and we cannot do better than to quote a paragraph from that reply. "Whence, I ask, does he [i.e., Rowley] learn that they [i.e., Daniel and his three friends] were admitted to any order? There is no indication in the Book that any of them exercised any but *political* authority (2:48, 49). Daniel was made 'rab-signin' (a political title) *over* all the wise men of Babylon—a very wise precaution. All the terms used of Daniel and the three other youths in Dan. 1:4, 17, 20 are of the most innocent kind, and relate in no way to either priesthood or magic."

If the book of Daniel really teaches that Daniel became a heathen priest, as apparently some critics think it does, would not such teaching be one of the strongest arguments against a post-exilic origin for the book? In the third century B. C. when Jewish nationalism was apparently being emphasized, how can we conceive of a "legendary" Jewish hero becoming a heathen priest? And if this narrative is from Maccabean times, how can such a representation possibly be accounted for?

IV

The Daniel of Ras Shamra

A little more than seven miles north of Latakia on the coast of Syria is the port Minet el-Beida (Whitehead), and about one mile to the southeast is a place which was called in the documents of antiquity Ugarit, but today bear the name Ras Shamra (Fennelhead). In 1929 serious excavation was begun which resulted in the discovery of clay tablets bearing a cuneiform alphabetic script, and coming from 1500-1200 B. C. Work upon the decipherment of the tablets began immediately and has progressed apace. The study of these tablets is still in the stage of infancy, but remarkable indeed is the progress which has been made.

In 1936 there appeared a volume *La Légende Phenicienne de Danel* by Charles Virolleaud, (Paris) in which one of these texts was edited, a text which apparently mentioned the name Daniel. It has been suggested (see Dussaud, *Syria*, XII, 77) that the Daniel of Ras Shamra and the Daniel of whom Ezekiel speaks should be identified.

It has been noted that Ezekiel, in addressing the king of Tyre, spells the name of Daniel in an archaic fashion which is really Phoenician and which is identical with the orthography of the Ras Shamra text. Thus, Ezekiel writes the name Dan'el whereas, in the book of Daniel it always appears Dani'el. On the Ras Shamra text it appears as in Ezekiel, Dan'el.

It should be noted that Ezekiel distinguishes this Dan'el because of his wisdom (28:3), and righteousness (14:14, 20). Furthermore, he classifies him with Noah and Job, both of whom were men of antiquity and not contemporaries. Is it possible, as Virolleaud suggests (*op. cit.*, p. 121) that the name Daniel was proverbial among the Tyrians, and that for them Daniel would be an ancient wise man and possibly an ancient king of Tyre (see the text I, 151) as Noah and Job were ancient wise men of the Hebrews?

The Ras Shamra epic deals with a character which is really mythological. How much foundation in fact there may be we do not know. But it is extremely questionable, to say the least, that Ezekiel had such a legendary hero in mind. It should be noted, as Virolleaud himself points out, that although the Dan'el of the epic was a just person, nevertheless, the attributes of wisdom (hkm) and *righteousness* (sdqt) are not predicated of him. Furthermore, the orthography of the proper name is by no means decisive.

The passages in Ezekiel are not without difficulty, but there is still much which can be said for that interpretation which holds that the prophet is speaking of the Biblical Daniel. Daniel, according to this interpretation, is deliberately placed between the two devout men of antiquity for the purpose of glorifying him. Noah was a just man (Gen. 6:9) and Job was upright and one who feared God (Job 1:1). Apparently, in the mind of Ezekiel, these characteristics were also found in Daniel. Surely the righteousness and piety of Daniel are exhibited by what is related in Dan. 1, and the fact that he walked with God is shown by his interpretation of the king's dream (Dan. 2). The wisdom of Daniel, mentioned in Ezekiel 28:3 is also exhibited in the life of the Biblical Daniel. These statements of Ezekiel would have enhanced the prestige of Daniel and would have told Ezekiel's readers of the mighty witness for the faith which Daniel was making in Babylon. I seriously question therefore any identification of Ezekiel's Dan'el with the Dan'el of Ras Shamra.

V.

The Identity of the Fourth Empire

It will be noted that in the commentary we have adopted the position that the fourth empire is the Roman. Historically this view has found wide acceptance, but it has by no means been universally embraced. Luther was probably guilty of overstatement when he said, "In this interpretation and opinion, all the world are agreed, and history and fact abundantly establish it."[1] Turretin was closer to the truth when he remarked that all Christians were in agreement in recognizing the fifth kingdom to be Messianic, but that they disagreed as to whether the fourth was Roman or that of the Seleucids and Lagidae.[2]

To the writer it appears that from the book of Daniel itself it is impossible to arrive with absolute certainty as to the identification of this fourth kingdom. Nevertheless there are considerations which make it appear that by the fourth empire Daniel *did not* have in mind the kingdom of the Greeks.

1. The correct method of procedure has been pointed out by Aalders in his excellent article to which reference has already been made (p. 268). It is to begin with that which is plain and explicit and in the light of the plain to interpret what is less clear. Thus, we may begin with the descrip-

---

[1] As given by Keil, *ET*, p. 245.

[2] "Agi enim de Regno Christi, quod obtinere debuit, eversis quattuor Monarchiis et Regnis in statua Danieli ostensis, Christiani omnes consentiunt, Sive per quartum Regnum intelligatur Romanum imperium, sive Seleucidarum, et Lagidarum Alexandri successorum Regnum, de quo inter eos non constat," Turretin, *Institutio Theologiae Elencticae*, 1847, Pars Secunda, pp. 431, 432. It is very interesting to note that Turretin makes no mention of any Christians who consider the fourth Kingdom to be that of Alexander himself.

tion of the horn in ch. 8. Nearly all expositors are in agreement that this horn has reference to Antiochus Epiphanes. Now, the basic question is, Are we to identify this horn with the "little horn" of ch. 7? If such identification can be made, then we must conclude that the fourth empire is Greece. If, however, such identification cannot be made, we are forced to the conclusion that the fourth empire is not Grecian. Such a comparison must, of course, be a just one. We must not overrate the importance of minor divergencies in the descriptions, but must seek to discover whether or not there are major divergencies. What, then do we discover? This question may be answered by presenting in tabular form the representations of the two horns.

Ch. 7	Ch. 8
1. The horn is called a little horn.	1. The horn is said to come forth from littleness.
2. Diverse from the horns which preceded.	2. No similar statement made concerning this horn.
3. The horn "comes up."	3. The horn "goes out."
4. In coming up, the little horn *uproots* three of the ten previous horns.	4. The horn goes out from one of the four horns which had come up in place of the great horn upon the head of the he-goat. It does not uproot any horns before it.
5. Personalized traits—eyes as the eyes of a man and a mouth speaking great things—are given to this horn.	5. No personalized traits, unless possibly the words "and trampled them" of 8:10 might be so considered.
6. Nothing is said about a growth in *size* of this horn. On the other hand, the little horn acts *as though* it were great. Its mouth speaks great things; it has a look more stout than its fellows, it makes war with the saints and prevails against them, it wears out the saints, and thinks to change times and laws, and the saints are given into its hand until a time, times and the dividing of a time, but *nowhere* is this "little" horn described as becoming great.[3]	6. Stress is immediately placed upon the great growth in size of this horn.

7. The little horn carries on his warfare until the final judgment. He, together with the fourth beast from which he rose, is destroyed by Divine judgment. In order to introduce the statement of his destruction the reader is given a majestic judgment — scene, and from this supreme judgment council the books are opened, and the beast was slain and given to the burning fire.

7. Wholly different is the end of this horn. Of him it is merely said that "he shall be broken without hand." Hardly any stress is placed upon his death.

8. The saints who are persecuted by the "little" horn receive the kingdom.

8. Nothing is said of any reward being given to those who were persecuted by this horn.

Of the various differences above listed, some are obviously more important than others. The purpose of ch. 7 seems to be to stress the unique character of the "little" horn. This appears first of all in the explicit statement of the diversity of this horn from those which had preceded it. Wholly in keeping with this description is the fact that the beast itself from which the horn grows, is diverse from the three beasts which had preceded it. In ch. 7 the reader's attention is thus drawn to the unique character of the beast and also of the "little" horn.

---

3 The explanation of this fact may probably be as follows:

The horn of ch. 8 obviously stands for a human king. This is the interpretation given in 8:23 ff. The description of his great growth is indicative of the fact that he should in a physical sense attack many countries, including Palestine. He wages physical warfare, and his warfare is directed against the historical Jewish people. Upon this point, there is little, if any, serious difference of opinion. Thus, he took away the daily sacrifices from the Temple at Jerusalem. The symbolism represents these conquests by describing the horn as growing in size.

Very different, however, is the case with the "little" horn of ch. 7. He does not take action against the historical Israelitish people. Nothing whatever is said of his taking away the daily sacrifices. Rather, his warfare appears to be primarily spiritual. Note that he comes up, not from another horn but from the head of the last beast. He is probably to be regarded, therefore, not as an individual man or king, but as a power. He makes warfare upon the saints of the most High, who belong to a kingdom that is spiritual, Divine in origin, universal in scope and eternal in duration. The warfare therefore, would seem to be spiritual in nature. It is perfectly true that this spiritual opposition will manifest itself in physical attack and persecution, but the warfare herein described appears to be basically spiritual. This appears to be brought out by stressing the blasphemous, presumptuous nature of the "little" horn. It has a wicked, hostile, defiant attitude toward God which results in its endeavor to destroy those who belong to a spiritual kingdom.

Very different, however, is the case in ch. 8. The beast from one of whose four horns the horn grows is said to be a he-goat. The beast which preceded the he-goat was a ram. Now, how can it be said that the he-goat was basically different from the ram? In fact, are not the ram and the he-goat essentially the same? The beast, therefore, is not characterized as unique. Furthermore, there is nothing particularly unique about the horn. It appears going out from one of the four preceding horns, and is described as growing in size, and finally being cut off without hand. But what is there about it that may be regarded as particularly unique?

The unique character of the "little" horn appears also from the fact that it possessed eyes like the eyes of a man and a mouth speaking great things. These features seem to point to an intelligence which is directed toward the overthrow of the kingdom of God.

But that which particularly stresses the solemnity of the description is the majestic scene of judgment, laid in heaven. The fourth beast, and its subsequent outgrowths, are to be destroyed in a two-fold manner:

1) Positively. The God of Heaven will erect a kingdom which will be truly universal and eternal. This fact, which receives such emphasis in ch. 7 is symbolized in ch. 2 by the Stone cut without hands, which smites the image and becomes a great mountain, filling all the earth.

2) Negatively. The enactment of judgment, by which the entire rule symbolized by the beast and its horns is given over to the burning of fire.

The scene in the vision is of course symbolical, and chronological events of history cannot be pressed. As the vision manifested itself in history we may note that the first great blow against the fourth kingdom came with the appearance of the Son of God upon earth. From the time of His death and resurrection His Kingdom has grown and progressed. When He again comes to earth He will come to judge, and the mighty oppressors of His people will be condemned in the judgment of eternity. The destruction of the fourth beast and its "little" horn is a matter of the utmost solemnity. Of this solemnity nothing whatever appears in ch. 8. There the horn is merely cut off without hand, and nothing is said of a destruction of the he-goat. Certainly there is no association in destruction of the he-goat and the horn of ch. 8 as there is of the "little" horn and the nondescript beast in ch. 7. It would apear therefore that the "little" horn of ch. 7 and the horn of ch. 8 are not to be identified.

The horn of ch. 8 is not expressly identified as Antiochus Epiphanes, but since the ch. goes on to lay stress upon the taking away of the daily sacrifice and since the he-goat is explicitly identified with Greece, we would seem to be perfectly warranted in discovering in this horn a symbolical representation of Antiochus. If, then, such identification is correct, and if the "little" horn of ch. 7 is not Antiochus, it therefore follows that the fourth beast of ch. 7 and the he-goat of ch. 8 are not to be identified. The last beast of ch. 7 therefore does not represent Greece, and the "little" horn must be recognized as symbolizing, not Antiochus, but one who comes forth from a kingdom which was in existence when the kingdom of the Son of Man was erected, namely, the kingdom which followed that of the Greeks, the Roman Empire.

— — — — —

2. The second step in the argument to show that the fourth kingdom is Rome and not Greece is found in a study of the second empire. This empire, we shall seek to show, is not merely Median, but rather combined Medo-Persia. If this assumption that the second empire is Medo-Persia is correct, then one of two results obtains. Either we have the order:

1. Babylon
2. Medo-Persia
3. Alexander
4. Alexander's successors.

or we have the order:

1. Babylon
2. Medo-Persia
3. Greece
4. Rome.

Let us consider the first alternative, namely, that the fourth kingdom is that of Alexander's successors. This position has been set forth for example by Stuart. However, it does not appear to do justice to the requirements of the text. In 8:8ff. the kingdoms of the Diadochi are clearly represented. They are represented, however, not as independently existing, but merely as offshoots of the Grecian empire. The he-goat is said to be the king of Greece (8:21). When the great horn is broken, four horns appear *in its place* (8:8, 22). These four, therefore, are represented merely as replacing the first, and all are outgrowths of the he-goat, the Grecian empire. This fact is decisive against any attempt to identify the fourth kingdom—which is said to be diverse from those preceding it—with the successors of Alexander.[4]

The second alternative, it seems to the writer, is alone tenable. However, those who refuse to admit that the fourth empire is Rome are faced with difficulty. Most such expositors well recognize the impossibility of

---

[4] In recent times this position has been capably discussed by Rowley (*DM* pp. 139-142). In this connection it should be remarked that the nameless beast of ch. 7 in no sense serves as a suitable symbol for the successors of Alexander. Cf. also Pusey, *op. cit.*, p. 139.

considering the fourth empire to be the successors of Alexander. They believe, rather, that it is the Grecian empire as such, i.e., the empire of Alexander and his successors. There then arises a problem, namely, what is the identity of the three preceding empires? If the scheme is 1. Babylon; 2. Medo-Persia; 3. ——?———; 4. the Grecian empire; the question arises, What is the third empire?

There is no point in considering some of the attempted solutions to this problem, such as those which endeavor to find a reference to four kings, instead of four kingdoms. Such interpretations fly in the face of the text, and Rowley (DM) has done admirable service in refuting them. Nor, for that matter does the position of Hitzig commend itself, namely; 1. Nebuchadnezzar; 2. Belshazzar; 3. Medo-Persia; 4. Greece. This position, also, by identifying the second kingdom with a king instead of a kingdom does violence to the text. Again the symbolism of chs. 2 and 7 obviously does not apply to Belshazzar.

What, therefore, is to be done by those who postulate Babylon as the first kingdom, and Greece as the fourth? This is the problem that arises. How is it to be solved? By many it is solved by adopting the following scheme. 1. Babylon. 2. Media. 3. Persia. 4. Greece. Instead, therefore, of considering Medo-Persia as a unit, many split up Media and Persia into two kingdoms. Now, the scholars who adopt this view are well aware that after the downfall of Babylon there never was an independently existing Median kingdom. According to them, however, the author of the book of Daniel did not know this, and erroneously assumed such to be the case. The basic question which we must therefore face is, What is the identity of the second kingdom? Is it Media or is it Medo-Persia? If it can be shown, and it can, that the second kingdom is Medo-Persia, then the advocates of the Grecian hypothesis are placed in an exceedingly embarrassing position. They must then identify the third empire, and this *cannot be done.* If, then, it can be shown that the second kingdom is Medo-Persia, the Grecian hypothesis is lost.

The arguments which are generally employed to support the position that the second kingdom is Median are as follows: 1) A Median king is said to have ruled after Belshazzar and before Cyrus; 2) A racial distinction between Darius the Mede and Cyrus the Persian is thought to be repeatedly emphasized; 3) The kingdom of Babylon is said to be divided (i.e., in the sense of partitioned) and given to the Medes and to the Persians (5:28). These are the principal arguments, and to them careful attention must be given. Before discussing them, however, we would make two preliminary observations.[5]

---

[5] The best recent presentation of this position is given by Rowley *DM*, pp. 138-160.

1. It is impossible to hold that the fourth kingdom is Greece (i.e., the Grecian empire as such and not merely the Diadochi) without positing historical error in the book of Daniel. Men like Stuart and Zöckler, who adhere to the trustworthiness of the book, do not regard the second kingdom as Median nor the fourth as Grecian. They consider the second to be Medo-Persia and the fourth to be that of Alexander's successors. It is not their position, however, which is now under discussion. It is rather the position that the fourth kingdom is the Grecian empire, and this view cannot be held today without the assumption that Daniel made an historical error, namely, positing an independent Median kingdom after the downfall of Babylon and the rise of Persia. The necessity of making such an assumption is one of the strongest objections against this view.

2. Even if the arguments above mentioned should prove to be correct, they would not in themselves suffice to show that the second kingdom of chs. 2 and 7 was Median, and the third Persian. They would of course go a long way toward supporting such an identification, but there are other considerations which must also be taken into account. Does the symbolism of the visions, for example, support this position? Are the Medes and the Persians ever regarded as a unit in Daniel? Such questions as these also have their proper place.

Let us now proceed to consider the arguments which are adduced in support of the position that the second-kingdom is Median. It is said in the first place that a Median king ruled after Belshazzar and before Cyrus. But nowhere in the book of Daniel is it said that Darius the Mede ruled before Cyrus. Such was undoubtedly the case, but this is not explicitly stated in Daniel. What are the facts?

1. Belshazzar was slain 5:30.

2. Darius received the kingdom, i.e., ". . . the kingdom passed to Darius, without the slightest indication as to the manner of the transfer" (*DM*, p. 51).

3. An event is dated by the first year of the reign of Darius 9:1, cf. also 11:1.

4. It is said that Daniel prospered in the reign of Darius and in the reign of Cyrus the Persian (6:28). What do these facts prove?

We may note that in the above references the kingdom is never identified as the kingdom of the Medes or the kingdom of the Persians. In one place (6:28) mention is made of the reign of Darius and the reign of Cyrus the Persian. This passage, however, requires special comment. The word translated reign is maleXuth from the noun maleXu. Now in the book of Daniel the word maleXu is employed with different connotations.

In 6:26 for example ("in every dominion of my kingdom") it obviously refers to a territorial realm. In fact, in this sense it quite approximates the equivalent of the English word "realm." In the latter part of the same vs. (i.e., 6:26b) however, the word is used with still a different connotation ("his kingdom that which shall not be destroyed"). Here the word does not refer to geographical or territorial extent, for Darius is clearly speaking of a spiritual kingdom. What Darius has in mind here is an organized kingdom that is eternal in duration. This is quite a different connotation from that which the word bears in the earlier part of the vs. In 4:23 (4:26) the word seems to bear still another sense ("thy kingdom shall be sure unto thee"). Here the question is not about the continuance of the kingdom of Babylon but about the rule of Nebuchadnezzar over this kingdom. In this passage, therefore, the word seems to express the idea of royal authority or kingship.

Now in the passage which is of immediate interest to us the word is employed in yet a different sense. Here it has reference not to the territorial extent of a kingdom, nor to an organized power as such, nor to royal authority, but rather to the actual reign of a specific king. We might paraphrase, "Now Daniel prospered while Darius was reigning and he also prospered while Cyrus the Persian was reigning." In other words, the passage is speaking not about a *kingdom* but about the *reign* of two kings and it states the fact that during the reign of *each* of these two kings Daniel prospered. This construction appears frequently in Hebrew. For example, we read, (Dan. 1:1). "In the third year of the *reign* of Jehoiakim." Now, the reference here is not to the objective kingdom of Judah but to the *reign* of Jehoiakim over that kingdom, and this fact is proved by the mention of a date. Similar uses also appear in Dan. 2:1 and 8:1, and outside the book of Daniel in Jer. 49:34; 52:31; Ezra 4:5, 6; 7:1; 8:1; Esther 2:16; I Chr. 26:31; 29:30; II Chr. 3:2; 15:10, 19; 16:1, 12; 29:19; 35:19. All of the above passages employ a Hebrew word, maleXuth, which is the precise equivalent of the Aramaic word maleXu.

With respect to this present passage, therefore, our conclusion must be that it says not a word concerning the identity of any kingdom. All it asserts is that Darius reigned and Cyrus the Persian reigned.

As to 5:30 and 6:1 it may be said that the kingdom here mentioned is probably to be understood in the same sense as "kingdom of the Chaldeans" in 9:1. This appears from the following consideration. Daniel has just been elevated to the position of "third" ruler *in the kingdom* (5:29). In the same night in which this elevation occurred, Belshazzar, king of the Chaldeans, was slain (5:30). The king was slain; what then happened to the kingdom? It was taken over (how, we are not told) by Darius the Mede (6:1) who immediately began to administer its affairs (6:2ff). Throughout this passage the kingdom *is the same*, the kingdom of the Chaldeans. It certainly is not a world-kingdom of the Medes. It is ruled over by a Chaldean, Belshazzar, and it is ruled over by a Median, Darius, but *it is still the kingdom of the Chaldeans*. This is explicitly stated in 9:1. The reason for this is apparent. The purpose of the writer is to stress the kingdom of the Chaldeans as the enemy of the people of God. He is not concerned to say, "This is now the kingdom of the Chaldeans, now the kingdom of the Persians." Rather to him, it is the kingdom of the enemy people, the Chaldeans. When foreign rulers are on the throne, he merely seeks to identify them. Darius was from the seed of the Medes, and was made king over the kingdom of the Chaldeans (9:1). This means that Darius was of Median ancestry and *that is all it means*. It does not mean that the writer erroneously thought that following the Babylonian empire there was a Median empire and following the Median empire there was a Persian. To insist upon this is to do a grave injustice to the writer of Daniel.

By way of summary, then, we may assert that the picture which the book of Daniel presents is as follows. There is a kingdom which is hostile to the people of God. It is the kingdom of the Chaldeans. When its king, Belshazzar, was slain, it passed into the hands of a certain Darius who was of Median ancestry. During his reign and also during the reign of Cyrus who was a Persian, Daniel prospered.

Such evidence, therefore, is not sufficient to establish the theory that the writer of Daniel erroneously considered Babylon to be followed by a Median empire. The purpose of the writer is to designate the ancestry both of Darius and of Cyrus, not to name the powers which took over the fallen kingdom of the Chaldeans.

An historian who wished to describe the vicissitudes through which Holland passed during the second world war might write somewhat as follows. "After the overthrow of the government of Queen Wilhelmina, an Austrian, Arthur Seyss-Inquart took control of the government." Upon the basis of a statement such as this it would be most unjust to maintain that after the downfall of Queen Wilhelmina, Holland was ruled by the Austrian government. All the above statement means is that the man who took the government was himself an Austrian. The same is true in the case of Daniel.

The second argument adduced in support of the position that a Median empire followed that of Babylon is that a racial distinction between Darius and Cyrus is repeatedly emphasized.

Cyrus is mentioned

1:21 Cyrus the King.
6:28 Cyrus the Persian.
10: 1 Cyrus King of Persia.

Darius appears:

5:31 Darius the Median.
6:1 Darius.
6:6 King Darius.
6:9 King Darius.
6:25 King Darius.
6:28 Reign of Darius.
9:1 Darius the son of Ahasuerus, of the seed of the Medes.
11:1 Darius the Mede.

What do these facts reveal? For one thing they do not lay particular emphasis upon the racial ancestry of Cyrus. Only in one passage is he called a Persian (6:28), and the reason for that is obvious. It is to show that Cyrus is of a different ancestry from Darius. This is the only passage in which a racial distinction between the two is emphasized. Daniel is however careful to stress the Median ancestry of Darius. But what does this prove? It proves nothing more than that the two men were of different racial origin. To deduce from this that there was an independent Median empire just preceding the Persian empire is to be guilty of a *non-sequitur.*

In the third place it is argued that 5:28 when properly interpreted, means that the kingdom of Belshazzar is to fall partly to the Medes and partly to the Persians. It is to be divided into two parts, one of which is given to the Medes and the other to the Persians. But is it the intention of the writer that such be our understanding? Obviously it is not, as the following considerations abundantly indicate.

1. The word *divided* (perisath) is employed because it sounds like *Persian* (paras). Now this word in Aramaic means to break in two. Some have taken it in the general sense of *break.* Thus Stuart aptly remarks "*Broken* is the better meaning here, for *divided* between the Medes and Persians, would convey the idea that each of these was a separate and independent power; which was not the fact when Babylon was captured." But even this is not necessary. As M points out, "when an empire is destroyed its unity is lost, even if it be absorbed as a whole by the conqueror."'

But what completely refutes this erroneous interpretation is the fact that in the immediately succeeding context, when Darius *the* Mede is upon the throne, the Medes and Persians are regarded as a *unit.* In 6:8 the king is reminded of the "law of the Medes and Persians, which altereth not." On the basis of this law Darius *the Mede* acts. Reference is again made to this law in vv. 12 and 15. Now it is the presence of this conception of the Medes and Persians as a unit *in this context* which destroys the erroneous idea that the author of Daniel believed that there was an independently existing Median empire immediately after the downfall of Babylon. If the references to Darius *the Mede* were placed in a different context, possibly there might be some justification for this assumption, but since he appears as one who is subject to the law of *the Medes and Persians,* this erroneous assumption must go completely.

For be it noted that in these words, *the law of the Medes and Persians,* we have the *only* clue given in this context, (except of course the clear statement in 5:28) as to the identity of the *power* which succeeded Babylon.[6] This supreme power, to which Darius the Mede was subject was the Medo-Persian government.

It would indeed have been strange if in 5:28 the writer had intended his readers to understand that Belshazzar's kingdom would be divided and given partly to the Medes and partly to the Persians, and then straightway in the immediately succeeding context had represented the kingdom as ruled over by a Median who was subject to the laws of a united Media and Persia. Yet it is precisely this which we are compelled to assume, if we adopt the interpretation of 5:28 which some advocate.

We have seen therefore, that the three principal arguments which have been adduced to support the position that the second world empire of Daniel is Media and not Medo-Persia fall to the ground. We must now give consideration to the manner in which in the book of Daniel Media and Persia are symbolized. In 8:20 we read, "The ram which thou sawest having two horns are the kings of Media and Persia." This vs. provides the interpretation of vs. 3, ". . . a ram which had two horns: and the two horns were high; but one was higher than the other, and the higher came up last." From these vv. two facts stand out. 1) A distinction between Media and Persia is made, thus revealing the composite nature of the kingdom. 2) The underlying unity of the kingdom is shown by the fact that *one* animal represents it. The reader's attention is first directed to the ram (i.e., to the unity of the kingdom) and then to its diversified aspect as represented by the two horns. One of these horns came up after the other, which signifies the fact that it became predominant. This is historically true. Persia did as a matter of fact become predomi-

6 Such passages as 8:3, 20; 10:13, 29, in reality support this identification.

nant over Media, and hence in passages such as Dan. 10:13, 20 the nation is referred to simply as Persia.

There is therefore in this symbolism a picture of a united kingdom with a two-fold aspect. In line with this *one* kingdom with its two-fold aspect is the representation of the second kingdom given in chs. 2 and 7. The representations of these chs. are certainly congruous with the view that the second kingdom is Medo-Persia, but it is difficult to see how they (particuarly 7:5) can apply to Media alone. Pusey goes so far as to say (*op. cit.*, p. 125) "Every lineament then of the description agrees with the Medo-Persian empire; the heavy fierceness and the destructiveness of the animal; the prominence given to the one side; the three ribs, which can receive no explanation as to any other empire." Rowley, in defense of the position that the second kingdom is Median says, "It is only claimed that where the meaning is so obscure, the verse cannot rightly be used to embarrass or to support either view" (*DM*, p. 153). For my part I am inclined to think that the truth lies somewhere between these two positions. Rowley is correct, it seems, in asserting that the vs. is obscure. The obscurity, however, applies to the details and not to the central meaning. (See com. in loc.) The central meaning is that an empire, represented by the bear, is to conquer much territory. Now Media alone cannot rightly be represented as an empire whose principal characteristic was that it conquered much territory. (See App. VI). If the writer of Daniel in 7:5 intended to represent Media alone, he has brought himself into sharp conflict with what he says in 8:3, 20, where Persia is correctly represented as coming up after Media and obtaining the supremacy.

On the other hand, the combined Medo-Persian empire (as in 8:3, 4) did conquer much territory, and the description in 7:5 is apt.[7] A further point should be noted. In 7:5 attention is called to the fact that the beast is raised up on one side (see *com.* in loc.). It is difficult to escape the conclusion that this indicates a double-sidedness. It fits in well if the writer was symbolizing Medo-Persia, but I completely fail to understand why it was mentioned if he was thinking merely of a Median empire. The conclusion to which we are led therefore is that the writer of Daniel had in mind by his second empire Medo-Persia and not simply Media.

— — — — —

3. The next step in the development of the argument is to show that the statements made concerning the fourth beast do not well apply to the Grecian Empire but do describe the Roman. We may take our starting-point from 7:7. In this vs. the fourth beast is nondescript, and we are explicitly told that "it was diverse from all the beasts which went before

[7] Pusey has admirably illustrated this fact, *op. cit.*, pp. 123-125.

it." Furthermore it is described as "dreadful and terrible and strong exceedingly." It is also introduced in a manner which immediately indicates that it is in a class by itself and is not to be likened to the three beasts which precede it. "After this I saw in the night visions"—these are the stately words which solemnize the introduction of the fourth beast. They prepare the reader for something unusual; they warn him of the solemnity of the revelation which is about to be made.

All such particular solemnity is lacking however in the manner in which the kingdom of Greece is introduced in ch. 8. In this ch. Greece is represented by a he-goat, and there is nothing particularly striking in the manner in which the beast is introduced. We are simply told that as the seer was beholding the ram, a he-goat came from the west. The kingdom therefore is not represented by a nondescript beast, nor can the he-goat be described as "dreadful and terrible, and strong exceedingly." But what is most important, not only is the he-goat not diverse from the ram, but it is *precisely the same* kind of beast. For what essential difference is there between a ram and a he-goat? One result is surely clear. The he-goat of ch. 8 and the nondescript beast of ch. 7 are *not the same beasts* nor are they intended to represent the same kingdom.

Furthermore, the description of the activities of the he-goat, found in 8:5-8, 21, 22, in no way corresponds to what is said of the nondescript beast in ch. 7.

The Nondescript Beast

Comes up from the sea.
Dreadful, terrible, strong exceedingly.
Had great iron teeth and nails of brass.
Devoured and brake in pieces.
Stamped the residue with its feet.
Had ten horns.
Another little horn arose among the ten horns.
Three of the first horns were plucked up by this little horn.
The beast was slain.
Its body was destroyed.
Its body given to the burning flame.
Represents a kingdom diverse from all kingdoms.
It shall devour the whole earth, and shall tread it down and break it in pieces.

The He-Goat

Comes from the west on the face of the whole earth.
Touched not the ground.
Had a conspicuous horn between its eyes.
Came to the two-horned ram.
Ran into him in fury.
Moved with choler against the ram.
Smote the ram.
Broke the ram's two horns.
Cast the ram to the ground.
Stamped upon the ram.
Waxed great.
Great horn is broken.
Four conspicuous ones come up in its stead.

The above contrasts should speak for themselves. Is it not apparent that by means of the symbolism of the nondescript beast in ch. 7 and the he-goat in ch. 8 the author intended to represent two entirely different kingdoms? In respect to the origin, nature and destiny of these beasts the representations differ. We are compelled therefore to conclude that if the he-goat of ch. 8 stands for Greece, the nameless beast of ch. 7, since it is the last beast in the vision must stand for the empire which followed Greece, namely Rome.

There is a reason for the fact that the beast was nameless, and this reason appears in the unique nature of the kingdom which is represented. Now there is nothing so unique in the Grecian empire either of Alexander or of his successors that it could explain the use of such symbolism. But Rome was unlike those kingdoms which preceded. Rome showed itself to be the first truly universal empire of antiquity. Rome was characterized by its conquering and crushing power and by its ability to consolidate the territories which it seized. In this respect appeared its uniqueness. As Pusey says, ". . . Rome had consolidated a dominion different in character from any before her and wider in extent" (*op. cit.*, p. 129).

4. One further point must be mentioned. In ch. 2:44 it is expressly stated that the Messianic kingdom will be erected "in the days of these kings," i.e., the four kingdoms (See the exposition in loc.). As a matter of historical fact, Christ did not appear upon earth in the days of the Grecian empire, but when Rome was mistress of the world. If then we are to regard these words (i.e., 2:44) as true prophecy, we are compelled to conclude that the fourth kingdom is Rome and not Greece.

By way of summary we may conclude: 1) A comparison of the horn of ch. 8 and the little horn of ch. 7 makes it apparent that the two horns are intended to represent different things. Since the horn of ch. 8 evidently stands for Antiochus Epiphanes, it follows that the little horn of ch. 7 does not stand for Antiochus Epiphanes; 2.) Since the second kingdom is Medo-Persia and not Media alone, it follows that the order must be Babylon, Medo-Persia, Greece, Rome; 3.) The fourth beast of ch. 7 and the he-goat (which represents Greece) of ch. 8 are obviously intended to symbolize different empires. Since, therefore, the fourth beast of ch. 7 is the last beast in the vision it must represent an empire which arose after Greece, namely, Rome; 4.) Daniel explicitly states that the Messianic kingdom will be erected during the time of these kingdoms. Since the Messianic kingdom was not erected during the days of the Grecian empire, it follows (if we at all take the words of Daniel seriously) that the last empire must be Rome.

It remains to consider the objections which have been urged against the position herein advocated and the arguments adduced in favor of the view that the fourth kingdom represents Greece. These are as follows:

1) It is argued that the Messianic kingdom does not begin until after the four dynasties are destroyed. Great stress is laid upon this point. Stuart, for example, says, "This is a circumstance too decisive to admit of any appeal. Unless then the Roman dynasty was destroyed before the coming of Christ, the fourth dynasty was not Roman" (p. 189). In recent times Rowley has restated this view, "Whether the fifth monarchy was to be the world dominion of the Messiah, as most hold, or whether it was to be a purely spiritual kingdom, as the Praeterist school holds, the prophecies clearly imply that all other world monarchies would end with its advent" (*DM*, p. 86).

In reply we would call attention to the time-honored rule of interpretation that the obscure must be interpreted in the light of that which is more plain. In this instance the symbolism of the visions must be explained in accordance with the accompanying interpretation and not vice versa. Such an interpretation appears in 2:44, where it is explicitly stated that the Messianic kingdom is to be erected in the days of the kings of the four empires. In other words, while these empires *are still in existence*, not after they have been destroyed, will the Messiah's kingdom be established. It is in the light of this clear statement of 2:44 that the symbolism of the visions must be interpreted.

Nor is there anything in the symbolism of these visions which conflicts with such an interpretation. Such symbolism, when rightly interpreted (i. e., in the light of 2:44) presents a warfare between the little horn and the saints of Messiah's kingdom. The outcome of this warfare ends with Divine intervention, and the entrusting of the kingdom to the saints forever. In the light, therefore, of 2:44 and of 7:18 and 7:21 we must regard the little horn as making war with the saints of the Divine kingdom. It follows then that the little horn and the saints of the kingdom of the Son of Man exist side by side. The little horn does not make war against saints who do not belong to a kingdom, for the only saints mentioned are those who belong to the kingdom of the Son of Man (7:14). It is therefore against the saints of the kingdom of the Son of Man that the little horn wages war, and the outcome of the warfare is that the saints possess the kingdom eternally.

We conclude that the interpretation which insists that the Messianic kingdom must follow the destruction of the four empires is erroneous.

2) Those who interpret the fourth kingdom as Greece generally posit Media as the second kingdom. This has already been shown to be untenable.

3) The principal objection to the Roman view, however, is that it is said to be historically incorrect. So Driver, "The great, and indeed fatal, objection to this interpretation is, however, that *it does not agree with the history*" (p. 97). Driver contends that the historical Roman empire came to a close in 476 A. D., and that no ten kingdoms arising therefrom can be identified. In reply we would point to the exposition of ch. 7. The figure ten is to be regarded as a round or whole number. It merely signifies that there will arise a number of kingdoms which may be said to have their historical roots in Rome. The little horn, itself, need not necessarily represent one king or kingdom. It may possibly signify a coalition of governments. Whatever its outward, historical form is to be, it is the manifestation of the spirit which exalts man and opposes Christ.

If, however, the number ten be insisted upon, as Driver apparently wishes to do, can we discover ten kings or kingdoms which have arisen from the Grecian empire? In the present writer's opinion this cannot be satisfactorily accomplished. For one thing, those who insist upon a literal interpretation of the number ten are surprisingly inconsistent when they do not also insist that the ten kings should be contemporaneous. For the ten horns appear upon the head of the fourth beast *together*, and three of the ten are uprooted by the little horn. If, therefore, we are to insist upon the number *ten*, let us also insist upon ten somewhat contemporaneous kings. The advocates of the Grecian view, however, do not do this, and thus show themselves to be inconsistent at this point. They seem satisfied if they can even find ten names which for the most part follow one another in historical order.

The latest attempt to identify the horns has been made by Rowley (*DM*, pp. 98-120). He regards the first seven horns as the first seven Seleucid kings, namely 1. Seleucus I, 2. Antiochus I, 3. Antiochus II, 4. Callinicus, 5. Ceraunus, 6. Antiochus III, 7. Seleucus Philopator. So far there is much agreement with Rowley among the advocates of the Greek view. Who, however, are the three kings which are uprooted by the little horn? According to Rowley, they are, 1. Demetrius, 2. Antiochus, the murdered brother of Demetrius and 3. Ptolemy Philometor.

Rowley has come to his identifications only after pointing out in a most able way the weaknesses in other attempts to identify the ten horns. What however may be said about Rowley's identifications? To the present writer they offer the same obstacles as do other identifications which seek to interpret the ten horns by a Syrian line of kings. What about Demetrius? He was the son of Philopator and a hostage at Rome, and after the death of Antiochus, did sit upon the throne. But how then can he possibly be regarded as having been uprooted by Antiochus? Rowley suggests that a writer at the time of Antiochus could not know that Demetrius would ultimately sit upon the throne, and hence might regard him as "uprooted" (p. 114). But the horns in the symbolism represent kings (see 7:24). Now if the writer did actually live at the time of Antiochus, how could he possibly regard Demetrius (although a legitimate heir) as a king, when Demetrius, as far as the writer knew, had not yet sat upon the throne? And furthermore, how could this writer possibly regard Demetrius as a king who had been uprooted? [Note the language "and he (the little horn) shall subdue three kings" (7:24)]. Antiochus did not subdue Demetrius.

As to the brother of Demetrius, there is a fragment of John of Antioch, (see Carolus Mullerus, *Fragmenta Historicorum Graecorum*, Vol. IV, p. 558, No. 58, Parisis 1885) which relates that Antiochus slew a son of Seleucus Philopator. However, nothing whatsoever is really known of this son (Muller remarks: Alter vero—filius, quem Antiochus occidit, aliunde, quantum scio, non notus est.) It should be noted that this son of Seleucus would not be the heir to the throne as long as his brother Demetrius was living.[8]

Rowley regards the third uprooted horn as Ptolemy Philometor. Even if it be granted, however that Ptolemy was entitled to a place in the Seleucid line, serious difficulties emerge. Suppose that Porphyry is correct in asserting that a Syrian party did endeavor to claim the throne for Ptolemy (see Jerome's comments on 11:21 in App. VIII), even so it does not follow that Antiochus had uprooted Ptolemy. For, as a matter of fact, Philometor was a ruler of Egypt, a Ptolemy, and not a Seleucid. Antiochus could not be regarded as subduing him and coming up in his place. As Pusey well remarks, "A boy-king, who falls into an uncle's hands is treated by him with show of friendship, and is restored at once, within the year, by his own people, is neither *subdued* nor *uprooted*" (*op. cit.*, p. 177).

It must be emphasized that our basic objection to this interpretation is not the difficulty found in identifying ten Syrian kings, but the endeavor to find a *successive line* of kings rather than a number of more or less contemporaneous kings or kingdoms. The symbolism represents, not successive kings, not a line, but merely a number of kings existing at approximately the same time, all belonging to the second phase of the beast's history.

---

[8] It is, of course, maintained by some scholars that this murdered son had been a king. See *CAH*, Vol. VIII, pp. 498, 713f. However, the evidence is scanty, and it is best not to be dogmatic. Even if there had been a co-regency of some kind, this does not fit in well with the symbolism of Dan. 7, which represents the "little" horn as coming up after the ten and uprooting three of them.

5. The Roman view is said to be due to a priori considerations. Thus Rowley, "But that the Roman view rests on *a priori* considerations is sufficiently proved by its history" (*DM*, p. 73). The prophecy, so runs the argument, had no fulfillment in the Grecian empire, hence it was necessary to reinterpret applying it to Rome. The earliest Roman interpretation is said to be found in Revelation 13 and the Apocalypse of Baruch (39), as also in 2 Esdras, Josephus and the Epistle of Barnabas. On the other hand the Greek view is thought to appear as early as the *Sibylline Oracles* (c. 140 B.C.). Upon the basis of this evidence, it is argued that the Greek view was first held, but that, since the prophecy was not fulfilled in Greece, it was necessary to reinterpret. Hence the origin of the Roman view. "To transfer the fulfilment to the termination of the Roman empire seemed a simple way out of the difficulty, and it was little wonder that the view became dominant in the Church—" (*DM*, p. 74).

Is the matter, however, so simple? The relevant passage in the Sibylline Oracles is as follows:

> "Yet after leaving one root, which the Destroyer shall cut off,
> He shall put forth a side-shoot of ten horns."[9]

The reference appears to be to Antiochus Epiphanes, who leaves a root (Antiochus Eupator) which is cut off by the Destroyer (Demetrius) and then from ten horns puts forth a side-shoot (Alexander Balas).

It has been suggested that the ten horns refer to the ten letters of *Alexandros* (see note in *AP*, p. 386). More likely, however, there is some allusion to the Book of Daniel. In fact, such seems almost unquestionably to be the case. In what sense, however, is this allusion to be taken? Is it to be understood as an *interpretation* of the book of Daniel or rather merely as an allusion which provides a suitable literary device for the writer? Without hesitation we would say the latter.

The passage in the Sibylline Oracles is confessedly difficult and the text not in perfect condition.[10] The common translation would imply that the side-shoot was to be planted from the ten horns.[11] But it appears better to construe the *ek deka de keraton* with *kopsei* of the preceding line and to translate,

---

[9] See Charles *AP*, Vol. II, p. 386; Rowley, *DM*, pp. 115-120. The Greek text reads: RIZAN IAN CE DIDOUS, 'EN KAI KOPSEI BROTOLOIGOS EK DEKA DE KERATON, PARA DE PHUTON ALLO PHUTEUSEI.

[10] As an example, the text of line (388) "—there shall come unexpectedly to Asia's wealthy land" has EX instead of EIS which would seem to be required. Rowley deserves the gratitude of all for the discussion of the text which he presents.

[11] i.e., The EK DEKA etc., is construed with PHUTON ALLO.

"Whom the Destroyer will cut off from ten horns."

Apparently, therefore, the writer understood the ten horns to refer to ten kings. But if this is the case, one is amazed that Antiochus Eupator (for apparently he is the one designated as the root) should be regarded as coming from ten kings. Is Demetrius the dreadful "little" horn or is Antiochus Eupator? And what about the three uprooted horns?[12] Is it not clear that the writer is not intending to interpret the book of Daniel? Apparently all that he wishes to say is that the Destroyer cuts down one root from among ten horns (i.e., of royal descent). Doubtless the writer knew of Daniel's use of ten horns to represent ten kings, hence he employs the same figure without intending to specify any particular kings. A root from among kings has been cut off! To say that, and that alone appears to be his purpose.

Even, however, if this passage might be regarded as a witness to the Grecian interpretation, it would not necessarily follow that it was widely held. For the interpretation, if it be such, is not clear-cut but very confused.

Suppose, however, that the Grecian view were widely held before the New Testament, this would only show that the prophecy in Daniel had been misunderstood. Now, it is perfectly true that from New Testament times on, the Roman view becomes prominent. To what, however, is this prominence due?

The real reason why the Roman view came to the ascendancy in New Testament times is due to two facts:

1) Our Lord identified Himself as the Son of Man, the heavenly Figure of Daniel 7, and connected the "abomination of desolation" with the future destruction of the Temple (e.g., Matt. 24).

2) Paul used the language of Daniel 7 to describe the Antichrist, and the Book of Revelation employed the symbolism of Daniel 7 to refer to powers that were then existent and future.

This is enough. This was the very voice of God interpreting the Prophecies of Daniel. The book of Daniel is woven into the warp and woof of the New Testament. When, therefore, the New Testament interprets the Old Testament symbolism as it does, the matter is settled. God has spoken. And the reason why the Roman view became so

---

12 The view of M, namely, that the three violent deaths in this context stand for the three horns is certainly unlikely. For, if this were the case, the root from the ten horns is himself one of those that is cut off. It should be noted that M's translation of line 396 is incorrect. He renders, "Yet after leaving one horn, which the Destroyer shall cut off." The original, however, is rizan (see M, p. 292).

prevalent in the early church is because this view is found in the New Testament, not because men thought they had found "—a simple way out of the difficulty" (*DM*, p. 74).[13]

For our part we desire to rest upon the clear teaching of the New Testament. We regard the New Testament, as also the Old, as the infallible, authoritative Word of the God of Truth. And with the statements of the New Testament, the other considerations which we have adduced are in agreement. To maintain the Grecian view one must posit error in Daniel. Surely a view which requires such procedure condemns itself.

VI

The Historical Background of the Book of Daniel

The four winds of heaven burst out in storm upon the great sea. The people of God were in tragic condition. Exile had already become the lot of the northern nation, and the children of Judah remained alone. The theocracy could no longer exist in its present form. God's people must be dispersed and sifted, that from them might come forth the true remnant. The slumbering nations whom God would use as His instruments must now arise to life. The heavenly powers and forces thus arouse to motion the nations of the world, and as a result the neo-Babylonian empire appears upon the horizon.

---

[13] In the early Church St. Ephraim the Syrian interpreted the kingdoms as follows: 1) Babylon, 2) the Medes, the kingdom of Darius King of the Medes (In Scripture, however, Darius is never called king of the Medes), 3) the Persians, 4) the kingdom of Alexander. The toes of the image are said to be ten kings, successors of Alexander. The three ribs in the mouth of the bear (Dan. 7:5) are the Medes. Persians and Babylonians. The ten horns on the nameless beast are ten kings which have sprung forth from it, and the little horn is Antiochus. The three horns uprooted are the seeds of horns. The judgment scene (Dan. 7:9ff) was set during the time of Judgment of the Greeks, and the Son of Man is the Messiah.

Ephraim however differs radically from the modern exponents of this interpretation in that he considers the prophecy to have been revealed by God to Daniel. In this connection attention may be called to a recent attempt (we must pronounce it a failure) to account for the origin of the idea of the five monarchies upon merely naturalistic grounds. See Joseph Ward Swain, "The Theory of the Four Monarchies: Opposition History under the Roman Empire" in *Classical Philology*, Vol. XXXV, Jan.-Oct., 1940, pp. 1-21 and the comments upon this article by W. Baumgartner, "Zu den vier Reichen von Daniel 2" in *Theologische Zeitschrift*, Vol. 1, 1945, pp. 17-22.

The Neo-Babylonian Empire.[1]

The death of Asshurbanipal in 626 B. C. left a greatly weakened Assyrian empire, one far departed from its ancient glory. Three unimportant rulers sat upon the throne, and Nineveh, the capital, was ready for destruction, as Zephaniah had prophesied, "And he will stretch out his hand against the north, and destroy Assyria; and will make Nineveh a desolation, and dry like a wilderness" (2:13).

Probably the most important figure in the assault upon Nineveh was a king from distant Media named Uvakhshatra or Cyxares who gave his aid to the ruler of Babylon, a Chaldean named Nabopolassar (625-605 B. C.). In 612 B. C., after a siege of over two months, Nineveh fell. In the division of territory the Medes took the land east of the Tigris river, whereas that to the west and south fell to the Chaldeans. For a time an Assyrian king, Ashuruballit II ruled at Harran in the west, but he too fell in 606 B.C. Thus the neo-Babylonian empire appeared upon the ruins of fallen Assyria.

A few years after the death of Ashurbanipal, when the shadows of dark night began to come over Assyria, the light dawned upon the weak kingdom of Judah. In the year 622 B. C. a copy of the Pentateuch (the book of the Law) was discovered in the Temple.[2] This resulted in a reform of the true worship of the LORD. At this time also the great prophet Jeremiah was active.

But Judah, as ever, was a buffer state between two great powers. Now that Nineveh had fallen, the ruler of Egypt turned his attention toward the East. Pharaoh Necho took the throne of his father Psammetik I in 610/09 B. C. In 2 Kings 23:29 we read, "In his (i.e., Josiah's) days

---

[1] The following account purports to be nothing more than a sketch intended to introduce the reader to the subject. Many details have naturally been omitted. The interested reader should consult *CAH*, Vol. III, 1925, pp. 206-225; Vol. IV, 1926, pp. 1-25, where he will find suitable bibliographies. Mention may also be made of Sidney Smith: *Isaiah Chapters XL-LV*, London, 1944, pp. 24-48; 115-157, 204.

[2] It is generally held that this book comprised only Deuteronomy or a part thereof. But the reader should note the force of the arguments adduced against this position. See O. T. Allis: *The Five Books of Moses*, 1943, pp. 176-182. The traditional critical position is given in *IOT*, pp. 178-187. Of particular interest are the two volumes of Adam C. Welch, *The Code of Deuteronomy*, 1924 and *Deuteronomy: The Framework to the Code.* These last two works, although not written from the standpoint of orthodoxy, nevertheless constitute a serious challenge to the position of the Graf-Kuenen-Wellhausen school.

Pharaoh—nechoh king of Egypt went up against the king of Assyria to the Euphrates."[3] There was a reason for this march. The surviving king of Assyria, Ashuruballit had made his residence in the city of Harran. In the year 610, two years after the downfall of Nineveh, Nabopolassar laid siege to the city, and Ashuruballit was forced to retreat to Syria. The city thus fell into the hands of the Chaldean.

In the following year (609 B. C.) Ashuruballit at the head of an Egyptian army laid siege to Harran but failed to capture it. Where did Ashuruballit obtain his Egyptian army? Without doubt it was from the Pharaoh himself who had now reached Syria. On his journey the Pharaoh had been opposed by Josiah at Megiddo, and Josiah had been slain (2 K. 23:29; 2 Chr. 35:20-24). Josiah had declared his freedom from Assyria and possibly had made his resistance against Necho in order to prevent Necho from bringing assistance to Ashuruballit.[4]

The city of Carchemish remained in the possession of Necho for some years. Meanwhile, Jehoahaz, the son of the dead Josiah, was made king. However, the choice was displeasing to Necho, who, after three months, took him prisoner and laid a heavy tribute upon the land (2 K. 23:30-34; 2 Chr. 36:1-3). Instead Necho placed upon the throne a brother of Jehoahaz, Eliakim, and changed his name to Jehoiakim. For eleven years Jehoiakim reigned, and began his reign as a vassal king to Necho (2 K. 23:34-37; 2 Chr. 36:4-8).

In the year 605 Necho marched to the Euphrates and was roundly defeated by the son of Nabopolassar, Nebuchadnezzar II, who then turned his attention to Palestine, taking captives from the city of Jerusalem (see App. I). Jehoiakim now became a vassal of Nebuchadnezzar. After three years however, (i.e., probably in the year following the vision of the colossus) he rebelled, and bands of marauders, doubtless at the instigation of Nebuchadnezzar who was used as an instrument of the Lord, were sent against him (2 K. 24:1-4). Jehoiakim was killed, and his body cast out to lie like an animal's carcass (Jer. 22:18ff.; 36:30).

The kingdom of Judah was now taken over by Jehoiachin, the eighteen year old son of Jehoiakim, who reigned for the brief space of three

---

[3] 2 Chr. 35:20 merely states that the Egyptian King "came up to fight against Charchemish by Euphrates." Rowley *RA*, p. 16, correctly points out that the Hebrew preposition in 2 K. 23:29 is ambiguous. It may be translated "Pharaoh went up *to the help of* the king of Assyria."

[4] In most of the reconstruction here given I follow Arthur Hjelt, *Die Chronik Nabopolassars und der syrische Feldzug Nechos* in the *Festschrift* for *Karl Marti,* 1925, pp. 142-147. But see note 3 *supra.* I disagree with Hjelt when he remarks that in the passage in Kings the expression in which the preposition occurs — "kann nur von Heranziehen im feindlichen Sinne verstanden werden" (*op. cit.,* p. 145).

months. In the year 598 B.C. (the eighth year of his reign) Nebuchadnezzar laid siege to Jerusalem and took it (2 K. 24:8-16; 2 Chr. 36:8-10). Mattaniah, the uncle of Jehoiachin, was appointed as ruler, and his name changed to Zedekiah. The best men had now gone into captivity, and Jeremiah spoke in scathing terms of those who remained (Jer. 24). Zedekiah did the foolish thing of forming an alliance with the Egyptian ruler Psammetich II. This rebellion brought on Nebuchadnezzar, "he, and all his host" against Jerusalem. From the recently discovered Lachish Letters, which vividly illustrate the background of Jeremiah, we learn how the Babylonian king took various towns in southern Palestine, before making his final siege against Jerusalem.[5] We learn also from excavations in southern Palestine that since the previous siege of Nebuchadnezzar (598 B. C.) the country was becoming increasingly poverty-stricken. In August 587 after holding out for a year and a half, Jerusalem itself was entered, and many were carried captive (2 K. 24:17-25:21; 2 Chr. 36:11-21).

Under the governorship of Gedaliah, only the poorest in the land now remained. He however, did not appear acceptable, and in the 7th month, a certain Ishmael slew him, with the result that the people, with Jeremiah as a captive, out of fear of the Babylonians, fled to Egypt (2 K. 25:22-26).

Of these conquests Nebuchadnezzar has left no detailed account. He has, however, given a general description of his exploits.

"In exalted trust in him (Marduk) distant countries, remote mountains from the upper sea (Mediterranean) to the lower sea (Persian Gulf), steep paths, blockaded roads, where the step is impeded, [where] was no footing, difficult roads, desert paths, I traversed, and the disobedient I destroyed; I captured the enemies, established justice in the lands; the people I exalted; the bad and evil I separated from the people."[6]

Nebuchadnezzar himself was more of a builder than a warrior, and is best known for his hanging gardens which were built for his Median wife.[7]

Nevertheless, he continued his warfare. After the conquest of Judah he fought against Tyre. In 585 he began the siege, and for thirteen years the Babylonians continued, unable to take the city. Finally, the ruler, Ethobal II, came to terms with Nebuchadnezzar.

---

5 See Torczyner: *Lachish I,* 1938. The present writer sought to give a popular account of these letters in Pr. Sept. 1938, pp. 165, 166.

6 As given by Barton: *Archaeology and the Bible,* 1927, p. 439.

7 A popular description ot Nebuchadnezzar's work is given by Jack Finegan: *Light from the Ancient Past,* 1946, pp. 185-187; see also *HBA,* II, 1901, pp. 316-353.

During this siege of Tyre the Babylonians again turned their attention toward Egypt. In 567 Nebuchadnezzar invaded Egypt, but it is not known how far he succeeded in going. In the year 562 this great monarch died, having made great the name of Babylon throughout the then known world. "When he died there died also the real power to live and grow in his empire. He left no son like himself, and the Chaldean people were unable to produce another man worthy to sit upon his throne and sway his sceptre" (*HBA* II, p. 353).

The throne was occupied by Evil-merodach (Apil-Marduk) the son of Nebuchadnezzar (562-560). Of him it is recorded that he dealt kindly with Jehoiachin (2 K. 25:27-30).[8] He was slain by his brother-in-law, Neriglisar, who ruled four years (560-556 B.C.), and was followed by his son Labashi-Marduk, who, after a few months was put out of the way by conspirators. Among these was Nabonidus, who ruled as the last king of Babylon. We have already discussed the relationship between Nabonidus and his son Belshazzar (see comments on Dan. 5). In 539 Babylon fell to Cyrus the Persian. Thus came to an end the great empire symbolized by the winged lion, the empire of Nebuchadnezzar.

The Medo-Persian Empire

Who was this Cyrus to whom the neo-Babylonian empire fell? From the sea there arose a second beast, like unto a bear. In the Iranian plateau to the east of Mesopotamia strange peoples had lived. Sometime during the second millenium B.C. (c. 1500) an Aryan group known as the Medes had come into this plateau from the North. The Medes occupied the north-western part of the country, and their capital later became known as Ecbatana. From the land of Parsua came the Persians who settled near Anshan. One of their rulers was Achæmenes (c. 700 B.C.) whose name was preserved by the later kings. While there is much obscurity about the early history of these peoples it may be remarked that for a long while the Persians were under the domination of the Medes. This domination, however, was broken with the appearance of Cyrus II, commonly known as Cyrus the Great.

The reign of Cyrus began about 559 B.C. He was not content to remain as King of Anshan, but extended his sway over the other peoples of ancient Persia. This was done by first decisively defeating Astyages, king of the Medes (—the final campaign was in 550-549 B.C.). Cyrus next seized the Median capital Ecbatana. It should be noted, however, that for the Medes all of this amounted to little more than the substitution of the house of Cyrus for that of Astyages. The great empire of the Medes

---

[8] The name of Jehoiachin has been discovered. See the present writer's *New Light from Babylon* in *PG*, Jan. 1946, p. 5.

and Persians was however, being created, the breast and arms of silver, the bear raised up on one side, the ram with the two horns, one of which was higher than the other.

In 547 B.C. Cyrus turned his attention toward Lydia, and in 546 the kingdom of Lydia was overthrown. Crœsus, its king, had entered into alliances with the Spartans, Egypt and Babylonia. Although Babylonia had not had time to aid Crœsus against Cyrus, nevertheless, the fact of the alliance was doubtless known to Cyrus, who now determined to attack Babylon. Thus Cyrus was fulfilling the prophecy of Isaiah, "Behold I will stir up the Medes against them, which shall not regard silver,—And Babylon, the glory of kingdoms, the beauty of the Chaldees excellency, shall be as when God overthrew Sodom and Gomorrah" (cf. Isa. 13:17-22).

It was not until 540 however that the attack upon Babylon took place, and in 539 the city fell. In this task Cyrus was assisted by the divisions which were present in the neo-Babylonian empire itself. Gobryas, a general of Cyrus, entered Babylon without fighting. On the 3rd day of Marchesvan Cyrus himself entered Babylon in peace, and Gobryas placed governors in charge of Babylon. On the night of the 11th of Marchesvan Gobryas died. Also some other prominent person died, possibly the wife of the king.[9]

For a time the administration of the land was under a certain Darius. All that is known of him is that he was of Median ancestry. Since his name has not been discovered upon the monuments, it has been suggested that he is an invention of the writer of Daniel. But this by no means follows. It is perfectly true that hitherto the name of Darius, apart from the book of Daniel, has remained unknown.[10] But surely the cuneiform evidence does make it clear that there was a period of some change shortly after the downfall of Babylon. It is quite possible that, because of the tremendous responsibilities and duties which the vast new empire placed upon him, Cyrus delegated the rule of Babylonia to a subordinate. And it is also perfectly possible that this subordinate may have possessed vast power, and may very well have been addressed as king by the conquered people and also may have been regarded by them as having been made king over the realm of the Chaldeans. There is not *one-whit* of extra Biblical evidence to show that such a state of affairs may not have existed.

---

[9] *NB*, p. 170ff.

[10] Rowley (DM) has argued that Darius was neither Cambyses, Astyages nor Cyaxares, and he has shown that in all probability Darius was not Gobryas.

The only real difficulty is that as yet it has been impossible to identify this Darius.[11]

Whatever the explanation of the identity of Darius the Mede may be it is a problem for secular history. There is no sufficient reason for doubting his historicity. While he was over the kingdom of the Chaldeans, Daniel was placed in the den of lions and also received the remarkable revelation of the seventy sevens.

Cyrus showed a policy of toleration toward his subjects, for two hundred years previously he had been predicted by Isaiah the Prophet as the shepherd and anointed one of the Lord, who should say to Jerusalem, "Thou shalt be built; and to the temple, Thy foundation shall be laid" (see Isa. 44:24-45:5).

Cyrus, in his first year issued a proclamation, permitting the Jews to return to Palestine to rebuild their temple (2 Chr. 36:22, 23; Ezra 1:1-4).[12] No objection can be taken to the fact that Cyrus uses the name of the LORD, for in proclaiming religious freedom to the Babylonians he had also used the name of their god Marduk.[13] The first group of exiles therefore set out. But Daniel remained in Babylon. In the third year of Cyrus he received the remarkable revelation recorded in chs. 10-12 of his book. Of his last days we know nothing whatsoever.

In 530 Cyrus died. His last years must have been filled with the great task of organizing and strengthening his vast empire. This work was herculean. In fact, it was while fighting against enemies in the distant eastern confines of his kingdom that he died.

---

[11] It is quite conceivable that, even if Darius was ruler only by virtue of delegated authority from Cyrus, he was permitted to be addressed as king, and was entrusted with tremendous power. In the Behistun inscription Darius (i. e. Hystaspis) speaks of the kings who had rebelled against him, and the 9 kings whom he took captive (see Col. IV, par. 2, 3). These were men who had ruled over districts which already belonged to Darius. Among these were some who in declaring their independency had used expressions such as, "I am the king of Sagartia, of the race of Cyaxares." In other words they apparently desired to be king, not merely in a subordinate, but in an independent sense. At any rate, this inscription does permit us to see that the word king might be used of one who had been a subordinate ruler.

[12] For a defense of the substantial historicity of this edict see Elias J. Bickerman, *The Edict of Cyrus in Ezra* 1, in *JBL*, Sept. 1946, pp. 249-275.

[13] See *NB*, pp. 175-179. Note the language of Cyrus, "The entirety of all the lands he (i.e., Marduk) surveyed and examined. He sought out a righteous prince, the desire of his heart, who would grasp his hand. Cyrus, the king of Anshan, whose name he uttered, he called for kingship over all."

Cyrus was followed by his eldest son, Cambyses (530-522 B.C.), who conquered Egypt (525), greatly assisted by aid from within the country itself, and pressed on also into Ethiopia, where he was not entirely successful. On his way back to Persia, he committed suicide.

When Darius Hystaspis ascended the throne (522) he found rebellion breaking out on all hands. Nor in Palestine was all satisfactory. Haggai and Zechariah now appeared, seeking to spur the people on in their task of building the Temple, and in 515 the Temple was completed (Ezra 6:15). The rebellions which had broken out were put down and Darius ruled as master of his empire.

Darius was followed by Xerxes, (the Ahasuerus of Esther) who suppressed a revolt in Egypt which had broken out in the year before his father's death. He also abolished the "kingdom of Babylon," and took away the statue of Bel (see App. III), as a result of which there followed two Babylonian rebellions.

From the waters of the sea another great beast was arising, the four-headed panther with four wings. When under Darius the Ionians had revolted, the Greeks had interfered, and it was up to Xerxes to punish them. Great preparations were made, and in 486 Xerxes set out from Sardis. At first all went his way, but at Salamis he was forced to turn back (480), and his army which had been left in Greece was defeated (479). Little is known of his later years. He was murdered in 465, and Artaxerxes I came to the throne.

Because his right hand was said to be longer than his left, Artaxerxes was surnamed Longimanus. His reign on the whole was rather peaceful, and he himself seems to have been somewhat of a weak ruler. Ezra 7:11ff gives a copy of his commission to Ezra, permitting him to obtain the necessary treasure for the house of God in Jerusalem.

In the 20th year of his reign Nehemiah appears as his cupbearer, and is appointed governor of Judæa. Artaxerxes died in 424, to be followed by his son Xerxes II, who was murdered within two months. The throne was then occupied by Ochus who called himself Darius. After a reign of 19 years he was followed by Artaxerxes II, surnamed Mnemon. In the beginning of his reign his younger brother Cyrus rebelled, and although this rebellion was quelled the way into the heart of the empire was opened to the Greeks. The result was that during the reign of Artaxerxes II there were almost continual rebellions, and the old Persian empire was gradually falling to pieces, although valiant attempts were made to restore it, and when in 359 his reign ended much had been restored.

He was succeeded by his son Ochus who took the title Artaxerxes III, and showed himself to be a vigorous ruler but very cruel. In 338 he was murdered, and his youngest son Arses placed upon the throne. But in 335 Arses also was murdered by Bagoas, who had murdered his father.[14] Bagoas now placed upon the throne one who became known as Darius Codomannus. Darius proceeded to do away with Bagoas, having feared lest he should suffer the same fate as Arses. In the spring of 334 Alexander began his campaign, and Darius went out to meet him, being defeated both at Issus and Arbela (331). In the next year he was killed, and Alexander regarded himself as the head of the Persian Empire.

The Third World Empire

It is obvious that the turning point in the history of the Persian world-empire was the defeat of Xerxes' expedition. Only once did Persia appear to equal the supremacy which she had had under Xerxes and that was at the close of the reign of Artaxerxes II. This situation, however, was largely brought about by means of the help of Greek armies and generals. Greece was looming larger and larger upon the horizon of world history.

It was through the work of Alexander III, known as the Great, the conspicuous horn of the he-goat (Dan. 8:5) that Greece became a world-empire. Alexander was the son of Philip II of Macedon, born in 356 B.C., and educated under Aristotle. In 336 he came to the throne, and soon established the supremacy of Macedon over the Grecian states. In 334 he set out into Asia Minor, defeating the Persians at Granicus, and freed many of the Greek cities of Asia Minor, grounding and establishing there his power. At Issus he roundly defeated Darius and in 331 could enter Persia itself, where at Arbela he won a great victory. He went from city to city, seizing treasure and destroying the royal palace at Persepolis. "The he-goat waxed very great." Alexander went on and on in his conquests until his death in 323. He had created a universal empire and a universal culture, but at his death his empire perished and was partitioned among his four generals.

Of importance from the Biblical viewpoint are the Seleucid and Ptolemaic dynasties. The Ptolemies were a dynasty which ruled in Egypt from 323 to 30 B.C., and the Seluecids a line which ruled in Syria from 312 to

---

[14] Bagoas, a eunuch, was the vizier of Artaxerxes III.

65 B.C. Between these two lines part of Alexander's empire was divided. The following table will be of aid in the study of this period:

Ptolemy I (Soter) 323-285 Dan. 11:5	Seleucus I. Nicator 312-280
Ptolemy II. Philadelphia 285-246 Dan. 11:6	Antiochus I. Soter 280-261
Ptolemy III. Euergetes I 246-221 Dan. 11:7, 8	Antiochus 11. Theos 261-246
Ptolemy IV. Philopator 221-204 Dan. 11:11, 12, 14	Seleucus II. Callinicus 246-226 Dan. 11:9
Ptolemy V. Epiphanes 204-181 Ptolemy VI. Philometor 181-145	Seleucus III. Ceraunus 226-223 Dan. 11:10
	Antiochus III The Great 223-187 Dan. 11:10, 12, 13, 14, 16, 17, 18
	Seleucus IV. Philopator 187-175 Dan. 11:20
	Antiochus IV. Epiphanes 175-164 Dan. 11:21-35
	Antiochus V. Eupator 164-162
	Demetrius I. Soter 162-150
	Alexander Balas 150-145

It was under the reign of Antiochus Epiphanes that the Jews particularly suffered. He was the son of Antiochus the Great, and indeed a strange figure. When he came to the throne the Jews were being subjected to a process of Hellenization, which Antiochus continued. Among them, however, were those who had no desire to fall in with such a policy. These became known as the Hasidim, or pious ones, and set themselves forth as champions of the Law.

Under the leadership of Joshua, a brother of the high priest Onias III, many of the Jews were willing to fall in line with Antiochus' policy of Hellenization. By means of a bribe, Joshua, who had changed his name to Jason, induced Antiochus to depose Onias and to place himself in the office of high priest. He immediately set about to permit an influx of Grecian customs, even establishing a gymnasium (an exercise-ground) under the citadel in Jerusalem.

For three years Jason continued in office until in 171 he was supplanted by another Hellenized Jew, one Menelaus who had secured the favor of

Antiochus. Jason was compelled to flee, taking refuge with the Ammonites east of the Jordan, and Menelaus immediately revealed his true character by stealing some vessels from the Temple to pay his debts to Antiochus. For this he was rebuked by Onias III, whose death was forthwith procured (see the introductory comments on Dan. 9:24-27, p. 193).

Shortly afterward it was falsely rumored that Antiochus had died, and Jason with 1,000 men attacked the city, shutting up Menelaus in the citadel. Antiochus evidently regarded this as rebellion, and on his way back from Egypt in 168, entered Jerusalem, and robbed the Temple.

After his Egyptian campaign, two years later, Apollonius, a general of Antiochus, on a Sabbath day attacked Jerusalem, setting it on fire.

"And he fell upon the city suddenly, and smote it very sore, and destroyed much people out of Israel. And he took the spoils of the city, and set it on fire, and pulled down the houses thereof and the walls thereof on every side. And they led captive the women and the children, and the cattle they took in possession.—And they shed innocent blood on every side of the sanctuary, and defiled the sanctuary. And the inhabitants of Jerusalem fled because of them; and she became a habitation of strangers, and she became strange to them that were born in her, and her children forsook her. Her sanctuary was laid waste like a wilderness, her feasts were turned into mourning, her sabbaths into reproach, her honour into contempt. According to her glory, so was her dishonour multiplied, and her high estate was turned into mourning" 1 Macc. 1:30b-32, 37-40).

Antiochus now determined utterly to root out Judaism. The Jews he sought to compel to observe the heathen rites and made a matter of death the observance of the Jewish worship. In line with this policy the Temple was dedicated to Zeus. Throughout the land Antiochus caused the erection of heathen altars, and on the 25th of December (Chisleu) in 168, a heathen altar was erected upon the altar of burnt offering in the temple. Martyrdoms became frequent, but there was also much apostacy.

Then something happened. In a little town named Modin, about 18 miles N.W. of Jerusalem Mattathias, an elderly priest, not only refused to take the lead in offering a pagan sacrifice, but slew both a renegade Jew who wished to take his place and also the king's commissioner, and then broke down the altar.

Mattathias, in order to encourage the people, "—called to mind the great deeds of their fathers and the faith that had inspired them. In the climax of his speech he referred to the fiery furnace and to Daniel in the den of lions. This recalled to them that their God could and would save those who put their trust in Him" (*SBD* II, p. 275). Thus revolt arose, and, under the leadership of Mattathias and his five sons, it rapidly spread. The heathen altars throughout the country were destroyed.

In 166 Mattathias died, and was succeeded by his third son Judas, known as Maccabæus (the hammerer). He was able to slay Apollonius and another Syrian general Seron, with the result that Antiochus now entrusted half of all his army to his general Lysias, charging him to wipe out of the Jews root and branch. However, it was to no avail, for Judas successfully routed him. As a result, on the 25th of December 165, the Temple altar was rededicated. One year later, on an expedition in Persia, Antiochus died.

The Fourth World Empire

The vision of the fourth world empire is introduced with particular solemnity. "After this I saw in the night visions, and, behold a fourth beast, dreadful and terrible and strong exceedingly." This beast is nondescript and unlike those which preceded it.

At first Rome was merely one of the city-states in Italy. However, as time went on she extended her conquests, both in Italy and abroad. Thus she came into conflict with the remains of the Grecian empire which she found in a weakened condition. In 63 B.C. the Roman general, Pompey, entered Jerusalem and thus the Jews came under Roman sway. In 37 B.C. an Idumean named Herod was placed upon the throne, and continued until 4 B.C. thoroughly subservient to Rome, yet not tampering with the Jewish religion as Antiochus had done. It was shortly before the death of Herod that our Saviour was born.

When the Saviour was "cut off" in His death, the veil of the Temple was rent in twain. Up until this moment the Temple had been the dwelling place of the Holy God. But when the veil was rent, the fact was proclaimed to all the world that the way of access into the presence of God had been opened. Men might now approach God directly, without the intervention of any earthly priest or mediator. Christ and Christ alone is the Way.

Furthermore the Temple itself was no longer the Divine Temple, but an abomination, a house of idolatry. The sacrifices which were henceforth offered were idolatrous abominations. The Temple was not merely a den of thieves; it had become a house of idolatry. In the providence of God, this abomination was soon to be brought to an end.

Shortly after the resurrection of Christ and His ascension to heaven, in the year 41 A.D., war broke out between the Jews and Romans. The climax came in the year 70. A few days before the Passover the Romans under Titus came near to Jerusalem. After preliminary engagements they attacked the wall of the city and fifteen days later succeeded in making a breach. For some two weeks the fighting went on, and the Romans had completely surrounded the city. On the 17th day of Tammuz the daily sacrifices ceased, and on the 9th of Ab (August) the Temple area was entered. The Temple was burned to the ground and the Jews were ruthlessly killed. Their blood, Josephus declares, ran down the steps of the Temple in a stream. On the wing of abominations the one who maketh desolate had come, and the Temple and city lay in ruins. The full end and desolations were determined and poured out.

The Messiah had been cut off; the sacrifice and oblation ceased, and the Temple had been destroyed. The mighty Roman power apparently stood supreme. But from that lowly land of Palestine there went forth Jews whose hearts the Spirit of God had touched, who declared that the Messiah whom death had cut off was alive, having risen from the dead, and who preached faith in His Name. The Kingdom of God was upon earth, and neither the Roman empire nor the very gates of hell could prevail against it.[16]

VII

The Commentary of Jerome on Daniel 11:21-45

vs. 21ff. *And there will stand in his place a contemptible one, and there will not be given to him the honor of the kingdom, and he will come secretly, and will obtain the kingdom through deceitfulness. And the arms of fighting will be laid waste before him, and there shall be crushed moreover even the leader of a covenant. And after the league with him he will practice deceit, and will come up and succeed with a few people. And he will enter the abundant and plentiful cities, and he will do that which his fathers have not done, nor his father's fathers: the spoil and booty and their substance will he scatter, and against the strongest plans will he plot, and this for a time.* Hitherto the order of history is followed, and between Porphyry and ourselves there is no controversy. Other things which follow to the end of the book he interprets as applying to Antiochus who was surnamed Epiphanes, the brother of Seleucus, son of Antiochus the Great, who reigned in Syria eleven years after Seleucus and obtained Judæa, under whom there was a persecution of the law of God, and the Maccabean wars are said to have taken place. We however think that all these things are prophesied concerning Antichrist who will come at the last time. And since to this there might seem to be opposed the fact that the prophetic word leaves such things in the middle, from Sel-

[16] In thus writing, I wish most emphatically to repudiate the Romanist notion of the identity of the Kingdom of God and the visible church.

eucus to the end of the world, it may be replied that in earlier history where it was speaking about the kings of Persia, it put only four kings after Cyrus the Persian, and, passing over many intervening events, suddenly came to Alexander the Macedonian king. This is the custom of the Sacred Scripture, not to relate everything but to explain those things which seem to be most important. And since there are many things which we must later read and expound, which do fit the person of Antiochus, he should be regarded as a type of the Antichrist, and those things which have partly applied to him as being completely fulfilled in the Antichrist. And this is the custom of the Sacred Scripture. It sets forth the truth of the future in types, as, for example, that which is said concerning the Lord as Saviour in the 71st Psalm[1] which is entitled, "by Solomon." All the things which are said by him cannot apply to Solomon: for neither will he remain *with the sun and before the moon for generation and generation* (Ps. 71): nor did he rule from sea to sea and from the river to the ends of the earth, nor did all people serve him, nor has his name remained before the sun nor are all the tribes of the earth blessed in him nor have all people magnified him. In part therefore and as though in the shade and image of the truth they are set forth concerning Solomon, that they may be more perfectly fulfilled in the Divine Saviour. Therefore just as the Saviour has both Solomon and other saints as the type of His advent, so also must we believe that Antichrist has as a true type of himself, the very bad King Antiochus, who persecuted the saints and violated the temple. We shall follow therefore the plan of exposition, and with each explanation, we shall note briefly what appears to belong to our opponent and what to ourselves. *There will stand,* they say, *in the place* of Seleucus, his brother Antiochus Epiphanes, who at first was not given the honor of the kingdom by those in Syria who favored Ptolemy but afterwards by a pretense of clemency obtained the kingdom of Syria. And Ptolemy's arms of fighting, and everything for plundering were laid waste before Antiochus and were broken. Moreover the arms are called strength. Whence also the hand is called a great army. And not only, are we told, did he conquer Ptolemy by fraudulence, but also the leader of a covenant namely, Judas Maccabeaus, did he overcome by deceit. And this is what is meant, when he himself had secured bread for Ptolemy and had become a leader of the covenant, afterwards he practiced deceit against him. Moreover the reference here is not to Ptolemy Epiphanes who reigned fifth in Egypt, but to Ptolemy Philopator, the son of Cleopatra, the sister of Antiochus whose maternal uncle he was. And when after the death of Cleopatra Eulaius the eunuch, the tutor of Philometor, and Leneus ruled Egypt, and sought for Syria which Antiochus had oc-

[1] The 72nd Psalm in the English Bible.

cupied by fraud, there arose a battle between the uncle and the boy Ptolemy. The leaders of Ptolemy who had begun the battle between Pelusium and Mt. Cassius were conquered. However, Antiochus, sparing the boy, and pretending friendship, came up to Memphis, and there, as was custom, receiving the kingdom of the Egyptians and declaring that he would take care of the boy and his affairs, subdued with a handful of people, the entire Egyptian people to himself and entered the wealthy and plentiful districts. And he did that which his fathers had not done, nor his father's fathers. For none of the kings of Syria had so devastated Egypt and scattered all their riches; and he was crafty, as to subvert by his deceit the wise plans of those who were the leaders of the boy. Porphyry, in following these things, has followed the very redundant account of the Sutorii, which we have given in brief compend. We however interpret better and more correctly, that in the end of the world Antichrist will do these things, he who is to rise from a small people, that is, from the people of the Jews, and he will be so lowly and contemptible; that there will not be given to him the honor of the kingdom, and through treachery and fraud he will obtain the sovereignty, and the arms of fighting of the Roman people will be laid waste by him and will be destroyed. And he will do this because he will pretend that he is the leader of a covenant, that is of the Law and Testament of God. And he will enter the richest cities, and will do what his fathers had not done nor his father's fathers. For none of the Jews except Antichrist had ever reigned over all the earth. And he will take counsel against the strongest plans of the saints, and will do all things for a time, as long as the will of God permits him to do them.

vv., 25, 26 *And his strength and his heart shall be aroused against the king of the South with a great army. And the king of the South will be called forth into war and with much aid and many forces; and they will not stand, because plans will be devised against them. And those who eat bread with him will destroy him, and his army will be oppressed, and many shall fall down slain.* Porphyry interprets these things of Antiochus who, with a great army set out against Ptolemy, his sister's son. But also the king of the South, that is, the leaders of Ptolemy, were called forth to war with much aid and many forces, and were not able to withstand the fraudulent plans of Antiochus, who pretended peace with his sister's son and ate bread with him and afterwards occupied Egypt. We however, according to the sense given above, interpret everything of the Antichrist, who will be born from the Jewish people and will come from Babylon and will first overcome the king of Egypt, who is one of the three horns concerning whom we have already spoken before.

vv. 27, 28. *Also the heart of the two kings will be set to do evil, and at one table they will speak a lie, and they will not succeed; for hitherto is the end in another time. And he will return to his land with great forces.* There is no doubt but that Antiochus would make peace with Ptolemy and would have a banquet with him and would plot treacherous things, and would accomplish nothing; because he would not be able to obtain his kingdom, but would be cast out by the soldiers of Ptolemy. But from the fact that the Scripture here says that there were two kings whose heart was deceitful, that they might do harm to one another, it cannot be shown to be in accord with history. For Ptolemy was of but youthful age, and, taken in by the treachery of Antiochus, how could he plot evil against him? Whence we wish to refer all these things to Antichrist and to the King of Egypt whom he first overcame.

vv. 29, 30. *And his heart will be against the holy testament, and he will do and will return to his land. At the determined time will he return and come to the South, and the last will not be like the first. And there will come upon him triremes, and Romans, and he will be slain.* Or as others have interpreted *And they will be threatened by him.* Both the Greek and Roman history declare that Antiochus turned, having been driven out of Egypt, and came into Judea, that is, against the holy testament, and despoiled the Temple, and bore away an immense amount of gold, and, having established a garrison of Macedonians in the citadel, returned to his land. And after two years he again gathered an army against Ptolemy and came to the South. And when the two brothers of Ptolemy, the son of Cleopatra, whose uncle he was, were shut up at Alexandria, the Roman envoys came. One of them was Marcus Popilius Lenas, who, when he found him standing on the shore, and had given him the decision of the senate by which he was commanded to depart from the friends of the Roman people and to be satisfied with his own kingdom, (and he, i.e., Antiochus in accordance with the answer of friends had delayed the advice), is said to have made a circle in the sands with the stick which he held in his hand, and to have surrounded the king and said, "The senate and the Roman people command that you here and now reply to what your plans are." When these things had been said he replied, frightened out of his wits, "If it pleases the senate and the Roman people, we shall depart," and so immediately he moved his army. Moreover, he is said to have been beaten, not because he died, but because he lost all his great arrogance. Concerning Antichrist there is no doubt but that he will fight against the holy Testament, and fighting first against the King of Egypt, will straightway be alarmed by the troops of the Romans. These things moreover under Antiochus Epiphanes took place as an image, so that this most wicked king, who persecuted the people of God, would prefigure Antichrist, who would persecute the people of Christ. Whence many among us think that because of the greatness of his wrath and shamefulness Domitius Nero will be the Antichrist.

And he will return and will become enraged at the testament of the sanctuary and will do and will return and will plan concerning those (*Vulg. against those*) *who have left the Testament of the sanctuary.* We read more fully of these things in the deeds of the Maccabees (1 Macc. 1): because, after the Romans had driven him out of Egypt, he came indignantly against the testament of the sanctuary and was invited by those who had left the law of God and had mingled themselves with the ceremonies of the Gentiles. This must be more fully completed under Antichrist who will be indignant against the testament of God, and will plan against those whom he wishes to abandon the Law of God. Whence, Aquila has more significantly interpreted, *And he will plan and will forsake the covenant of the sanctuary.*

Vs. 31 *And arms from him will stand, and they will pollute the sanctuary of strength, and will bear away the perpetual sacrifice and will give an abomination into desolation.* Instead of *arms,* others have interpreted, *seed,* so as to signify root or offspring. They moreover have reference to those who were sent by Antiochus after two years when he despoiled the temple that they might exact tribute from the Jews and take away the worship of God and might place in the temple of Jerusalem the image of Zeus Olympus and statues of Antiochus, which are here called the *abomination of desolation* when the whole burnt-offering was removed and the perpetual sacrifice. We contend that all these things have transpired as a type of Antichrist who will seat himself in the temple of God and will act as God. Moreover, the Jews wish this to be understood neither of Antiochus Epiphanes nor of Antichrist but of the Romans, concerning whom it was said above: *And triremes will come,* both Italian and Roman, and he will be humbled. After much time concerning these same Romans who came to aid Ptolemy and threatened Antiochus, it is said that there will arise a king Vespatian; his arms will stand, and his seeds, (i.e., Titus his son with an army), and will pollute the sanctuary and will bear away the perpetual sacrifice and will hand over the temple to eternal solitude. SIIM of course and CHETHIM which we have interpreted *triremes and Romans,* the Hebrews take in the sense of *Italians* and *Romans.*

Vs. 32 *And the wicked ones against the testament will pretend fraudulently, the people however which knows its God will obtain and will do.* This we read in the books of the Maccabees, that they had pretended to be custodians of the Law of God, and afterwards had made a pact with the Gentiles, but others should remain in the religion which I think will be future in the times of Antichrist, when the love of many will grow cold. Concerning which the Lord says in the Gospel: *Dost thou think that when the Son of Man comes, He will find faith upon the earth?* (Luke 18:8).

And the learned among the people will teach many and they shall fall by the sword, and the flame, and in captivity and in the plundering of days. The books of the Maccabees refer to how many things the Jews suffered by Antiochus and are a testimony of their triumph, who, for the care of the Law of God sustained flames and swords, and slavery and plunderings and the severest punishments. No one doubts that these things will take place in the future under Antichrist when many resist his power and flee into different places. The Hebrews interpret them of the last overthrow of the Temple which took place under Vespatian and Titus, when there were many of the people who knew its God and were killed for the sake of His Law.

Vs. 34, 35 *And when they fall, they shall be raised up by a little help, and many will attach themselves to them fraudulently. And some of the instructed ones will fall, that they may be refined and purged and made white up to the time appointed, for hitherto will be another time.* Porphyry thinks that the little help signifies Mattathias from the village of Modin, who rebelled against the leaders of Antiochus and tried to serve the worship of the true God (1 Macc. 2). Moreover, we read, he is called a little help because Mattathias was killed in battle, and afterwards his son Judas, who was called Maccabæus, fell in battle and his other brothers were deceived by the fraud of the adversaries. Read Maccabees. All these things therefore, we are told, were done that the saints might be tried and refined and made white until the determined time, because to another time would the victory be deferred. We think that the little help should be understood as having reference to the time of Antichrist because assembled saints will resist him and will use a little help, and afterwards many from the instructed ones will fall. And this will occur, so that, it will be as though they were refined in a furnace and made white and refined until a determined time should come, because the true victory will be in the advent of Christ. Certain of the Hebrews understand these things to have reference to the princes Severus and Antoninus, who greatly loved the Jews. Others, however, apply it to the emperor Julian, because, when they had been oppressed by Gaius Cæsar and in the distress of captivity had endured many things, he, pretending to love the Jews, arose, promising that there would be sacrifice in their temple: in which they will have little hope of help, and many Gentiles, not in truth, but in falsehood, will attach themselves to them. For the worship of idols they will pretend friendship with him. And they will do this, that those who have been proven may be made manifest. For the time of their true salvation and help will be Christ whom they falsely think will come when they will have received Antichrist (I Cor. XI).

Vs. 36 *And a king will do according to his will, and will be exalted, and will be magnified against every God, and against the God of Gods will he speak marvelous things and he shall direct, until wrath be completed, for a prescribing has been accomplished.* Or as others have interpreted: *for in himself will be the consummation.* From this place the Jews think that what is said is about Antichrist, that after the little help of Julian a king will be raised who will do according to his will, and will be exalted against all which is called God and will speak marvelous things against the God of gods, so that he will sit in the temple of God and will make himself God, and his will will rule until the wrath of God is fulfilled, because in himself will be the consummation. We also understand this of Antichrist. Porphyry however and others who follow him think that the reference is to Antiochus Epiphanes, in that he was raised against the worship of God, and came into such great haughtiness that he ordered a likeness of himself to be placed in the temple at Jerusalem. And as to what follows, *And he will direct, until wrath is completed, because in himself will be the consummation,* they thus understand, that he has power so long, until God becomes enangered with him and orders him to be killed. Polybius and Diodorus who write historical collections, relate that he not only acted against the God of Judea, but also inflamed by the incitement of greed, tried to despoil the temple of Diana in Elymais, which was very rich. He was attacked by the people who kept guard about the vicinity of the temple, and by certain phantasies and terrors was cast into insanity and at last passed away into death. This they declare happened to him, because he tried to violate the temple of God. We however say that although this happened to him, it happened, because he exercised much cruelty against the saints of God and polluted His temple. For we must believe that he was punished, not because of that which he tried to do, and having repented, ceased to carry out, but for what he actually did do.

Vs. 37 ff. *And he will have no regard for the God of his fathers, and will be in the desires of women: nor will he care for any of the gods, because he will rise against all. Moreover he will venerate the god MAOZIM in his place, and the god whom his fathers have not known he will worship with gold and silver and precious stones and valuable things. And he will act that he should fortify MAOZIM with a foreign god whom he has known and will multiply glory, and will give to it power in many things, and will freely divide the land.* Instead of that which we have rendered, *and he will be in the desires of women,* the LXX have translated, *and he will not be subject to the desires of women.* Again, instead of MAOZIM, which appears in the Hebrew, Aquila has translated, *God of forces,* the LXX, *the bravest god.* For indeed, in the Hebrew, instead of that which we have said, *and he will be in the desires of women,* it is ambiguous, when Aquila says, rendering word for word, *and concerning the God of his fathers he will not understand, and concerning the desire of women, and concerning every god he will not understand.* By these words we may understand both that he has the desire of women and that he does not have. If we should read and understand *apo Koinov, and concerning the desire of women he will not understand,* it is easier to interpret of Antichrist, since he will therefore pretend chastity, in order that he may deceive many. But if however we thus read, *and concerning the desire of women,* in order to supply *he will be,*[2] it will fit better the person of Antiochus, who is said to have been most dissolute, and through debauching and corruption of the royal dignity to have come into such shame that he would associate publicly with actresses and even with prostitutes, and in the presence of the people, would satisfy his lust. Porphyry has ridiculously interpreted, the god MAOZIM, so that he would say that in the village Modin, from whence came Mattathias, and his sons, the leaders of Antiochus had placed a statue of Jupiter, and had compelled the Jews to offer sacrifice to it, that is, to the god of Modin. But as to what follows, *and the god whom his fathers did not know will he worship,* this fits the Antichrist better than it does Antiochus. For we read that Antiochus held the worship of the idols of Greece, and compelled the Jews and Samaritans to worship his gods. Likewise, also, as to what is said, *and* he will act that he should fortify MAOZIM with a foreign god whom he has known, and he will multiply glory, and will give to them power in many things and will freely divide the *land,* Theodotion has interpreted, *and he will do these things in order to fortify garrisons with a foreign god, and when he will make a display for them, he will multiply honor, and will bring it about that they are ruled by many, and will divide the land freely.* Instead of *garrisons,* Symmachus has interpreted *places of refuge.* It is thus explained by Porphyry, he will do all these things in order to fortify the citadel of Jerusalem, and will place garrisons in the other cities, and will teach the Jews to worship a foreign god; there is no doubt but that he means Jupiter. When he will have shown him to them and will have persuaded them to worship him, then to these deceived ones will he give honor and much glory and will accomplish for others who had been dominated in Judea and will divide possessions through duplicity and will distribute gifts. The Antichrist also will abundantly bestow many rewards upon the deceived ones, and will divide the land with his army, and those whom he has not quieted with terror, he will subjugate with greed.

Vv. 40, 41. *And at a determined time one will wage war against him from the South: and like a tempest will the king of the North come against him with chariots and horsemen and a large fleet: and he will enter countries, and will overflow and will pass through. And he will enter into the*

---

[2] i.e., to express the thought, he will concern himself with the desire of women.

glorious land, and many will fall. For which Symmachus has interpreted, *and many thousands will fall,* Theodotion, *and many will be weakened.* But take the many who fall in accordance with Aquila, either cities, or regions or provinces. Porphyry refers these things to Antiochus, because in the eleventh year of his reign he fought again against Ptolemy Philometor the son of his sister. For when he heard that Antiochus was coming, he gathered many thousands of the people. But like a strong tempest Antiochus entered many lands with chariots and horsemen and a large fleet and devastated them all in passing through them. And he came to the glorious land, that is, Judæa, which Symmachus has interpreted, *land of strength.* Theodotion has retained the Hebrew word itself SABAI (others SABAM and SABA), And he fortified the citadel from the ruins of the walls of the city, and thus he proceeded into Egypt. We however, referring these things to the Antichrist, say that he will first fight against the king of the South, that is, of Egypt, and afterwards will conquer Libya and Ethiopia, which we have above applied to the three horns from the ten horns, and because he will come into the land of Israel and many cities or provinces will surrender to him.

These only will be saved from his hand, Edom and Moab and the chief of the children of Ammon.

Antiochus, they say, making haste against Ptolemy, the king of the South, did not touch the Idumeans, Moabites and the Ammonites who were to one side of Judah, lest, becoming engaged in another battle, he should cause Ptolemy to become stronger. Antichrist also will leave intact Idumea, and the Moabites and the children of Ammon, that is, Arabia, because the saints will flee there to the deserts.

Vv. 42, 43 *And he will send his hand against the lands, and the land of Egypt will not escape and he will be lord of the treasures of gold and silver and of all the valuable things of Egypt. He will also pass through Libya and Ethiopia.* We read that Antiochus had in part done these things. But what follows, namely, *he will also pass through Libya and Ethiopia,* we assert is more applicable to the Antichrist. For Libya, which many refer to Africa, and Ethiopia, Antiochus did not hold, unless by chance, when the Egyptians were captured, even those provinces were alarmed, because in that very region are the provinces of Egypt and neighborhoods far away through the deserts. Whence it is not said that he would take them, but that he would pass through Libya and Ethiopia.

Vv. 44, 45 *And a report will disturb him from the East and from the North. And he will come with a great multitude, and will destroy and kill many. And he will fix his tabernacle in Apedno, between the seas above the glorious and sacred mountain, and he will come even to its height, and no one will help him.* Also in this place Porphyry dreams I know not what wild things about Antiochus. Fighting, he says, against the Egyptians and passing through Libya and Ethiopia, he will hear from the North and East that battles are being stirred up. Hence he returns and will capture the resisting Aradii and will devastate the entire province along the seacoast of Phœnicia. And immediately will he proceed to Artaxes, the king of Armenia, who will be moved from the regions of the Orient, and after many have been killed by his army, will place his tent in the place Apedno, which is situated between two very broad rivers, the Tigris and the Euphrates. And when he will have proceeded hither, he is not able to say in what glorious and holy mountain he will dwell. Nevertheless he is not able to prove that he dwelt between two seas, and it would be foolish to interpret the two rivers of Mesopotamia as two seas. He has passed over the glorious mountain, therefore, because he has followed the interpretation of Theodotion, who says, *between the middle seas above the holy mountain Saba.* And if he should think that Saba is the name of a mountain, either of Armenia or of Mesopotamia, he is not able to say why it is holy. Even by means of this license in lying we are able to say that he has remained silent. It is called a *holy mountain*, because in accordance with the error of the Armenians, it is consecrated to idols. *And he will come*, he says, *up to the summit of this very mountain*, in the province of Elymais, which is the most remote district of the Persians eastward. Wishing there to despoil the temple of Diana, because it possessed infinite wealth, he was put to flight by the barbarians, because they esteemed that temple with particular regard; and he died in Tabæ, a city of the Persians, destroyed upon the walls. As an affront to us he has made up these things in a most artificial discourse, which, even though he should be able to prove that they are spoken of Antiochus and not of the Antichrist, what is that to us, since we do not attempt to prove either the advent of Christ or the falsehood of Antichrist from all the passages of Scripture? For suppose that these things were spoken of Antiochus, what harm does that do to our religion? And in the previous vision, where the prophecy was fulfilled in Antiochus, was anything said concerning Antichrist? Wherefore, let him forego doubtful matters and cleave to those which are plain. Let him declare who that stone is, which, having been cut from the mountain without hands, grew into a great mountain and filled the whole earth and destroyed the four-fold image. Let him declare who is that Son of Man, who will come with the clouds of heaven and will stand before the Ancient of Days, and there is given to him a kingdom which has no end, and all peoples, tribes and languages will serve him. He passes over these things which are plain and asserts that they are prophesied concerning the Jews, whom we know are serving even unto today. And he says that he who wrote the book under the name of

Daniel lied for the sake of reviving their hope.[3] Not in that he would not be able to know the entire future history, but that he would have mentioned events which had already occurred. And he lingers in false statements in the last vision, substituting rivers for a sea, and the glorious and holy mountain Apedno, but can bring forth no history where he has read this.

We, however, thus explain the last chapter of this vision of the Antichrist, because when he fights against the Egyptians, Libyans and Ethiopians, and, uprooting three horns from the ten horns, will hear from the regions of the Orient that wars are being waged against him. Hence he will come with a great multitude, in order that he may destroy and kill many, and will fix his tabernacle in Apedno near Nicopolis, which was formerly called Emmaus, where the mountains of the province of Judea begin to rise. At length he will stir himself up to the mount of Olives, and will ascend the district of Jerusalem. This is what the Scripture here says, *And when he will fix his tabernacle* at the base of the mountainous province between two seas, namely, the sea on the East which is now called Dead, and the Great Sea on whose coasts are situated Cæsarea, Joppa, Ascalon and Gaza. Then he will come unto the summit of its mountain, that is, of the mountainous province, that is, the top of the Mount of Olives, which is called glorious, because from it the Lord and Saviour ascended to the Father. And none will be able to give aid to Antichrist, since the Lord is enangered against him. And it is claimed that Antichrist will perish there, where the Lord ascended to heaven. The word *Apedno* is compound, because, if it is divided, it may be understood thronou autou, that is, of his throne. And the meaning is, And he will fix his tent and his throne between the seas above the glorious and holy mountain. Symmachus has thus interpreted this place: *And he will extend the tents of his cavalry between the seas unto the holy mountain of strength, and will come unto the top of the mountain.* Theodotion: *And he will fix his tent in Aphedano, between the seas in the holy mountain Saba, and will come unto its part.* Aquila: *And he will plant the tabernacle of his tent* (prætorium) *in* Aphadano *between the seas, in the glorious and holy mountain, and will come even to its end.* The Septuagint alone has interpreted, disregarding any question of the name, *And he will erect his tent then between the seas, and the holy mountain of will, and the hour of his end will come.* Apollinarius has followed, for he is completely silent about the name *Apedno.* I have gone into this somewhat at length in order that I may show both the sophistry of Porphyry who has ignored

[3] The Latin word is *mentitum.* All honor to Porphyry for thus candidly and accurately stating the case. (There seems no sufficient reason for denying this language to Porphyry). For if an unknown author, living at the time of the Maccabees, wrote under the name of Daniel, he did just what Porphyry declares he did — he lied.

all these things, or has pretended that he does not know them, and the difficulty of Holy Scripture, the understanding of which without the grace of God and the teaching of the elders, the most unskilled in the highest degree arrogate unto themselves. Moreover it must be noted that the Hebrew language does not possess the letter P, but instead uses PH which has the sound of the Greek PH. In this very passage it is written by the Hebrews as PH, but is read P. Moreover, as to the fact that Antichrist should come to the summit of the holy and glorious mountain and should perish there, Isaiah speaks more fully, *The Lord will cast down in the holy mountain the face of the ruler of darkness over all nations, and him who rules over all peoples, and the anointing wherewith he is anointed against all nations.*

VIII

Porphyry and His Criticism of Daniel

In the commentary several references have been made to the opinions of Porphyry, who was one of the earliest hostile critics of the Old Testament. This noted antagonist of the Christian Faith was probably born in 232 or 233 A.D.[1] It appears also that he was from the city of Tyre in Phœnicia, for he speaks of himself as a Phœnician. However, some of the early writers refer to him by the designation *Bataneotes*, probably indicating thereby that he was from the region of Batanea, within the Hauran. Although this name was evidently intended to be a term of disdain, it may also possibly contain an illusion to the fact that his birthplace was not Tyre, but some obscure section of the Hauran.

He was named Malchus after his father, and probably spent his early years in Tyre where he received a careful education. It is not known whether his parents had at one time been Christians.

Porphyry may have learned Hebrew. At any rate he became at home in the Chaldean, Persian and Egyptian mysteries. As a youth he met the great Origen, whom he regarded as a "Greek brought up in Greek learning," whose course of life was Christian but who in his opinions about God and material things "acted as a Greek," and introduced Greek ideas into foreign fables (i.e., the Scriptures). Above all Porphyry condemned the allegorical method of interpretation which Origen employed.

It was Porphyry's privilege to journey to Athens which was then a renowned center of study. Here he received instruction from many dis-

[1] At the end of the tenth year of the reign of Gallienus, who celebrated his decennalia in 262, Porphyry appears to have been thirty years of age.

tinguished men, but the one under whom his critical faculties greatly developed and at whose feet he spent most of his time was the philosopher Longinus. It was Longinus who bestowed upon him the name Porphyry (i.e., purple). On the whole the sojourn at Athens was a valuable preparation for the next stage in Porphyry's life, his study at Rome with the neo-Platonist philosopher, Plotinus, who was to exercise great influence upon his pupil.

Such was the background and training of this great antagonist of Christianity. His magnum opus was the monumental work *Against the Christians,* comprising fifteen books and written in Sicily when Porphyry was about forty years old. It was suppressed by Constantine, but apparently copies still existed at a later date, for in 448 the emporer Theodosius II and Valentine again decreed that it be destroyed. From this time on, copies are no longer to be found, and it is even questionable whether Jerome himself actually possessed one.

The work brought forth several replies, the first of which, as far as we know, being by Methodius of Olympus. According to Jerome he wrote ten thousand verses. Eusebius soon followed, composing a work of twenty-five books. Finally, Apollinarius of Laodicea produced a powerful reply in thirty books. All of these, except for scattered fragments, are lost.

It is difficult to determine whether Porphyry actually denied the Mosaic authorship of the Pentateuch. Quite probably he did. At least there is evidence extant to show that he did believe in the historical existence of Moses.[2]

Some of Porphyry's criticism was very superficial. Why, he asked, should God forbid eating of the tree of the knowledge of good and evil? It is understandable that God might prohibit evil, but why should He forbid the knowledge of both? Sacrifice was thought to be foreign to true piety, an opinion which Porphyry believed he had obtained from the prophetical books. Moses, he asserted, said nothing about the Deity of Christ, nor is any prophecy of the crucifixion to be found in the books of the prophets.

Most important, however, of Porphyry's criticisms of the Old Testament is that which he directed against the book of Daniel. "Porphyry," says Jerome, who in his commentary has preserved this criticism, "wrote his twelfth book against the prophet Daniel, denying that it was composed by him whose name it bears, but rather by someone who was in Judea during the times of Antiochus, who is called Epiphanes." What we have

---

[2] One of the latest statements of the position that Porphyry denied the Mosaic authorship of the Pentateuch is made by Robert M. Grant in his article, "Historical Criticism in the Ancient Church" in *The Journal of Religion,* vol. xxv, no. 3, July 1945, pp. 183-196. This position is based upon a passage in the *Apocritica* of Macarius Magnes. In all probability the one against whom Macarius is writing is Porphyry.

in the book are not prophecies uttered by Daniel, but a narration by an unknown author of events which had already transpired. Consequently, according to Porphyry, in the narration of events up to the time of Antiochus, we have true history, but anything beyond that time is false, since the writer could not know the future.

Like the other prophets, continues Jerome, Daniel predicts that Christ will come, but more than this, he even teaches at what time He will come, and arranges the kings in order, enumerates the years and predicts the clearest signs. Porphyry has seen that these things have come to pass and so contends that they were fulfilled at the time of Antiochus. Consequently, reasons Jerome, his assault upon the book of Daniel is in reality a testimony to the truth. Hence, whenever occasion requires, Jerome intends to reply to his opponent's "calumnies, and the arts of philosophy; rather, the pagan ill-will, by means of which he endeavors to overthrow the truth, and with certain deception to take away the light of clear eyes, I shall endeavor to confute by means of simple explanation."

Apparently Porphyry thought that the book of Daniel was originally composed in Greek, for he used the version of Theodotion. He sought to explain the etymology of a word in the legend of Susanna, in order to show the Grecian origin of Daniel. According to Jerome, both Eusebius and Apollinarius had answered this charge by pointing out that the fable of Susanna and also of Bel and the Dragon were not to be found in the Hebrew. Jerome further remarked that, when translating Daniel several years previously, he had himself marked these sections with an obelus. In addition, he asserts, Origen and other Greek doctors and ecclesiastics had also declared that these sections were not to be found in the Hebrew.

However, although on this point Porphyry was in error, it is evident that in preparation for his attack upon Daniel he had read widely. Jerome mentions some of the secular authors, the knowledge of which is necessary for an understanding of the background of Daniel, and states that Porphyry claims to have known some of these.

In general it may be said that Porphyry follows the procedure mentioned by Jerome, i.e., the predictions of Daniel he interprets, not as referring to Antichrist, as did Jerome, but to Antiochus Epiphanes. Furthermore, the passages which Christians have traditionally regarded as Messianic, Porphyry would apply to the people of Israel.

In his detailed exposition Porphyry sometimes shows himself as a serious interpreter, nor are these detailed interpretations always at variance with those of Christian expositors. In fact, as far as detailed exposition is concerned, we find in Porphyry an approach to grammatico-historical exegesis.

Nevertheless, Porphyry cannot be regarded as a truly scientific interpreter of the Bible. His work is founded upon the presupposition that predictive prophecy is impossible (si quid autem ultra opinatus sit, quia futura nescient, esse mentitum). It is upon the basis of this assumption that Porphyry came to his conclusion that the book of Daniel was a product of the second century B.C. This date has been accepted by many in recent times. But let us never forget that the "modern" date for the composition of Daniel was first advanced by one whose heart and soul were hostile to supernatural Christianity.

Bibliography

The following bibliography in no sense pretends to be exhaustive, but merely limits itself to works of authors to whom reference is made in the commentary. Unless otherwise noted such references in the commentary are to works herein listed. Those who desire fuller bibliographies will find them in *DM*, and in M. They should also consult the interpretative article by Walter Baumgartner, "Ein Vierteljahrhundert Danielforschung" in *TR*, 1939, pp. 59-83; 125-144; 201-228.

Aalders, G. Ch.: *Het Herstel van Israel volgens het Oude Testament*, Kampen, n.d.

Allis, O. T.: *Prophecy and the Church, Phila.*, 1945.

Anderson, Sir Robert: *The Coming Prince, The Last Great Monarch of Christendom*, London, 1881. *Daniel in the Critics' Den*, New York, n.d.

Auberlen, K. A.: *Der Prophet Daniel und die Offenbarung Johannes*, 1854, ET by Adolph Saphir, Edinburgh, 1856.

Barnes, Albert: *The Book of the Prophet Daniel* in *Notes, Critical, Explanatory and Practical on the Old Testament*, Edinburgh, n.d.

Baumgartner, W.: *Daniel* in Kittel, *Biblia Hebraica*,[3] 1937, pp. 1255-1283.

Bevan, A. A.: *A Short Commentary on the Book of Daniel*, 1892.

Behrmann, G.: *Das Buch Daniel*, Gottingen, 1894.

Boutflower, C.: *In and Around the Book of Daniel*, London, 1923.

Butler, J. Glentworth: *The Bible-Work*, vol. ix, New York, 1894.

Buxtorf, J.: *Lexicon Chaldaicum, Talmudicum et Rabbinicum*, Basileae, M.D.XXXIX.

Calvin, J.: *Praelectiones in librum prophetarium Danielis*, ET by T. Myers, 2 vols., 1852-53.

Charles, R. H.: *A Critical and Exegetical Commentary on the Book of Daniel*, 1929.

Cooke, G. A.: *A Text-Book of North Semitic Inscriptions*, 1903.

Darby, J. N.: *Synopsis of the Books of the Bible*, New Edition, Revised, Vol. II, New York, n.d.

Deane, H.: *Daniel* in Ellicott's Commentary on the Old Testament.

Delitzsch, Franz: *Daniel*, art. in *Realenzyklopaedie fuer protestantische Theologie und Kirche.*

de Wette, W.: *Einleitung*, ET, *A Critical and Historical Introduction to the Canonical Scriptures of the Old Testament*, 2 vols., Boston, 1859.

Driver, S. R.: *Daniel* in *The Cambridge Bible*, 1922.

d'Envieu, J. F.: *Le Livre du prophete Daniel*, 4 vols., Paris, 1888-1891.

Ephraim of Syria: *Opera omnia quae extant, Graece, Syriace, Latine, in sex tomos distributa*, Syriacum textum recensuit Petrus Benedictus, Tomus Secundus, Romae, M.DCCXL.

Ewald, H.: *Die Propheten des Alten Bundes,* ET by J. Frederick Smith, vol. 5, 1881.

Fuller, J. M.: *Daniel* in Commentary on the Bible, edited by F C. Cook, New York, n.d.

Gaebelein, A. C.: *The Prophet Daniel,* New York, 1911.

Goettsberger, J.: *Das Buch Daniel uebersetzt und erklaert.* 1928.

Haller, Max: *Das Judentum, in Die Schriften des Alten Testaments, Goettingen,* 1925, 2 Abtheilung, 3 Band, *Daniel,* pp. 271-310.

Haevernick. H. Ch.: *Commentar ueber das Buch Daniel.* 1832.

Heidel, A.: *The Babylonian Genesis,* Chicago, 1942.

Hengstenberg, E. W.: *Die Authentie des Daniel und die Integitaet Sacharjah,* 1831. ET, 1848: *Christology of the Old Testament,*[2] Tr. from the German by James Martin, Vol. iii, 1858, pp. 77-264.

Hippolytus, in Bonwetsch's ed. in *Die griechischen christlichen Schriftsteller der ersten drei Jahrhunderte.*

Hitzig, F.: *Das Buch Daniel,* 1850.

Ironside, H. A.: *Lectures on Daniel the Prophet,* New York, n.d.

Jephet Ibn Ali, *Daniel,* ed. by D. S. Margoliouth, 1889.

Jerome, *In Danielem Prophetam,* in *PL,* ed. Migne, vol. 25, 1865.

Keil, C. F.: *Commentar ueber den Propheten Daniel,* 1869. ET, 1877.

Kennedy, J.: *The Book of Daniel from the Christian Standpoint,* London, 1898.

Kliefoth, T.: *Das Buch Daniel,* 1868.

Kranichfeld, Rudolph: *Das Buch Daniel,* 1868.

Lacunza, M.: (Published under the name of Juan Josafat Ben-Ezra) *The Coming of Messiah in Glory and Majesty,* tr. from the Spanish by Ed. Irving, 2 vols., 1827.

Lang, G.: *The Histories and Prophecies of Daniel,* London, 1941.

Langdon, S.: *The Babylonian Epic of Creation,* Oxford, 1923.

Lenormant, F.: *La Divination et la Science des Presages chez les Chaldeens,* 1875.

Maurer, F.: *Commentarius grammaticus criticus in Vetus Testamentum,* vol. 2, Leipzig, 1838.

Mauro, Philip: *The Seventy Weeks and The Great Tribulation,* Rev. ed., Swengel, Pa., 1944.

McClain, A. J.: *Daniel's Prophecy of the Seventy Weeks,* Grand Rapids, 1940.

Montgomery, J. A.: *A Critical and Exegetical Commentary on the Book of Daniel,* New York, 1927, in ICC.

Paton, L.: *A Critical and Exegetical Commentary on the Book of Esther,* New York, 1916, in ICC.

Pfeiffer, R. H.: *Introduction to the Old Testament,* New York, 1941.

Prince, J. D.: *A Critical Commentary on the Book of Daniel,* Leipzig, 1899.

Pusey, E. B.: *Daniel the Prophet,* New York, 1891.

Rollock, R.: *In Librum Danielis Prophetae,* Genevae, M.D.CX.

Rose, H. J., co-author with J. M. Fuller, see under *Fuller* above.

Rosenmueller, E. F. C.: *Scholia in Vetus Testamentum,* 10. 1882.

Rowley, H. H.: *Darius the Mede and the Four World Empires in the Book of Daniel,* Cardiff, 1935

Schurer, E.: *Geschichte des Juedischen Volkes im Zeitalter Jesu Christi*, 3 vols., 1901-09.

Scofield, C. I.: *What Do the Prophets Say?* Phila., 1916.

Scofield Reference Bible, New York, 1917.

Stuart, Moses: *A Commentary on the Book of Daniel*, Boston, 1850.

Theodoret, *Commentarius in visiones Danielis prophetae*, in *PG*, vol. lxxxi.

von Lengerke, C.: *Das Buch Daniel*, 1835.

Vos, G.: *The Pauline Eschatology*, Princeton, 1930.

Walvoord, J. F.: *Is the Seventieth Week of Daniel Future?* in *Bibliotheca Sacra*, Vol. 101, Jan. 1944.

Wilson, Robert Dick: *Studies in the Book of Daniel*, New York, I, 1917; II, 1938.

Wright, C. H. H.: *Daniel and his Prophecies*, 1906.

Zoeckler, Otto: *Daniel* in Lange's *Theol-homiletisches Bibelwerk*, 1870, *ET* by James Strong, New York, 1876.

INDICES

General Index

(to Introduction and Appendices)

Index of Scripture References

(to Introduction and Appendices)

Geneva